NAVIGATING THE OLD ENGLISH POOR LAW

The Kirkby Lonsdale Letters, 1809–1836

Records of Social and Economic History is a British Academy Research Project.

RECORDS OF SOCIAL AND ECONOMIC HISTORY
NEW SERIES 62

NAVIGATING THE OLD ENGLISH POOR LAW

The Kirkby Lonsdale Letters, 1809–1836

EDITED BY
PETER JONES
AND
STEVEN KING

Published for THE BRITISH ACADEMY
by OXFORD UNIVERSITY PRESS

Oxford University Press, Great Clarendon Street, Oxford OX2 6DP

First edition published in 2020

British Library Cataloguing in Publication Data
Data available

Library of Congress Cataloging in Publication Data
Data available

Typeset by
New Leaf Design, Malton, North Yorkshire
Printed in Great Britain by
TJ Books Ltd, Padstow, Cornwall

ISBN 978–0–19–726681–6

Foreword

Historians have long appreciated the social and economic significance of the English and Welsh Old Poor Law. One of its key requirements was that relief was sought from parishes where people were legally settled, which may not have been where they lived. It is clear that many 'out-parish claims' were made, though few of their written pleadings, whether petitions or letters, have survived. However, the records of Kirkby Lonsdale in the historic county of Westmorland are unusually rich for the period covered by this edition, mainly because of the care taken at the time by Stephen Garnett, the local official overseeing the process. These are letters claiming relief from people with little formal education who found themselves in dire circumstances. Their moving pleas, sometimes made by interlocutors, and the annotations on them by Garnett, open a window onto the perilous existence of many people at a time associated with war and demobilization, rural upheaval, and industrialization in nearby towns and cities.

From this rich cache the Editors have selected cases relating to twenty individuals, families, or networks for which multiple letters survive, averaging about twenty-seven each, sometimes sent over many years. This allows, as the Introduction makes clear, the life cycle of poverty to be seen as a process rather than scattered events, expressed in the language of the poor themselves. This volume adds, therefore, considerably to two earlier volumes in this series, one edited by Thomas Sokoll on pauper letters from Essex, the other edited by Joseph Harley on pauper inventories from Norfolk. It is additionally welcome that records of the workings of the Old Poor Law in Northern England have been added to the series.

Professor Craig Muldrew, a member of the Series' steering committee, liaised with the Editors to advance this volume. The General Editor, Professor Vanessa Harding, then ironed out remaining lacunae. I am very grateful to both colleagues for their considerable efforts.

Julian Hoppit, Chair, Records of Social and Economic History Committee
April 2020

Contents

List of Figures

Acknowledgements

The material for this volume was originally collected as part of a research project (funded jointly by the AHRC and the DFG in Germany, AH/I500561/1) entitled 'Pauper Letters and Petitions for Poor relief in Britain and Germany, 1770-1914'. We are grateful to both organisations and to the co-PI on that project, Professor Andreas Gestrich, for their support. Disentangling and interpreting the letters reproduced here has been a considerable task and we are grateful to both the Cumbria Archive Service and to Dr Carol Beardmore (who did much of the final editorial work for this selection of letters) in that task. Directly and indirectly, this work owes much to the two people who blazed a trail on pauper letters and their value to social and cultural historians, Thomas Sokoll and James Stephen Taylor. Of course, preparing a volume of this magnitude while also trying to do a 'day job' incurs many personal debts. Peter Jones would like to thank Karen Thompson for her unfailing support and encouragement. Steve King would like to thank Professor Keith Snell and Dr Paul Carter for their always insightful perspective on the nature and meaning of pauper language and also Dr Elizabeth Hurren for supporting another step in his reinvention as a storyteller.

Introduction

> The Humble Petition of Eleanor beck a Pauper of your Parish
> To the Churchwardens and Overseers of the Parish of Kirby Lonsdale
>
> Humbley Shew that your Petitioner has been dangerously ill this 3 Weeks and not able to get out of the House and is redused to the greatest want
>
> Your Petitioner humbly prays that you will be pleased to send her some relief or she must inevitably Perish ...[1]

So begins the first letter in the Kirkby Lonsdale parish collection from Eleanor Beck, a widow with a young son who was living in Mold, Flintshire. Beck was down on her luck, unable to provide a subsistence for her family and without sufficient local resources (kin, doctors or the means to pay for them, and work) to help her through a difficult time. She did what many of those in the same position would have done, writing to her place of settlement (in this case Kirkby Lonsdale in Westmorland, now Cumbria) asking them for something from the parish funds to tide her over until her fortunes improved. On its own, Beck's letter is unremarkable. We now know that there are in parish collections up and down the British Isles tens of thousands of similar letters from the poor and those who wrote on their behalf. They were a particular feature of the late-Old Poor Law in England and Wales.[2] Beck's supplicatory tone, her rhetorical use of 'dangerous' illness to establish her deservingness, and an insistence that parish relief was the last resort lest she should perish, will all be very familiar rhetorical vehicles to those who have used pauper letters in their work or who have followed trends in demotic history over the last two decades.[3]

[1] Letter 17, below.

[2] The letters in this volume were originally digitised and transcribed during a three-year project, jointly funded by the AHRC and the DFG in Germany, entitled 'Pauper Letters and Petitions for Poor relief in Britain and Germany, 1770–1914' (AH/I500561/1).

[3] This field of study owes much to the research and writing of Thomas Sokoll and James Stephen Taylor. Sokoll's magisterial survey of pauper letters in Essex appeared as a volume in this British Academy Series and between them Sokoll and Taylor have explored the experiences of numerous sub-groups of the poor through the lens of letters like that of Eleanor Beck. See T. Sokoll, 'Writing for relief: Rhetoric in English pauper letters 1800–1834', in *Being Poor in Modern Europe: Historical Perspectives 1800–1940* ed. A. Gestrich, S. King and L. Raphael (Bern, 2006) pp. 91–112;

Setting Beck's letter in the context of the Kirkby Lonsdale collection as a whole, however, reveals something more striking. This is the first of forty pieces of correspondence relating to Eleanor Beck and her family, a series which, as far as we can tell, is all but complete. Overall, there are more than 1,200 individual pieces of correspondence in the Kirkby Lonsdale collection relating to 131 individuals, families or kinship networks like the Becks', and spanning twenty-eight years between 1809 and 1836.[4] Although it would be optimistic to suggest that every one of the interleaving letters, invoices, memoranda, and other ephemera received by the parish in relation to these people were retained or have remained in the collection since it was first compiled, the Kirkby Lonsdale archive is one of the three most complete sets of parochial correspondence from the Old Poor Law for England and Wales.[5] Its survival is a matter of historical serendipity, but the fact that it was compiled so conscientiously in the first place was down to the efforts of one man: Stephen Garnett, who was the parish officer in charge of the day-to-day administration of relief in Kirkby Lonsdale throughout the period when these letters were received and about whom we have much more to say below.

In most cases, only a handful of letters by or relating to individual claimants and their families were written.[6] Yet in a significant minority, including the Becks, the number is such that it is possible to follow ordinary

T. Sokoll, 'Negotiating a living: Essex pauper letters from London, 1800–1834', *International Review of Social History* 45 (2000) pp. 19–46; T. Sokoll, 'Old age in poverty: The record of Essex pauper letters, 1780–1834', in *Chronicling Poverty: The Voices and Strategies of the English Poor, 1640–1840* ed. T. Hitchcock, P. King and P. Sharpe (Basingstoke, 1997) pp. 127–54; T. Sokoll *Essex Pauper Letters 1731–1837* (Oxford, 2001); J. S. Taylor, 'Voices in the crowd: The Kirkby Lonsdale township letters 1809–36', in Hitchcock, King and Sharpe, *Chronicling Poverty*, pp. 109–26; J. S. Taylor, 'A different kind of Speenhamland: Non-resident relief in the Industrial Revolution', *Journal of British Studies* 30 (1991) pp. 183–208; and J. S. Taylor, *Poverty, Migration and Settlement in the Industrial Revolution: Sojourners' Narratives* (Palo Alto, 1989).

[4] Taylor counted the number of individuals and families represented in the letters at 257. Although this is far more than we have been able to identify, given the idiosyncratic orthography of much of the correspondence and the difficulty of triangulating evidence at times, it is likely that the true number lies somewhere between our figure and his: Taylor, 'Voices in the Crowd', p. 111. In common with all other parish collections, that of Kirkby Lonsdale includes letters from or about paupers (that is, someone already in receipt of relief), and letters from or about those who were applying for relief, as well as official correspondence and associated material such as bills relating to both groups.

[5] The other two are Hulme (Lancashire) and Tetbury (Gloucestershire). See S. King, *Writing the Lives of the English Poor 1750s–1830s* (Montreal, 2019) pp. 32–60.

[6] For example, in the case of 90 of the 131 individual pauper/pauper families we identified in the overall collection, the number of pieces of correspondence totals five or fewer; and in the case of 42 individuals only a single letter exists. This is a 'normal' profile for parochial collections. See King, *Writing the Lives*, p. 24.

lives and relief 'careers' in great detail over extended periods of time.[7] Serial letter writers/subjects of correspondence dominate numerically all of the parochial archives that we are aware of, and the Kirkby Lonsdale collection is no different in this respect. Against this backdrop, the letters selected for inclusion in the present volume represent almost half of the entire Kirkby Lonsdale township collection, but the 599 pieces of correspondence relate to just twenty individual claimants and their families. Our selection criteria (and the nature of the resultant sample) are detailed at greater length below but at their core is a desire to allow readers to engage with the most complete life-cycles in the wider collection while at the same time including the full epistolary interplay between claimants, parish officials and others – those we have described elsewhere as the 'advocates' of the poor under the English and Welsh Old Poor Law.[8]

Serial subjects like these provide a unique lens through which to view wider issues such as the experience of being poor, the nature of pauper agency, chronologies of the development of sustained literacy, and the nature and limitations of state power in the long eighteenth-century. Through correspondence by or relating to them, it is possible to follow the fortunes of widows (like Eleanor Beck); abandoned wives; labourers without work and those too old or too sick to earn a living; families in periodic crisis; and others facing chronic long-term hardship. The lives of paupers already in receipt of relief, and poor people applying for relief either for the first time or after some time had elapsed since their last application, are played out here and the stories they tell are correspondingly complex and affecting. Through these case studies, the reader can: trace the intricacies of negotiation for relief under a discretionary system of welfare; follow the development of rhetorical strategies by the poor in their own letters, and the reactions and responses of parish officials to those strategies; and discover for themselves the importance of a much wider network of social relations and cultural influences in mediating the relief relationship. Taken as a whole, the correspondence has the power to demonstrate once and for all that the poor were far from passive or powerless in their dealings with the parish under the Old Poor Law, and that they were able to marshal a formidable armoury of sentiment, linguistic sophistication and community support in their negotiations for relief.

[7] For examples of work that has used this sort of extended letter series in other places, see P. Sharpe, 'Survival Strategies and stories: Poor widows and widowers in early industrial England', in *Widowhood in Medieval and Early Modern Europe* ed. S. Cavallo and L. Warner (London, 1999) pp. 220–39 and S. A. King, 'The residential and familial arrangements of English pauper letter writers, 1800–1840s', in *Accommodating Poverty: The Housing and Living Arrangements of the English Poor, c.1600–1850* ed. J. McEwan and P. Sharpe (Basingstoke, 2011) pp. 145–68.

[8] S. A. King and P. Jones, 'Testifying for the Poor: Epistolary Advocates and the Negotiation of Parochial Relief in England, 1800–1834', *Journal of Social History* 49 (2016) pp. 784–807.

Eleanor Beck used all of these strategies in her battle to survive the hardships of a difficult life, and was very successful in doing so. She and her family managed to eke out a living in North Wales, seventy-five miles from Kirkby Lonsdale, for the best part of three decades despite long periods of unemployment, regular bouts of sickness, long-term disability and the vagaries of old age. At times it is clear that they did little more *than* survive; but the correspondence leave us in no doubt that even this would have been impossible without the support of Eleanor's parish allowance and other small grants of relief from Kirkby Lonsdale.[9] When her long association with the parish finally came to an end in May 1836, a daughter-in-law, Charlotte, wrote to the overseer 'to inform you of the death of my poor mother Elenor Beck[.] She died this morning affter a Long Illness' [Letter 55]. But Charlotte's real purpose in writing was far more pragmatic and, in the context of this collection, far more interesting than simply notifying the parish of Eleanor's death: 'I most Humbley Implore your Goodness to help [me] out of this Distress to Bury my Old aged Mother as I asure you I have nothing Twoards her funeral and Cannot get any Without your assistance'. Thus, the parish of Kirkby Lonsdale, which had for so long supported Eleanor Beck in her home in North Wales, remained the last resort for Eleanor (and her family) at the very end.[10]

Pauper Letters and Settlement under the Old Poor Law

Pauper letters and associated correspondence from epistolary advocates and poor law officials were in large part the product of a particular set of structural conditions that governed the organisation of relief under the English and Welsh Old Poor Law. In the founding Act of 1601 each parish was made responsible for the relief or maintenance of its own poor. It was not, however, made clear in this crucial piece of legislation who actually 'belonged' to a parish for relief purposes.[11] Inevitably, disputes arose within parishes about the lodging and maintenance of the migrant poor, and between parishes about who should be held responsible for vagrants and those with no fixed or

[9] Her experience speaks to Peter Solar's construction of the Old Poor Law as a critical safety net in eighteenth-century England and Wales: P. Solar, 'Poor relief and English economic development before the industrial revolution', *Economic History Review* 48 (1995) pp. 1–22.

[10] On the active and positive part that parishes played in the funerals of paupers in this period, see E. Hurren and S. A. King, 'Begging for a burial: Death and the poor law in eighteenth and nineteenth century England', *Social History* 30 (2005) pp. 321–41.

[11] *An Act for the Relief of the Poor* (43 Elizabeth I c. 2), 1601.

clear place of belonging.[12] As a result of this lacuna, a further act was passed in 1662 (and amended or augmented several times thereafter) which sought to replace the amorphous concept of 'belonging' with the more certain (and legally enforceable) one of 'settlement'.[13] Under the 1662 Act, paupers and prospective paupers were tied to a specific parish for relief purposes by a number of 'heads of settlement'. These included being: born in a parish; resident for 40 days or more; hired as a servant for a year and a day; or a lessee of property to the value of £10 a year. Furthermore, women lost their own settlement and took that of their husband on marriage.[14] The result of these two key pieces of legislation is that, although parishes had an obligation to address the problem of poverty and hardship on their doorstep, they only had a responsibility to relieve or maintain their own poor. Moreover, even by the 1660s the definition of who was poor and who not lay with parochial officials, albeit that those turned down for relief or given less than they felt they needed could apply to magistrates for remedy, a matter to which we return below.[15]

This intertwining Black Letter law meant that parish officers were supposed to be vigilant both in making sure that people did not gain a settlement in a place and thus become a potential burden at some point in the future, and that those applying for relief or (less systematically) at risk of doing so actually had a settlement and thus a right to be heard. For those found to have no settlement rights, dependence or sometimes even the threat of dependence could result in removal from a host parish back to a place of

[12] On the ubiquity of this question for European welfare systems, see J. Innes, S. A. King and A. Winter, 'Settlement and Belonging in Europe, 1500–1930s: Structures, Negotiations and Experiences', in *Migration, Settlement and Belonging in Europe, 1500s–1930s* ed. S. A. King and A. Winter (Oxford, 2013) pp. 1–28.

[13] *An Act for the Better Relief of the Poor of this Kingdom*, better known as the *Settlement and Removal Act* (14 Charles 2 c. 12). On the various issues surrounding 'belonging', chargeability (that is parochial responsibility for the poor) and settlement under the early English poor law, see Steve Hindle, *On the Parish? The Micro-Politics of Poor Relief in Rural England, c.1550–1750* (Oxford, 2004), Chapter 5. A key summary of the situation post–1662 can be found in K. D. M. Snell, *Parish and Belonging: Community, Identity and Welfare in England and Wales, 1700–1950* (Cambridge, 2006) pp. 84–86.

[14] For an excellent introduction to the structural conditions of the *Settlement and Removal Act*, as well as to its background and the impact that it had on the lives of the poor, see J. S. Taylor, 'The Impact of Pauper Settlement, 1691–1834', *Past and Present* 73 (1976) pp. 42–74. Specifically on the problem that transferred settlement posed for women see P. Sharpe, 'Parish women: Maternity and the limitations of maiden settlement in England, 1662–1834', in *Obligation, Entitlement and Dispute under the English Poor Laws* ed. P. Jones and S. King (Newcastle, 2015) pp. 168–92.

[15] P. King, 'The rights of the poor and the role of the law: The impact of pauper appeals to the summary courts 1750–1834,' in Jones and King, *Obligation, Entitlement and Dispute*, pp. 235–62.

legal settlement.[16] In this sense settlement was vital for the poor, an aspect of their identity and allegiance which could mean the difference between survival and starvation in times of hardship. Yet, as local case law interpreting the rules of having, gaining and losing settlement multiplied, and as the scale of migration and urbanisation intensified in eighteenth-century England, the compelling simplicity of removal was rapidly lost. Inevitably, and increasingly, many of those who established a settlement in one parish (having been born there, for example) spent long periods (perhaps even decades, and, occasionally, whole lifetimes) in another.[17]

One solution to the problem of a person or family being 'out of their place' when falling into poverty was that those who migrated from their settlement parish could apply for a certificate to prove that they 'belonged' to that place should they become dependent on relief. Certification was intended to facilitate migration: holders could only be removed from their parish of residence when they actually became chargeable, not simply because it looked as though they might. However, for a variety of pragmatic and self-interested reasons parishes were always reluctant to issue settlement certificates, and there is considerable evidence that by the middle of the eighteenth century their use, never particularly widespread, was in steep decline.[18] Nonetheless, by the final years of the eighteenth century, the combination of a rapidly industrialising economy, migration and significant population growth meant that the numbers of the migrant poor in England and Wales had risen to unprecedented levels.[19] In so far as it is possible to imagine a 'typical' community in the early 1800s, its membership would have included variable proportions of, *inter alia*: the definitively and obviously settled poor already in receipt of relief; people with settlement who were on the verge of dependency; those who held certificates; vagrants and sojourners; those who were clearly without any claims of settlement; and a group – sometimes a very large group – of families whose settlement would be ambiguous and contestable if they ever fell into poverty and applied to their host parish. Against this backdrop it is clear from other studies that in some places and at some times the poor were still liable to be removed in large numbers to their settlement

[16] The question of when settlement examinations were taken to determine parochial liabilities is a complex and contested matter, especially for the later Old Poor Law. For a good rendering of the issues, see R. Wells, 'Migration, the law and parochial policy in eighteenth and nineteenth-century southern England', *Southern History* 15 (1993) pp. 86–139.

[17] This is the clear inference to be drawn from C. Pooley and J. Turnbull, *Migration and Mobility in Britain since the Eighteenth Century* (London, 1998).

[18] Snell, *Parish and Belonging*, pp. 98–100. A further Act was passed in 1795 which removed the clause in the 1662 legislation whereby those who were only likely to become chargeable could be removed to their parish of settlement, thus finally dispensing with the theoretical need for parish certificates. 35 George III c. 101.

[19] I. D. Whyte, *Migration and Society in Britain, 1550–1830* (Basingstoke, 2000) pp. 138–41.

parish on becoming chargeable.[20] Yet, it is also clear that even larger numbers were not routinely removed at all. Instead, they were relieved (temporarily and, sometimes, in the long-term) at a distance.[21]

Thus, from the 1780s onwards a system of 'out-parish' relief was increasingly the norm for existing paupers, those applying for relief who lived away from their settlement parish, and for many parishes which sought (or agreed) to keep them there.[22] The poor remained chargeable to their parish of settlement, but rather than travelling back to receive relief it was sent to them where they lived by means of an intermediary, or was administered by the parish of residence and then repaid by their 'home' parish.[23] A number of reasons have been suggested for the development and rapid adoption of the out-parish system from the 1780s onwards. It may (and probably did) have something to do with the fact that legal settlement and removal activity was relatively costly for parishes, and was therefore something they wished to avoid if possible.[24] In growing urban centres, and particularly in London, it could well be that the sheer pace of population growth and casual migration made formal removal unworkable and unrealistic.[25] And it almost certainly had something to do with the needs of the growing industrial labour market: it made little sense for a parish of residence to eject large parts of its labour force during temporary downturns in trade, or for a settlement parish to force unemployed families to return 'home' and face long-term dependency when a stop-gap payment might tide them over until trade improved.[26] Yet none of these explanations is wholly sufficient to explain either the huge growth, or the nature, of the out-parish system of relief as it developed after the 1780s, not even when taken together. It is for this reason perhaps, that Craig Muldrew and Steven King have suggested that it was a shift in the availability of small change and the development of other reliable money transmission mechanisms

[20] Snell, *Parish and Belonging*, pp. 100–101; Taylor, 'The Impact of Pauper Settlement', p. 53 n. 31.

[21] S. A. King, 'Poor Relief, Settlement and Belonging in England, 1780s to 1840s', in King and Winter, *Migration, Settlement and Belonging*, pp. 83–93.

[22] It is important to note, however, that the 'out-parish' system of relieving certain paupers at a distance had existed since at least the 1720s. The earliest 'classic' pauper letter we have found (conforming to the rhetorical and formal model of the majority of those in this volume, and in Sokoll's) was sent in 1728: East Sussex County Record Office, PAR 496/37/3, Mary Harte of Alresford, Hampshire, to Mr. Eagle of Uckfield, West Sussex, 1 February 1728.

[23] This is, of course, a process that generates extensive chains of correspondence between parish officials, the poor and those who advocated for them.

[24] King, 'Poor Relief, Settlement and Belonging', p. 83; Taylor, 'The Impact of Pauper Settlement', p. 57 n. 40.

[25] D. Green, *Pauper Capital: London and the Poor law, 1790–1870* (Aldershot, 2010) pp. 20, 51.

[26] King, 'Poor Relief, Settlement and Belonging', pp. 83–4; S. A. King, '"It is impossible for our Vestry to judge his case into perfection from here": Managing the Distance Dimensions of Poor Relief, 1800–40', *Rural History* 16 (2005) pp. 163–65.

that underpinned the development of this extra-legal network. Crudely, officials, the poor and advocates were only likely to have written in sustained fashion if there was a realistic hope of money following letters.[27]

However, as Steven King has also demonstrated elsewhere, the decision of whether or not to relieve an applicant at a distance was a complex one, and influenced by many more factors than simply whether such a transaction made economic sense. One consideration that appears to have been of real significance relates to the family ties binding the poor to their place of residence or parish of settlement. King found that for the parishes of Sowerby and Calverley in Yorkshire, for example, bilateral removal activity (or the lack of it) seems to have been closely tied to extended family networks, so that paupers and poor families were far more likely to be removed if they had significant kin in their *settlement* parish, and far less likely if their kin networks were more firmly rooted in their parish of *residence*. It could be argued that this, again, was an economic decision made by both applicants and parochial officers based on the long-term likelihood of kinship help in support of or substitution for parochial welfare. Yet taken alongside other evidence relating to the importance of sentiment and the continuing influence of notions of 'belonging' under the Old Poor Law (about which we will have more to say later in this Introduction), it seems clear that paupers and the prospective poor – and, in particular, certain categories or classes of poor people – were able to negotiate relief at a distance over considerable periods of time on terms favourable to themselves.[28] In the case of Eleanor Beck, for example, we do not know how much weight the vestry gave her wishes when deciding to relieve her at arm's length, but we do know that she managed to remain in Mold, with the support of Kirkby Lonsdale parish funds, for twenty-eight years, raising a family there, at least some of whom later became distantly dependent on the same parish. This is despite the fact that her situation changed dramatically during that period, from partial economic independence to, at one stage, total dependence on the parish [Letters 17 to 56].

Both in the national context and the Kirkby Lonsdale sample, the question of whether (and how quickly) pauper letter writers were successful in securing new, renewed or different allowances is a complex one. The authors of these letters (officials, other advocates, existing paupers and the prospective poor) invariably stressed the need for urgency of action or a prompt reply, or

[27] C. Muldrew and S. A. King, 'Cash, wages and the economy of makeshifts in England 1650–1800', in *Experiencing Wages: Social and Cultural Aspects of Wage Forms in Europe since 1500* ed. P. Scholliers and L. Schwarz (Oxford, 2003) pp. 32–56.

[28] S. A. King, 'Reconstructing lives: The poor, the poor law and welfare in rural industrial communities', *Social History* 22 (1997) pp. 318–38.

both, from the recipient. In some cases we can see that officials did act, and presumably at speed once the letter arrived. Stephen Garnett, in his capacity as Guardian of the Poor, annotated many of the original letters with his decisions or the amount awarded, and where we have the replies of officials systematically recorded (as, for example, in the nearby town of Lancaster) it does seem that they appreciated the need for rapid action in some cases.[29] Where we do not have such a paper trail, the issue becomes more opaque. This is not helped by the fact that individual payments for out-parish relief might appear in the accounts of the settlement parish, the host parish, both or neither, depending on what sort of allowance was awarded and who actually delivered it into the hands of the pauper or their representative. Sometimes, notably where a settlement parish had several dependent paupers in a single host community, the allowances might simply be recorded as a lump sum under the name of the person conveying the allowances. Without a note to this effect, the person named appears in the same way as any other supplier of goods and services to the poor law and the nature of official responses to the claims of the out-parish poor is obscured. In practice, then, we do see some rapid and substantial responses (though these are not generally calibrated either to the amount requested or the circumstances described) but we also see letters persistently ignored such that writers had to renew their appeals time and again. Most letters, however, do seem to have received a response of sorts, something which is evident in Kirkby Lonsdale letters that open with an acknowledgement of prior relief or correspondence. These responses probably arrived less quickly than the writer or advocate thought necessary (something which is often noted in further correspondence) but there are good reasons why such delays should occur. These included problems of getting and sending small change, addresses for the poor which were out of date or imperfectly specified, the need to convene a vestry, officials being away from home, and letters being lost in the post.

Of course, for poor writers a central concern was how to ensure that their letters arrived promptly at the required destination, as King has shown in a wider context.[30] In our period this was by no mean an unproblematic matter. While postage costs were generally paid by the recipient (and many letter writers complain about the costs of receiving their relief enclosed in letters from the overseer) the postal system itself was susceptible to thefts, misdirection, and loss. There is perhaps a sense that in the very last decades of the Old Poor Law, poor writers came to imbue 'the post' with more trust than had been the case in the 1790s or early 1800s, and it is certainly clear that the majority of Kirkby Lonsdale letters were conveyed through this system. Yet,

[29] Lancashire Record Office, PR 866 and 867, Lancaster Letter Books, 1809–1840.
[30] King, *Writing the Lives*, pp. 61–89.

in common with all other places where large collections of texts survive, the post was only one way for letters to travel. Thus, they might be conveyed by trusted parties (relatives, neighbours and friends), tradesmen who plied their trade between a host community and a place of settlement, by officials themselves, on packet boats, or via itinerant hawkers who were coming in the general direction of the settlement community. Sometimes these modes of conveyance were explicitly recognised in the text itself, as for instance where the writer asked for an immediate reply to be sent via 'the bearer'. Such avenues had the advantage for the poor writer that the overseer would not have to pay for receipt of the letter and might thus be in a better mood when he read it. For Kirkby Lonsdale, as with other communities, there was no inevitable correlation between the distance from which the poor wrote, and the mode of conveyance. Some people used the postal system even though they lived close by and could easily have walked the letter over. Others, sometimes at considerable distance, either brought letters themselves or got trusted others to bring them rather than use the postal system. This was doubtless a calculated act designed to emphasise the depth of need and the fact of their belonging to a place. Intermediaries might also be able to provide first hand testimony of suffering and urgent need to back up the stories told in the letters themselves. In the broadest sense, therefore, the decisions that the poor made about how to convey letters can be understood as part of the very negotiation process rather than a simple mechanical decision rooted in considerations of cost or distance. In the end, and as King has argued elsewhere, it is clear that it was of the greatest importance to paupers that their letters arrived promptly and safely, and it is equally clear that parish officials generally reacted to the letters of poor writers in a timely fashion, not least because the costs of failing to do so could occasion ever more correspondence and ever more cost.[31]

It is the out-parish system, then, that explains why large numbers of pauper letters were routinely received by parishes in England and Wales under the later Old Poor Law, and why quantities of surrounding correspondence by other parties to the relief relationship was also generated.[32] In this context (and as we have already observed), the collection of parish correspondence for Kirkby Lonsdale is remarkably complete. It is important to understand, however, that this is merely an artefact of preservation or lack of it. We know from other parochial sources that many more letters were

[31] King, *Writing the Lives*, pp. 93–106.

[32] It is important to note that some paupers and prospective paupers who lived in their settlement community also chose to send letters to officials. This happened when the person was too sick to move, when they could not leave work, or where the topography of large parishes (for instance in West Yorkshire or Wales) was such that walking to find officials or attend a vestry would be a considerable task.

received by officials than were retained. In some parishes (Thrapston in Northamptonshire, for instance) original letters have been lost but an overseer or clerk took the trouble to copy incoming correspondence and some replies into a bound copy letter book. The fact of the book being bound goes some way to explaining its survival, but the act of copying reveals several hundred pauper letters that would otherwise be lost to us. Where comprehensive vestry minutes survive (as, for instance, at Garstang in Lancashire) these record the receipt and reading out of letters now lost.[33] Overseers' accounts record the costs of paper, ink, candles, and postage, with in some places (Calverley in West Yorkshire, for instance) the scale of spending such as to indicate that a collection at least comparable in scale to that of Kirkby Lonsdale once existed. In some parishes, our project found letters still in the parish chest at the local church, a mass of unbound paper which simultaneously shows the likely scale of the original collections, were we only able to view them at the time they were created, and the ease with which such an archive might be lost. Annotations and drawings on some letters show that, after a time, this correspondence might literally become scraps for recycling. It seems likely, then, that many hundreds of thousands of letters by, about or for the poor circulated throughout England, Wales and Scotland from the 1780s.[34] Yet, if such material was created and necessitated by the structural conditions of the Elizabethan poor and settlement laws, its character and content was shaped and mediated by the ongoing and evolving relationship between paupers, prospective paupers, parish officials and others who were drawn into its sphere of influence. How these relationships unfolded, and how we can trace them in the correspondence collected here, is the subject of the next section.

Pauper Letters, Negotiation, and Agency under the Old Poor Law

As we have noted, under the English and Welsh Old Poor Law the poor had an absolute right to apply for relief from their parish of settlement when they

[33] Vestries were meetings of ratepayers, usually convened to consider and sign off the annual accounts of parochial officials such as overseers of the poor or to deal with strategic issues such as decisions over whether to build workhouses after an Act of 1723 facilitated such institutional relief. Over the eighteenth century these potentially large gatherings were slowly replaced with 'select vestries' in which much smaller groups of taxpayers convened to undertake more detailed and frequent oversight of parochial officials and processes. Many such meetings considered the appeals (written and in person) of the settled and out-parish poor. The rules for select vestries were regularised in 1818–19, with the passing of the Sturges-Bourne Acts. See S. Shave, 'The impact of Sturges Bourne's poor law reforms in rural England', *Historical Journal* 56 (2013) pp. 399–429.

[34] For more on these issues see King, *Writing the Lives*, *passim*.

faced economic hardship. But most of those who have worked closely with parish sources acknowledge that this was very different from the right to *receive* relief. The distinction is a fine one, and it relies on an understanding of the Old Poor Law as an essentially discretionary system of welfare.[35] Thus, while parishes had a statutory duty to relieve or maintain their poor when destitute, the actual implementation of these key concepts remained fluid and open to interpretation. There was no clear definition of 'poverty', no universally applicable measure of 'destitution', and so the question of who should or should not be relieved was, in the final analysis, left to the discretion of parish officials or select vestries. Similarly, the Old Poor Law gave little direction as to what or how much should be given by way of relief, and how regularly it should be given, simply placing a requirement on parishes to respond to legitimate cases where they arose.[36] Hence, parishes have been described, in relief terms, as 'welfare republics' in which the needs or wishes of rate payers, the depth of local resources, variable local demand and different interpretations of statutory and customary rules and norms were constantly held in balance.[37] Indeed, some historians now view local and regional variability of practice as a defining characteristic of the Old Poor Law.[38]

Within this discretionary system, if poor applicants disagreed or were dissatisfied with the decision of the overseer or vestry they could appeal to a local magistrate for arbitration and a further ruling, as we noted briefly above. There are intuitive reasons to suppose that this element of appeal to an independent third party would have been well-used.[39] In practice, however, recourse by 'wronged' paupers and applicants to higher powers under the Old

[35] The debate over the rights of the poor under the Old Poor Law was recently revived with the publication of Lorie Charlesworth's legalistic review of the historiography in *Welfare's Forgotten Past: A Socio-Legal History of the Poor Law* (Abingdon, 2010). Charlesworth maintained from the outset that the fact that 'Poor law was law ... has slipped from the consciousness of those researching and publishing on the history of welfare in England and Wales' (p. 1), and she went on to claim that settlement law gave paupers an absolute right to receive relief. We would argue that this perspective understates the deep understanding and serious engagement of welfare historians with Black Letter and case law in the past, and also fails to comprehend the actual conditions under which relief was negotiated locally. For a more detailed discussion of this view see King's review in *Rural History*, 22 (2011) pp. 271–78.

[36] Hindle, *On the Parish?*, pp. 13–14, 379–98; S. A. King, *Poverty and Welfare in England, 1700–1850: A Regional Perspective* (Manchester, 2000) pp. 18–22.

[37] On the way that this balance could vary according to the exact causes of poverty see S. A. King, *Sickness, Medical Welfare and the English Poor 1750–1834* (Manchester, 2018) pp. 1–18.

[38] S. A. King, 'Negotiating the Law of Poor Relief in England, 1800–1840', *History* 96 (2011) p. 433; P. Jones and S. A. King, 'Introduction: Obligation, Entitlement and Dispute: Navigating the English Poor Laws, 1600–1900', in Jones and King, *Obligation, Entitlement and Dispute*, p. 3.

[39] On this issue see P. King, 'Social inequality, identity and the labouring poor in eighteenth century England', in *Identity and Agency in England, 1500–1800* ed. H. French and J. Barry (Basingstoke, 2004) pp. 60–87.

Poor Law appears to have been statistically quite rare, in contrast to the impression now emerging for the New Poor Law.[40] Rather, the picture that has emerged of negotiations for relief from the study of pauper letters, particularly between 1780 and 1834 (the relevant period for this volume), is that they were highly complex and nuanced and more likely to be characterised by courtesy, familiarity, dogged determination, and the interplay of subtle cultural markers, than by direct contestation, vehement denunciation, or outright threats.[41] This is not to suggest that the poor were unwilling or unable to use complaint or the threat of further action if negotiations with vestries and overseers broke down; rather, it is to make the crucial observation that, in general, by '[filtering] their material and practical needs through a fine rhetorical mesh', and by fostering and maintaining an ongoing dialogue with parish officials, they avoided conflict and the need to deliver ultimata.[42] This is attested by the fact that in the last decades of the eighteenth century the formal petition (for a long time the predominant form for written appeals for local relief) had been overtaken by the familiar letter, an epistolary form which (as the name suggests) not only fostered familiarity between senders and recipients, but also established a dialogic relationship which, in practice, was hard to break.[43]

[40] The early results from a new AHRC-funded project analysing letters sent to the central board of commissioners in London after 1834 suggests that paupers were more likely to appeal to this higher authority after 1834 than they were to the magistrates before. See http://intheirownwrite.org for further details.

[41] See, for example, P. Jones, '"I Cannot keep my place without being deascent": Pauper Letters, Parish Clothing and Pragmatism in the South of England, 1750–1830', *Rural History* 20 (2009) pp. 31–49; P. Jones, 'Widows, Work and Wantonness: Pauper letters and the Boundaries of Entitlement under the Old Poor Law', in Jones and King, *Obligation, Entitlement and Dispute*, pp. 139–67; S. A. King, '"Stop This Overwhelming Torment of Destiny": Negotiating Financial Aid at Times of Sickness under the English Old Poor Law, 1800–1840', *Bulletin of the History of Medicine* 79 (2005) pp. 228–60; S. A. King, '"I Fear You Will Think Me Too Presumptuous in My Demands but Necessity Has No Law": Clothing in English Pauper Letters, 1800–1834', *International Review of Social History* 54 (2009) pp. 207–36; King, *Writing the Lives*; Sokoll, 'Negotiating a Living', pp. 42–46; Sokoll, *Essex Pauper Letters*, pp. 56–61; Sokoll, 'Writing for Relief', pp. 91–102.

[42] King, 'Negotiating the Law', pp. 423, 428–34; Jones, '"I Cannot keep my place"', p. 31.

[43] We are not concerned in this Introduction or volume with petitions. These crop up occasionally in parochial collections but by the 1780s their formulaic language and structure, a mainstay of appeals to magistrates/courts and elite groups in earlier periods, are almost completely absent. On petitions, see J. Healey, *The First Century of Welfare: Poverty and Poor Relief in Lancashire, 1620–1730* (Woodbridge, 2014) and R. Houston, *Peasant Petitions: Social Relations and Economic Life on Landed Estates 1600–1850* (Basingstoke, 2014). On the decline of petitionary cultures see P. Jones and S. A. King, 'From Petition to Pauper Letter: The Development of an Epistolary Form', in Jones and King, *Obligation, Entitlement and Dispute*, pp.70–5.

Of course, it is important not to confuse this fostering of familiarity and the conscious establishment of dialogic networks by the poor and their advocates with uncritical notions of 'friendship' or harmony in relief negotiations. It is axiomatic that the relationship between the poor and parochial officials and vestries was underpinned by a contest for limited resources, so that while the latter might have expected to keep a constant eye on opportunities to restrict or limit outlay from hard-won local taxes, the former might deploy a formidable armoury of rhetorical and strategic tools to gain competitive advantage in negotiations for relief. To this end, the poor showed a keen awareness of the laws relating to parish responsibilities in relief matters, and of the established rules governing the actions and behaviour of overseers and other parish officials. Even though they only rarely resorted to magistrates' appeals, for example, the settled and absent poor were not averse to using the threat of an appeal when more emollient strategies to secure relief had failed.[44] Yet, far more frequently deployed (in fact, almost universal) was the implied threat (usually in the less confrontational form of a prediction) that an applicant would be forced to bring themselves and their family 'home' to their parish of settlement should they be refused relief at a distance. This would establish a dependent relationship which might last years rather than a few weeks or months if the parish had acted when it could and should have.[45] We see this time and again in pauper (and advocate) letters, and it is no less of a motif for those represented in this volume. Thomas Robinson, for example, wrote more than once that 'without your assistance I see no prospect but to sell whatever few things we have and come back'; but he did so only to emphasise that 'if I could stay here I think I can perhaps get some thing to do by and by' [Letter 487]. As was so often the case, the 'threat' to come home was, in fact, framed as a promise to stay away with a little 'assistance' from the parish.

In the first instance, however, the poor generally avoided either threats or coercive predictions, instead deploying a range of universally recognised yardsticks of deservingness to build their case. Old age, infirmity and widowhood were the strongest of these measures, along with sickness, disability, and abandonment by the heads of households. Deployment of these core indicators was also the norm for the settled poor who could attend the vestry or the office of the overseer in person. For the out-parish poor such criteria were developed within letters and series of letters that used sophisticated narrative strategies and rhetorical constructions to further enhance their chances of

[44] King, 'Negotiating the Law', pp. 418, 420, 432.

[45] Poor writers frequently referred to the fact that peeling themselves off from a host community would mean the loss of financial credit, work, childcare and reputation. They also often noted the need for parishes to pay accumulated debts and the costs of finding them new accommodation and furnishing should the writer have to return 'home'.

success.[46] The rhetorics of 'nakedness' and 'starvation' were thus common, and often deployed with a great deal of strategic insight.[47] Eleanor Beck's son, Robert, wrote in May 1832 that 'the Children are all nearly naked, and starving', and later the same year he again asked for relief as 'we are all nearly starved' [Letter 30]. 'Starvation' was also used as a metaphor for extreme need in letters by, or relating to, Richard Garlick, Christopher Grime, Betty Langhorn, Thomas Robinson and James Wilson; and 'nakedness', too, is directly deployed many times in the letters in this volume.[48] But other, more complex, motifs to establish deservingness and entitlement are also integral to the correspondence. For example, notions of 'belonging' and 'friendship' were constantly referenced and deployed by the poor in their written appeals and personal vestry appearances. Moving beyond the simple, legal definition of belonging by settlement, these more fluid but no less important usages were constantly in play.[49] They were founded on indicators such as long residence in a host or settlement community; demonstrable connections with neighbours, family, and friends; ongoing practical, economic, or emotional support from within the host community; and a long-established contribution by poor people themselves to their place of residence, whether through employment, raising a family, or by supporting or being supported by, friends and neighbours. Grace Nelson, for example, was described by her doctor as being in particular need, for not only was she very ill and without means to take care of her three children, but the 'resources of her friends' nearby were said to be 'spent' [Letter 419]. Thomas Robinson constructed his claims for periodic assistance carefully, weighing the debt he owed the Kirkby Lonsdale vestry against the support he could call upon in Preston. He was particularly mindful to point out to the overseers that 'we could not possibly have done so long as we have done but for the assistance of our friends at Halton', but 'as they have nothing [more] to spare without injuring themselves we cannot expect them to maintain us altogether' [Letter 485]. Any or all of these yardsticks might be deployed by the poor in an effort to persuade officials of their

[46] For the particularly sophisticated rhetorical approaches adopted by the sick, see King, *Sickness, Medical Welfare*.

[47] Jones, '"I Cannot Keep my Place"', pp. 33–5; Jones, 'Widows, Work and Wantonness', pp. 160–61; King, '"I Fear You Will Think Me"', pp. 220, 223–25, 227; Sokoll, 'Negotiating a Living', pp. 31, 39–40; King, *Writing the Lives*, pp. 204–16.

[48] Claims of nakedness spoke to the neglect of the most basic of parochial duties, that of keeping the respectable and deserving poor actually respectable. The symbolism of nakedness, notably of children, was also used as a means of admonishing parishes by the epistolary and personal advocates of the poor.

[49] S. A. King, 'Friendship, Kinship and Belonging in the Letters of Urban Paupers, 1800–1840', *Historical Social Research* 33 (2008) pp. 249–77; K. D. M. Snell, 'Belonging and Community: Understandings of "Home" and "Friends" among the English Poor, 1750–1850', *Economic History Review* 65 (2012) pp. 1–25.

deservingness to be relieved away from their parish of settlement. Conversely, they might also be deployed in the context of a writer's settlement parish in order to establish a sense of obligation at a distance. In particular, letter writers routinely asked overseers and parish officials to stand as their 'friend' when no others could be found to assist them, and reminded recipients not only of the legal connection between the writer and their parish of settlement, but of long personal connections as well.[50] Ann and John Thistlethwaite wrote that 'I hop you will beffriend me at this time or it is up with Me on all sides', and William Lowry was keen to recall the overseer's 'Kind Generosty upon which Sir I have always found you to be a friend' [Letters 530 and 332]. In this way, the importance of attachment and belonging to both the host community, and the place of settlement, were constantly emphasised and rehearsed, not in opposition to each other but as different aspects of a complex patchwork of emotional and cultural resources to be drawn on in times of need.

As these examples suggest, poor writers lacked neither guile nor sophistication in their written appeals for relief, but the letters in this volume also demonstrate convincingly that they exercised a surprising level of agency in their negotiations as well. Ascribing historical 'agency' to the actions of the poor is fraught with the dangers of assumption and misconception, and Megan Webber is right to point out that '[h]istorians regularly refer to agency, yet very rarely do they explicitly define it'.[51] However, she herself also points towards the most comprehensive and compelling definition of agency with regard to the poor when referring to the work of E.P. Thompson at the very beginning of her discussion.[52] Thus, in the context of the eighteenth-century food riot, Thompson famously asked the question: 'being hungry, what do people do?' In expanding his query, he constructed a concise framework for understanding the concept of the agency of the poor across the board:

> How is their behaviour modified by custom, culture and reason? And (having granted that the primary stimulus of 'distress' is present) does their behaviour contribute towards any more complex, culturally-mediated function, which cannot be reduced ... back to stimulus again.[53]

[50] In one instance Robert Beck specifically addresses Stephen Garnett, the overseer of Kirkby Lonsdale as 'Dear Friend', and in another laments that he has 'no other friend to send but to you' [Letters 53 and 47]. See also King, 'Friendship', p. 258; Snell, 'Belonging and Community', p. 19, *n*.258.

[51] M. C. Webber, 'Troubling Agency: Agency and Charity in Early Nineteenth-Century London', *Historical Research*, 91 (2018) p. 116.

[52] Ibid., 117.

[53] E. P. Thompson, 'The Moral Economy of the English Crowd in the Eighteenth Century', *Past and Present* 50 (1971) pp. 77–8.

Bearing in mind Thompson's succinct definition, it is clear that by the early years of the nineteenth century, in their sophisticated deployment of rhetorical cultural markers, in the shift from the supplicatory petition to the dialogic familiar letter, and in the constant (and consistent) rehearsal of accepted touchstones of belonging and attachment, the out-parish poor were masters at negotiating for a share of scarce communal resources. It is even more remarkable that they honed these skills at precisely the point when, we are told, their claim for consideration under the Old Poor Law was at its most precarious, and that they had 'lost much of the legitimacy they had earlier enjoyed'.[54]

Across the discipline of social history, there has recently been a revival of interest in a 'new history from below', and the study of social interactions and negotiations through pauper letters, petitions and other demotic sources are central to this movement.[55] Without minimising the huge structural disadvantages that the parish poor faced during our period, the correspondence in the Kirkby Lonsdale collection points forcefully to the fact that they did have agency in the context of the relief relationship. They exercised it to mitigate the worst excesses of poverty, periodic unemployment, growing urbanisation, and industrial expansion, and they were often very successful at negotiating a living even at a distance. Taken together, this correspondence also shows us that those negotiations were conducted within a shared linguistic register founded on consensus and compromise. Direct and open conflict was rare, and it is clear that all sides in these negotiations recognised and respected the fact that the local state was, and was intended to be, malleable and flexible in approaching the claims of the poor.[56] When officials and vestries failed to act, or acted in ways other than the writer thought they should, further letters

[54] L. Hollen Lees, *The Solidarities of Strangers: The English Poor Laws and the People, 1700–1948* (Cambridge, 1998) p. 82. Indeed, this assessment is, perhaps, something that needs to be revisited in the light of what we now know about parish relations through pauper letters.

[55] The phrase is Tim Hitchcock's, and comes from 'A New History from Below', *History Workshop Journal* 57 (2004) pp. 294–98. For examples of this focus, in addition to the work already cited, see J. Bailey, '"Think Wot a Mother Must Feel": Parenting in English Pauper Letters, c.1760–1834', *Family and Community History* 13 (2010) pp. 5–19; L. Earner-Byrne, *Letters of the Catholic Poor: Poverty in Independent Ireland, 1920–1940* (Cambridge, 2017); P. Jones and S. A. King, 'Voices from the Far North: Pauper Letters and the Provision of Welfare in Sutherland, 1845–1900', *Journal of British Studies* 55 (2016) pp. 76–98; M. Lyons (ed.), *Ordinary Writings, Personal Narratives: Writing Practices in 19th and Early 20th Century Europe* (Bern, 2007); A. Tomkins, '"I mak Bould to Wrigt": First-Person Narratives in the History of Poverty in England, c.1750–1900', *History Compass* 9 (2011) pp. 365–73.

[56] It was only when this 'malleability' broke down, and parish officials began to draw back from tacitly agreed norms of behaviour towards the poor, that open conflict resulted. See, for example, P. Jones, 'Finding Captain Swing: Protest, Parish Relations, and the State of the Public Mind in 1830', *International Review of Social History* 54 (2009) pp. 449–53, and King, *Writing the Lives*, pp. 90–115.

would follow, often framing increased demands consequent on the inaction of parishes in the first place. Poor writers expected officials and others in 'their' parish to at least give their letters a hearing. The analogue to this expectation can be seen in a core feature of overseers' correspondence, which is that officials went to great lengths to explain lack of action or delayed response to the poor and their advocates. There was, in other words, a shared framework of expectations and, certainly by the late eighteenth century, a shared rhetorical infrastructure for exploring the boundaries of entitlement and deservingness in a discretionary welfare system. It is in part for this reason that the Kirkby Lonsdale collection, unlike that of Thomas Sokoll in the same record series, brings together *all* of the different components of the correspondence relating to individuals and family groups who applied for, and were often given, relief at a distance. For this community, these components were gathered together and coordinated by one man over the whole of the twenty-seven years covered by this volume, and it is to him, and the context of the parish in which he worked, that we now turn our attention.

Stephen Garnett and the Township of Kirkby Lonsdale

By the early years of the nineteenth century, Kirkby Lonsdale was an established and prosperous market town, having held a charter for its markets and fairs for at least 600 years. In 1849, five fairs were said to have been held there annually, signifying its importance as a trading centre and hub for the farmers and small manufacturers in the Lune Valley that surrounded it. While the letters in this volume were being written, Kirkby also had a carpet and blanket manufactory and many of its poorer inhabitants were employed in weaving basic linen and cotton cloths. Its general prosperity was attested by the fact that it was home to a free grammar school (established by letters patent in 1591), a book club (1794), a savings bank (1818), and the Royal Hotel, which housed the petty sessions for the Lonsdale Ward every Thursday.[57] By 1811, the town also had a workhouse, built under the terms of the Relief of the Poor Act, 1782 (22 George III c. 83, more commonly 'Gilbert's Act'), at a cost of £2,500.[58] The workhouse was incorporated for the use of paupers from seventeen parishes and townships thereabouts, and in

[57] P. J. Mannex, *History, Topography, and Directory, of Westmorland; and the Hundreds of Lonsdale and Amounderness in Lancashire* (London, 1849) p. 348.
[58] Ibid., p. 351. Also *Report from His Majesty's Commissioners for Inquiring into the Administration and Practical Operation of the Poor Laws: Appendix (B.2.). Answers to Town Queries, in Two Volumes, Vol.1*, Parliamentary Papers, 1834, vol. 44.

1834 it housed sixty-five inmates: twenty-three men, twenty-two women, and twenty children from nine years upwards.[59]

Yet, the history of the town is of far less interest to us here than that of a single individual who lived there. All of the letters in this volume – and, indeed, all of those in the Kirkby Lonsdale collection overall – were received by Stephen Garnett, who was appointed overseer of the parish in 1809 or thereabouts, and who later took the title of 'Guardian of the Poor' in or around 1814. As was mentioned at the beginning of this Introduction, the survival of the collection appears to have been almost entirely down to him. Unusually, though not uniquely, and for reasons that remain unexplained, Garnett kept just about every piece of correspondence that was sent by, or related to, the out-parish poor between 1809 and 1836. He did so more or less in date order, and he bundled the correspondence annually.

We know little about Garnett as a man, and what we do know is down the work of James Stephen Taylor, who has done more than anyone to shine a light on the Kirkby Lonsdale collection up to now. It is thanks to him that we know that Garnett was born in 1763 in the West Riding of Yorkshire, that he was resident in Kirkby Lonsdale in 1787, the date of his marriage, and that he was a grocer, seedsman, and auctioneer with a house and premises on the main street of the town.[60] This background is important if we wish to understand the Old Poor Law as essentially comprised of a matrix of welfare republics, because in this context the personalities of the overseer and (if convened) select vestry members are important to the basic sentiments that framed how the claims of both the out-parish and proximately settled poor were received. In this sense, Taylor's further characterisation of Stephen Garnett may need to be revised. In his volume on *Sojourner's Narratives*, in which he presents fifteen brief case studies drawn from the Kirkby Lonsdale collection, Taylor describes Garnett as 'apparently a hard case', moving on to say that, on the evidence of the letters, he was 'quick to suspect and slow to trust', and was 'largely insensitive to the pleadings of others'.[61] This construction of a harsh personality is in keeping with many early characterisations of overseers which saw them as corrupt, venal, hard-faced, incompetent, and decidedly on the side of the rate-paying classes.[62]

[59] *Report from His Majesty's Commissioners for Inquiring into the Administration and Practical Operation of the Poor Laws, Appendix (B.2.). Answers to Town Queries, in Two Volumes', Vol.1*, q.15 p. 243, Parliamentary Papers, 1834, vol. 44.

[60] Taylor, 'The Impact of Pauper Settlement', p. 68; Taylor, 'A Different Kind of Speenhamland', p. 195; Taylor, 'Voices in the Crowd', pp. 109–126.

[61] Taylor, *Poverty, Migration and Settlement*, p. 144.

[62] Such characterisations, for instance, dominate the work of D. Marshall, *The English Poor in the Eighteenth Century* (New York, 1969) and S. Webb and B. Webb, *English Poor Law History Part I: The Old Poor Law* (London, 1963 reprint).

In fact, there seems to be very little evidence, either in the letters or in the wider parish records, to support this view. Even though he kept very few of his own responses and replies to incoming correspondence, those that do remain paint a rather more humane and conscientious picture of Garnett as a man and a parish officer, especially when set in the context of the tens of thousands of other letters collected as part of the AHRC project outlined earlier in this Introduction. For example, in one of the earliest letters (1809) reproduced below, he received an invoice from the parish of Clayton, near Bradford, for relief paid to the Nelson family [Letter 359]. In the copy reply, written on the reverse of the Clayton overseer's invoice, Garnett observed that 'yours I Recd. and by it I observe what as you Have allowed Joseph Nelson appears like a weekly pension', and he went on to note that the parish 'never authorised you to Give him a pension [although] we have paid his House Rent regularly'. Nonetheless, Garnett continued:

> not doughting what...you have advanced him was done from motives of Humanity and I Concive it a very Necessary thing for one Overseer to place a sort of discretionary pour [*power*] or Confidence in another[,] and on that account I wish you to Relive Joseph Nelson as in your Judgement seems most proper[,] not doughting but that you will do the same as if you was doing for your own Township.

Thus began a relationship between Garnett and the Nelsons which lasted until at least the end of the period during which the letters were collected, and which, according to Taylor, cost the Kirkby ratepayers over £400 in relief.[63]

It is clear from elsewhere in this letter that in 1809 Garnett was very new to the job. He noted that he only became aware of the arrangement to pay the Nelsons' rent 'on Conversing with the late Overseer'. Yet, there is no sense that his approach towards them was the result of his status as a novice in these affairs, and these were not the words and actions of a man who had set his mind to oppose the claims of the poor. Indeed, he was to continue his constructive engagement with poor writers, advocates and officials in host parishes throughout his tenure.[64] Sixteen years later, in 1825, for instance, he wrote to the overseer of Ardsley, near Wakefield, in relation to Isaac Middlebrook who had made a claim for relief and had clearly told the Ardsley authorities that his settlement was at Kirkby Lonsdale. Even though Garnett maintained that that he could find no record of the man, and that his name

[63] Taylor, *Poverty, Migration and Settlement*, p. 161. Taylor's account also contains further useful details about the Nelsons, and about the nature of John Haley's relationship with them (pp. 161–64).

[64] It must also be noted, though, that in the early Nelson correspondence John Jenkinson, overseer of Clayton, does betray a degree of impatience at Garnett's tardy responses to his requests for reimbursement for relief paid to the family [Letters 360 and 366].

was not even known 'by the oldest Inhabitant' of Kirkby Lonsdale, he went on to say that:

> On this account I cannot authorise you to relief him on our account, but i wish to ^be^ rightly understood it is not our wish to put any obstackels in the way or cause any unnecessary trouble, if he can tell whear his parents lived or with whoom he himself lived and by what means he gained a settlement it will be attended to.[65]

Generally, all we hear from Garnett himself in the letters is a perfunctory 'Granted' or 'Not granted' appended here or there to a request for relief, but this narrative vacuum should not be taken as taciturnity or a lack of feeling towards the poor in his charge, not least because such silences are duplicated across the corpus of pauper letter collections even where we have clear evidence of officials acting with extraordinary generosity to the in- and out-parish poor. There is nothing in the content of the appeals he received, or in the ongoing correspondence from the poor, advocates and overseers, to suggest that they held him in anything other than high regard, and there are enough references (as noted above) to his being a 'friend' to both applicants and their intermediaries, and to his kind treatment of them, to dispel any notion that he was a particularly harsh member of his tribe. Overall, Stephen Garnett seems to have been a thorough, meticulous, and, as far as it is possible to tell, fair-minded man; which, it turns out, is greatly to our benefit, as well as to that of the poor whose letters and appeals he so painstakingly kept, for without his diligence we would be bereft of the case studies in this volume. Which case studies are represented here, and how and why they have been selected, is the subject of the next section.

The Kirkby Lonsdale Corpus and Editorial Selection

It has already been noted that, while this volume does not contain all the letters from the Kirkby Lonsdale collection, it does represent the full range of parochial correspondence arising from, and relating to, selected out-parish individuals and families. As such, it not only reflects negotiations between the poor, their advocates and parish officials, but also those between parishes in relation to the discharge of their responsibilities to the poor and to each other. In addition, it brings into view other voices crucial to the establishment and maintenance of entitlement, such as landlords requesting the payment of rent for poor residents [Letters 111, 150 and 194, for example], surgeons and

[65] Kendal Archive Centre, WPR19/7/18/29, Stephen Garnett to John Scorah, 1 November 1825. This letter falls outside the scope of the case studies in this volume.

doctors who wrote to confirm details of sickness and disability [Letters 7, 152 and 220], and third-party intermediaries (such as shopkeepers and neighbours) who received relief a distance, and who then passed it on to the out-parish poor [Letters 349 and 380]. Some, though by no means all, of these third-party letters include advocacy on behalf of claimants, confirming details of hardship and sickness, or simply stating that the writer believed the applicant to be a worthy object for out-parish relief [Letters 290 and 365]. This is true of many parish-to-parish communications as well, confirming our findings elsewhere that overseers very often wrote letters which strayed beyond their official capacity, and acted as advocates for the poor of other parishes in relief negotiations.[66] The collection also includes many pro-forma invoices alongside less formal requests from host parishes to receive reimbursement for relief paid on account. In short, any and all correspondence that was received and retained by the overseer on behalf of the parish of Kirkby Lonsdale relating to our case studies has been included in this volume. Only by doing so can we really track the strategic shifts in the rhetoric of individual writers and those close to them, as well as the fluctuating tides of sentiment and pragmatism in the correspondence of those who responded to their appeals.

It follows, then, that not every classic 'pauper letter' in the Kirkby Lonsdale collection is reproduced. The volume is not intended as simply another collection of pauper letters, an analogue for a single parish of Thomas Sokoll's pioneering collection for the whole county of Essex.[67] Rather, we have chosen to include all letters that are part of a series of correspondence from, about, or relating to a single individual or family group, as in the case of Eleanor Beck with whose story we started this Introduction. We have focused particularly on series amounting to ten or more items, including letters from the poor and advocates, but also third-party correspondence such as that originated by officials.[68] The volume thus consists, as observed above, of 599 letters relating to twenty individual poor people, poor families and/or poor kinship networks. The largest number of items in a single series is ninety (in the case of the Nelson family, who we have already encountered)

[66] King and Jones, 'Testifying for the Poor', pp. 12–17.

[67] Sokoll, *Essex Pauper Letters*.

[68] Ten items is an arbitrary cut-off, as would be the case in any greater or smaller number of pieces. The approach is informed in part by practical considerations (a smaller cut off would have made this volume unwieldy) but mainly by a sense from the whole corpus of parish collections we have seen that ten items represents the threshold at which we can determine that parishes, advocates and the poor are in fact in a process of correspondence. It is this process and the negotiating and rhetorical canvas that stands behind it which is important for understanding wider questions about the experiences and agency of the poor. See King, *Writing the Lives*, pp. 145–58.

and the smallest series relates to Ruth and John Kitchen (living at Preston in Lancashire), for whom there are twelve pieces of correspondence. In almost every series in this volume, the nature of family and kinship relationships is explicit or can be readily deduced as the correspondence unfolds. However, there are exceptions, and an explanation for the rationale behind the inclusion of these particular case studies is required:

- **Nancy Bainbridge** sent a single letter from Manchester to Kirkby Lonsdale in 1822 [Letter 6]. George and Ann Bainbridge were the subject of fifteen letters, also sent from Manchester, between 1811 and 1829 [Letters 1–5, 7–16]. There is no indication from the content of the letters of a family connection between Nancy, and George and Ann. But all of them asked for their relief to be supplied through a Mr. Craston who lived in Oldham Street, Manchester, suggesting the likelihood of a personal connection in the parish of residence and holding out the possibility that it may have been a kinship connection.
- **William and Elizabeth Langhorn** wrote letters from Lancaster: two relate to William [Letters 290 and 291], and twenty-nine to Elizabeth [Letters 292 to 320]. Neither mentioned the other in their letters, but both mentioned a local overseer named Darwen. In addition, both of William's letters were sent shortly before Elizabeth began her correspondence with Kirkby Lonsdale, and by the date of her third letter it is clear that Elizabeth was by then a widow. There is, therefore, a strong likelihood that they were man and wife, and that William wrote for both of them before his death, with Elizabeth continuing the correspondence in her own right afterwards.
- **Rachel Boothman** was the author or subject of twenty letters between 1825 and 1836 [Letters 75–76, 86–103]. George Boothman, James Boothman senior and James Boothman junior generated twenty-six letters between 1809 and 1828 [Letters 57–74, 77–85]. George was the son of James senior and the father of James junior (who died in 1819). All three, along with their families, lived in or just outside of Carlisle for the duration of the correspondence. Rachel (née Robertson) was married to another James Boothman who, we are told in the letters, died in 1824. Even though there is nothing in any of the letters to suggest a direct connection between Rachel or her husband and George, James senior and James junior, there is circumstantial evidence that strongly suggests it. Rachel, already a widow, first wrote for relief from her home town of Glasgow, signing the letter under her maiden name of Robertson. However, she, too, eventually settled in Carlisle, from which fourteen of her letters were sent, all of which were written in her married name of Boothman.

An exercise to map the locations of communities from which correspondence was sent is instructive. Figure 1 takes the *entire* Kirkby Lonsdale corpus and maps the *discrete* places from which correspondence was sent. We can see that letters and other material were received from as far away as London to the south, Glasgow to the north, Hull to the east and Mold to the west, but that the vast majority of sending communities were to be found within a radius of 100 kilometres around Kirkby Lonsdale itself. This broad situation, including the presence of London and the fact that letters were often sent from places within walking distance of a settlement parish, is common to all large letter collections that we have encountered.[69] Figure 2 conducts the same exercise for the sub-sample of correspondence reproduced in this volume and we can see that the effect of our sampling is to cut out the farthest-flung communities (including London) while keeping the broad pattern of essentially regional correspondence networks. In terms of discrete 'sending' places, the great majority can be found within a triangle bounded by Carlisle to the north, Mold in North Wales to the south-west, and Bradford to the east. Within this triangle lay many of the newly industrialising centres of northern England – including Bradford, Manchester, Wigan, and Preston – and all of these places are well represented in our sample of letters. Other correspondence was sent from less obviously industrial though nonetheless still important commercial centres such as Whitehaven, Lancaster, and Carlisle. Intriguingly, Kirkby Lonsdale sits very close to the centre of this triangle, which is approximately 190 kilometres at its longest, north to south, and 110 kilometres at its widest, west to east.

Figure 3 changes the focus, setting out for the entire Kirkby Lonsdale collection the *volume* of correspondence sent from each discrete community. The switch to volume indicators clearly shows that the Kirkby Lonsdale archive was dominated by correspondence sent from relatively close 'localities' and this observation can be made even more keenly when we focus on the sub-sample reproduced in this volume (Figure 4). We know from Pooley and Turnbull's pioneering study of general migratory characteristics in Britain that the mean distance travelled by the whole of their cohort during this period was approximately 40 kilometres.[70] This is certainly reflected in our sample of letters, the majority of which were sent from within a circle of about this radius from Kirkby Lonsdale. Thus, it is clear that our sample provides a good rendering of the underlying collection and population from which it is drawn.

Among the likeliest explanations for the geographical concentration of material is that the boundaries of the triangle of core sending communities

[69] King, *Writing the Lives*, p. 24.
[70] Pooley and Turnbull, *Migration and Mobility*, Table 3.4, p. 56.

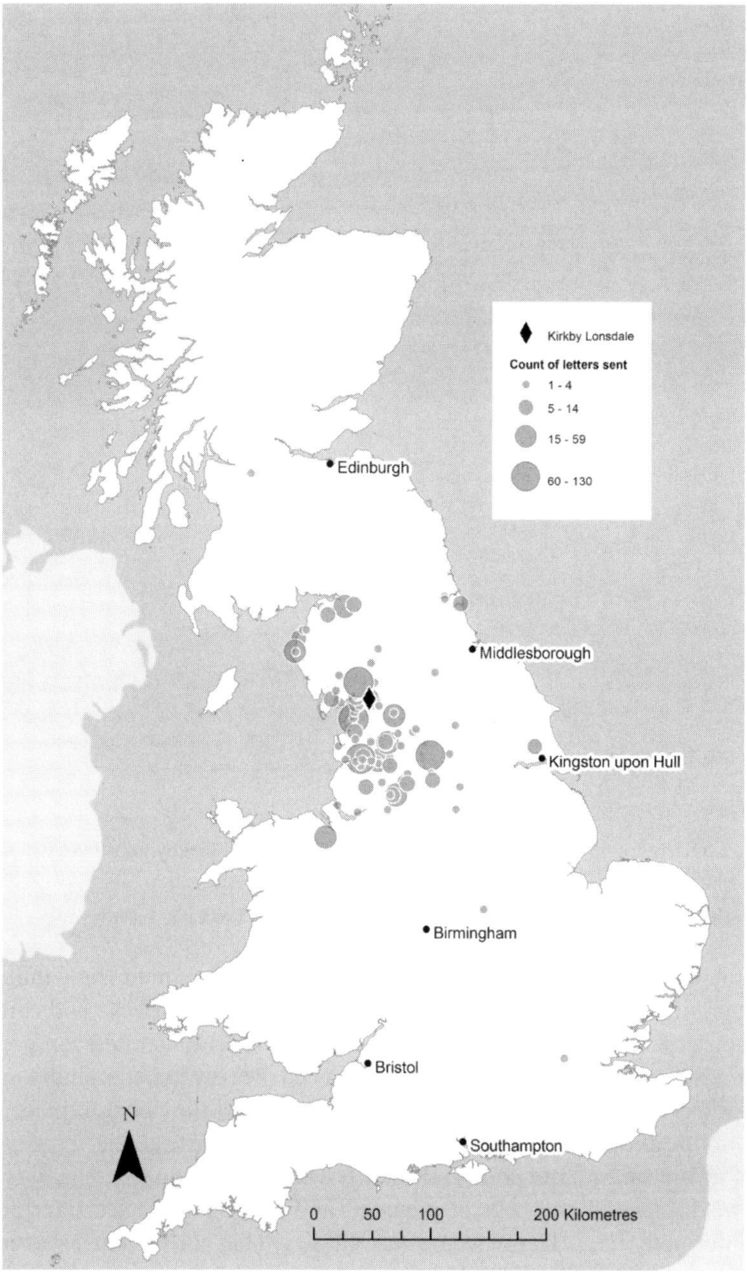

Figure 1: Discrete communities from which letters were sent to Kirkby Lonsdale: whole collection.

Acknowledgement: Drawn by William Farrell, University of Leicester Library.

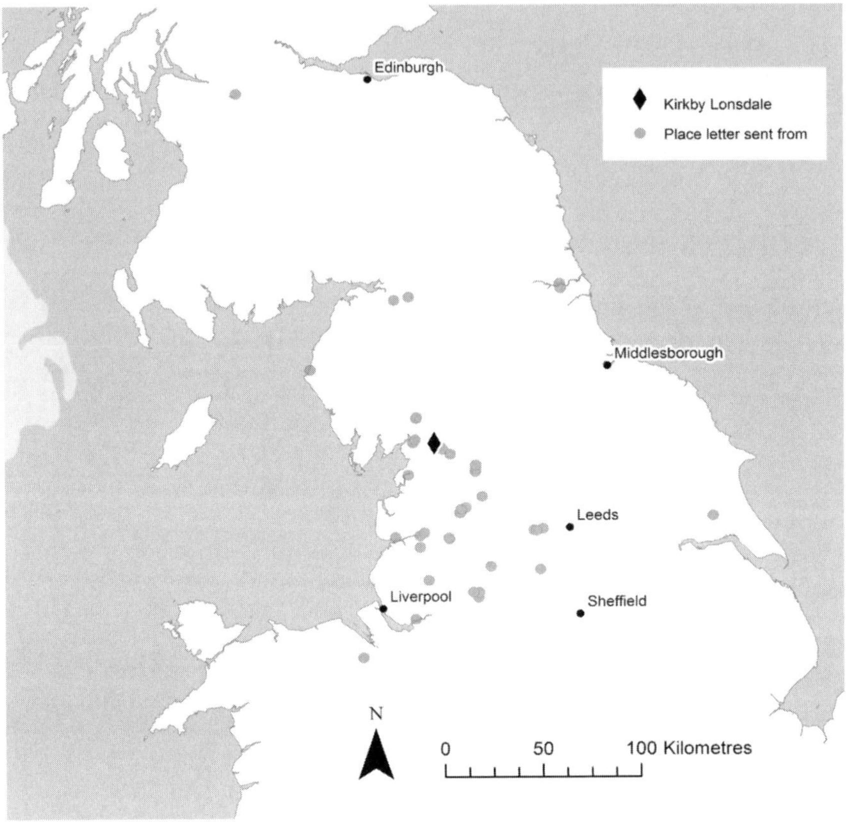

Figure 2: Discrete communities from which letters were sent to Kirkby Lonsdale: sub-sample for this volume.

Acknowledgement: Drawn by William Farrell, University of Leicester Library.

broadly coincide with the outer limits of the township's immediate influence thereabouts, and hence with its ability to provide proper checks and controls on the claims of its out-parish poor. As King has demonstrated comprehensively elsewhere, the out-parish system relied heavily on the ability of all parties (relieving parishes, parishes of residence and the poor) to place their trust in one another, but also on their ability to demonstrate the veracity of a claim in the case of the poor and their advocates, and on the reliability and trustworthiness of networks of payment and credit for overseers and financial intermediaries.[71] Hence, there was an inevitable correlation between the

[71] King, '"It is impossible"', pp. 173–75, and S. A. King, '"In these you may trust". Numerical information, accounting practices and the poor law, c.1790 to 1840', in *Statistics and the Public Sphere: Numbers and the People in Modern Britain, c.1750–2000* ed. T. Crook and G. O'Hara (London, 2011) pp. 51–66.

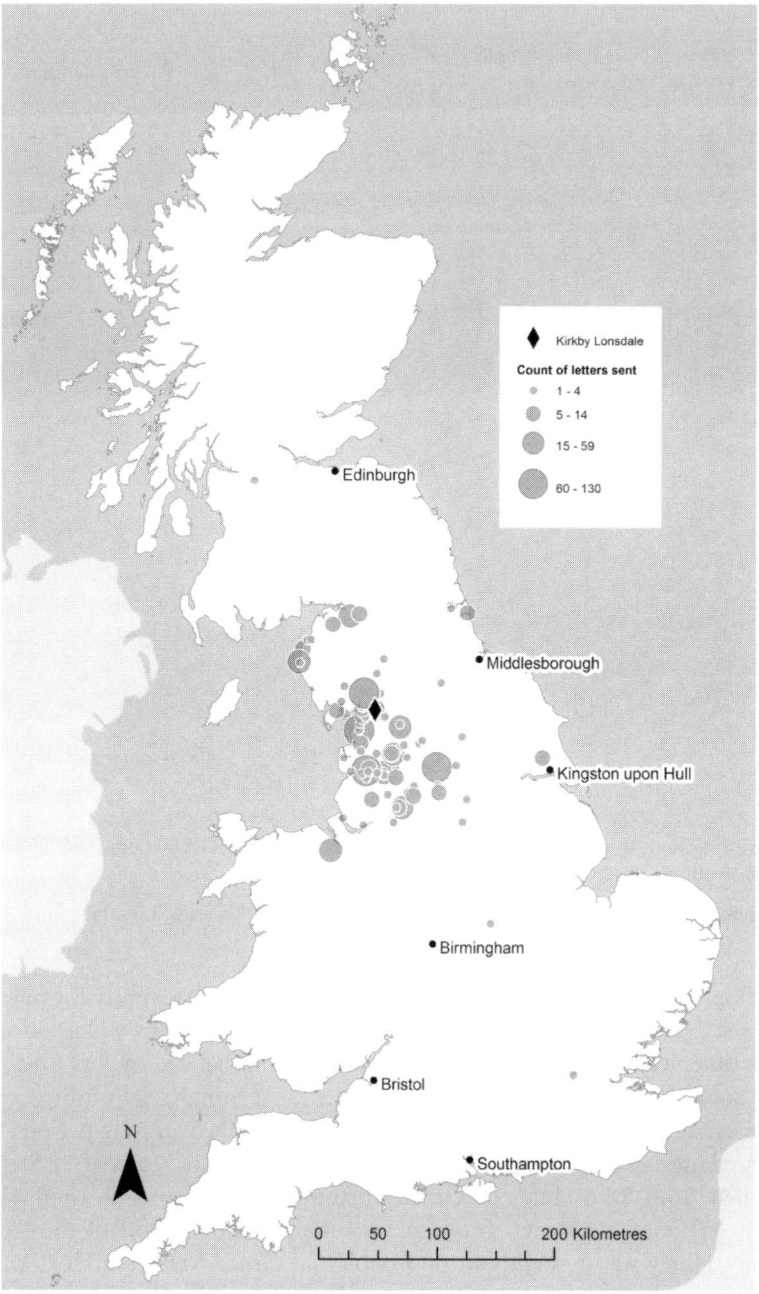

Figure 3: Volume of letters sent from different communities to Kirkby Lonsdale: whole collection.

Acknowledgement: Drawn by William Farrell, University of Leicester Library.

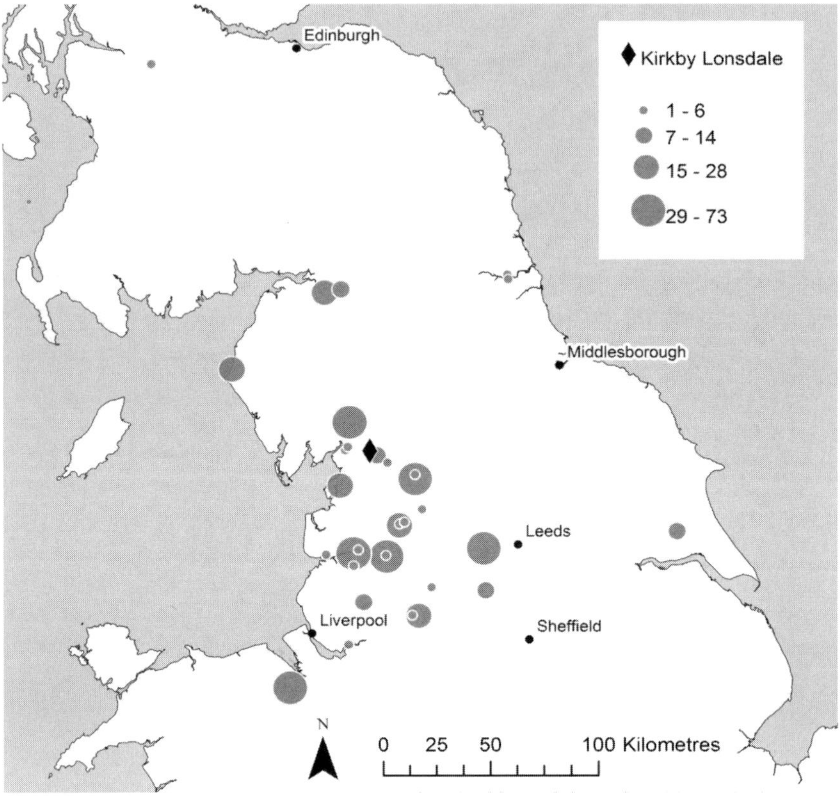

Figure 4: Volume of letters sent from different communities to Kirkby Lonsdale: sub-sample for this volume.

Acknowledgement: Drawn by William Farrell, University of Leicester Library.

development of networks of trust and relatively close proximity for relieving parishes, particularly in terms of inter-parish relationships which persisted over time. These networks were also, however, influenced by less obvious – and sometimes less visible – factors, such as personal relationships which were established and maintained between individuals over long periods. One such relationship is clearly visible in the correspondence received by Stephen Garnett from John Haley of Great Horton, near Bradford. In total, Haley wrote 37 times to Garnett between 1814 and 1831 on behalf of the Nelson family. Haley was a neighbour of Joseph and Grace Nelson in Horton, and throughout his correspondence he wrote detailed accounts of their hardship and travails and acted as a conduit for the money sent by Garnett for their relief. His letters show a deep concern for the family, particular after Joseph's death in 1814. In 1815, for example, he wrote to inform Garnett that Grace Nelson's eldest daughter had been badly burnt in a domestic accident. In the course of this letter he gave intimate details of how she had been attended by a reluctant doctor at the pleading of other neighbours, and how those same neighbours treated her wounds and cared for her until she recovered [Letter 385].

Over the years, Haley's letters to Garnett grew in familiarity. Initially, they were polite but formal and without any obvious personal embellishment, but by 1819 Haley was addressing the Kirkby Lonsdale overseer as 'Frend Garnett' and was offering his blessing to Garnett and his family [Letters 401 and 412]. By this point, he was also using his detailed accounts of the Nelsons' predicament to direct Garnett's orders for their relief, a measure which seems to have met with some success judging by the correspondence between the two men. By 1829, the relationship between Haley and Garnett was such that he did not simply act as an advocate for the Nelsons, but was very much concerned for the interests of both parties. In September of that year, for example, he wrote to Garnett to tell him that Ruth Nelson, Grace's widowed sister-in-law, 'keeps a Verry Disorderly House ... and her Children is Verrey Idle and Naughty'. He went on to advise that soon enough she would come to him again for money, but that 'She deserves none as now they are weell and in Work and Able to Work if they were not Idle' [Letter 431]. A month earlier, he had written to advise Garnett that Grace's daughter, Betty, 'is a Verrey Great Lier and not fit to Come in a Neighbour House. But if you take her to the Workhouse She may Grow Better with Care' [Letter 430]. Clearly, John Haley, who had begun his epistolary relationship with Kirkby Lonsdale parish as a straightforward advocate for Joseph and Grace Nelson, became much more integral over time, both to the extended Nelson family in its attempts to continue as out-parish paupers (the majority of the content in his letters remained positive in its advocacy for them), and to the parish itself, as a trusted intermediary and source of information about the Nelsons' situation, including moral judgement in matters of deservingness. It is only when we view this body of correspondence in its entirety that Haley's complex role in the Nelsons' pauper careers becomes clear.

Another significant advantage of being able to view the unfolding lives of the poor over a long series of correspondence is the opportunity to trace the different triggers for, and the shifting nature of, hardship. The concept of 'life-cycle poverty', and its importance in the development and maintenance of entitlement to relief, under the Old Poor Law is something that has received a great deal of scholarly attention over recent years but it is rare to see it played out in such detail over the lifetimes of specific individuals, and even rarer to be able to trace its effects, not only on those individuals, their families and extended support networks, but also on their relationships with relieving parishes.[72] In the case of the Nelsons and the Becks, for example, we have already noted that wives became widows over the course of their correspondence, and that those widows moved from partial independence (able to earn something towards their living) to total dependence on family, friends and parish relief. When the extended family on which they came to depend also faced hardship (due to unemployment, for example, or sickness, or premature death) the dynamic changed yet again. What strikes one most forcefully in these accounts of shifting fortunes and interconnected lives is not only the precariousness of the 'makeshift economy' for those who found themselves temporarily or permanently at the margins of independence, but also their tremendous resourcefulness and resilience.[73]

It is clear from this correspondence that, very often, those who wrote back to their 'home' parish for relief did so reluctantly, and only as a last resort. Even as a regular recipient of intermittent relief William Winder was anxious to assure the parish that 'I have always done my utmost endeavour to Maintain my Family'; but failing health and family sickness gave him little choice: 'if no answer returns by next market day', he wrote, 'I shall be Obliged either to come myself or be removed[.] I should have been very sorry to trouble you but I realy am forced' [Letter 575]. It would be easy to regard these and other claims of honesty, character, intense need, the exhaustion of all other possibilities, and a wish to regain respectability, as simply strategic, rhetorical vehicles designed to speak to the expectations of officials and ratepayers; but such claims could easily be checked and dishonesty exposed. Equally, it could be argued that the poor were writing (or were getting others to write on their behalf) according to a template that was well understood and perhaps even circulated. Yet, the internal dynamics and continuities of handwriting apparent in our sample suggest persuasively that most of those who signed letters also wrote them, and that most letters retained the sort of individuality that would throw into doubt the existence of a well-understood template.[74] Rather, the correspondence gives an insight into the lived experience of being poor and into the life-cycles of dependence and partial independence in which

[72] The literature on life-cycle poverty is extensive. For some recent examples, see: King, *Sickness, Medical Welfare*; A. Levene, *The Childhood of the Poor: Welfare in Eighteenth-Century London* (Basingstoke, 2012); B. Moring and R. Wall, *Widows in European Economy and Society, 1600–1920* (Woodbridge, 2017); L. Murdoch, *Imagined Orphans: Poor Families, Child Welfare, and Contested Citizenship in London* (New Brunswick, 2006); D. M Turner, *Disability in Eighteenth-Century England: Imagining Physical Impairment* (London, 2012); and S. Williams, *Poverty, Gender and Life-Cycle under the English Poor Law, 1760–1834* (Woodbridge, 2011).

[73] For the most comprehensive discussion of the 'makeshift economy' of the English poor under the Old Poor Law, see S.A. King and A. Tomkins, 'Introduction', in *The Poor in England, 1700–1850: An Economy of Makeshifts* ed. S.A. King and A. Tomkins (Manchester, 2003) pp. 1–38.

[74] On this matter, see King, *Writing the Lives*, pp. 116–44.

marginal people were often enmeshed. It demonstrates agency, rhetorical sophistication, and the idea that poor relief was, and was meant to be, negotiated. But at the most basic level these letters also tell a story about the social world of the parish, and not one that sits easily with contentions that in the last decades of the Old Poor Law the claims of the poor lost their legitimacy in the eyes of ratepayers. As material documents, however, letters and other forms of parochial correspondence were probably not easy to read at the time they were sent, and this problem has been magnified by the passage of time. It is to this issue that we will turn in the following section.

Editorial Conventions

Much has been written about the nature of pauper letters, stylistically and as a historical source, particularly by Thomas Sokoll, and as a result it is unnecessary to go into too much detail here.[75] However, some explanation is needed regarding the editorial decisions which have been made about the correspondence reproduced in this volume. Although we have followed many of the conventions used by Sokoll, there are some key differences to the way that he presented his letters from Essex. We have, for instance, tried to remain as faithful as possible to the overall layout of the original text. To this end, and in common with Sokoll, where aspects of a letter were indented by the writer (the author's address at its head or foot, the date of the letter, or the opening salutation and closing peroration), this formatting has been retained. However, unlike Sokoll, where a letter writer crossed through or scrubbed out a word or words in the original, we have followed their lead in this volume and crossed them through in the transcription.[76] Similarly, where a word or words were inserted as an afterthought, either as subscript or superscript, we have included them in the transcription and placed them inside carets (^^) or reverse carets ($_{v\,v}$) to emphasise that fact. Of course, it is impossible to represent all of the material and physical characteristics of a hand-written letter, but we have tried wherever possible to give at least an indication of the process of letter-writing and construction in the appearance of our transcriptions.[77] This approach gives readers a clearer sense of the effort and care (or other-

[75] Sokoll, *Essex Pauper Letters*, pp. 45–70; Sokoll, 'Old Age in Poverty', pp. 130–35; Sokoll, 'Writing for Relief', pp. 93–104; Sokoll, 'Negotiating a Living', pp. 25–30. See also S. A. King, 'Pauper Letters as a Source', *Family and Community History* 10 (2007) pp. 167–70, and Jones, 'Widows, Work and Wantonness', pp. 141–47.

[76] Here we impose the uniform convention of a single-line strikethrough for all crossings through and erasures.

[77] The originals of the letters transcribed in this volume can be viewed at Kendal Archive Centre, which is a branch of Cumbria Archive Service.

wise) that went into the writing of a text, the way that letters might have been viewed and read when received, and the thought processes that likely went into the strategy and rhetoric embodied in these letters. In turn, such considerations give a sense of the complexity and nuance of the negotiation for relief on the one hand and the essential and personal 'character' of letters and letter writers on the other.

While the process of representing the letters with a degree of fidelity is relatively straightforward, the accurate interpretation of words and meaning is sometimes far less so. As has been noted many times by those who have used them, pauper letters, the letters of advocates, and even the letters of officials are very often idiosyncratic documents, written phonetically, with unruly punctuation and syntax, and with little regard for standard orthographic conventions.[78] At times, the handwriting can be very difficult to read, and even when it is intelligible the sense of what a writer intended to convey can easily be mislaid in a thicket of literary eccentricities. Take, for example, this brief extract from Richard Garlick's letter, dated 24 August 1834:

> I do not no until I in quard and that the could not medel aney <m>oar [*page torn*] of a month and with that my Land Loard was Drunkin at that time and was for a month be foar that I could not a quent Im with my Shiften until last Thursday [Letter 136]

Some of Garlick's intended meaning may be discerned here – and, of course, it becomes much clearer when one is able to contextualise this passage with the rest of the letter, and all of the attendant correspondence that goes with it. In essence, it might be 'translated' into standard English as follows:

> I do [*did*] not know until I inquired that they could not meddle any more of [*than?*] a month, and with that my landlord was Drunken at that time, and was for a month before [*so*] that I could not acquaint him with my shifting [*economic situation*] until last Thursday.

Nonetheless, the interpretation of some of the documents in this volume will inevitably remain open to question. This is both a disadvantage and a great joy of using correspondence as evidence. In the unschooled writer's interpretation of what they understood to be the conventions governing the epistolary form – what Susan Whyman has labelled 'epistolary literacy' – we get the opportunity to hear the individual 'voices' of the poor in history; though it does, of course, raise questions about precisely what those 'voices' represent.[79]

[78] Sokoll, 'Negotiating a Living', pp. 25–6, 29; Sokoll, 'Writing for Relief', pp. 93–9; Jones and King, 'Petition to Pauper Letter', p. 64.
[79] S. Whyman, *The Pen and the People: English Letter Writers 1660–1800* (Oxford, 2009) p. 16.

Sokoll has described pauper letters as having been written in the manner of the author's speech: 'Not just [the] heavy phonetic spelling, but also the rhythm and the pace of the writing, convey the sound of the spoken word'.[80] We might modify his analysis by suggesting that the idiosyncratic letters reproduced here often have less of the feel of the spoken word, and more of cognitive struggle. For example, it is likely that many of Richard Garlick's letters are so dense and difficult to disentangle precisely because he was working in a medium in which he was far from comfortable. It is obvious from the extract above, and from much of the content of the other letters sent in his name, that Garlick was quite clear what he wanted to say to the overseer of Kirkby Lonsdale; but it also obvious that he was not at all confident as to how his thoughts might properly be committed to paper. Letters such as these might therefore be described, not so much as documents recording speech-types, but as *thought records*. In the manifest struggle to convey complex meaning, they seem to speak very eloquently of the effort that was required for semi-literate writers to organise their thoughts within an unfamiliar medium.[81] There is, in the end, something very human, and very affecting, in the courage that it must have taken to commit pen to paper in letters such as these. It was certainly no easy option for many poor people. The results would in turn have been far from simple to read and understand from the point of the overseers who, in a system of negotiation, could only act on the contents of the letters before them.

Given the limited writing ability of some of the writers represented (the poor, advocates, *and* officials), and the fragile nature of the evidence, it is not only the meaning contained within the letters which is sometimes open to question. On occasion, a word or words may be completely unreadable and irrecoverable, either because of poor handwriting or for some other more mundane reason. Over time, letters became torn or water damaged, their edges frayed, and sometimes sealing wax obscured parts of the text. Occasionally, one word was overwritten by another, and either might therefore be rendered illegible as a result. Under these circumstances, we have striven to make sense of what is missing wherever possible by placing suggested text (suggested by us, that is) in between angle brackets < > or italicised square brackets *[ ]*. Where no immediately obvious suggestion is possible we have simply replaced the missing word or words with asterisks in square brackets, the number of asterisks representing or, where it is impossible to be certain, estimating, the number of letters in each missing word. On occasion, where suggested or replaced text occurs we have also provided an explanation

[80] Sokoll, 'Writing for Relief', pp. 95–6.

[81] This observation develops ideas about the effort required to write as set out in King, *Writing the Lives*, pp. 61–89.

as to why the original text is obscure or illegible. These editorial insertions appear in the transcriptions within square brackets, and are italicised to distinguish them from original letter text. Finally, here and there in the original correspondence letters, words and passages have been underlined for emphasis, and once again (and consistent with our desire to highlight the process of writing and thought that stands behind the physical text) we have endeavoured to remain as faithful as possible to the originals in this respect.

In addition to the above conventions, relating to the core letter text, other content appears in these letters which is not part of the intended text itself. Some of this content is familiar to anyone who has sent a letter by mail: the address of the recipient, for example, and the postmark. As Sokoll noted in *Essex Pauper Letters*, the only significant structural difference between the letters represented in this volume and their modern equivalent is that, before the widespread adoption of the envelope in the 1840s, the address of the recipient was written on the reverse of the paper which contained the message. This was then folded and sealed to display only the address to which it should be sent.[82] As a result, although the recipient's address is materially integral to the letter, it cannot be considered to be part of its essential message. Not all of the letters in the Kirkby Lonsdale collection have recipient's details written on them. In those that do, in almost all cases these details fall into one of three conventions: the letters were addressed either to Stephen Garnett at Kirkby Lonsdale, to the Overseer(s) of Kirkby Lonsdale, or to the Overseer(s) and Churchwardens of Kirkby Lonsdale. As a result, in the transcriptions below we have taken the decision to include addressee's details only in the few cases where they differ from these three conventions – in other words, where the recipient of the letter was *not* Stephen Garnett (or the unnamed parish official) at Kirkby Lonsdale. Similarly, we have chosen not to transcribe any postmarks which appear on the obverse of the letters *unless* they give an indication of the date of the letter which is missing in the core letter text. Content such as this, along with any other annotations or additional writing which cannot be considered to be part of the text itself, has been included in an additional field below the core letter text entitled 'circumtext'. Occasionally, annotations by Garnett are included, and in this case they are identifiable by the initials [SG] before the transcribed circumtext (e.g. **Circumtext:** *In different hand [SG]:* Granted). Any further explanatory notes relating to the content of the letter, or observations about the letter, its author or subject, have been included in a separate field below the core letter text and circumtext, though we have sought to keep these to a minimum in accordance with the general principle that the letters and associated correspondence should be allowed to speak for themselves wherever possible.

[82] Sokoll, *Essex Pauper Letters*, p. 45.

We have endeavoured to keep our explanatory headings for each of the items of correspondence as simple as possible, following Sokoll's lead. The correspondence is presented in case study groups which are ordered alphabetically according to the subjects' names. Within each case study group, the items are ordered chronologically with each ascribed a basic identifying number that develops numerically across the whole corpus from 1 to 599. In each letter's heading, its identifying number is followed (wherever possible) by the sender's name and the place from which the letter was sent, along with the recipient's name and place of reception. As far as can be estimated, the date of the item is also given. Where any of these details is missing from the text itself, but can be deduced from the wider context (for example, where only an initial is given for a sender's forename, but the full forename is known from elsewhere) the missing details are included in square brackets. Finally, these details are followed in the headings by the original archive reference for Kendal Archive Centre in parentheses.

Transcription Conventions

In common with the editorial decisions detailed above, the conventions for the transcription of the letters and items in this volume have been kept as basic and as simple as possible. Most are recognisable from Thomas Sokoll's methods in *Essex Pauper Letters*. They are:

[ ] — Insertions of editorial text have been placed within square brackets. Such insertions take two forms:

- In the headings of the letters, material in normal square brackets with normal (non-italicized) text indicates an editorial insertion of material (a line of the address for instance) which is not in the original letter text.
- In the transcribed letters themselves, material which appears in normal square brackets with *italicized* text indicates an in-text editorial explanation or commentary (e.g. [*page torn*]).

[ ] — Material in italicized square brackets indicates a suggested reading of a word or words which are present in the original but ambiguous, indecipherable or illegible. The text inside such brackets is not italicized (e.g. 'There *[*was*]* a mistake') so as to differentiate it from editorial explanations or commentaries.

< > — Conjectured readings of physically destroyed/obscured parts of the text have been placed within angle brackets.

^ ^ or v v — Caret or reverse carets have been be used to indicate superscript or subscript words or phrases in the text.

[***] — Illegible words where no editorial suggestion is possible have been replaced by asterisks in square brackets. The reason for employing asterisks rather than the dashes [- - - - -] used by Sokoll to indicate irre-

coverable text is because we have transcribed words which have been crossed through, partly erased or scrawled out in the letter text, rather than moving them to the 'Notes' section. Single dashes cannot be struck through without covering them completely. There are two forms to this convention:

- Where a word is indecipherable or illegible, and where no suggested reading is possible, square brackets with asterisks have been used to indicate the estimate number of letters.
- In the case of more than one word or a whole sentence, each word has been placed within its own square brackets. This is most likely when words or a sentence have been crossed through or partly erased, e.g. ~~[****] [********] [***] [**]~~.

~~Crossings through or rubbings out~~ Where a word, words or sentence has been crossed through, partly erased, or scrawled out in the original, this has been uniformly indicated by a single line strikethrough in the transcription.

<u>Underlinings</u> Underlined words and sentences in the text are also underlined in our transcriptions.

Example

These abstract editorial conventions can be brought to life through a worked example. Figures 5 and 6 are thus photographs of a letter written by Margaret Gill to Kirkby Lonsdale on 5 June 1827. The letter claimed that Gill had been badly treated by her host parish in Beverley. She was heavily pregnant and sick, her existing child was on the brink of starvation and her husband had been unable to find work. Gill now appealed to the friendship and Christian philanthropy of her settlement parish to rescue her given that she had no one else to come to her aid. The breathless tone, lack of punctuation and remarkable spelling are all classic signatures of pauper letters and testify to the sense (explored above) of cognitive struggle that the barely literate faced when trying to convey their situation. Even a cursory glance at these pictures shows the complexity of the editorial interventions needed to make these documents intelligible. Here we see torn pages, obscured texts, ink blots, words that are simply meaningless to a modern reader, superscript text and missing or unreadable letters within words.

Transcriptions of Figures 5 and 6:

166 Margaret Gill in Beverley to Stephen Garnett in Kirkby Lonsdale, 5 June 1827 (WPR/19/7/6/20/9)

June 5 1827 Beverley

Margret Sorah which is now the wife of John Gill Dear frend i now take up my pen to right theis fuw lines to you to inform you how Beverlay parish has behaved to me sens i came too them it is throw having the Child with me that dos not bellong to them they will neither take me into the house nor giv me nothing ought nor they will not let him go too seech work and i am viry neear hungrid to death and can get no suport in the world i have not been ought of bed for too days and if you Would be so cind as to send me the money for the Child that i can have sumthing to eat for [an] i can not liv for i expect to be confined every day Dear frend pitty my case in the time of need for for [wim] starving for he has not had a but one weeks Worke sins we left Kendale and he has tramped a bove six hundred miles sins we seed you at Kirkby Lonsdale Dear frend if you would send them a s<h>arp [*page torn*] lettr i think it would doo them some good for they will not doo any thing for hus my husband was theare on monday night last and they told him they would not doo any thing so long as we ke<p>t [*page torn*] this Child and what can i doo with <the> [*obscured by wax seal*] poor little thing i took the burding [****]ry [*obscured by wax seal*] fit a hundrid and fifty miles my self but i doo not expect to live long for their is a viry trien time coming on for me in my situa^tion^ i am so poorley Dear frend i hope you will thin^k^ when you reed this few lines pleas to giv my cind love to my father William Sorah the ostler at the red Dragon in Kirkby Lonsdal^e^ and i hope he will think on my poor little sistrs so long as he doos live tell him that i doo not think that ever he will see me a live again in this world for i hav been for three days withought meat and the money would be of viry great servtis <to> [*page torn*] me pleas to send it as soon as posable if you can

When you right Direct
for John Gill Hattr [Mr]
John Wilson hattr Market
place Beverley Yorkshire

and so i remain your hum
ble sirvent

Margaret
Gill
Bevrley

Mr Stephen Garne^t^
if in office

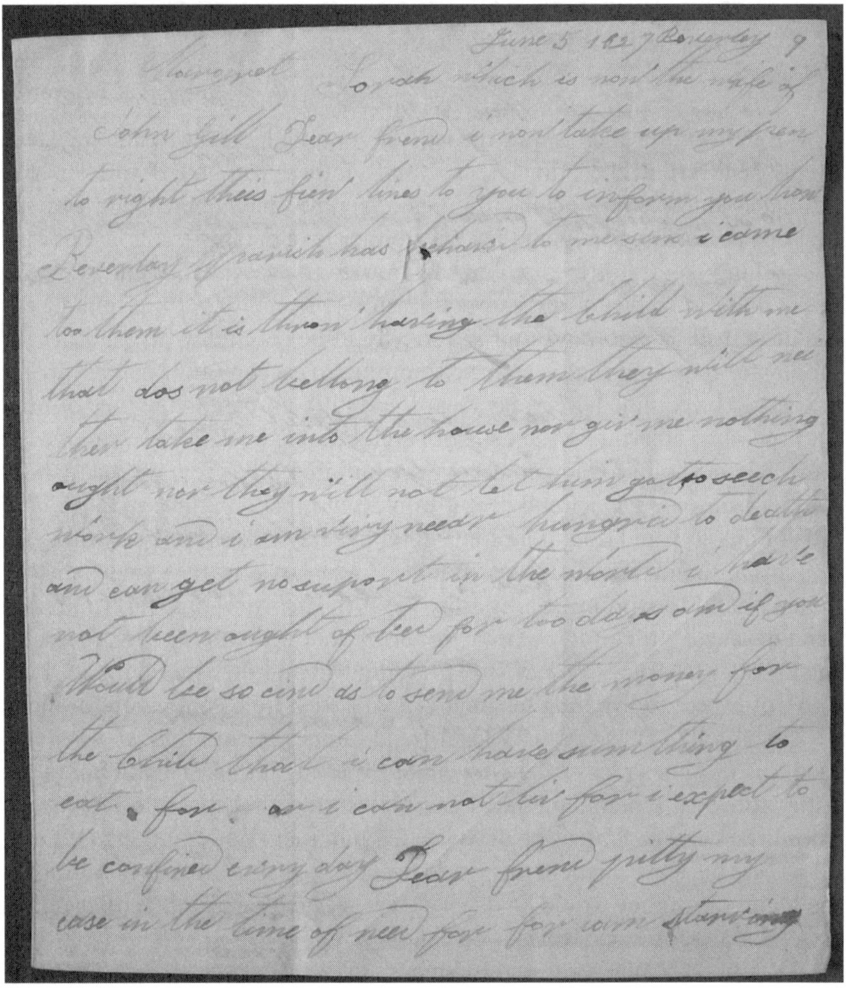
June 5 1827 Beverley 9
Margaret Sorah which is now the wife of
John Gill Dear frend i now take up my pen
to right theis fiew lines to you to inform you how
Beverley parish has behaved to me sinc i came
too them it is throw having the child with me
that dos not bellong to them they will nei
ther take me into the house nor giv me nothing
aught nor they will not let him get to seech
worke and i am viry needy hungrie to death
and can get no suport in the worlde i have
not been aught of bed for two days and if you
Would be so cind as to send me the money for
the Child that i can have sumthing to
eat for as i can not liv for i expect to
be confined evry day Dear frend pitty my
case in the time of need for for i am starving

Figure 5: Letter from Margaret Gill (first page).

Acknowledgement: Courtesy of Cumbria Archive Service (WPR/19/7/6/20/9).

Figure 6: Letter from Margaret Gill (subsequent pages).

Acknowledgement: Courtesy of Cumbria Archive Service (WPR/19/7/6/20/9).

Applying the broad transcription conventions outlined here yields a transcript like that above. Thus: superscript text is enclosed in carets (situa^tion^); letters which are missing from words because of damage to the document but which can be implied are inserted with an explanation of the nature of the problem (ke<p>t [*page torn*]); words that have to be interpreted are enclosed in square brackets (can have sumthing to eat for */an/* i); and words where we can make out some letters but not others are mapped out using square brackets and placeholders (i took the burding [****]ry). Such interventions notwithstanding, it is easy here to perceive the voice and strategic rhetoric employed by Gill as she attempted, in the very late stages of pregnancy, to convince Stephen Garnett that her case was deserving of relief. And it is to her story and others like it that the rest of this volume turns.

THE KIRKBY LONSDALE LETTERS, 1809–1836

1.

BAINBRIDGE, letters 1–16

1 Geo[rge] Grundy in Manchester to the Overseers of Kirkby Lonsdale, 16 November 1802, 20 February 1803 and 4 September 1811 (WPR/19/7/6/4/20)

Overseers of Kirkby Lonsdale

To Manchester Overseers, Dr.

Names	*From*	*To No. of Weeks Per Week.*				*£.*	*S.*	*D.*
		Weeks						
George Bainbridge	9 Novr. 1802	3 at 3/. 1 at 4/. 4 at 5/.				1	13	
ditto	27 Decr 1802	6 at 5/. 1 at 4/. 2 at 3/.				2		
ditto	13 March 1804	Coffin for child aged 5 years					6	8
ditto	14 ditto 1805						7	
ditto	17 June						10	6
ditto	23 Septr. 1805	Coffin for a boy aged 10 years					12	
ditto	3 Decr	Coffin for a girl aged 4 years					10	
ditto	9 Decr	Coffin for a child aged ½					6	
			£	s	d	6	5	2
		12 Feby. 1805 by cash		7				
		12 June ditto by ditto		10	6			
				17	6		17	6
		due Manchester				£5	7	8

~~[*******]~~ [*scored out*] Kirkby Lonsdale 16 Novr. 1802 1st Letter

Gentlemen I received a letter from you concerning the distressed State of George Bainbridge & his family which we have taken into Consideration & from the Complaint as you State as being a bad Cold we hope that he will not have Occasion for support from the town any length of time as perhaps by this time he may be got better but be so Kind as to support him with a little money for a week or two not to exceed 5 or 6 Shillings a week if he has Occasion & I will remitt the money to you but I hope by this time he may be got better but be so Kind as to let me Know how they go on I am with respect your Obdt. Servt. Miles Craston

Kirkby Lonsdale 20 Feb^ry 1803, 2nd Letter

dear Sir you I think long of me giving you an answer concerning the family of Geo Bainbridge You write that they are not able to get out of bed which is a bad situation if they are in Sickness they must have what is necessary or else george is not a man that Can be much depended on, you'l relieve them as nearly as you can and as soon as they can be able to travel if they cannot support themselves where they are they must come here and we must provide for them with work and necessarys I am with respect Miles Craston Overseer

Overseer of Kirkby Lonsdale

Sir

We now furnish you with a copy of orders for the payments made to George Bainbridge and his Family – as we are desirous to have all old accounts settled without delay – we must request you will remit a Post Office order for the balance, or pay Messrs. John Coates & Son of your Town, taking a receipt from them and sending ^it^ to us soon as possible – Mr Coates will know the writer of this and will no doubt see the propriety of this account being settled –

Yours obedient

Manchester Geo. Grundy

4th Septr. 1811

Circumtext: *Address of recipient:* Overseers of Kirby Lonsdale Westmorland

Notes: *This is a printed proforma invoice with correspondence added. The content of the invoice in italics (outwith brackets) represents the printed text.*

This letter is particularly complex. What is clear from the text beyond the invoice is that the first two entries are copies of letters written previously by Miles Craston, who was the conduit for the Bainbridges' relief payments in Manchester. These appear to be advocate letters to Stephen Garnett, written on behalf of, and respecting, the Bainbridges. The final letter, overleaf, is written in a different hand and is from George Grundy on behalf of the Manchester overseers, asking for settlement of the invoice.

2 Geo[rge] Grundy in Manchester to the Overseers of Kirkby Lonsdale, 13 November 1811 (WPR/19/7/6/4/23)

To Manchester Overseers, Dr.

Relief given to		*From*	*To*	*Weeks*	*Per Week.*	*£s.*	*S.*	*D.*
George Bainbridge		Novr. 9 1802	20 Novr. 1802				6	
do.	do.	20	29				12	
do.	do.	29	20 Dec^{r}.	3	5/-		15	
do.	do.	Decr. 20	31 Jany. 1803	6	5/-	1	10	
do.	do.	Jany. 31 1803	21 Feb^{y}				10	
do.	do.	March 13 1804 aged 5 years	Coffin & dues for Child				6	8
do.	do.	14 1805	received by Letter				7	
do.	do.	June 17	received by Letter				10	6
do.	do.	Septr. 23	Coffin &c. Boy 10 years old				12	
do.	do.	Decr. 3	do. Girl 4 years old				10	
do.	do.	9	do. do. 1 ½ do.				6	
						6	5	2

1805 Feby 12th	By Cash p. Letter	0.7.0		
June 12	By do.	0.10.6		6 5 2
1811 Sep. 27	By do. p. Mr. Coates	5.7.8		

Overseer of Kirkby Lonsdale

Sir

I send you another statement of your account having been informed by George Bainbridge that there was an error in the one sent before – You will observe that the 7/ & 10/6 were paid to George, being Cash received by letter from your Township and paid over to him. – In the former account it might appear as a charge for Coffins but you notice there was not the age of the deceased mentioned. – You will please inform Mr. Wilson the Magistrate of this circumstance by which he will see that the payments made to Manchester are perfectly correct

I remain for self and the other Churchwardens Yours obedient

Manchester Geo. Grundy

13 Novr. 1811

Notes: *This is a printed proforma invoice with correspondence added. The content of the invoice in italics (outwith brackets) represents the printed text.*

3 G[eorge] and Ann Bainbridge in Manchester to an Unknown Clergyman, 6 March 1814 (WPR/19/7/6/7/2)

Manchester 6 March 1814

Revd Sir
We Return you thanks for the 12 shillings that we recived of Mr Creston from you – Ann Bainbridge [***] [*page torn*] you have alredy been informd had a in port brock in October – but got reather better till about five weeks since the desorder returned on hir again which has brought hir to a state of great destress – likwise G Bainbridge is much afflicted with fits several times a Day which has brought him quite unsensibld so that neather knife nor weapen must be in his way had you sent them somthing weekly as you promised it might a been a mens of keeping him from being in such a Lunickt state if you will not send them somthing shortly he must be sent to the Manchester Lunick on your expence Ann is in such a state that She cannot be removed

So no more at present
from your
G & Ann Bainbridge

Pleas to send by
Return of Post
to G Bainbridge
No.7 Spittle Street
or J. Duest No.10 C<an>on St

Circumtext: *Part-printed certificate in italics and from one of the infirmary physicians, enclosed with the letter. The content in italics (outwith brackets) represents the printed text.*

To the Overseers of the Poor.
I Certify that Ann Bainbridge
^16^ Spittal St *is a*n out *Patient*
of the Manchester Infirmary under
the Care of <T Miller>
One of the Physicians to the Infimary
G Stock March 6 1814

4 George and Ann Bainbridge in Manchester to Isaac Grundy in Kirkby Lonsdale, 8 April 1816 (WPR/19/7/6/9/3)

Manchester Apr 8 1816

Dear Sir

We have taken the liberty of aqui^t^ing you of our destressed surcumstance & Ann Bainbridg have been upwards of six weeks in a deep decline which makes me unable to walk and George is so werry much afflicted with the head Strruck fitts that it drives him to a state of derengment we have had a docters advice and he informs us that it is uncurable he is worse then when Mr Grundy saw him and continues to worsing and we have don as long as we can without trubling you you may Judge of our state which is wery destressing at present we hope that you will send us a little of the poor householders relief

So no more at present from your
George & Ann Bainbridge

Pleas to direct to Mr Creston N°37 ~~Old~~ham Oldham Street or n°55 Georgelee St to G Bainbridge

Circumtext: *Addressee*: Mr Issiack Grundy Woolling Manuf^turs^ Kirby lonsdane Weastmoorland

5 Ann Bainbridge in Manchester to the Parish of Kirkby Lonsdale, 4 August 1816 (WPR/19/7/6/9/8)

Manchester 4th Augt. 181$_{v}$6$_{v}$

Dear Sir

I have taken the liberty of Writing to you as i have no other friend to depend upon for any information of my Husband as i understand he is with you in the work house i wish to know how he is going on and whither it will be nessery to send his clos as they are but a few which I have left as i have been under the nessety of laying some of them past i have rec^{d}. all the nine shillings and sixpence at a trifle pr week ^from Mr Creston^ and I still continue under the affliction of an Inpost break in my side which makes me unable to git my living or travel about i disire that you will consider my state and be so kind as to send me ^a^ triffel more Sir pleas to send by return of post as i wish to be deiricted by you in all things

So no more at present from
your respectfulley
Ann Bainbridge

Pleas to direct
to N°55 George Lee Street

6 Nancy Bainbridge in Manchester to the Reverend Joseph Sharp, 11 December 1822 (WPR/19/7/6/15/44)

To the Revd. Joseph Sharp

Revd. and dear Sir/

I beg permission to inform you that one evening returning home from a place I had been *[charing]* at I had the misfortune as I was passing by an unguarded Cellar, to fall into it, the night being very dark I was not aware of danger, I Recivd by the fall such injury as to render me totally unable to do anything towards a livelihood, I am consequently under the necessity (very reluctantly) to apply to you for a little Parochial Relief, and beg you ^will^ have the goodness at Christmas, to remit me a little to Mr. Crastons Oldham Street, Manchr. and your benevolence will be ever rememberd with gratitude by,

Revd. and Dear Sir,
Your Humble petitioner –

Manch^{r}. Decr. 11th
1822

Nancy Bainbridge

Circumtext: *Same hand:* The above is a true statement Witness Edwd. Davies

7 Geo[rge] Garden in Manchester to the Parish of Kirkby Lonsdale, 22 May 1823 (WPR/19/7/6/16/36)

I Certify, that Ann Bainbridge
was *an* Out *Patient of the Manchester Infirmary*
in October 1822 for a Contus^{xd} Arm

Geo. Garden
House *Surgeon to the Manchester Infirmary*
May 22 *18*23

Notes: *This is a printed proforma certificate. The content of the certificate in italics (outwith brackets) represents the printed text.*

8 Ann B[ain]bridge in Manchester to the Parish of Kirkby Lonsdale, 10 May 1824 (WPR/19/7/6/17/22)

Manchaster May 10 1824

Sir

I have taken the Liberty of Informing you that I was not Able to undertake the jorney to Carbeylondall at Ester for I was very Ill and still Contiuneys in a very Poor state of Halth I recived Eight shillings the beginin of Spring and I was very thinkfull for it

Sir I should be very much Oblidge to you to send me sum Present relife or sattle ~~wake~~ Wakely money on me as I hame gratley in want at Prasent I ham still lame in my Harm you will Plase to sand it to Mrs Crasdall OIdham Street No38 no more at present from

Ann Benbridge

9 Ann Bainbridge in Manchester to S[tephen] Garn[ett] in Kirkby Lonsdale, 17 January 1825 (WPR/19/7/6/18/2)

Manchester January 17 1825

To Mr. S. Garner

Sir,

I take this opportunity to request of you the favour of sending me some money over, I should not have troubled you with writing but that otherwise you might not know whether I was still alive. I am at Mrs. Owen's No16 Loom Street. I am exceeding low in circumstances and very short of work which urges me to request the favour of you ~~sen~~ sending the money. Please to send it by Mr. William Butler carrier to be left at <Mr> [*obscured by wax seal*] Craston No38 Oldham Street Manchester where I shall receive it.

Yours with due
respect
Ann Bainbridge

10 Edw[ar]d Davies in Manchester to the Parish of Kirkby Lonsdale, 26 May 1825 (WPR/19/7/6/18/16)

Manchester May 26th 1825

Dear Sir/

I am requested by Ann Bambridge to inform you, that for some weeks she has been so much indisposed, as not to be able to do anything towards procuring a maintenance, is now in great distress, and humbly begs you will have the goodness to send her some Parochial relief as early as possible, to Mr. Crastons, Oldham Street as usual –

I am
Sir Yr^{s}. Respectfully
Edwd. Davies

11 Ann Bainbridge in Manchester to Stephen Gar[nett] in Kirkby Lonsdale, 20 September 1825 (WPR/19/7/6/18/23)

Mr. Stephen Gardner

Sir

I Beg leave to write You and to say I have rec^{d}. your Welcome Letter with the inclosed £1.-.-. which I am thankful to you for I feel myself obliged to apply to you again for being so bad with a Typhus fever at Witsuntide that I remain as yet very weak and poorly, having little or no nourishment, and am very incapable of doing work I shall forward this Letter by Pr. favor Mr. Craston which I hope you will in return send me an order soon and be pleased to take into consideration my present state of Health in making some addition to my stated allowance for this indeed is a time of need, which I hope I shall not forget to pray that the Blessing of the Widow may Come upon you in causing her heart to sing for joy

I Beg to remain
Y^{r}. Ob^{t}. Humble
Servant
Ann Bainbridge

P.S. Should Mr. W. Craston of Carby Lonsdale shortly send any Packet to Mr. Edwd. Craston 38 Oldham Street Manchester be pleased to forward my relief by them it will save me if it is not inconvenient to you the Postage of the letter ¼ -

I remain Yr.
Humble Serv[t].
Manchester 20[th] Sepr. Ann Bainbridge
1825

12 Edw[ar]d Davies in Manchester to Stephen Gar[nett] in Kirkby Lonsdale, 15 November 1825 (WPR/19/7/6/18/31)

To Mr. Stephen Gardner

Sir/

Ann Bainbridge desies me to write, to inform you that She is very poorly and in great distress, and will be greatly obliged to you if you will have the goodness to send her some relief –

I am
Sir
Yours Respectfully
Edw[d]. Davies

55 Oldham
=Road
Manch[r]. Nov[r]. 15th
1825 -

13 Edw[ard] Davies to the Parish of Kirkby Lonsdale, 12 January 1826 (WPR/19/7/6/19/1)

Manch[r]. Jany. 12th 1826

Dear Sir/

I am desired by Ann Bainbridge to inform you that she rec'd your kind Letter, and Money safe for which she returns you her grateful thanks, and, also, she desires me to acquaint you with her present distressed situation, She has been a long time very unwell, but for several weeks past she has been so ill, as not to be able to feed herself: she is not in a state that will admit of a removal by any conveyance whatever, or she would be for now comfortable and much better served for, if she was with you. She humbly begs you will be so Kind as to take her case into consideration, and be so kind as send her a little more relief, to all human appearance she will not need it long.

I am D[r]. Sir yours Resply.
No.55 Oldham Road Edw[d]. Davies

14 Ann Ba[i]nbridge in Manchester to Stephen Garn[ett] in Kirkby Lonsdale, 22 March 1826 (WPR/19/7/6/19/13)

Manchester March 22nd 1826
To Mr Stephen Garner
Sir,

I send you these few lines, to inform you that I have been a very poor State of Health for some time past; which Obliges me to remind you that I am in the greatest necessity, and to request you to forward my Weekly allowance with all expedition.

I am with the Greatest Respect
Yours &c, Ann Banbridge

P.S. I received the last money in perfect safety

15 W. H. Craston to the Parish of Kirkby Lonsdale, 1 January 1827 (WPR/19/7/6/20/29)

Manchr. Jany. 1st 1827

Sir

Yours came to hand yesterday enclosing an one pound Note for Mrs Bainbridge but have thoughts ^proper^ to withold the payment untill your answer to this. I have supposed by your direction to her in her former husbands ^name^ that you are not acquainted with her recent marriage to a pensioner she has been married three or four months, consequently must concur that she falls chargeable to some other Township I shall not part with it untill your reply is made

I am for father
ys most Obdt.
W.H. Craston

16 Geo[rge] Salkeld in Manchester to the Parish of Kirkby Lonsdale, 11 March 1827 (WPR/19/7/20/37)

Manchester March 11th 1827

Sir

According to your directions I went to Mr Craston's and received from him one pound which I understand was originally intended for Mrs. Bainbridge but which luckily, and much to the credit of Mr. Craston, fell into my hands. Mr. C, wants two shillings for postage which is all the demand I understood him to have against you. in answer to your question respecting the rent two shillings and ninepence pr. week is the highest sum I have paid since I came here, during the interval betwixt my writing to you and me receiving yours I was so pressed for money to procure what was necessary for my family that I went to the Board Room to see if you had sent to there, I was answered in the negative, after which they sent a person to visit us who having ascertained our situation made his report to the Board who Kindly gave me five shillings, a free gift, without any reference to its repayment, thus you will perceive my not belonging to this place is a misfortune, I cannot help remarking on the impolicy, if so I may call it, of sending a pound to a single woman in possession of perfect health (who, if willing, need not want work ten minutes) while the same sum is awarded to a family of eight persons contending with a dangerous ~~and~~ and exceedingly troublesome disease.

my wife continues bedfast but is something better than she was, the children are fast recovering, or rather recovered, but their emaciated frames proclaim the danger of a relapse for want of proper nourishment, I hope the better feelings of those who are called upon to relieve the sick will see the necessity of sending us another pound at least, and thus enable me to restore my family to their wonted health.

Waiting for your further kindness

I am yours respectfully

Geo. Salkeld

Notes: *This last letter relating to Ann Bainbridge is curious, in that Salkeld, the sender, admits that he intercepted a £1 note which was intended for her, and used it for his own family's relief. There is some indication in the letter that Salkeld was expecting relief from Kirkby Lonsdale, but unfortunately this is the only letter either from, or relating, to him in the collection, and as a result it is impossible to follow his case through in the correspondence. No further correspondence relating to Bainbridge was sent after this date, perhaps suggesting that Salkeld's disparaging assessment of her needfulness was heeded by the Overseer.*

2.

BECK, letters 17–56

17 Eleanor Beck in Mold to the Churchwardens and Overseers of the Poor of Kirkby Lonsdale, 21 July 1809 (WPR/19/7/6/2/22)

The Humble Petition of Eleanor Beck a Pauper of your Parish

To the Churchwardens and Overseers of the Parish of Kirby Lonsdale –

Humbley Shew that your Petitioner has been ^dangerously^ ill this 3 Weeks and not able to get out of the House and is redused to the greatest want

Your Petitioner humbly prays that you will be pleased to send her some relief or she must inevitably Perish I am afraid of getting relief from Other persons least they should through your Parish to some extraordinary expences pray let me beg for God's sake that you send me some relief by return of Post – and your Petitioner will ever pray

Mold July 21st 1809

18 El[ea]nor Beck in Mold to the Parish of Kirkby Lonsdale, 7 September 1809 (WPR/19/7/6/2/28)

Mold Septr. 7th 1809

Sir)

I am Surprising that I had no answer from you after I have Send before but I hope that you will Consider little towards me for I am in Great distressd and my Eldest Son is very poorly this long while, for I expect that you will be so Good as to Give little towards in assistance for it is impossible for me to do with my two little ones, which I hope that this will put you in Consideration to a distressed family that are much i<n> [*page torn*] Want of Necessity So I Remain

Sir

I am your Hble Servt.
Ellianor Beak

19 Steph[e]n Garnett in Kirkby Lonsdale to Eleanor Beck, 8 September 1812 (WPR/19/7/6/5/24)

Kirkby Lonsdale Septr. 8th 1812

Eleanor Beck

Yours I rec^{d}. ^and^ in consideration of the present high price of provisions the Gentlemen present at a late Township meeting thought proper to allow you ^{s}10/ as extra relief, You may let the Gentleman that pays You see this and ~~which~~ wish him to give you as above and we will repay him

I am Yours &c.
Steph^{n}. Garnett Overseer

20 Eleanor Beck in Mold to the Churchwardens and Overseers of the Poor of Kirkby Lonsdale, 20 August 1812 (WPR/19/7/6/5/36)

To the Church Wardens and Overseers of the Poor
of the Parish of Kirby Lonsdale

The Humble Petition of Eleanor Beck wife of John Beck a Parishioner of your Parish

Humbly complains Shew that that your Petitioner is in great Distress and want being in a bad state of Health and my Eldest son lying dangerous ill of a feve<r a>nd [*page torn*] provisions very dear

My humble Petition to you is that you will be pleased to send me some Money by way of relief in my present distressed situation otherwise I must inevitably be removed to your Parish which will be very expencive to the Parish (if I get any relief here from the Overseer of this Parish they will be sure to remove me) and to prevent and to put you to as little expence possible I beg you will as soon as possible send me relief and your Petitioner will for ever pray for you and your Family –

Please to direct
Eleanor Beck
Mold
Flintshire

Circumtext: *In different hand:* Granted 10s/

Address of recipient (overleaf): The Overseer of the Poor of the Parish of Kirby Lonsdale near Burton Westmoreland 20th Augst 1812

21 Eleanor Beck in Mold to the Parish Minister of Kirkby Lonsdale, 6 September 1822 (WPR/19/7/6/15/23)

Mold Septr 6 1822

Revd. Sir

As the last recource I apply to you, the charecter of whose Sacred office is charity and benevolence; the applications of the Vicar and the Overseer of the Parish of Mold on my behalf have fail'd to obtain any relief from the Overseer of Kirby – he is not a stranger to my case – he Knows that I am destitude and aged – still he singles me out as an object worthy of nothing but to be a prey of adversity he deigns not to drop the least ingredient of comfort in bitter cup of affliction which I am doom'd to quaff –

Though the Parish of Kirby sent a letter the overseer of Mold some years ago to relieve my necessities – they have now forgot their boon when age and infirmities and the loss of my children have conspired to make more in need of their assistance I trust Sir that obeying the dictates of your benevolent heart you will my case before the parishioners – Let me not be understood as making any claim upon their generosity No the least mite will be repaid by thousand blessings – I would not wish to put the parish to any unnecessary expence by applying for relief to Mold parishioners who of course would send me to Kirby – And I could with less allowance in native place here ~~then~~ than any where else – should you, Sir, take my case into consideration and obtain for me a little to blunt the shafts of penury you will ensure yourself the blessings of Him who is styled the Judge of the Widow" and daily prayers of your most

Hmble Sert.
Eleanor Beck
Mold
Flintshire
N Wales

Circumtext: *Address of recipient:* To the Parish Minister of Kirby ~~Lonsdale Nr Kendal~~ Westmoreland

Postmarked: <C>hester 7SE7 1822, 790

22 El[ea]nor Beck in Mold to the Parish of Kirkby Lonsdale, 10 September 1827 (WPR/19/7/6/20/48)

Mold Flintshire
10th Sept 1827

Sir
I respectfully beg to state that I am the Wife of John Beck ^White smith^ of Burton in Kendal in the Parish of Kirkby Lonsdale and that I am so reduced by age and Infirmity that I am unable to support myself any longer. I therefore humbly implore that you will be pleased some small Relief as I really am in very great Poverty and my Sons having married and left me, I have now no one to give me the smalles Relief and have had none from the Parish these four years.
Your favourable answer will be most gratefully received by
Sir
Your very Poor & humble Servant
Elinor Beck
Milford St.
Mold
Flintshire

23 C. B. Clough, Vicar of Mold to the Parish of Kirkby Lonsdale, 19 October 1827 (WPR/19/7/6/20/46)

Dear Sir/
As it appears that two or three applications have been made to the overseer of your parish without receiving any answer on behalf of Elinr. Beck now residing here may I beg the favour of you to mention her case to the overseer. She is not able to go out to work & get her livelihood so well as formerly on account of her increasing years & is very destitute of proper clothing for the winter particularly shoes to obtain which necessaries her endeavours must prove completely inadequate. She lives close to my house & I am well acquainted with her state. The overseer may direct to Elenr. Beck
Milford St.
Mold
Of course the overseer will repay your postage
I must apologize for intruding upon your time upon this occasion but unless the clergy exert themselves on behalf of the poor they are too often neglected

I am kind Sir
Your ob^{t}. Servant
Mold Vicarage C.B. Clough
Oct. 19 1827 Vicar of Mold

24 Robert Beck in Mold to the Parish of Kirkby Lonsdale, 20 December 1831 (WPR/19/7/6/24/41)

Sir

I send this to inform you that we arrived home yesterday and the Money that you gave us is all done on the Journey and my Mother and my Wife and three of the Children is very bad no better than keeping their Beds we were Oblige to Walk to Bristol before I could get shoes for the Children only I beg a Pair of Old shoes for two of them I beg on you to send us some relief as soon as ever you can or else we must come back again and you must pay the expences and Keep us as we do not know when this Work will go

I am Sir your &^{c}. &^{c}.
Robert Beck

Mold
Decr. 20th 1831

25 Robert Beck in Mold to Stephen Garnett in Kirkby Lonsdale, 9 January 1832 (WPR/19/7/6/25/2)

M^{r}. Stephen Garnett
Sir

Please to pardon my Boldness in troubling you once more I received the Kind letter you sent me and the ~~[***** *****]~~ [*Illegible, overwritten by*] One Pound in it I feel myself very much obliged to you for your Kindness, I am sorry to inform you that our Work is not started yet their is no inteligence when it will start till after the 20 of this Month when the meeting of the Creditors will be I hope Sir you will have the goodness of relieving us for we are in a disstresing State the Children are barefooted I cannot help sending to you for relief as soon as the Work will start I shall let you Know of it hoping it will not be long their is s^c^ores of men out of employ at this neighbourhood I can not get a days work in any where about here – I beg of you to send as soon as posible

I am Sir your Humble Servt.
M^{r}. Stephen Garnett Robert Beck
Maesydre
January 9th 1832 Mold

26 Robert Beck in Mold to [Stephen] Garnet[t] in Kirkby Lonsdale, 30 January 1832 (WPR/19/7/6/25/7)

Mr. Garnet
Dear Sir I am Sorry that I am under the nesesety of Troublng you as I dow But I am verry Thankfull to you for All your Past, favours for which I shall feel my Self in Duty Bound to Pray with you and yours I am Sorry to Inform ^you^ of the Distress of this County as hear is in this Town of mold three more has fail since I was with you that is Thos Jones Peolsmelyn mold allso Willard Jones mold and George Evans Do Besides My masters Samuell and James Knight Cotton Spinners & Bankers With and Through all the above Dear Sir you never See Such Distressed Place all the above Employed many Hundreds Hands and now hear is not a Days work for any Sort of men My masters Prommes to Pay 13/4 Per Pound And the Crediters wou^l^d not Singd at that and We must waite for Sale if all ther Property that is all the Estate and the Cotton mill and all therefore Dear ^Sir^ if you Can get me work I Shall be verry hapy to Come again in Hops you will Send me Some Relife again as Soon as Posable and in hopes you will Send Some to to get Shoes or Clogs for we are quite Bare Feet, and we Shall be verry thankfull to you and Please to Send Some money to Cary us as we Cannot dow without Comming to you

Dear Sir I wished you had Known hear was a gentlemen from Kendal at Mold To Day he Could Certify to you that all in this is nothing But the Truth in hopes your goodness will Consider Our Distress and Send as Soon as you Can ~~a~~ in so dowing you will greatley Oblige your Humble Serv$^{t.}$ Robt. Beck Maesydre Mold Jan^{ry} 30th 1832

Circumtext: *In different hand [SG]*: Granted £2.0s.0

27 Robert Beck in Mold to [Stephen] Garnett in Kirkby Lonsdale, 19 March 1832 (WPR/19/7/6/25/15)

Mr Garnett
Sir I am under the nessesty of Troubling you Once more as I asure you Dear Sir that I am In great Distress at Present as my Wife got her Bed of a Child burth on the 16th Instant, and I had nothing of any One Kind nether Bread nor Buter But few Potatoes and Salt and hear is nine of us now in the famely as we have Six Children my self and Wife and my mother and I have been fare and near Looking out For Some sort of work and Cannot get any thing to Dow therfore Dear Sir I hope youll Consider our distress and send us some Releif as soon as Posable Or els we shall Certainly Perish for want of Bread

and Indeed my wife is Verry ill now and I have nothing to give her Dear Sir I have Regrentit many times that I have Come from you We should had meat With you But I Trust you will send this time as Soon as this Comes to hand I Remain Dear Sir

Your Distresed Humble Servant
Robert Beck Maesydre near Mold
March the 19th 1832

28 Rob[er]t Beck in Mold to [Stephen] Garnet[t] in Kirkby Lonsdale, 10 April 1832 (WPR/19/7/6/25/19)

Mr Garnet

Sir I am Sorry To Trouble you as I dow Asure you my wife is verry Poorley and the Little Child evar Since I wrote to you Last as I Mention to you in my last I had nothing but few Potatoes When my Wife got her Bed and Dear Sir hear is nothing to dow hear is Hundreds out of employment, and I have Been fare and near and Cannot get nothing To dow and Our factory Was on Sale at Manchester on the third Instant, but it was not Sold god only Knows what will be Come of us therfore Dear Sir I hope Somthing Will Turn out Soon you mae Depend that I Shall not Trouble you if I Can get Work And I humbley beg you will help me as Soon as you Can as I am and the famely verry Bare for mate and Clothing So Dear Sir I am Your Humble Servant Robt Beck Maesyde near Mold April the 10th 1832

29 Robert Beck in Mold to [Stephen] Garnett in Kirkby Lonsdale, 22 April 1832 (WPR/19/7/6/25/23)

Mr Garnett

Sir, I am Sorry that I am under the nesesety of Troubling you as I done I have Sent to you Dear Sir this three Weeks nearley When all that I had was quite done and my Wife and the Little Child was Very ill for want of meat and I Could get none for them and from that day to this we have had nothing But What my Poor nebour give a little One Day and without any the 4 next day and Through that distress my famely are all in great want I hope you will Send Some Relife by the Return of Post asure you this Day and I and my famely we have nothing that a man or Child can eat therefore I hope you Will Send or I must Troube this parish and must Come to you as my famely Will die for want as hear is Hundreds of men that Cannot get any work and not Likely to meet with any if Please god we shall Be With you by your neak meeting and We have Repent that ever We left you but We Shall not dow So any more if once Shall See Kirkby I Shall Sell all the What few things I have this next Week unless Your letter Will Come soonner as hear is nine of us in famely So Dear Sir I Remain your Humble Distresd Servent Robert Beck Maesydre near Mold april the 22nd 1832

30 Robert Beck in Mold to the Parish of Kirkby Lonsdale, 8 May 1832 (WPR/19/7/6/25/25)

Mold 8 May 1832

Sir

I write to inform you that my Mother, is now lying extremely ill at the present time, as has been so for sometime past – I am also very sory to say that there is no prospect of my getting any work round this neighbourhood, so many people being out of employment, and there is no hope of the Factory starting for some time yet – the last money I rec[d] I have nearly expended all myself going round the Country in search of Work, and am no better – and the Children are all nearly naked, and starving – So I will thank you to find me some work to do at your place, and I will imediately come over – as it is no use stoping here = but I cannot leave here without money to bring me on my jurney so I will look anxiously for some from you for that purpose – because I can get none here – I am very sory at being so troblesome to the parish, but cannot help it, for I would much rather work if I could get any to do

I remain
Sir
Your Ob[t] Serv[t]
Robert Beck

Circumtext: *Below, in pencil*: Maesyrdre near Mold

31 Robert Beck in Mold to Stephen Garnett in Kirkby Lonsdale, 19 June 1832 (WPR/19/7/6/25/32)

M[r]. Stephen Garnett

Sir

Please to pardon my Boldness in troubling you this time there is no Sign for this mill to start nor any other Employ to be had it is very hard with us at present there is about 400 men from this County gone to Cumberland to the Coal & Mine Works if I had Shoes on my feet I would have gone with them myself and the Children are barefoot you Know Sir it is imposible to go to seek Work in this Condition I feel myself much obliged to you for your Kindness in times past, you promised in your last you would send in 4 Weeks time, having that confidence in you that you will pity me in my distress and relieve me and my family out of it you would be surprised if you was to see ^the^ distressing state of us here my Clothes are done I had but wat you see when I was over if I could do for myself & family I would not trouble you Dear Sir please to send as soon as possible I remain Sir your Humble Servt

Robert Beck

June 19th 1832 Maesyrdre near Mold

32 Robert Beck in Mold to Steph[e]n Garnett in Kirkby Lonsdale, 9 August 1832 (WPR/19/7/6/25/41)

Maesydre Mold Augst 9th 1832

M^{r}. Steph^{n} Garnett

Sir

I hope you will pardon my Boldness in troubling you – I receved the last letter and the sovereign for which i return you my gratefull thanks for your Kindness to me and my Family I am obliged Sir to ~~[*****]~~ [*illegible, overwritten by*] trouble you again there is scorces out of employ in this little place there is not a days Work to be had if I could get employ I would not trouble you there is a Law going on at Lancaster concerning the writings of this Factory we dont Know how it will be after indeed Sir myself and Children are quite barefoot it is imposible for me to go from home to seek Work if you think that I could be employed by you I shall very willingly come I beg of you Sir to send a little to get few things for us to Change beside what you Kindly *[*ave*]* as the Colera is ranging through the Country many died within the last 2 months it is the opinion that poverty causes many disease among the lower Casses I hope Sir you will not forget us, may the Blessing of Almighty God rest upon you and your family

the prayer of Your Humble Servt. Robert Beck

33 Rob[er]t Beck in Mold to [Stephen] Garnet[t] in Kirkby Lonsdale, 10 September 1832 (WPR/19/7/6/25/46)

Mr Garnets

Sr I am Sorry that I am under the nesesety of Troubling you again asure you hear is nothing that a Poor man Can get to dew and the Farmers that has

Little Work The tel me and my Old Shopmates that we are the Factory Men the will give us nothing to dow and by that and So many year Out of Employment it is has hard now as ever and Dear Sir Povart Stears in our faces is *[at]* this time as bad as ever i feel my self in duty Bound to Pray with you and the gentlemen of the Parish for all Past favours and I Could wish Dearley if you Could Send by Some of the gentlemen From your nebourhood to Call and See our distress you Could belive them I wish i had nevar Come From you as for this Factory i belive it will be Long to time again before any thing will be done hear thirfore Dear Sir I hope you will Relive my Poor Famely as Soon as Posable or we must Perish and the allmighty will Reward you for your Goodness I am your Humble Servt Robt Beck

Maesydre Mold Septr. 10th 1832

34 Rob[er]t Beck in Mold to Stephen Garnett in Kirkby Lonsdale, 15 October 1832 (WPR/19/7/6/25/57)

Maesydre Mold Octr 15th 1832

Mr Stephen Garnett

Sir

I hope you will pardon my Boldness in troubling you this time I am under the necesity of sending to you for further relief there is no sign of our Work to start their is no Work to be had about here if you think it best for me and Family to come over to the Parish I am very Willing to come if you will have the Kindness to send us the means we stand in need of the Chilldren are all barefoot and quite without clothes to change I hope Sir you will deliver us out of our distress you Know Sir there is nine of us the Winter is coming on and no means of providing for my poor Family ~~y~~ having that confidence in you Sir I trust you will take our case under your notice –

I am Sir

Your Humble Servt.

Robt. Beck

35 Robert Beck in Mold to Steph[e]n Garnett in Kirkby Lonsdale, 12 November 1832 (WPR/19/7/6/25/62)

Maesydre Novr. 12th 1832

Mr Steph^{n} Garnett
Sir

Permit me most humbly to address you with these few lines, I Rec^{d} the letter you sent, and the sovereign inclosed therein, I feel very much obliged to you for your Kindness towards me I am obliged to send these lines to you, hoping Sir you will have the goodness to send us the means of getting shoes, we are all barefoot, we cannot get any otherwise, I have no other place to apply to but to you for relief out of any distress, I ^am^ very willing to come to Kirby if you think that I could get work to Keep my Family, there is no work to be had here, hoping Sir you will relieve me and my poor family out of our distress

I am Sir
your Humble Ser^{t}.
Robert Beck

36 Robert Beck in Mold to Steph[e]n Garnett in Kirkby Lonsdale, 24 December 1832 (WPR/19/7/6/25/72)

Mold Decr 24/32

Mr Steph^{n} Garnett
Sir

I am obiged to send to you again for further relief we are nearly starved in Want you promised to send a mon^th^ and 5 weeks is past since I had the last I hope Sir you will consider our state there is 8 of us beside our mother to live upon the little we receive from you Dr Sir I further beg of you to send little for my Mother hoping Sir you will answer this without fail I remain your Humble Ser^{vt} in distress

Robert Beck

37 Ele[a]nor Beck in Mold to [Stephen] Garnett in Kirkby Lonsdale, 4 January 1833 (WPR/19/7/6/26/13)

M[r] Garnett Mold Jan 4[th] 1833

Sir

I hope you will pardon my Boldness in troubling you poverty compels me to send to you I need not tell you of my weakness you are conc^s^. of that when you saw me being above 63 years of Age I have no clothes to cover me to Keep me warm neither on myself nor on the Bed this Parish is very Willing to relieve me I am to Weak to be rem[d] but I thought it is my duty to acquaint you first you have not allow me any since I came from Kirby the little you send my son is not enough to find ther Bread I hope Sir you will Pity a poor Widow in distress your Humble ser[t].

Maesydre Elenor Beck

Circumtext: *In different hand [SG]*: Granted 2[s]/ a week

Notes: *Same handwriting as Robert Beck's correspondence.*

38 C. H. Clough in Mold to the Parish of Kirkby Lonsdale, 14 January 1833 (WPR/19/7/6/26/12)

Sir/

I beg to inform you that the Family of Rob[t]. Beck is very much in want of clothing, which it is impossible for him to purchase out of his Parish Allowance, & he scarcely is able to get any work here as we have numbers out of employ & I fear that the Cotton mill is not likely to start again soon. I feel convinced that you might keep them at a lower rate in your own Parish. Perhaps you may be able to send them an additional sovereign with your next remittance to enable them to get absolutely necessary clothing. I would not write to you unless I know that they were badly off

I am Sir your *[Hl]* Servt.

C.H. Clough

Mold Vicarage

Jany 14th 1833

Circumtext: 1/9 out of every sovereign goes for the Postage 1d of which pr extra delivery.

39 Robert Beck in Mold to Stephen Garnett in Kirkby Lonsdale, 23 January 1833 (WPR/19/7/6/26/9)

Mr Stephen Garnett Mold Jany 23/33

Sir

I rec^{d} your letter and the Sovereign you sent me I feel very much oblige to you for your loving Kindness towards me and family in distress, I would be very Glad if I could get employ but there is so many out in this place it is impossible to meet with any, I feel very much oblige to you for your Kindness towards my mother in her old age Dear Sir I went with the letter to the Overseer of this place and he said th~~at~~^at^ he would not accept of it he had enough to trouble him in his own Parish, but Mr Parry Draper & Gocer Mold said if you will agree to pay the 2^{s}/ p^{r} Week to M^{r} C Medcalf & Sons Linsey Manufacturers Kendal, that he will pay my Mother here place to let us Know soon if that will be the Case

Your Humble Servt. Robert Beck

40 Robert Beck in Maesydre to Stephen Garnett in Kirkby Lonsdale, 5 February 1833 (WPR/19/7/6/26/8)

Mr. Stephen Garnett

Sir

I feel sorry that I am obliged to trouble you so often for relief, indeed poverty compels me to do there is no Work to be had here, I am quite bare-foot and my little Children naked I have no other place to apply to but you Dear Sir I feel thankfull to you for the Kindness you have shewd to my aged mother, having that confidence in you Sir that you will assist your humble Servt. in distress believe me to be Sir

Yours &.

Robert Beck

Maesydre Feb 5th 1833

41 Robert Beck in Mold to [Stephen] Garnett in Kirkby Lonsdale, 27 March 1833 (WPR/19/7/6/26/58)

Mold March 27 1833

Mr Garnett

Sir I have wrote these few lines to you to Inform you that we are in very Bad State I have my Children very Ill with the Mazles and I Can assure you that it is very hard and I hope you will think of me and my Poor Distress family I have *[them]* 4 of them we afever to up in our turns to Attend them which we Beg on you to Send as Soon as you Can as I shall Be over myself if in Case you Cant Assist me

I am your Humb[le]
Servt Rob[t]. Peck

Notes: *There is a sense that the distress of the illness afflicting Robert's family has affected his ability to commit his thoughts legibly to paper. Note the confusion towards the end of the letter, and the fact that he clearly signs his surname 'Peck' rather than 'Beck'.*

42 Robert Beck in Mold to [Stephen] Garnett in Kirkby Lonsdale, 26 May 1833 (WPR/19/7/6/26/44)

Mr Garnett
Sir
I hope you will Pardon My Boldness in troubling you as i dow I asure you Dear Sir if I Could any ways Dow to get little Bread for my selfsh and fameley i Should not 5 of my Children was down of the fever in march and April last and the are not well as yet One Died and Buried and asure you the Coffin is not Paid yet through so long illness and Cannot Get a Days work for my life not hear nor near this Ᵽ Small Town therfore I humbly beg your goodness will send us Releif as Soon as Posable for we ^are^ Rely in want in so dowing you Will greateley Oblige your very Humble Servant in Distress Robert Beck Maesydre near Mold 26th of may 1833

43 Robert Beck in Mold to the Parish of Kirkby Lonsdale, 18 August 1833 (WPR/19/7/6/26/26)

Maesydre Mold August 18th 1833

Dear Sir
Your Letter Came safe to hand on the 14th Instant and I am verry thankfull to you for your goodness at all times and I shall forevar feel my self in Duty Bound to Pray with you and your Famely for all Past favours Dear Sir I am hapy To Inform you that on Friday last I was Calld to the mill to get my frame Redy to Start once again I am a Stretchar in hopes I shall earn little Bread for my Self and famely according to your Disire

I shall Send the age of my Childeren
Elizth Beck was born 22nd may 1821
Jno. Beck was born 31st Dec$^{r.}$ 1822
Ellen^{r}. Beck was born 1st may 1824
Jane Beck was born 7th Jan^{ry} 1827 Died last april
Edwd. Beck was born 26 Septr 1829
Marg^{t} Beck was born 16 March 1832

I had none of my Childeren in the mill as the was to Small when the mill Stop
I have 2 in Servis if I Could get little Clothes for them But I Cannot
Dear Sir I most Humbley Beg your goodness will help me for to get some Clothes for my my Two ouldest or els the must be Send home again belive me we are all near necked as we have not had any Clothes for this Two years Past in hopes you will help ^me^ for this time In hopes you shall not be Troubled by me any more for my lifes time

I am your Humble Servt Robert Beck

44 El[ea]nor Beck in Mold to the Parish of Kirkby Lonsdale, 16 March 1834 (WPR/19/7/6/27/3)

Dear Sir

I hope you will pardon my boldness in Trubbling you after all your goodness unto us In all past fevours I asure you i am verry bare for Clothing as i got nothing to Change and my Daughter in law Cannot Keep me clean my weekly alowance is all gone before the Weeks end that i Cannot get anything to my back therfore Dear Sir I hope you will for this Once again as you have send to Keep me from hunger that you will send me some Clothing to Keep me from the Cold In so dowing you will greatly ablige your Humble Servent and be blesed of the lord

I am Dear Sir your Humble servent Ellinor Beck
Maisydre near Mold 16th March 1834

45 Rob[er]t Beck in Mold to [Stephen] Garnett in Kirkby Lonsdale, 24 June 1834 (WPR/19/7/6/27/43)

Mr Garnett
Sir

I am sorry that I am under the nesesety of troubling you my wife got her bed of a Cheild burth and She is Wake and Poorley and asure you Dear Sir We Could not Spare any of my low wages against this time in hopes you will not take unkind of me for this time after so maney that you have Send to Keep me and my famely Comfortable in hopes Dear Sir you will help this time in so Dowing I shall forevar feel my self in Duty bound To Pray with you & yours I am Dear Sir your Humble Servent Rob[t] Beck Maisydre Mold 24[th] June 1834

46 Rob[er]t Beck in Mold to [Stephen] Garnett in Kirkby Lonsdale, 20 October 1834 (WPR/19/7/6/27/23)

Mr Garnett

Sir I hope you will pardon my boldness in troubling you I am under the nesesety of dowing as my famely Has been verry poorley and One of my Childeren is verry Ill at this Present time in hopes Dear Sir your goodness Will Help me again as my wages is but Low and My self wife and Six childeren to live on I should not have Trubled you if it was not rather hard on me I have sent To you when my wife got her Bed you have not send any I asure you it was verry hard with us at that time In hopes Dear Sir you will not forget me at this time

I am your Most Humble Serv[t] Rob[t] Beck

Maesydre near Mold

October 20[th] 1834

47 Rob[er]t Beck in Mold to [Stephen] Garnett in Kirkby Lonsdale, 14 December 1834 (WPR/19/7/6/27/10)

Mr Garnett Dear Sir

I hope you will Pardon my boldness in troubling you at this time I asure you my mother Ellenor Beck is very Ill and been verry likely in our sight to Depart with this World and certify to you She has been in this ill estate this three weeks Past that we are obliged To have One up we with her night and Day that we Are unable to get fire and little nurishment which such Illness requirs and asure you Dear Sir I Rob[t] Beck I am verry Poorley this 9 Days Past and am Verry ill this Day therefore I most Humbley Implore your goodness With some relife in this needfull time So Dear Sir I have ~~a~~ no other friend to Send but to you and I return to you Many and my sincare thanks for all Past favours and I trust to your goodness at this time I am your most Humbley Serv[t] Rob[t]. Beck Maesrdre near Mold

Decr. 14[th] 1834

48 Rob[er]t Beck in Mold to the Parish of Kirkby Lonsdale, 15 January 1835 (WPR/19/7/6/27/53)

Dear Sir
I hope you will Pardon my boldness in Troubling you after all your goodness to me and my famely for which Fevours I feel my self in duty bound to Pray with you and your famely as long as I shall live Dear Sir I Bless god I and my famely is in Perfect Steate of Health And I get for my wages Bread for us all But I asure you we are verry bare for Clothing my self and the Childeran especialy shoes and all wering aparel is verry bare and Poor therfore as I had no other To help me in time of need, but you in hopes that you will help us to get a little nesesarys that is most wanting in hopes you will not fail for this time in so dowing Dear Sir you will greatley Ablige your Humble Distresd Servent Robt Beck

Maesydre near Mold 15^{h} Jan^{ry} 1834

Notes: *Although this letter is dated January 1834, its place in the sequence strongly suggests that it was actually written in January 1835 and mistakenly dated for the year just past.*

49 Robert Beck in Mold to the Parish of Kirkby Lonsdale, 11 February 1835 (WPR/19/7/6/28/2)

Dear Sir
I am Sorry that I am under the snesesety of Trubling you as our Water Wheel is Broke and I doue not Know how long we must be Idle but In hopes We Shall not be verry long as the millwrights From manchester is arived hear and the are Working at night and Day therfore Dear Sir I hope you will help us for the time again and verry thankfull we are for your goodness and Past fevours in hopes the allmighty will Prosper you and yours is the Prayer of your Humble Servent, Robert Beck Maesydre near Mold
11th February 1835
Allso my mother Ellen Beck is verry Poorley and she has been so this four months and she is not lickley to recover but nearer to the other World Dayley asure you Dear Sir we are with her Illn<ess> [*obscured by ink blot*] and Other things verry low Ellin Beck

50 Robert Beck in Mold to the Parish of Kirkby Lonsdale, 19 August 1835 (WPR/19/7/6/28/34)

Dear Sir

I am Sorry to Inform you our Cotton mill is Standing again to Repare the watter wheel and other Shafts the most of the driveing parts in the mill We have 15 men from manchester as millwrights Smiths and & the think the can Complete the Job In two months therfore Dear Sir I am under the nesesety of Troubling you for Relife again in hopes you will not take unkind of me in so dowing who I feel my self in Duty bound to pray with you and yours for all Past fevours and in hopes we Shall not have any more Stopage after this for Some years I am your Humble Servent Robert Beck

Maesydre near Mold 19th august 1835

51 Robert Beck in Mold to [Stephen] Garnett in Kirkby Lonsdale, 25 October 1835 (WPR/19/7/6/28/18)

Mr Garnett

Sir

I am Sorry to Inform you that our Cotton mill is standing yet and will be for another month In hopes it will be a Lasting work when Finish that I can dow without Troubling you as i dow I must Implore Dear Sir your goodness at this time again in hopes you will Pardon My boldness for asure you it is Rather Hard with me and my famely at this Present time in hopes with god s blessing I can be abel to Maintain my famely without troubling you after this time So Dear Sir I trust to your Goodness and remain your Most Humble Servant Robert Beck Maisydre near Mold

25th October 1835

52 Robert Beck in Mold to [Stephen] Garnett in Kirkby Lonsdale, 11 January 1836 (WPR/19/7/6/29/12)

Mr Garnett

dear Sir I am under the nesesety of Troubling you as Our Our mill is verry unregular the maen shaft that turns the Work from the Water Wheel is broke in the midle and not Long since [**] [*page torn*] We was stoping for thirteen Weeks to Put the above Shaft and wheels up But I hope this will not be long before it will be done again In hopes the will make a lasting job of it that I can Dow without Troubling you as I have done and I hope Dear Sir that you will forgive me for this time again and help me and my famely in so dowing I trust the allmighty will reward you for your Goodness for this and all Past fevours I Shall Forever feel my self in duty bound to Pray with you and yours I am Dear Sir your verry Humble Servt Robert Beck Maisydre near Mold

Jan^{ry} the 11th 1836

53 Rob[er]t Beck in Mold to [Stephen] Garnet[t] in Kirkby Lonsdale, 5 March 1836 (WPR/19/7/6/29/4)

Mold March 5th 1836

Dear Friend i send these few lines to you hoping to find you in a good health And i am very Much oblige to you for what i had and i hope you'll never be in the want of them I let you Know that My Mother is very poorly since a Month very ill and My Wages is very little and very Poor Work i ve got now and we have 6 children and the Are very naked and i've got nothing at all just coming Sir because its so very Poor in this place now no Stir at all and the Work very scarse and this work where i am is Standing just half of the time –

For Mr Garnet

So No More at
Present from your affectionate
Firend Robt Beck
Mold 5 March

54 Charlotte Beck in Mold to [Stephen] Garnett in Kirkby Lonsdale, 21 March 1836 (WPR/19/7/6/29/1)

Mr Garnett
Sir
I am sorry to Trouble you at this time I must Inform Dear Sir My Husband Robert Beck is gone to some Part of Lancashire to Try to meet with a situation as he was out of Employment at Mold Cotton mill. I cannot let you Know what was the reson of my Husband to leve mold as he went of unknown to me I hope he will not be long Before he will meet with a Situation and will Send for his Small and distresed famely asure you Dear Sir I dow not Know what to dow as I have but one Boy that Gets any thing he gets Two Sheelings and Six Pence Per week and 1^{s}/6^{d} from the 2/6 weekley for Rent and i have But 1^{s}/- for 5 of us the Oldest of 4 is 10 years of age at may Next and the other 6 and the other 4 are the youngest One I must Trust to your goodness and

mercy in hopes you will help me in my Distress I thoat it was my Duty To let you Know my situation before I trouble this Parish as the above is nothing but the truth and in hopes I shall have a letter from you and as soon as I shall hear from My Husband I shall let you Know for I dow feel my Self as long as i shall live in duty bound to Pray with you and yours for all Past faveurs and i Trust you Will not forget me this time in hopes with gods Blessing I shall hear from my Husband verry soon My Husband Mother Ellenor Beck is verry Poorley and has baing this Two months Past and she is not likley to remain hear But for short time

Dear & Honer^{d} Sir I ~~b~~ Conclude my Distresed letter And Remain your very Humble Servent

Charlotte Beck Maesydre near Mold

21st of march 1836

Notes: *It seems clear from the handwriting and phraseology in this, Charlotte Beck's first signed letter to Garnett, that the letters previously sent in her husband, Robert's, name were in fact written by her.*

55 Charlotte Beck in Mold to [Stephen] Garnett in Kirkby Lonsdale, 8 May 1836 (WPR/19/7/6/29/31)

Mold 8th May 1836

Mr Garnett

Dear Sir I have ^through^ my Sorrow to Inform you of the Death of my Poor mother ^Elenor Beck^ She Died this morning affter a Long Illness of Two month leing that I dow not Know what is One night Rest and I had a woman with me nearley all the Above time and my Husband has left me this 7 weeks To day he was some time at manchester before he meet With a Situation I am hapy to Inform you I have Receved a Letter from My Dear Husband that he has got into work this fortnight back with Mr Wm Latham Cotton Spinner in hopes Dear Sir we Shall dow well if Please god that we Shall Be Twogethar Once again I most Humbley Implore your Goodness to help out of this Distress to Bury my Old aged Mother as asure you I have nothing Twoards her funeral And Cannot get any Without your asistance in hopes you Will not forget me at this Sorrowfull Distress and Mr Parry has behaved well he didnot Leve my Mother in want of any thing in all her Illness and he give us much more then what was Due I hope Dear Sir you will Send me Some Relief as Soon as Posable and Direct your Letter eathar to me or to Mr Thos Parry Grocer new street mold I am your Distresd Humble Servent

Charlotte Beck Maesydre near Mold

8th May 1836

56 Charlotte Beck in Mold to [Stephen] Garnett in Kirkby Lonsdale, 21 June 1836 (WPR/19/7/6/29/21)

Mr Garnett

Dear Sir

I am Sorry that I am under the nesesety of Troubling you I hope it will be the ~~the~~ Last time as I have Sent to you before My Husband has met with situation in Manchester this 2 months back and he wants his famely there very much which i Trust and Belive will be better for us but Dear Sir I Cannot Posable go as I have Six Small Childeren and in Buring My Husbands mother and my Husband Came Over to mold On wisin week as his Work was starting that Week with One thing and the Other I am very law and Paying Rent hear and my Husband Paying much for his Lodgin at Manchester a we got no better therfore I most Humbley Impele your goodness for this Once again To help me and my Small famely to manchester in hopes with gods blesing I shall not Trouble you as long as the allmightly spare Our health in hopes you will send as soon as you Can for we get none forward as we are and I am verry thankfull to you for all Past fevours and feel My self in duty bound to Pray with you and yours and Remain your Humble servent

Charlotte Beck Maisydre near Mold

21st June 1836

Circumtext: *In different hand [S. G.]*: Nothing Granted

3.

BOOTHMAN, letters 57–103

57 Ja[me]s B[o]othman in Carlisle to the Parish of Kirkby Lonsdale, 23 October 1809 (WPR/19/7/6/2/36)

Carlisle 23^{d} October 1809

Sir/ Your petitioner James Boothman is at present under the necessity of aplaying To ayou for his parish money as he is still In the same lame sitwation not being able to do any work and if you will be so Kind as send the same from the 7th of May To the 12th november it will very much Oblidge me as I have my Rent to pay at that Time, being 27th weeks which amounts to $\underline{2^{s}. 6^{d}}$. I sinserley hope you will not fail to send it as soon as possible as you may be asured it is very much wanting my wiff being in In a very poor situation as well as myself having a lame arm which Disables her Greatly and if you would be so Good as make some small addition to the former allowance it would ad Greatly to our Releiff I Remain, Sir
Your Humble Petitioner, Jas Bothman
N.B. Please direct as follows to Jas Bothaman at the Back hill without the English Gates Carlisle

58 James Boothman in Carlisle to the Parish of Kirkby Lonsdale, 20 June 1810 (WPR/19/7/6/3/16)

Carlisle 20th June 1810

Sir/ I Recived your letter bearing date the 18th Nover <u>1809</u> In which I Recived in inclosed $^{£}$2.1^{s}. which paid Me up to the 17th January 1810. I Beg sir that you will be so kind as make my next payment From the 18th January to the 11th July inclusive. At the same time I trust much to your Goodness To Lay my situation before the Commatee in order To Get some augmentation to my allowance as I do asure you sir my Distress is very Great Provisions house

Rent and every thing else at Present being very high, and my wiff and me Being both in a very frail situation.

I Remain Sir your most
Obed$^{t.}$ Humble Servant
James Boothman

P.S. Be pleased to direct to James Boothman ~~at~~ at the Back Hill without the English
Gates Carlisle

59 W[illia]m McWilliams in Carlisle to Stephen Garnett in Kirkby Lonsdale, 13 August 1810 (WPR/19/7/6/3/24)

Carlisle 13th Augt. 1810

Mr Stephen Garnett

Sir

I take the liberty of writing you respecting Geo Boothman who at this time is agood deal distressd having his wife laying in Childbed on which Acc^{t}. he cannot follow his work so close as he might otherways do – he requests you will have the goodness to remit to Me his Pension ^to this time^ with the House Rent I ashure you ~~at this time~~ he is very needful & appears sorry to give you trouble

I am
Sir
Your &c
Wm McWilliams

NB be kind enough to send a statemnt to me of the remitt^{an} that I may shew him what has been received & how apply'd

Circumtext: *Address of recipient,* Mr Stephen Garnett Parish officer Kirby Lonsdale *Postmarked:* Carlisle

Overleaf, in different hand [SG]:

Sir/

Yours I Recd and in reply my agreement with George Boothman was to allow him 2/ P week for a littel ~~ass~~ while till he Got better in his health, after he left Kirkby I sent him ten weeks pay I think it was adresed to you and never hearing aney thing but that he was Got well I Cannot Concive that he has any just Claim on our township for a Regular pension But we are will^ing^ to assist him a littel in his presant distress Inclosed I send him 2.2.- which I hope will Enable him to do for himself hereafter

60 W[illia]m McWilliams in Carlisle to [Stephen] Garnett in Kirkby Lonsdale, 14 February 1811 (WPR/19/7/6/4/6)

Mr Garnett Carlisle 14th Feby 1811

Sir

I am desired by Boothmans Landlord to write you respecting his Rent he is now more than 12 Mos. behind & in fact he is not able to pay it neither to suport his Family during the [****] [*page torn*] times he has been very much out of Health this Winter in Consequence was oblig'd to leave the Loom & for sometime has been Working as a Nailor, his Master told me he was not able to make more than 7 or 8 Pr Week which was literaly starving his family Supose he has wrote you on this Subject – I think you had better give him a little assistance than have the whole Family to suport

I am Sir Your Obed Serv.
Wm McWilliams

Circumtext: *Address of recipient,* Mr Stephen Garnett Overseer Kirby Lonsdale
Postmarked: Carlisle 298
In margin: Mr. Thos. Pierson Carlisle 11th Feby 1811
In different hand [SG]: Granted £2.0s.-

61 W[illia]m McWilliams in Carlisle to [Stephen] Garnett in Kirkby Lonsdale, 15 June 1811 (WPR/19/7/6/4/17)

Mr Garnett Carlisle 15th June 1811

Sir/

From the distressd Situation of Geo Boothman & Family I am requested by him to Write you for relief, he has not been able to follow his employment for sometime back owing to a Severe Swelling in one of his Legs & having a Bone wrought out of his Ancle & had it not been for the goodness of his Neighbours he wou'd have been literally Starv'd he has a Wife & 4 Children to Support therefore you may easily judge of his wants which shoud be done immed'y when in health he is a very infirm Creature & not able to work for such a Family the last money you sent him the One half was paid to the Landlord for Rent the other apply'd to find him in necessarys there is now one Years rent due I trust you will have the goodness to send him immedeate relief, or the Parish will be apt to remove him

I am
Sir
Your Obed^{t} Ser^{v}
Wm McWilliams

62 W[illia]m McWilliam[s] to [Stephen] Garnett in Kirkby Lonsdale, N.D. (WPR/19/7/6/4/28)

Mr Garnett
Sir
I duly rec^{d}. yours covering a Guinea note for Boothman deducting the Postage 19^{s}/10 which have been apply to his relief.

Since writing you he is a great deal worse as you will find from the above Certificate he is realy in Such a State it is impossible to remove him he has not been in Bed for 3 weeks & with such a Family as I describ'd to you in a former letter he is in a Most Miserable Situation besides his rent he is ^in^ Debt with Some of his Neighbours for Groceries I ashure you he appears a very honest fellow & seems Sorry to make this application the Small Sum you sent him will do little for Such a Family being Several Weeks bad before making this application, if not taken into Consideration Soon he will be Oblig'd to apply to a Magistrate to get relief in the Parish where he resides

I am
Sir
Your Obed^{t} Ser^{v}
Wm McWilliam

Circumtext*: At top of letter, in a different hand:*

This is to certify that George Boothman is not able to be removed from a swelling in his left Leg
J. Holmes Surgeon

Notes: *Although this letter is not dated, its place in the sequence strongly suggests that it was sent sometime between letter numbers 61 and 63.*

63 W[illia]m McWilliams in Carlisle to Stephen Garnett in Kirkby Lonsdale, 13 May 1812 (WPR/19/7/6/5/15)

Carlisle 13th May 1812
Mr. Stephen Garnett

Sir/

I duly rec^{d} yours covering two Notes 7-7 on acct of Jas. Boothman after paying Postage leaves a bal^{ce} of a few Shillgs.

I have Sent him a Copy of your Letter telling him I cou'd not continue his allce untile I heard further from you therefore in all probability he will apply to the quarter were he resides he must be in a wretched Situation there being Six of Family which from the high price of Provision Six Shillgs is a Small Pittance as you gave me no instructions when you wrote last I did not consider it right to Continue paying him

I am
<Sir> [*obscured by wax seal*]
Your Obe^{d} Servt
Wm McWilliams

NB Shall give
Boothman the Ball$^{ce.}$

Circumtext: *Address of recipient:* Mr Stephen Garnett Guardian to the Poor Kirby Lonsdale

Postmarked: Carlisle, 13 MY13 1812, 298

In margin: NB he lives at Little Corby near Warwick Bridge and I think in Warwick Bridge Quarter in the Parish of Wetherall, about 6 miles from Carlisle

64 John Keysham in Carlisle to the Parish of Kirkby Lonsdale, 15 May 1812 (WPR/19/7/6/5/16)

Carlisle May 15th 1812

Sir

Mr McWilliam communicated to me your letter of the 10th Inst. & I have this day seen James Boothman the Pauper who is from disease altogether unable to follow any kind of employment whereby he could contribute to the support of himself and family.

As a Medical man and a Magistrate I cannot say that it would be impossible to remove him without danger but I am confident such a step would be the means of increasing his complaints and would occasion him much pain. Under these circumstances I seriously recommend you to allow him 8^{s} per week which is a small sum considering the state of his family (which consists of himself his wife and 4 children and his wife I understand is now pregnant) and the situation of the times. I am in no manner interested in his case, & consequently give this advice from the best motives

I remain Sir
Your humble Servt.
John Keysham M.D. J.P.

P.S. Be kind enough
to write to Mr. McWilliam

65 Jane Boothman to the Parish of Kirkby Lonsdale, 24 May [1812] (WPR/19/7/6/5/18)

May the 24

Sir i am Sory to trubel you with this Leter but it is a month Come whensday since i roat to you for my money that whas due but i never as recived it and i am in grat whant of it for work is bad and meat is dear and the one and 6p you alow me is Litil a nughs for hous rent in this place you sent me word you had a work hous i should Like to Come to it with my litil girl til times doth mend and do my best at aney thing i whas put to but i whas wiling to do as Long as you sent what whould pay my rent but i Can do no Longer without it

Your humbel servant
Jane Boothman

Notes: *Even though the year is missing from the date of this letter, its place in the sequence strongly suggests that it was sent in 1812.*

66 W[illia]m McWilliams in Carlisle to Stephen Garnett in Kirkby Lonsdale, 16 September 1812 (WPR/19/7/6/5/25)

Mr Stephen Garnett Carlisle 16th Sepr. 1812

Sir

As under I send you Geo. Boothmans a/c which trust you will find Correct, a remittce for the amount will Oblige

I call'd at his House a few Days ago & think he looks considerably better and my oppinion is that he might be remov'd . I afterwards enquird of the Doctor he told me he had not seen him for a few Days back but he thought him something better Shall wait your instructions concerning him

I am
Sir
Yours &c.
Wm McWilliams

From the 1st Augst to the 18th Sepr. 1812 £2.2.0

Circumtext: *Address of recipient:* Mr Stephen Garnett Guardian to the Poor Kirkby Lonsdale

Postmarked: Carlisle 298

In the margin: I Shall Shew him your letter in Answer to this therefor say whether you mean to continue his 6/ [****] he will never be better of his lameness

67 W[illia]m McWilliams in Carlisle to Stephen Garnett in Kirkby Lonsdale, 27 September 1812 (WPR/19/7/6/5/27)

Mr Stephen Garnett Carlisle 27 Sep <u>1812</u>

Sir/

Jas Boothman request me to inform you that he has a Child Scalded to death and woud be much oblig'd to you to assist him a little to pay the expence of the Coffin &^{c}. Since receiving yours have Advanc'd him one Weeks Subsce I find it will be inconvenient ^for me^ to continue Advancing him any further in future what you chuse to Send, ~~him~~ Shall be carefully given to him, Your letter was Sent to him at the Same time I told him I shoud have Nothing more to do in paying him but was induc'd to Advance him 6/ on Acc^{t}. of his present distress, what you remit say it is the W<hol>e [*page torn*] you mean to let him have until he comes over

Yours &^{c}, Wm McWilliams

Circumtext: *Address of recipient:* Stephen Garnett Guardian to the Poor Kirkby Lonsdale

Postmarked: Carlisle 28 SE 28 1812, 298

In the margin: NB He was over at Carlisle last week

68 W[illia]m Foster in Little Corby to the Parish of Kirkby Lonsdale, 21 October [1812] (WPR/19/7/6/5/32)

Little Corby Octr 21 [*page torn*]

Sir

In case you send me two or three ^Notes^ on hand I will have no objection to the paying weekly to Geo. Boothman 3/ or what you please to allow – Three Shillings P. week will do very little for them my opinion is that you ought to allow them 5^{s}. or 6^{s}. at least & then they might have some ~~likeliness~~ chance of doing –

Wm Foster

Geo: Boothman Dr. to Jno. Wilson	£	S	d
To 1 Coffin	0	8	6
To other Funeral <expe>nces [*page torn*]	0	6	6
	0	15	0

Notes: *Even though the year is missing from the date of this letter, its place in the sequence strongly suggests that it was sent in 1812.*

69 Tho[ma]s Randleson Overseer of Carlisle to the Parish of Kirkby Lonsdale, 15 October 1817 (WPR/19/7/6/10/39)

Carlisle 15 October 1817

Gentlmen/

a person of the name of James Bouthman belonging your Parish is very Poorly and Requires your Attention he produced a letter from you with are-mittance of 3.3.0 Due the 14 August 1816 you will please to remitt him 14 Months due at 6^{s} P month if not Complied with we will be under the Necessity of having a Removal Order suspended against your Parish you will Direct with the Money ~~to~~ and Oblige yours

Thos. Randleson
Overseer

English Street
Carlisle

70 George Boothman in Little Corby to Stephen Garnett in Kirkby Lonsdale, 9 June 1819 (WPR/19/7/6/12/13)

Little Corby 9th June 1819

Sir,

I hope your goodness will excuse me for Troubling you with this letter, but I have to inform you that my oldest son James departed this life about four weeks since after a very long and painfull illness, which has thrown ^me^ into a debt that I am not able to pay without your kind assistance Mr Dixon with whom he was employed (at his cotton Mill) has been very kind for he ordered the Doctor to attend him at his own expence, but his Coffin and Funeral expences being still to pay, and my rent likewise being due to the Landlord renders me unable to satisfy their demands, as my son was the chief that could assist in my famely who is great distress, therefore if your wonted goodness will assist me with what your consideration may think adiquate for the above purposes it will much

oblige your distressed
humble servant
George Boothman

Circumtext: *Address of recipient:* Mr. Stephen Garnett Parish Overseer Kirby Lonsdale Westmoreland

Postmarked: Carlisle JU9, 298

71 Geo[rge] Boothman in Little Corby to the Parish of Kirkby Lonsdale, 10 September 1819 (WPR/19/7/6/12/19)

Little Corby, Sep 10th 1819

Sir)

As I get my Shop good on Mr. Hugh James Carlisle, it would oblige me if you would have the goodness to transmit my next three Payments to him as it would save Postage and likewise oblige me, and Certify) in an answer to this as soon as possible) what time the three Payments becomes due, please to direct to me to the care of Mr. Hugh James Scotch Street Carlisle

I remain your humble
Servant
Geo. Boothman

72 Geo[rge] Boothman in Little Corby to the Parish of Kirkby Lonsdale, 30 May 1822 (WPR/19/7/6/15/14)

Little Corby May 30th 1822

Sir

According to your request I send you a statement of my Family, which is this, I have had 7 Children all came to a good age, 4 of them Boys, but the third died first and then the eldest in his 14th Year left only the second fit for Work which is in his 15th Year & is employed in a Cotton Mill at 4/6 Pr Week. The youngest Boy is in his 11th Year but being unhealthy is very small of his age and is in no regular employment I have 3 Girls the eldest in her 9th Year the second in her 7th and the youngest in her 5th – In regard to my own Health I am always forced to Walk with Crutches and must so long as I live Since Winter 1819 I have been much worse I can safely say that I am not 1 Hour without pain and frequently forced to sit up for whole Weeks together for I cannot rest in Bed so in regard to stating a regular income for myself I cannot for the little I can do in the Shoe business I am frequently disappointed by sickness so I will rely on your Wisdom & goodness in relieving my necessities – hoping your goodness will continue ~~towards~~ towards me

Yours &c. &c.
Geo. Boothman

Circumtext: *Below, apparently in the same hand:* I believe the above statement to be true Richard Rice Perp: Curate of Hayton

Further addition, in a different hand

Robert Milburn Church Warn
Geo Irving a neighbour

73 George Boothman in Little Corby to [Stephen] Garnet[t] in Kirkby Lonsdale, 10 May 1823 (WPR/19/7/6/16/32)

Little Corby 10th May 1823

Mr Garnet,

I am under very great necessity to make application to you for my money that you have the goodness to allow me, to be here on Saturday the 17th Instant as I am particularly in want of it

I am Your
humble servant
George Boothman

74 Geo[rge] Boothman in Little Corby to [Stephen] Garnett in Kirkby Lonsdale, 16 February 1824 (WPR/19/7/6/17/8)

Little Corby Feby 16th 1824

Mr Garnett

Sir it Will mouch oblidge me at this time if you Will pleas to lett me have my allowance to pay my Candlemass Rent houses is very Der in this place and Landlords is not Willing ot wait there Rent after the time –

Sir it is against my mind to make a Complaint But We have hard Shiften for a Bitt of Bread –

Sir if you will please to grant my ~~requested~~ request as soon as this Comes to hand it Will much oblidge your humble Servent

Geo Boothman

75 Rachel Robertson in Glasgow to the Parish of Kirkby Lonsdale, 25 February 1825 (WPR/19/7/6/18/6)

No.11 Princes Street
Glasgow 25 Feby 1825

Dear Sir

It is with the utmost pain that I am Compelled to make the present application to you as overseer of a district in the Parish of Westmoreland, But as my husband belongs to your parish & was regularly married to me in June 1821 as the attended Certificate will shew, and my said Husband having departed this life upon the 12 day of March last leaving me a helpless Widow with a Child not two years of Age & another Born a few weeks after his Death I am compelled to make this application humbly Craving such assistance as the Regulations of the Parrish admits of which will be thankfuly received by your most Ob^{t}. Sert.

Rachel Robertson
turn over

NB my deceased Husband is James Boothman Son of James Boothman */*Washing*/* house Keeper Carlile, R.R.

Circumtext: *Below, in the same hand:* I, James Marshall one of the Ministers of Glasgow hereby attest that James Boothman & Rachell Robertson were by me duly Married on the thirteenth day of June eighteen hundred and twenty One years

Below, in a different hand: Glasgow 25 Octr. 1825 James Marshall Muir Outer Hide Church Parish Glasgow

76 Rachel Boothman in Glasgow to the Parish of Kirkby Lonsdale, 22 May 1825 (WPR/19/7/6/18/15)

Glasgow May th 22 1825

Sir)

this comes to Lett you know that I have wrote to you some time ago and never received any answer, But I hope you will not Delay any time of writing me as I have Nothing to Suport me and my too helpless Children and I expect some little Suport for them as they are not able to want and if not I must be at the Trouble of Comming to See you as I ^am^ Lawfully Married which you would See in my first letter, and I Supos you will be Aquint with my Latte husbands father, James Boothman in Carlise

I hope you will ^write^ Return me a answer by the return of Post as I am rely needful of some suport

So no more
from
Your
Respectfull
Rachel Boothman

PS
Direct to me No.11 Princess Street
Miss Riddles Land

77 Tho[mas] Randleson Ass[istan]t Overseer in Carlisle to the Parish of Kirkby Lonsdale, 10 March 1826 (WPR/19/7/6/19/12)

Carlisle 10th March 1826

Gentlemen/

A person of the name of James Boothman ^has applied for relief^ belonging your Parish is Unwell and Cannot be Removed to you – he is 80 years of Age, he gained his Settlement by being 7 years an Apprentice to a linnen Weaver, he had relief from You about 7 years ago –

You will please to Say what we must relieve him with weekly Otherwise we must have an Order of removal suspended against your Parish, Waiting Gentlemen your Answer will Oblige yours respectly

Tho. Randleson
Assist. Overseer

78 Tho[ma]s Randleson Assistant Overseer in Carlisle the Churchwardens and Overseers of Kirkby Lonsdale, N.D. (WPR/19/7/6/20/22)

County of Cumberland *The CHURCH-WARDENS and OVERSEERS of* Kirkby Lonsdale *to the CHURCHWARDENS and OVERSEERS of the Poor of English Street Quarter, Parish of St. CUTHBERT'S, CARLISLE.*

	Dr. for Money paid as per Order to						
Names	*From*	*To*	*No of Weeks*	*Per Week*	*£*	*s.*	*D.*
	1826						
James Boothman	17 March	Novr 10th Inclusive	35	2/	3	10	–
do-----	10th Novr 1827	March 30	20	4/–	4	–	
					7	10	–

Boothman has been Confined to his bed for upwards of 20 Weeks for which his Daughter was Obliged to leave her place and wait upon him 4/- weekly is as Small Allowance as he possible can do with

Attention being paid to the Settlement of the above, will much oblige the Church-wardes and Overseers of English Street Quarter, St. Cuthbert's, CARLISLE, otherwise the pay will be discontinued; they having made a Resolution not to continue Payment for those Townships who do not pay immediate attention to the Settlement of their Accounts; and if any alteration in the Allowance to your Paupers, please to signify it, for our future Government.

I am, Gentlemen.

Your obedient Servant,

Thos. Randleson Assist *OVERSEER*

C. THURNAM, PRINTER, CARLISLE.

Notes: *This is a printed proforma invoice with correspondence added. The content of the invoice in italics (outwith brackets) represents the printed text.*

Although the letter itself is not dated, the dates on the invoice suggest very strongly that it was sent between letters 77 and 79.

79 Tho[ma]s Randleson, Assistant Overseer in Carlisle to [Stephen] Garnet[t] in Kirkby Lonsdale, 5 May 1827 (WPR/19/7/6/20/18)

Carlisle 5 May 1827

Mr Garnet

Sir/

You will please to remitt the Money due us for the maintance of Jas. Boothman, Bill sent due March ^30^th^ for March 30 to May 4th 5 weeks 4/-

7.10.0
1. 0 .0
8.10.0

Boothmans Son has taken him in to the Country last Week as his Daughter could not do with him, in all probability you will be hearing from his Son in the course of a Week or two as we have Discontinued his Weekly Allowance

Your immediate Attention to the remittance will Oblige your by Order of the Select Vestry

Thos. Randleson
Ass[t]. Overseer

Circumtext: *Next to figures on account, in different hand [SG]:* Agreed to be paid

80 Geo[rge] Boothman in Little Corby to the Parish of Kirkby Lonsdale, 12 May 1827 (WPR/19/7/6/20/19)

Little Corby near Carlisle
May 12th 1827

Gent,

Be pleased to remit me on account of my Father Jas. Boothman who is now living with me 5/- a week as it is as little as I can do with He is obliged to be lifted in and out of bed –

I called upon Mr. Randleson for some relief for him but he inform me he can do nothing for him as I reside out of his Parish If you will write an order to the Overseer here he will pay me

Your Obed[t]. Serv[t].
Geo: Boothman

81 Tho[ma]s Randleson Assistant Overseer in Carlisle to [Stephen] Garnet[t] in Kirkby Lonsdale, 18 May 1827 (WPR/19/7/6/20/17)

Carlisle May 18[th] 1827

Mr. Garnet
Sir/

Yours on the 15 Inst Ireceived requesting an explanation with respect to James Boothman Your first order was to allow him 2/ or 2/6 P week as our Vestry thought most proper he accordingly was allowed 2/- weekly from

March to Novr. when he was taken extreemly ill and confined to his Bed and not any person to Attend him, Consequently application was made to our Vestry, and on examining him and finding his Situation most deplorable, Dr. Heysham J.P. Ordered along with the Vestry 4/ weekly which has been paid since that period – you may rest assured that it was as little as possible he could do with having his Weekly rent to discharge and his Daughter to wait on him – it was in contemplation to have an Order of Removal Suspended but referring to your Letter on the 17 March 1826 giving us power to advance him as we wood do our Own paupers the Order was dispensed with you would Observe the Bill I sent you in March last was Charged 4/ weekly which you never Answered

Boothman was taken to his Son in a Cart to Little Corby about 4 miles from Carlisle, which was done with great Difficulty if you are not Satisfied with this letter you may write to John Heysham Esqr. Magistrate which is the ~~[******]~~ [*overwritten by*] Chairman of our Vestry and was that Day when the extra allowance was granted, I requested Mr Grundy when he was at Carlisle last to call and see Boothmans Situation

Your remittance is requested and
Oblige your Respectfully
Thos. Randleson
Assis^{t}. Overseer
order of Vestry

82 Geo[rge] Boothman in Little Corby to Step[hen] Garnett in Kirkby Lonsdale, 2 July 1827 (WPR/19/7/6/20/1)

Little Corby July 2^{d} 1827

Mr. Step Garnett Sir Will you plese to send my Fathers penson it being Due a little time Back for my Father Came to me the 20 April Last, He is a veary Hold Man and Very Febel Can not Make aney Help for Him Self He is to Lift in and Hout of Bed –

and a Very great Burding to us – But We Are Wiling to Help Him all We Can and make is Burding as Lite as posabel We Can for you, and if you Will ples to send is alowance as sown as this Comes to Hand you Will mouch oblige your Houbel Servent

Geo: Boothman

83 Geo[rge] Boothman in Little Corby to Step[hen] Garnett in Kirkby Lonsdale [20] October [1827] (WPR/19/7/6/20/45)

Mr Little Corby Oct. <20> [*page torn*]
Step: Garnett Sir, Will you plese to My Fathers penn., I aplyed to Mr Ranilson But He i tould me He Head Nothing to do with Him Now, and He though my Father Would only Be payed once Quarters which Made Me Be so Long a aplying for it.

Sir Will you plese Send Mine a Long with My Fathers as I Have to pay My House rent as Sowen at Comes to Hand –
and you will Mouch oblige your
Houmbel Servent
Geo: Boothman

Notes: *Although this letter does not have a year, its place in the sequence strongly suggests it was sent in 1827.*

84 Geo[rge] Boothman in Little Corby to Steph[e]n Garnett in Kirkby Lonsdale, 13 November 1827 (WPR/19/7/6/20/42)

Little Corby Nov 13 1827

Mr Steph^{n} Garnett

Sir My Father and My ~~did~~ own alowance Which you plesed to ~~Ba~~ Sattel on us not Coming in Due time has being a great trouble to us and a great Disapointment to those that i Kned to pay tow – for i ~~he~~ had My Landlord to pay and My Bread Corn that i had got on trust not Being abel to pay – My Cradet is stoped and we har in Veary great Want Deer Sir be plesed to Wrile as sown as this Comes to hand – and you Will much oblige your poor houmbel servent
Geo Boothman

85 Geo[rge] Boothman in Little Corby to Step[hen] Garnett in Kirkby Lonsdale, 1 January 1828 (WPR/19/7/6/21/7)

Little Corby Jany 1 1828
Mr
Step Garnett Sir this Will inform you that my Father Died on the 14 of Last month – and as I have no Frand to Help me to pay the Fournell Expenss you Will I hope Consader my Saituation and ~~no~~ send me What you think is right

to pay the Expnss of the Sam – With regard to my Self I am Depened on my Famley and as Long as thay have Work and Bides with me I will try to dow my Self – Sir ples Write as sowen as posabel you Can and you Will Mouc^h^ oblige your hombel Servent

Geo. Boothman

86 Rachel Boothman in Newcastle to [Stephen] Garnett in Kirkby Lonsdale, 5 January 1829 (WPR/19/7/6/22/14)

Newcastle Jany. 5th 1829

Mr Garnett

Sir/ I am sorry to inform you that when I come here to Newcas^tle^ I did not find my friends as I expected and I am very ill off at present but I hope you will have the goodness to send me my two months allowance it being rather before the time but on account of the Distress I am in I hope you will remit it unto me otherwise I will have to throw myself upon the parish here – you may let Mr Parkinson know that I received all the things safe along with the Bundle I hope you will remit the money as soon as possible as I wish to go home to my own place as it will make little different to you only to be longer in sending the next

I remain yours obediently Rachael Boothman

her mark X

Circumtext: *Below, in different hand*: Please direct the letter to Rich^{d}. Petch Overseer Gateshead

87 Rachel Boothman in Newcastle to [Stephen] Garnett in Kirkby Lonsdale, 19 January 1829 (WPR/19/7/6/22/13)

Newcastle ^Jan^{y}^ 19th 1829

Mr Garnett

Sir this comes to lett you know that I wrote to you Concerning ^my^ money a fortneth ago but you never answered my letter but it was a little before it was Dew but by the time you receive this it will be Dew me and I hope you will have the goodness to Remitt the Same as it will be Dew on the 21 of this month and I have been very poorley of and if I Do not gett it Imeadetly I will be under the nessetey of making aplication for a Remov^ell^ to Kirkby Lonsdale

I [~~*****~~] [*overwritten by*] Remain your^{s} Rachaell Boothm^an^
Her Mark X
Direct to Rich^{d}. Petch Overseer Gateshead
newcastle on Tyne

88 Rachel Boothman in Newcastle to the Parish of Kirkby Lonsdale, 15 March 1829 (WPR/19/7/6/22/3)

Newcastle March 15th 1829

Sir)

this Comes to lett you know I received the money you sent to me ~~in Dew time~~ from Mr Gleghorn ^Overseer^ and It was a fortneth after Date and a letter Directed to Richd Petch and you mentioned about not paying any more money forehand but I hope you will have the goodness to Remit me the same at this time as I am Verry Poorly of and I will be everly Oblidged to you, as I have had letter from George Boothman and he wishes me to go to Carlisle and if you will Oblige ^me^ at this time I will be very thankfull to you as it will be all I will have to take me and my Children to Carlisle –

Please to write soon and By So Doing you will much Oblidge your humble S^{t}. Rachaell Boothman

Direct to the Care of Richd Petch
Overseer Gateshead Newcastle on
Tyne

89 John Cleghorn Assistant Overseer in Gateshead to the Parish of Kirkby Lonsdale, 6 April 1829 (WPR/19/7/6/22/37)

~~Newcastle~~ ^Gateshead^ 6th 1829

Sir) this is to Certfiy that Rachaell Boothman has made applycation to hus last weak and got some relief and apperently Distitute and if she Does not gett relief emedietly from you She must have a removell Imedietley and I hope you will not Delay writing as her money was Dew on the twenty first of Last month

Gateshead John Cleghorn
Ap 6th 1829 Assistant oversear

90 Rachel Boothman in Carlisle to [Stephen] Garnett in Kirkby Lonsdale, 6 [****] 1829 (WPR/19/7/6/22/50)

Carlisle 6th 1829

Mr Garnett)
Sir) I hope you will have the Godness to Remit my Money as Soon as Convenient as it will be Dew on the 15th of this month and if you will you will Much Oblidge me at preasant as I am a little putt about at the Mean time as it onley ^will^ be a few Days before the time I received the last money at Newcastle on the 16th of April and was Much Oblidged to you and Direct to Me Care of Robert Hill Shaddon Gate Carlisle I hope you will write as soon as posible and by So Doing you will Oblidge Yours

Rachael Boothman

Notes: *Although there is no month given for this letter, its place in the sequence suggests it was sent between April and September 1829.*

91 Rachel Boothman in Carlisle to [Stephen] Garnett in Kirkby Lonsdale, 7 September 1829 (WPR/19/7/6/22/44)

Carlisle 7th $Sept^{r}$. 1829

Mr Garnett

Sir) I received your letter and ~~more~~ [*overwritten by*] my money this Day Eight weaks I hope you will have the goodness to Remit my Alliment as Soon as Convienent and by so Doing you w<ill> [*obscured by wax seal*]

Much Oblidge your Humble &c.
Rachaell Boothman

Direct to me Care of Robt. Hill Mill Burns Row
Shaddongate Carlisle

92 Rachel Boothman in Carlisle to [Stephen] Garnett in Kirkby Lonsdale, 23 September 1829 (WPR/19/7/6/22/30)

Carlisle $_v$Septr$_v$ 23th 1829

Mr Garnett

Sir) I take the Liberty of writing you a few lines letting you know my preasent situation I am Living in with another person and it Does not answer my work as I am in a way of Making a little suport by washing and Dressing and I Could gett a little place ~~of~~ to my self if ^in^ ~~I~~ Case you would have the Goodness to advance me one pound and I will look for no more from you, untill the month of Janeray as it is to Gett a few small things ~~to~~ towards furnishing a house if you will Grant me this small favour you will much Oblidge

Your Humble Servent Rachel Boothman

Direct to me Care of Robt Hill
Shaddongate Carlisle

93 Rachel Boothman in Carlisle to [Stephen] Garnett in Kirkby Lonsdale, 1 November 1829 (WPR/19/7/6/22/56)

Carlisle Novr. 1th 1829

Mr Garnett

Sir) this Comes to lett you know I rec^{xd} my last money in Dew time Safe, I wrote you a few lines Concerning a months money in advance but never Rec^{d}. any answer I have had a very hard time latley my little Girl has been laying this fortneth with a broken leg and I Can get nothing Done for waiting upon her and if you would have the godness to Send me a few Shillings more then my aliment you would much Oblidge your

Humble S^{t}. Rachaell Boothman

Direct to me Care of Robt. Hill head of
Shaddon Gate Carlisle

94 Rachel Boothman in Carlisle to [Stephen] Garnett in Kirkby Lonsdale, 26 December 1829 (WPR/19/7/6/22/21)

Carlisle ^Dec^r^.^ 26th 1829

Mr Garnett
Sir,

I receved your last in Dew time and if you will have the godness to remit me my money a few days before Dew it will advantige me at the meen time and by so Dooing you will Oblidge Your Humble St.

Rachaell
Boothman

Direct to me Care of Robert Hill
Shaddon Gate Carlisle

95 Rachel Boothman in Carlisle to [Stephen] Garnett in Kirkby Lonsdale, 11 March 1830 (WPR/19/7/6/23/55)

Carlisle March 11th 1830

Mr. Garnett
Sir I write you thees few lines wishing to know the Delay of my money as it is above a weak Dew or if you have Sent it their is Some Mistake in the Post office when you write lett me know if their is any need of writing everey time it Comes Dew – as long as I Continue in the Same Place or not I hope you will not Delay writing and Direct to

Rachaell Boothman Care of Robt. Hill
Millburns Row Shaddon Gate Carlisle
So no More But Remains &c
Rachaell
Boothman

96 William Rees in Carlisle to the Parish of Kirkby Lonsdale, 12 April 1831 (WPR/19/7/6/24/31)

Carlisle
April 12 1831

Gentlemen

I write at the request of Rachael Boothman to beg that you will without delay forward to her as before the amount of her weekly parish relief for the want of which she has been greatly distressed, having a sick child to attend I trust therefore you will consider her necessities and send her the amount

I remain Gentlemen
your obed^{t}. Servant
William Rees
Min^{s}. of S^{t}. Mary

97 William Rees in Carlisle to the Parish of Kirkby Lonsdale, 24 March 1832 (WPR/19/7/6/25/14)

Carlisle
March 24
/32

Sir

I am requested by Rachael Boothman to beg you will be good enough to forward to her the amount the Parish allowance now due to her as they stand in g^{t}. need of it, the times being so very hard, in the course of a few days there will be three months due. it is a considerable hardship that the cost of the Postoffice order sh^{d}. be deducted from the poor womans small pittance each time the money is remitted as by sending ^a^ £5 note at once to the Overseer here it might be paid them weekly without any other deduction than the one postage

I remain Sir
Your obed^{t}. Servant
William Rees
Min^{t}. of St Mary
Carlisle

98 Rachel Boothman in Carlisle to [Stephen] Garnett in Kirkby Lonsdale, 21 July 1833 (WPR/19/7/6/26/29)

Carlisle July 21th 1833

Mr. Garnett
Sir)

I recieved yours Dated June the 19 and one Soverign which I was very thankfull you wished to know My Childrens ages Mary Boothman was Born Decr. 15th 1823 – James Boothman was Born Octr 14th 1825 – Likewise you wished to know their earnings But their earnings never has amounted to aney thing as yet, for Mary has had a Dry Scald in her head ever Since I left your house which has Caused me a Great Deal of Trouble and expence Both and James Likewise has Been under the Dispensrey Doctors ~~for~~ at Different times for the space of eight and nine Month at a time ~~they~~ – and he a Very Small Delicate Boy – But thank God Marys head has ^Got^ a Sound Cure if you think they are of aney use to you you may have thim at aney time as they never have been of aney use to me as Yet in Regard of Earning aney thing as Yett – I hope you will have the goodness to write as soon as Convienient as I am onley Very Poorley Situated –

I am Yours &
Rachaell Boothman

99 Rachel Boothman in Carlisle to Steph[en] Garnett in Kirkby Lonsdale, 20 May 1835 (WPR/19/7/6/28/47)

Duke Street
Carlisle
May 20th 1835

Sir

I acknowledge the recipt of your Letter bearing date 25th March Instant, and you may depend its Contents very much Surprised me, when you Say, that you have been informed I am Married again, I could like well you would give up your informant, so as I could bring him or her face to face – as Marriage is Such a change in Circumstances as I have not yet had the imprudence to contemplate therefore I hope and trust, that this candid dictaration will be Sufficient to enable the Vestry to believe, that no Marriage has taken Place – If the Vestry Persistes in discontinuing my weekly allowance, it must unavoidably force me to break up my House, and Come with my Family altogether, for how is it possible that a Single woman ^can^ ~~to~~ support her self and 3 helpless Children, winding bobbins for weavers and pay House rent and find firing, without the weekly allowance I have had –

Please turn over

I beg leave further to State, that my oldest Girl is now fit to be Put to Some business or other but then who will taken her without some remuneration, not any Person in Carlisle, for that I have tryed, therefore if the Vestry would condescend to advance Something on that head, I think I could get a Person to take ^her^ but without some remuneration I cannot therefore I will leave it for you to deside what is best to be done in that Case, as for the oldest Boy, I think he will never be fit for any thing he is so dilicate I have had the Doctors attending him for 9 Months together – as for the Child I was Carring when with you, I have never yet asked any thing for him, altho he now takes almost as much to Support him as any of the rest, so that if I am forced to come, in consequence of the discontinuence of my weekly allowance, I will be found to be but a heavy charge – however I must leave all these matters to your Superior judgement which bids me conclude and Subscribe myself

Sir

your most obedient
humble claimant
Rachel Boothman

To Step^{h} Garnett
Kirkby Lonsdale
Overseer of the Poor

Circumtext: *Overleaf, in different hand [SG]:*

Rachel Boothman admitted to the workhouse on the 9th Octr 1828 left the House 27 Nov^{r}
Mary Boothman then aged 5 ½ years
James -------do---------------- 4 do
James Bootham died in Novr 1827

100 Rachel Boothman in Carlisle to [Stephen] Garnett in Kirkby Lonsdale, 1 June 1835 (WPR/19/7/6/28/46)

Carlisle 1th $_{v}$June$_{v}$1835

Mr. Garnett,

Sir I rec^{d}. yours Dated 23 of May I am Sorry to Observe the Contents which has Put me to a great Deal of unesseary trouble as to applying to Mnnesters or Churchwarden they told me the onley ones to aply too was to aply too Respectble neighbours and house^holders^ was the Best to Sertify whether I was Married or not you mention Concerning the Childrens ages Mary was Born Decr. 15th 1823 – James Born Octr the 14 $_{v}$1825$_{v}$ as I have had perticular word from my Brother in Glasgow which he made perticular Enquirie at the Church wheir they ~~wheir they~~ weir Both Reg^e^stred, I am willing at aney time to Make Oath Before aney Majistrate what ever that I was never Married Since I was Married on James Boothman you Mention Concerning the Child I was Carring when with you But wheir I belong he Belongs But he has neither Cost you nor me aneything as yet and as for James by all apperance he will Trouble no on very long, But without your help a little longre Iam not able to Exist with them aney longer So I hope you will answer this Shortley or I will be forced to gett a Remouvell for me and my fammiley Emeidtley I have made apycation to gett Mary to Service But I can fall in with no place for ^her^ as ~~yett~~ yett – I am Yours &c. Rachaell Boothman

[*in different hands*] we the undersign[d] have known Rachaell Boothman upwards of four Years, and has been Single Since

Samuell Jarden writer
Robert Lawson Landlord of Dwelling
Wm Armstrong Queen Street Cooperative Society
James Winikill Grocer
Robert Hill

Circumtext: *Below, in further hand [SG]:* Granted 2s/ a week

In margin: You mentioned Concerning Directing my Letters to another Man But I was under an Obligation to him at Diffrent times

101 Rachel Boothman in Carlisle to [Stephen] Garnett in Kirkby Lonsdale, 4 August 1835 (WPR/19/7/6/28/35)

Carlisle 4th Augs[t]. 1835

Mr. Garnett)

Sir I take the Libertey of writing to you hoping you will not take aney thing Amiss I should Been Verey Sorey to Troubled You at this time But my situation at preasent, I wished to lett you know I have Been Verey Poorley Since Before I rec[d]. your last letter and a Soverign which I Shourley was verey much Oblidged to you and the Gentlemen of your Vestrey I am Verey Much put about paying my rent and My Landlord threat[s]. me if I Doo not pay on or Before Monday next he will take my few articules from me which Troubles me verey much the Some I am in dew is 18[s]. which I am not able to pay, Like wise the Children is particular Ill of for Cloathing, I thought you would have the goodness to advance me tenn weakes aliment ~~is~~ along with the other tenn that I will be due Shortley it would Much Oblige me at this time as I amm onley in a verey poor State of health, I hope you will Excuse me for writing at this time I would have Been sorey to put you to aney trouble if it had not have Been Compleet nessetey

I am You[r] Humble
& Obidient S[t]
Rachaell Boothman

102 Rachel Boothman in Carlisle to [Stephen] Garnett in Kirkby Lonsdale, 1 March 1836 (WPR/19/7/6/29/10)

Carlisle March 1th 1836

Mr. Garnett

Sir) I am sorry that I am under the nessety of writing you at this time But on the account of me Being poorley this some time I am ~~under~~ Compeled to lett you know my situation I am endue my Landlord a trifle for Rent and he is a Very Sever man and wishes to have it Emeadietley So if you would favour me with my alliment at this time you would Much Obidge your Humble

Sir^{t}

Rachaell Boothman

PS I am sorry ~~if~~ to inform you that my Son James has been bedd fast ever since Christimys Last untill this few Days and he is in a way of Recovery

103 Rachel Boothman in Carlisle to Ste[ph]en Garnett in Kirkby Lonsdale, 22 August 1836 (WPR/19/7/6/29/19)

Carlisle August 22th 1836

Steven Garnett

Sir) I rec^{d}. yours Dated June the 7 and Observed the Contents which I thought You Should have write me before this time you Mentioned about Reducing my pension which I Could expect nothing Els But not to Stopp it all to gether as I have a verey helpless Boy to Maintain & has Been for this Some weeks Verey poorley My Self, so I hope you Gentle$_{v}$menn$_{v}$ will take it to Consideration of my Distressed Situation at preasant as I am not able to maintain My Self at preasant So what ever you are going to allow me I hope you will ^Relieve me^ as soon as Possible please to Direct to the Care of Robt. Hill Duke S^{t}. Shaddongate Carlisle

I am Your Parrisoner Rachaell Boothman

4.

GARLICK, letters 104–137

104 Rich[ar]d Garlick in Chatburn to the Parish of Kirkby Lonsdale, 25 December 1816 (WPR/19/7/6/9/22)

Sir/
I ham forst to wright to you a bought the remander of my Rint for my Landlord will ^not^ put of no longar and I am shour that i cannot get it my silf the times so very bad so I would have you to considar to send it and a trifell be side wilst the times is beter and the remandar of my Rint is 38^{s} shillings and he as one gen me one week to pay it and he tould me to Day that if I dodnot get it agane weekend he would sell me my things so I would have you to consider to send it a gane the time for if the times would mend that i could do I would never want you to do aney thing we are very il set to get meat this time you may consider with in your self and 7 of famley pleas to send me answor back as sone ~~s~~ as you can
Decr 25th 1816 from Richd Garlick
Chatburne

Circumtext: *Overleaf, different hand [SG]*: Granted to 2.0.0 and to write him upon it
Same hand, in pencil [SG]: 1817 Jan^{r}, 19th Gave to George Clark of Bolton by Bolland the above sum

105 W[illia]m Hitchen, Overseer in Chatburn, to the Parish of Kirkby Lonsdale, 30 April 1819 (WPR/19/7/6/12/5)

Chatburn 30 of April 1819
Sir/ I hope you, & they other Gentlemen of the Town, will take It in to Considiration, and send Rich^{d}. Garlicks Rent as It is Impossible for him to pay It, his having a wife & six Children & the times so very hard, his Rent Day, is on Monday the 3^{d} Day of May. Sir you may send It by the post to Settle & they will forward It, by way of Skipton to Chatburn
From yours
Respectfully Wm Hitchen
Overseer

Circumtext: *In different hand [SG]*: To write to the Persons for the account of the ammount of Rent

106 Rich[ar]d Garlick in Chatburn to the Parish of Kirkby Lonsdale, 15 November 1819 (WPR/19/7/6/12/27)

Gentlamen   My Rent <w>as [*page torn*] due to Mr Braswell of Walley on the 8th of Novr and I hame not habel to pay it my self as my familey is large a Wife and 6 small Childran and my sumer jobe is over the next week and work wise very case so I hope you will have the goodness to send ~~I~~ it and a trifel be sides as my Children is all nacked all most and I ham not abell to get them aney Cloathes my self for there is non of them abell to adell me aney thing the Thrade is so bad at present and my Wife as scodan her Lege that she as not ben habel to adall aney thing this 6 weeks back so I hope you will have the goodness to send it by the Beare with out me coming ~~of~~ over as it is long way

from

Novr. 15th 1819   Richd Garlick

Chatburn

Circumtext: *Below, different hand*: James Wilson
Further hand [SG]: Rent Granted

107 Jonathan Farrer, Overseer of Clitheroe, to the Parish of Kirkby Lonsdale, 3 February 1820 (WPR/19/7/6/13/1)

Sir,

I write to you on behalf of Richard Garlick a pauper belonging to your Town, who is now residing in Clithero out of employment, and in very great distress, and not able to support himself and his family without some parochial relief. And if you consider to relieve him, after I have stated to you his distress, and you will give me an order to pay him some casual relief, or a Weekly Sum whether you may think more proper whilst he is out of employment I will lay it down for your Town – you will favor me with an answer on this subject as early as possible and am

Your most obed^{t}. Servt.

February 3rd 1820   Jonathan Farrer

Overseer of Clithero

Circumtext: *Overleaf in different hand [SG]:* ~~To~~ send the Overseer one pound to be given as he thinks proper to Richard Garlick

108 Rich[ar]d Garlick to the Parish of Kirkby Lonsdale, 2 May 1820 (WPR/19/7/6/13/9)

Gentalmen my Rint is Due on the 11th of May and I ham not Hable to pay it my self my Famley is so large for it is verey hard work to get meat for ~~us~~ them let a lone aney thing els whitch I hope you will have the gudness to send my Rint and a trifell be sides for we are most nacked for Cloathing and wear all of want of shorting we have non casley of aney sort and I hame not habel to get them aney for the times is so verey bad for ther is nothing to be hadled with weving with Children ate present but I hame Hired with my Hould Master a gane for the sumer ~~Cesan~~ Cesan that is wilst ould Martlsmess so I hope you will have the Goodness to send It by the Beare for I hame in Great nessitey at present ~~I~~ and I am not hable to get out of it with out the help of you If I could I schud think it verey gret shame to send to you

from yours

Richd Garlick

1820 May 2th

Circumtext: *In different hand [SG]:* Granted Rent and 10s/

109 Rich[ar]d Garlick and James Wilson near Clitheroe to St[ephe]n Garnett in Kirkby Lonsdale, 27 August 1820 (WPR/19/7/6/13/22)

Gentlmen I hame in great nessity of wrighting to you for some relife for wear all nacked and we have not aney thing to spare to get Clothing with for is verey har<d> [*page torn*] worck to get meat of any cind & Children is forst to go bare foot and bare leg for I cannot get nader Cloggs nor stockings for them not out of my wages and as for ther other clothing is as raged as they the ar shame to sethem and I my self and it cannot be helped with out the help of you and I hope you will have the considation to send me some money to get them sum Clothing to cep them warm for the Backend is coming on I have one ridey to Larn to weve if we hade aney Lomes to Learn on but I have non nor cannot get aney with out the help of you but if I could get one to Larne to weve a pice a week it would a great help in our Famley

from yours

Richd Garlick

Agu^{t}. 27th 1820
near Clithero

Circumtext: *Below signature, different hand*: James Wilson
In further hand [SG]: Granted £1.0.0
Address of Recipient (overleaf): Mr Stip^{n} Garnett Kirkby Lonsdall Westmorland

In margin, by address:

~~3 6~~
36 0 0
2 14 0
2 0
2 4 ½
38 18 4 ½
3 12 0
35 6 4 ½

110 Rich[ar]d Garlick in Pimlico, near Clitheroe, to the Parish of Kirkby Lonsdale, 29 November 1820 (WPR/19/7/6/13/35)

Gentalmen I hame in nessity for my Rint and I have nothing for it with out the help of you and my wages will be verey small for 12 weeks for ward and my Famley large I hope you will have the godness to give me it the Rent day is 3 weeks past and the are verey strick a bout their Rints in this part and if you would given me a pare of Blankets it would a ben a gret Cind <nes>s [*page torn*] as we are of want of a pare and nothing to get aney with and we are very ill starved this Winter

from

Novr 29th 1820 Rich^{d}. Garlick

Pimleyco ner Clithero

Circumtext: *In different hand [SG]:* Granted $^{£}$2.2^{s}.0^{d}.
Overleaf, in same hand [SG]: 1819 Decr. 18th Half years Rent $^{£}$2.5^{s}.0^{d}.

111 H Brasewell in Swan [W]abey to the Parish of Kirkby Lonsdale, 6 December 1820 (WPR/19/7/6/13/37)

Sir, as you are in the Abet of Paying Richard Garlick Rent wich was due the alf year the 11 Nov ~~I~~ Shall thank you to Send itt by the bearer the Rent is 5 Pounds a year and you Have only Send $^{£}$2.5^{s} for the alf years Rent Be fore and I Canot get it of them I can not get itt except I destres them and I do not like that you will Reclect they are a large famely you must Pay the other for ^them^ if you Please

and by so doin you will a blige
Me H Brasewell Swan Mabey
desem 6 1820

112 H Brasewell in Swan Wabey to the Parish of Kirkby Lonsdale, 9 May 1821 (WPR/19/7/6/14/19)

Swan Wabey May 9 1821

Sir I have sent you a line Respectin Richard Garlicks Rent Wich is due the 12 May to now the Reasen you do not Send ^~~rent~~^ the ^rent^ in ful the Rent is 5 Pound and the first 2 alf years you Sent the 2 Pound five then there Remaned 10 Shilins the Last alf years alf years Rent I only Reseved 2 Pound then there Remaned 10 Shilins there fore there is due to Me $^{£}$1.0^{s}.0^{d} Sins I Entered to that Property I thought Proper to Let you now a bout it to See wether you wod Settel the same or Else I Shall be ablige to distres them you will Please to Send by the bearer Next week and then I Shall be habel to say wat to do I Shall want of you

£3 – 10 – 0

So no more from your
H Brasewell

113 Rich[ar]d Garlick to the Parish of Kirkby Lonsdale, 30 May 1821 (WPR/19/7/6/14/20)

Gentalmen

I ham under the obligation of wrighting to you for my Rent as it was due on the 16th of May and my Landlord is very servear a bought it for there is sum rears be hind and I hame not hable to pase it without the help of you and my Famley is verey large and wagis is very small so I hope you will have the godness to send it by the berar or otherwise it will case me to comover for my Landlord is very sharp and I have nothing for Rint wilst my Famley is so very small for as sone I cand Do on my self I shoul be very glad

from Richd Garlick
May 30 1821

Circumtext: *In different hand [SG]:* Granted $^{£}$3.10^{s} – ^{d} Being the whole of his Rent then due

114 H Brasewell in Swan Wabey to the Parish of Kirkby Lonsdale, 14 November 1821 (WPR/19/7/6/14/42)

Swan Wabey Nov 14 1821

Sir, I thought it Proper to a Cuant you that Richard Garlick Rent is due to Me and the Poor Man sais he canot Pay any thin so I hexpect you will Send it as usal and by so doin you will a blige Me H Brasewell

The alf years Rent is 2 12 6

Circumtext: *In different hand [SG]:* Granted

115 H Brasewell in Swan [W]abey to the Parish of Kirkby Lonsdale, 8 May 1822 (WPR/19/7/6/15/10)

Sir I thought it Proper to a Cuant you that Richard Garlick Rent will be due on the 16 of May and ops at our Convenian$_{v}$ce$_{v}$ you will Send it by the bearer and by so doin you will a blige Me

H Brasewell Swan Mabey

May 8 1822

Circumtext: *In different hand [SG]:* Granted $^{£}1.10^{s}.0^{d}$

Below, in further hand, and in pencil: 2.12.6

116 Rich[ar]d Garlick in Pimlico near Clitheroe to the Parish of Kirkby Lonsdale, 3 July 1822 (WPR/19/7/6/15/20)

Gentlmen I undarstand that your ar informd that I have sum Benfit from the Lime Ciln be side common waggis but you ar rong informd it is but $14^{s}/^{d}$ P week and $16^{s}/^{d}$ shillings is all that I have coming in of any account a week and wee are 9 of Famley seven Childaren & Wife me self and Wife ar very Porley 6 weeks and lickley for continey a wille she as not ben out of Doar this 6 weeks and I hope you will con~~d~~sider my sitewation do sum thing at this time I have Doctor Cannon Bill of nearly 30^{s} shillings & Mr Bracewell be hind of rint whitch he is very angrey and I shure I can not pay nethar of them out of my Waggs I hope you come over & se my my sitwation & then you woul^d^ be lefe defrant to sum one as informed you I ham scertan that I must com over if you do not ^~~come~~^ send me sum thing to pay Doctor & Bracewell I must a comd over be for now but for my Mastar Giles Hoyle lend me a Pound Noat I was in destris for sum thing to Nurishe her and you may be lefe me that I must come & Famley as sone as Wife gets betar if you will not pay my

Rint but ~~you~~ <my> [*page torn*] Wife get out of Doar I would trie to do if you would pay my Rint will my Childran gets up a bit and you will not pay it be so cind as send me ~~not~~ word and we will comeall of Famley as sone She is fit to come for I ham suer I can not pay it my self we have a nuf to do get a bit of meat and so Gentlmen I hope you will have mersey on hus at this time

Pimblico   from your
near Clithero   Richd Garlick
July 3th1822

Circumtext: *Overleaf, in different hand [SG]:* Granted on account of the Sickness of his wife $^{£}$1.2^{s}.6^{d}. the Remainder of his Rent

117 Rich[ar]d Garlick in [C]litheroe to the Parish of Kirkby Lonsdale, 27 February 1823 (WPR/19/7/6/16/17)

G Gentalmen I ham in nessetey of wrigting to you for the rint witch is Dew to Mr Braswell for he is determend to have it he will tey hout of ~~to~~ [*overwritten by*] no longar & if you will not tack it in to considdurtion to pay him he will sell my few things and ham not hable to pay it my self you may considur your self 7 Childar & 6 of them very Smal ones and I have no work but what as be out of doar whitch I have not adled mor than 6 shilling a week and meat to find out of it with the frost & Snow ben so long on ground so I hope Gentlmen you will consider me at this time and I will trie to do my self at hafter if i can upon any acount I had Mr Brasewell at me last week and he would have to com over to you to se if I could get it if not he would be very scivere with me and I have not one shilling to wards it and no frind for I borowed sum wen my wife was Porly so long that is not paid back yet so I hope you will do it at this time & will want you no moare if I have my helth and you do not send it you may depend he will sell my things & then I shall be forst to Come to you and I think shall be bether of if I get this sumar over

from yours
Rich^{d}. Garlick

Feby. 27th 1823 <C>lithero [*page torn*]

Circumtext: *Below signature, in different hand*: Jas Wilson
In further hand [SG]: Granted $^{£}$1.0.0

118 W[illia]m Life in Pimlico to the Overseers of Kirkby Lonsdale, 4 December 1823 (WPR/19/7/6/16/56)

Pi<ml>ico [*page torn*] Decr 4 1823

To the Overseers of Kirby Lonsdale
I wrote to you about fortnight ago Expecting some relief for Rich^{d}. Garlick Family and not hering from you since except you send Immediatly some relief they will be Oblig^{d} to be remov^{d} to their Settlem^{t} he has been attended by the Dockter for this last 3 week but he is rec<ov>ering [*page torn*] and got to do a little of somthing but the family is quite in a most distrest situation for Clothing so I hope you will delay no time in Sending Something for their Support as their situation is realy distressing from your Hble Servt

Wm Life

Circumtext: *In different hand [SG]:* Granted 10^{s}/ out of Rates and 10^{s}/ from donation money

119 Rich[ar]d Garlick in Pimlico near Clitheroe to the Parish of Kirkby Lonsdale, 15 December 1827 (WPR/19/7/6/20/39)

Pimlico near Clitheroe Decr 15th 1827

Gentelmen I hope you will have the goodness to send me sum of the *[dow]* money to wards sum Clothing for the Boy that had his legs tacken of for he is very near naked and wagges is very low that I can not get hime any my self and he as not Earned nothing the three years to ward is mentance and he is goten a great strong Boy fit to go to sum trade but im not able to get him one pliace to send it by the Post

from your Homble sirvant
Richd Garlick

120 Rich[ar]d Garlick in Pimlico near Clitheroe to the Parish of Kirkby Lonsdale, 13 December 1828 (WPR/19/7/6/21/16)

Gentlemen I him under the nessety of whrighten to you for sum money for Relif for the Lame Boy the times is so very bad and work scace that we adlin is smaley and provison as dear and the Boy is 16 years of age now and I canot get aney work for him that he can do for the time so bad and I ham not hable to get him a trade so I hope you will have the Goodness to send him sum for Clothing and sumthing towards is mentance

I am yours Richd Garlick

Decr 13th 1828 Pimlico near Clitheroe

121 Mary Life to the Overseer of Kirkby Lonsdale, N.D. (WPR/19/7/6/23/27)

To the overseer of K<irkby> [*obscured by wax seal*] Lonsdale
I am wrighting ~~f~~ to you Informing you of the situation of Richd Garlick Wife who has been very poorly for a month back and except she can have a little asistance she is not likely for getting better I desire you will not delay as the recomend her to wear Flannels and they are not able to get any they have very little mony coming in so they are in a very distrest situation except you send them something Immediately they will be Oblig^{d} to get reliev^{d} from this town the truth of this you may refer to Mr Grundys as the Know I shou^{d} not write false

Mary Life

Note: *Although this letter is undated, its place in the sequence suggests it belongs between letters 120 and 122.*

122 [John] Life in Clitheroe to the Overseer of Kirkby Lonsdale, 4 February 1830 (WPR/19/7/6/23/51)

To the overseer of Kir<by Lon>sdale [*obscured by wax seal*]

This to acquaint you that Richd Garlick Famely is in a very distres^{d} Situation They have only 5^{s}/ a week coming in and they are 8 a famly his Wife is getting better and cou^{d} eat if she cou^{d} git any thing to eat but they are I will asure you in a very distrest situation they are all out of Work but Rich^{d} him self If you wou^{d} be so good as send them a note they think by the Middle of this Month they may some of them be got into work you may depend in the truth of the above

[Jn] Life

Clithro 4 feby 1830

Circumtext: *In different hand [SG]:* Granted 12^{s}/

123 Rich[ar]d Garlick in Pimlico near Clitheroe to the Parish of Kirkby Lonsdale, 30 November [18]31 (WPR/19/7/6/24/44)

Sir/ I ham very sorrey to say that I am in nessety of Wrighten to you my wife has been Porley hever since May 30th last she was 5 week and never was out of Bed and I have a woman to have in to House to do work at meat and wages we have 7 Children at home and non of them Can do the House work the are all lads but the two of youngs is gerles and the Doctor as oder me to get her sum thing to nourish her and I am not able for I have Paid the Dockter 3 Pounds for is Charge at this time and I have paid and geten un til both money and Cradet is don for I have ben in the Habet of Lime Burnen and the sesen is out for this year and thear is no work to be geten a bout has the times is so very bad only a day nou and then and I hav only one Boy in regler in ploy and will not have welest Candlmes next that is the time we begin at Lime Kilns a gane Gentlmen I hope you will look on me at this time with a pare of Blankets for we are porley of for *[*hosen*]* and I am not able to get them and I have not paid my Rent but if you will be so good to send me a Pound at this time to get sumthing for to nurish her at this time and I shall be very thankful for I will do with out trubling you if I Can be so Good as to send as soon as you Can for she is in great ned of it and I Cannot get any thing more for her from yours
Pimlico near Clithero Novr 30th 31 Richd Garlick

Circumtext: *In different hand [SG]:* Granted $^{£}$1.0^{s}.0

124 Will Gearsley in Clitheroe to the Parish of Kirkby Lonsdale, 26 January [18]32 (WPR/19/7/6/25/6)

Gent^{m}.

Richard Garlick has applied to me for relief, he has been very ill for upwards of a month & his wife has been confined to her Bed 34 weeks, he has 7 Children and only one of them works and he gets 3^{s}/6^{d} a week.

They are very ill off at the present Time & if you say what shall be done with them, by writing I will attend to it for you

His youngest Child is obliged in consequence of his wife's Illness to be fasted out –

Clitheroe In haste
26th Jan^{y}. '32 Yours obedtly
Will: Gearsley
Overseer

125 Rich[ar]d Garlick in Pimlico near Clitheroe to the Parish of Kirkby Lonsdale, 14 April 1832 (WPR/19/7/6/25/21)

Gentlemen, I ham under the Oblgaiton of wrighten to you wich I ham verey sorey to say my wife is Departed this world this morning after a lond and tides Ilness I have never ben with Sickness in this House two and three never since 30 of last may and I Desier you would be so Good as to releve me with sum mony to wards Berien her for i ham not able to Berier my self I have had a woman to ł here in to House all the time and if you will be so good as send me sum at this time I will cep of you as well as I can I ham il at want of Blankes if you would be so cind as send me a pair I ham not able to By a pare I hope you will have the Good to send me sum thing with out me have to come over from your Humble servent

Rich[d] Garlick

Pimblco near Clitheroe
April 14 – 1832

126 Rich[ar]d Garlick near Clitheroe to the Parish of Kirkby Lonsdale, 29 June [1832] (WPR/19/7/6/25/35)

Gentlemen I ham very sorey to say that I ham under the nessecty of trubling you at this time it is my mind to do with out if I could on any account but I hope you will tack me into consideration and my Famley I have seven Children at Home and a woman to pay Half a Crown a week for the ar all Boys but two of youngs I hope you will have the goodnes to send me sum thing at this time and I will in dever to do with ł [*overwritten by*] if I can on any Account if the trade would mend I Could do with out trubling you I have one that only gets 3 Days a week for want of the trade Staring and credet I have non with my Famley

June 29th I ham your Humble Servent
near Clitheroe Rich[d] Garlick

Circumtext: *In different hand [SG]:* Granted 10[s]/

Notes: *Although there is no indication of the year in which this letter was sent, it's content and place in the sequence strongly suggest it was sent in June 1832.*

127 Henry Bracewell in West Clough near Clitheroe to the Parish of Kirkby Lonsdale, 30 October 1832 (WPR/19/7/6/25/60)

Gentlemen thear is a poor Laberin man the name of Richard Garlick a Tenand of mine wich is not able to pay is Rint if is mind whas ever so good which he owes to me two years Rint within 15 ten shillings at 3 Pound a year and I think it your duty to do ~~shall~~ [*overwritten by*] Sum thing to wards it yo<u> [*page torn*] may think well that be cepes of you as he do with his Famley Five Littl Children that cane earn nothing with out mother and his House as not ben with out sickness for this last two years you may consider your selves that he canot pay aney Rint him self at prisind and I can~~t~~ not let him live Rent free but I shall give him ten Days to pay it in and if not I shall Destriss is goods and sell them for one year Rent unles you will pay sum thing for him and If you will you may ~~a~~ write by the Post to let me no for I ham determed to have a part of it or sell and you may think well that he do with a lettel as he dos with is Famley Richd Garlick

From Henry Bracewell

Octr 30th 1832 West Clough near Clitheroe

Circumtext: *In different hand [SG]:* Granted $^{£}$3.0^{s}.0^{d}

128 Henry Brac[e]well in West Clough near Clitheroe to the Parish of Kirkby Lonsdale, 1 May 1833 (WPR/19/7/6/26/46)

Gentlemen my Rint Day is on the tent of May and the Tenand Richard Garlick is not able to pay is owne Rint if is mind was so good is famley is so great and at litle adles he is a man that is well respecded with is Masters and a man that would pay if it lay in is power we have many Famley with us that is les than is that as her Rent pa~~y~~id and Five shillings a week and I inquard of is Masters what he Erned per week and the tould me that all that ad coming per Week was a Seven Shillings a week in winter time to mentan is Famley on but now he as 4 Shillings more and the are 8 of Famley the Ould end of Children as left him and go~~n~~t servis and I think it is your duty to do sum thing to this Famley in payin is Rent I no doubte but he will pay as sone as he can but it is out of is power at present and the Rint we must have and he as one Child as ben porley nearly two years be so kind to let me now wether you will pay it or not for it I must have

May 1th 1833

from yours Henry Bracwell

Wes Clough near Clitheroe

129 H[enry] Bra[c]ewell in West Cl[ough] to the Parish of Kirkby Lonsdale, 22 May 1833 (WPR/19/7/6/26/38)

Sir I Reseved yours of the 13 Respectin Garlicks Rent is Rent is Three Pound Per year but there is Six Pound Six Shilin howin for Rent at this Present time I all ways thought he would be habel to Pay and as been to Good but I see there is no Chans of Im Payin is self He as not a verey Good fameley and one as laid An a Poor State long I be leeve he is verey Ill of

I am yours Respectfuley
H Brasewell
West Cluf

Please to
Send Me word wat you May 22 1833
will do for im

Circumtext: *In different hand [SG]:* Granted $^{£}3.0^{s}.0^{d}$

130 Rich[ar]d Garlick in Pimlico near Clitheroe to the Parish of Kirkby Lonsdale, 5 June 1833 (WPR/19/7/6/26/41)

Sir I am in Great nessety of wrightin to you I have a Child Ded that as ben porley a bove 18 months and I ham not able to Bury it f<o>r [*page torn*] I have ben porley my self 3 weeks and this last week intirley of my work that I have nothing com in so I hope you will have the goodness to send me sum thing to Bury it and if you would send a few lines to John Garfetts In Keeper Clitheroe wear Kirby Lonsdale Carrier stops at he would li it Down for you or John Nuttle the Overseear of Clitheroe

from Richd Garlick

June 5th 1833
Pimlico near Clitheroe

Circumtext: *In different hand [SG]:* Granted 20^{s}/

131 H[enr]y Bra[c]ewell in West Clough near Clitheroe to the Parish of Kirkby Lonsdale, 15 June 1833 (WPR/19/7/6/26/36)

West Clough near Clitheroe June 15 1833

Sir) I have sene the letter that you send to Richard Garlick saying ~~[****]~~ [*over-written by*] that you would pay the Half year Rent if I would tack the Reares by Degrees of Richd Garlick that I will look of of them a while for the man is not able to pay any thing at present but I will not hurt him for the Rears as I think he will pay me by Degreeas as sone as he can so be as cind to send it by the carrery the next week

Rich[d] garlick Retornes you many thanks for the Pound noat that you send him towards Buring is Child

I am yours H[y] Brasewell

132 Henry Bra[c]ewell in West Clough near Clitheroe to Stephen Garnett in Kirkby Lonsdale, 1 November 1833 (WPR/19/7/6/26/72)

West Clough near Clitheroe Nov[r] 1[th] 1833

Sir/ My Rint Day is on the 10[th] Day of this month hopin you will have the goodness to pay this Half year Rent for the Poor man Rich[d] Garlick as he is not able to pay the Rears yeat but that I will lock of if the Rent be paid until he can Pay he is not able to Pay aney thing at Prisent no any this winter and you may think well If he indivers to cepe of you this winter and I hope you pleas to send it by the Carrier with given the pore man truble

I ham yours

West Clough Henry Brasewell

near Clitheroe

Circumtext: *Address of recipient:* Stephen Garnett Kirkby Lonsdale Westmoreland

In different hand [SG]: Granted [£]1.10[s].0[d]

Overleaf, in same hand [SG]: 1832 Jany. 26[th] Richard Garlick had for rent 3.0.0 which was all the Rent he had that year

133 Rich[ar]d Garlick in Pimlico to the Parish of Kirkby Lonsdale, 7 February 1834 (WPR/19/7/6/27/50)

Pimlico Feby 7[th] 1834

Dear Sir

A fortnight since, while working at the lime Kiln a splinter of Stone struck my left eye and so seriously injured it that I shall in all probability lose it. the pain and inflamation extends to the other eye and has totally deprived me of sight and has disordered my whole frame –

This serious accident has reduced my family to great distress being wholly dependent on my earnings for support

I am desirous of trying the Witworth Doctors, but am unable to do so without some charitable friend would help me at this crisis – from the

Kindness I have experienced from you heretofore encourages me to hope that you will assist <m>e [*page torn*] on the present occation

Yours Sincerely

Richd Garlick

Notes: *This letter is clearly written in a different hand to Garlick's other signed correspondence: not only is it orthographically very different, it is also much more confident stylistically, and in terms of spelling, grammar and syntax. Presumably, Garlick was unable to write this letter because of the injury to his eye, and therefore enlisted a scribe locally to write it for him.*

134 H[enr]y Bra[c]ewell in West Clough near Clitheroe to the Parish of Kirkby Lonsdale, 7 May 1834 (WPR/19/7/6/27/45)

Sir My Rent Day is on the tent Day of the month for the Cottege that Richd Garlick lives in and the Pore man is not able to Pay himself he as nothing but bad Forten he as got cut with a stone on his Eye and as lost it and the Paine of it as mede him very tinder of the other that he canot mentane is Laber at all times for is Helth as not ben so well Since the Eye was cut but he as very good master if he can go to do a little the will give him Wages I so is master and he tould me that Rich was a hard Labrin man win he was hin Helth he woud not mis is work and the had let him have a little money before hand seen he was in want and he me himself that you had send him a pound be fore and he was verey thankfull for and I think it is your Duty to send him a trifel more money [***] [*overwritten by*] the Docter tould me that that is Helth would not be so good wilst is Eyes got well and hardend I shall Expect you will send the Rent by the Carrier

I ham yours H^{y} Brasewell

West Clough near Clitheroe

May 7 1834

Circumtext: *In different hand [SG]*: Granted £1.5s.0d

135 Rich[ar]d Garlick in Pimlico near Clitheroe to the Parish of Kirkby Lonsdale, 21 July 1834 (WPR/19/7/6/27/36)

Sir I ham under the nessetey of writing to you I cannot Ern nothing with my Famley wear I ham but I have a sister at Tormbind wich I made aplication to hir to get me a pace that would Imploye me and Famley at and she as getin one to go to a Cotton mill If I can get thider and I think that I should Earn a living with out trublen you any more if you would lose me at this time as I have nothing to go with it is twenty two miles from Clitheroe and I have not one shilling of my own to go with and they would not Earn no~~t~~ thing the first mounth with not ben a qunted with the work and that it is unposebilety for to get with out help of you as I have not a Frind in the worald that will do me this Goodness without you will pay my Rint to Mr Bracewell and lend me three ~~[*****]~~ [*overwritten by*] Pounds until I can my Famley lerned to ther work and I hope I shall be able to pay you the three Pounds Back at after a little will which I hope it will be better boath for you and me If I can do with trobling you any moare and the time is set to go on the 4 of Month next if I can get the money to go with and I hope will consider to send it be tween and then for the carriage is Expences and we cannot live with out money wen we get thear for the First month and I ham in a nother Dificulty wen my Famley was Poorley a bout Five years a go I got in to Det seven Pounds which I was never able to pay it since and the have sirvede me with Law that I cannot stop a bove three weeks in the Borrow of Clitheroe if I do and cannot pay the will sill my goods and put mee in Prisen in the Borowe of Clitheroe and I shall stop thear sixteen week and must pay or */shole/* and no a lounce and it will cost 15 pounds to get out and will consider it better way to help me to this place as the cannot folle me to this place with ther ~~[******]~~ Low be so cind to send me a Answer as sone as posibly you can for I will not be inprisend I will get out of Clitheroe my self but I cannot get the Goods out of the Borow with out ben Reasted if I let them stop that time be over for the have Castle cort of the Owen and law of the owen so I hope will send me a Answer as sone as posebel that I may not get in the troble

Pimlico near Clitheroe

I ham Humble servent Rich[d] Garlick

July 21[th] 1834

136 Rich[ar]d Garlick in Pimlico near Clitheroe to the Parish of Kirkby Lonsdale, 24 August 1834 (WPR/19/7/6/27/30)

Pimlico near Clitherow Aug[t] 24 1834

Gentlemen I Receaved your letter with Great Cindness expecd that I should be forst to shift every Day but I went to the place and the House would not be not Bide of a three weeks from that time that I could not shift and the Clitheroe Low I do not no until I in quard and that the could not medel aney <m>oar [*page torn*] of a month and with that my Land Loard was Drunkin at that time and was for a month be foar that I could not a quent Im with my Shiften until last Thursday and he said that I how him a bove a years rint but he is sopin my Goods for 3 pounds and I must go in the morning my self If not I shall lose by job but he will be satifid If you will say that you will Give Im three pounds and If I leave my Famely be hind it will be 8 shillings out of my wag a week, and I have no Goods that will satifie him and I have no goods that I cannot do with out that I have ben forst to sell be for by /sickness/ that I have nothing /convinintel/ and if you will satifie Im at this time I will do my verey best to do with out trubling you of any acount be so Kind to send Mr Bracewell a ancwer by the Poast as soon as posabilly as I am Gon and my Famley is left be hind

from Rich[d]. Garlick

137 Henry Bracewell near Bradford to [Stephen] Garnett in Kirkby Lonsdale, 26 August 1834 (WPR/9/7/6/27/27)

Mr Garnett
Sir/ I have to Inform you that Richard Garlick your poper as left my House in a verey Shaby maner, as taken of all his goods in the night, and gone to Burnley Without paying me any thing – I therefore Hope you Will do what Lays in your power for me as I have rents and arears against im to near seven pounds which is a Hard Case –

I remain your Humble Serv[t].
Henry Bracewell
near Bradford
Yorkshire
August 26 1834

Notes: *This letter seems to be written in a different hand from the previous correspondence signed by Bracewell.*

5.

GARNETT, letters 138–165

138 John Jackson, Overseer of Kendal, to the Overseer of the Poor of Kirkby Lonsdale, 14 December 1816 (WPR/19/7/6/9/21)

Overseer of the Poor of Kirkby Lonsdale

To the Churchwardens and Overseers of Kendal, Dr.

Relief Given to	*From*	*To*	*Weeks*	*Per Wk.*	*£*	*s.*	*d.*
Widow Hall	5 Apl 1816	13 Decr	36	@ 4/	7	4	
William Garnett	Do	28 June	12	@ 2/	1	4	
					£8	8	0

The above is our Account against your Township, which I trust you will find correct; by favouring us with an early remittance, you will oblige the Churchwardens and Oveseers of Kendal.

I am your obedient Servant,

14 Decr 1816 John Jackson *OVERSEER.*

NB) Will thank you to advance James Metcalf Pension 1/ P week

Note: *This is a printed proforma invoice with correspondence added. The content of the invoice in italics (outwith brackets) represents the printed text.*

139 James Garnet in Kendal to St[ephen] Garnet[t] in Kirkby Lonsdale, 1 February 1817 (WPR/19/7/6/10/27)

Kendale Feby 1 1817

Mr Garnet Sir

at the Request of Thos & William Garnet I write to you traid is now so verey Bad it will not Be in my power to Give them full worke for the saime waigis as Shoes and Waigis is so much droped on the acount of so maney men Being out of worke which Belongs to this town and is Glad to worke at aney price – there is no Les then 3 or 4 plaise that I sent shoes too has failed that owes me a Good diale of mony theirfore I is nearly at a Stand at present Thos was so poorley after he Got to Kendale that I take Both him and fameley to my own hous as they had nothing But 1^{s} for 5 of them and not able to work and I have setled the 12^{s} Shilings that was short of his rent there fore I hope you will ple<e>as [*page torn*] to give them som thing weekely till traid takes a Better turn as it is out of my power to do aney more for them at preasant only I will Give them what worke Lais in my power the one is 5 and the other 6 of famley they think if you would a Low them 6^{d} a head they would Be able to dow turn over

pleas to Lay this Before your meting and Let me know the result By Georg Hall on wednesday next and you will much Oblidg

youres respectfuly

James Garnet

Mr S^{n} Garnet

Over Seare

Kerkby lonsdle

Payd

Circumtext: *In different hand [SG]*: Not Granted

140 John Jackson, Overseer of Kendal to S[tephen] Garnett in Kirkby Lonsdale, 20 September 1817 (WPR/19/7/6/10/37)

Mr S. Garnett

Sir,

William Garnett and als his brother Thomas have boath left Kendal owing to ^a^ dispute with the Masters about wages – William has a wife and four Children and Thomas a Wife and three Children boath of which are left without any means <to> [*obscured by wax seal mark*] suport theirselves and Children in Sconsequence thereof the are obliged to beg that you will allow them some thing for a few weeks say a Shilling a head P week and they will do there best till things are settled –

Your early reply will much oblige yours &c

John Jackson

Kendal Overseer

20 Sept 1817

Circumtext: *Address of recipient:* Mr S Garnet Overseer of the Poor K. Lonsdale
Postmarked: Kendal 26<1> [*smudged*]

141 John Jackson Overseer of Kendal, to the Overseer of the Poor of Kirkby Lonsdale, 6 November 1817 (WPR/19/7/6/10/43)

Overseer of the Poor of Kirkby Lonsdale

To the Churchwardens and Overseers of Kendal, Dr.

RELIEF GIVEN TO	*FROM*	*TO*	*WEEKS*	*Per Week*	*£*	*S.*	*D.*
Widow Hall	4 April 1817	24 Octr.	29	@4/-	5	16	
Mary Winder	20 June	4 July	2	@5/-		10	
Do. Do.	4 July	25 July	3	@4/-		12	
Do. Do.	25 July	29 August	5	@3/-		15	
Ann Hall	11 July	24 Octr	15	@2/6	1	17	6
~~Ann Webster~~	25 July	12 Sept	7	@5/-	1	15	
Widow Allen	22 August	3 Octr	6	@6/-	1	16	
William Garnett	19 Septr	10 Octr	3	@5/-		15	
Thos Garnett	Do.	Do.	3	@4/-		12	
					£14	8	6

The above is our Account against your Township, which I trust you will find correct; by favouring us with an early remittance, you will oblige the Churchwardens and Overseers of Kendal.

I am your obedient Servant,

6 Nov. 1817 John Jackson *Overseer*

Note: *This is a printed proforma invoice with correspondence added. The content of the invoice in italics (outwith brackets) represents the printed text.*

142 W[illia]m Crosthwaite in Kendal to the Parish of Kirkby Lonsdale, 6 July 1820 (WPR/19/7/6/13/15)

Kendal July 6th 1820

Sir)

W^{m}. Garnett belonging your Township is at this time in want of your assistance himself and two Children being in the Scarlet Fever I have relieved him with 2/- Shilling's to day your answer immediately will much oblige

Sir, Your H^{ble} S^{t}.

W^{m}. Crosthwaite

Overseer

143 W[illia]m Crosthwaite in Kendal to the Overseers of the Poor of Kirkby Lonsdale, 25 October 1820 (WPR/19/7/6/13/28)

Overseers of the Poor of Ky Lonsdale

To the Churchwardens and Overseers of Kendal, Dr.

RELIEF GIVEN TO	*FROM*	*TO*	*WEEKS*	*Per Week*	*£*	*S.*	*D.*
Widow Hall 1819	April 2nd	Octr. 20	81	3/-	12	3	
Wm Garnett 1820	June 21	July 21	3	10/-	1	10	
"	July 21	Augt 4	2	8		16	
"	Augt. 4	Oct. 8th	9	6/-	2	14	
"	Octr. 6	" 20	2	5/-		10	
April 14th to Cash					10		
					27	13	
By Balance from last acc^{t}.						13	
					£27 –		

The above is our Account against your Township, which I trust you will find correct; by Favouring us with an early remittance, you will oblige the Churchwardens and overseers of Kendal.

I am your obedient Servant,

Overseer.

Dear Sir,

The above is an Acct. is our acc^{t}. drawn out from the 2nd April 1819, since which date you have had £10 remitted, the pensions paid by you for Kendal, has been neglected to be entr^{d}. to your C^{r}. will thank you to hand me your acc^{t}. from same date and if there be a balance I will remitt it

Dear Sir Your H^{ubl}. S^{t}.

Kendal 25th Oct. 1820 Wm Crosthwaite

Notes: *This is a printed proforma invoice with correspondence added. The content of the invoice in italics (outwith brackets) represents the printed text.*

144 W[illia]m Crosthwaite in Kendal to the Overseers of the Poor of Kirkby Londsale, 25 Ja[nuary] 1821 (WPR/19/7/6/13/44)

Overseers of the Poor of K^{y}. Lonsdale

To the Churchwardens and Overseers of Kendal, Dr.

RELIEF GIVEN TO	*FROM*	*TO*	*WEEKS*	*Per Week*	*£*	*S.*	*D.*
To Balance						13	
1820 Widow Hall	Octr. 20	Jany. 19	13	3/-	1	19	
W^m^. Garnett	Decr. 1st		6	6/-		10	
	as per order				£4	2	

The above is our Account against your Township, which I trust you will find correct; by Favouring us with an early remitance, you will oblige the Churchwardens and overseers of Kendal.

I am your obedient Servant,
Wm Crosthwaite *Overseer*

3 15 6
6 6
4 2 9

Circumtext: *Address of recipient:* Overseer of the Poor Ky. Lonsdale

Postmarked: Kendal JA25 1821, 261

Notes: *This is a printed proforma invoice with correspondence added. The content of the invoice in italics (outwith brackets) represents the printed text.*

145 Tho[ma]s Walters Overseer in Kirkland to the Parish of Kirkby Lonsdale, 14 February 1821 (WPR/19/7/6/14/28)

Kirkland 14th Feby 1821

Gent^n^

Thomas Garnett Shoe Maker a Pauper of yours residing in this Township having a Wife & five Children two of which are very Ill applies to us for Relief stating their wants owing to the sickness of the Children, We gave them 2/- untill we hear from you please to say by return of post what is to be done in this case, if we are to advance them Relief on your a/c, or you will send them a little during their indispossition, Should we not hear from you before Saturday next we shall put them under an order of removal and Suspend it untill they are in a state fit to remove at which time we shall remove them in course waiting your answer

We are Yours &c &c
Thos Walters
Overseer of the Poor
T,ship of Kirkland

146 W[illia]m Crosthwaite in Kendal to the Overseers of the Poor of Kirkby Lonsdale, 21 February 1822 (WPR/19/7/6/15/4)

Overseers of the P<oor> [page torn] of K^{y} Lonsdale

To the Churchwardens and Overseers of Kendal, Dr.

RELIEF GIVEN TO	*FROM*	*TO*	*WEEKS*	*Per Week*	*£*	*S.*	*D.*
		1822					
~~1821 Widow Hall~~	~~March 30th~~	~~March 29th~~	~~52~~				
1821 Widow Hall	March 30	Augst. 24	21	3/	3	3	
Do.	Augst. 24	March 29th	31	1/6	2	6	6
W^{m}. Garnett under a suspended order of Removal					2	8	
					£7	17	6

The above is our Account against your Township, which I trust you will find correct. By favouring us with an early Remittance, you will oblige the Churchwardens and overseers of Kendal.

I am your obedient Servant,
Overseer

Sir
An answer by return will much oblige
Wm Crosthwaite
Kendal 21st Feby 1822

Note: *This is a printed proforma invoice with correspondence added. The content of the invoice in italics (outwith brackets) represents the printed text.*

147 W[illia]m Crosthwaite in Kendal to the Churchwardens and Overseers of Kirkby Lonsdale, 1822 (WPR/19/7/6/15/46)

Overseer of Poor KY Lonsdale

To the Churchwardens and Overseers of Kendal, Dr.

RELIEF GIVEN TO	*FROM*	*TO*	*WEEKS*	*Per Week*	*£*	*S.*	*D.*
Widow Hall	March 30th 1821	Augst 24th	21	3/–	3	3	
do	Augt 24th 1821	Decr 28th	18	1/6	1	~~5~~7	
William Garnett	– 31 do	Octr 5th	5		1	19	
Other expenses on Garnett						8	6
					£6	17	6

The above is our Account against your Township, which I trust you will find correct. By favouring us with an early Remittance, you will oblige the Churchwardens and Overseers of Kendal.

I am Your obedient Servant
W[m] Crosthwaite
Overseer

Note: *This is a printed proforma invoice. The content of the invoice in italics (outwith brackets) represents the printed text.*

Although the invoice is undated, its contents and place in the overall sequence suggest it was sent sometime in early 1822.

148 John Johnson in Kendal to Edw[ar]d Wilson, 5 [July] 1822 (WPR/19/7/6/15/37)

Kendal 7[th] mo. 5[th] 1822

Resp[d]. Friend
Edw[d]. Wilson

I feel desirous of trubling thee with a few lines respecting a Poor man that belongs to you ^W[m] Garnitt^ & whome I know to be in great destriss, he hath been in a [****] [*obscured by wax seal*] state of health for a considerable time back and not able to Work much, but for about a month back he hath been Quite off Work with a lame hand & is not attole likly to Work for sometime yet. If thou is not in office I hope thou will be so kind as speak to them that is. Thay are a very destrisd family & wanting releff. I hope thou will excuse the liberty I have taken

I am with respect my Fri[d.]
John Johnson

Circumtext: *In margin*: I expect his Wife will be the Bearer of this

149 Thomas Garnett in Kendal to the Parish of Kirkby Lonsdale, 3 June 1823 (WPR/19/7/6/16/39)

Kendal June 3[d] 1823

Sir my Goods been Scheduled this day for Seven pounds Ten Shillings which is Rent due and in Arear unless you will Considder to do Sum thing for me I must Be obliged to Bring my famley to Kirkby on Sattarday first But if you will pay thirtey Shillings I may Leav the house and take my Goods along with me by order of Jacob Wakefield I have A wife and 5 Children in a very Sickley way so that I cannot Pay aney thing my self

I am yours

Thomas Garnet

150 A Greenwood in Kendal to the Parish of Kirkby Lonsdale, 15 November 1823 (WPR/19/7/6/16/53)

Kendal Nov 15 1823

Sir

This is to inform you that Wm Garnett has payed Me the one half years Rent as soon as I shall Receive the other half which is $^{£}$2.2^{s}.0^{d}. Which you have agreed to pay as appea<rs> [*page torn*] By your letter then All Rent due to Me from Wm Garnett will then Be payed

I am sir your humble ^servent^

A Greenwood

NB Please direct for James Braithwait House of Corection Hill Kendal

151 J[oh]n Garnet in Kendal to the Parish of Kirkby Lonsdale, 31 March 1827 (WPR/19/7/6/20/23)

Kendale March 31 1827

Gentlemen

I am sory to inform you that it is not in my power <to> [*page torn*] employ Thos and Wm Garnet any Longer on the acount of the Dpesen of treide I have a very Great /slak/ at pesint and Goods that I have sauld I Cannot get pay for them so I am very at a stand I hope you will conider theire Case and do somthing for them and as sone as it is my poure I will Give them worke agane so /Cinder/ from yours

Respectfully

Jn Garnet

152 W. Gawthorp to the Parish of Kirkby Lonsdale, 29 [*****] 1828 (WPR/19/7/6/21/36)

29 – 1828

Dispensary

I certify that Wm Garnetts' family has been for some time Patients in the Kendal Dispensary & his Daughter is at present unfit to be removed

W. Gawthorp

Surgeon

Notes: *Although no month is given for this letter, its place in the sequence strongly suggests it was sent in early 1828*

153 W[illia]m Garnett in Kendal to the Overseer of the Poor of Kirkby Lonsdale, 29 June [1828] (WPR/19/7/6/21/37)

Kendel June ^th^ 29

Sir

I have to inform you that my Daughter is now lying dead in my house and that I ham not Able to Bear ^the^ expence of Burring hir myself so I hope you will excuse my Applying to you for As much mony as you think nessery for that purpos having undergon so Much fetague ~~and so~~ with Afflictions in my famely that I am so poorly ~~week~~ As not to Able to come over myself so I shal thank ^you^ to send me as much Mony as you can allow as I am in great Distris at prisent

So I Remain your well Wisher ~~W^{m}~~

Wm Garnett

to the overscer of the poor of

Kerby Lonsdal

Notes: *Although there is no year given in this letter, its place in the sequence strongly suggests that it was sent in 1828.*

154 Rob[er]t Boyd in Kendal to the Parish of Kirkby Lonsdale, 1 May 1830 (WPR/19/7/6/23/12)

Kendal May 1st 1830

Gentlemen

Haveing Wm Garnett liveing in house of mine & being 12 months rent due, I should thank you to do as much for me as possible, or I shall be obliged to sell them up, he as been a great deal out of work and has left Kendal

I remain yours &c
Rob[t]. Boyd

Circumtext: *In different hand [SG]*: Polock Hall Yard Kendal

155 Robert Boyd to the Parish of Kirkby Lonsdale, 14 July [1830] (WPR/19/7/6/23/1)

July 14

Sir
I was informed By William Garnett wife that you agreed to pay the half years Rent dew to me at your meeting in June last if it Be so I shall take it as a favour if you would Be so kind as to Send it with the Carier as I have no way of geting it of them But By Comming upon their goods as I am sure thay have no money at present

Robert Boyd
Rope Maker

Notes: *Although there is no year given in this letter, its place in the sequence strongly suggests that it was sent in 1830.*

156 Joseph Gunson in Kendal to the Parish of Kirkby Lonsdale, 4 December 1830 (WPR/19/7/6/23/35)

Gentlemen,
The Bearer Tho[s]. Garnett, tho' an industrious man; seems to be quite unable to maintain his family – the wife and younger children seem to be all-most famishing – and nearly naked –
He farms a cottage house of me at three pounds a year rent – and is now three half years in arrear – and there is no prospect whatever of his paying off what he is behind or payeing any rent at all for the future without some assistance – Under these circumstances I hope you will allow him something rather than put me to the necessity of selling them up
Gent[n] Your Mo Ob[dt] Serv[t]
Joseph Gunson
Kendal Dec[r] 4 1830

Circumtext: *In different hand [SG]*: Granted 3.0.0

157 John Garnett in Kendal to the Parish of Kirkby Lonsdale, 2 April 1831 (WPR/19/7/6/24/1)

Kendal Aprel the 2 1831

Sir

I take the liberty of Returning you my most sinsear thankes for your kind assistance allredy Recived and Beeg the libirty of making Appleaction for your further kind <as>sistance [*page torn*] as I feel my Boodly weekness still to incrace hoping that you will Be so kind as to send me what my township pleaces to alow me By Mr procter on wednsday next

I am your humbel servent

John Garnett

Circumtext: *Apparently in the same hand:*

Sir

you was saying some thing to my wife about Binding my son Thomas to wich I can have no objecations But I think I shal have to Come over sone and then we can have it settled at once

Wm Garnett

In different hand [SG]: Granted ^{s}10/ out of Donation Money

158 John Garnett in Kendal to the Parish of Kirkby Lonsdale, 30 April 1831 (WPR/19/7/6/24/28)

Kendal Aprel the 30 1831

Sir

I thank you for the 10^{s} you sent me By Mr procter and I again find my self under the nessety of applying for your further kind assistance as my affliction still Increases I am now got so weak that I Canot leave my Beed please be so kind as to send By Mr procter

I Remain your humble servant

John Garnett

Circumtext: *In different hand [SG]*: Granted ^{s}10/ out of Donation Money

159 Sam[uel] Radcliffe in Kendal to the Parish of Kirkby Lonsdale, 30 April 1831 (WPR/19/7/6/24/27)

I certify that John Garnett is a Patient of the Dispensary and that he is not in a fit state to travel

Kendal Sam Radcliffe

April 30 1831 Surgeon

160 Robert Boyd in Kendal to the Overseers of the Poor in Kirkby Lonsdale, 3 June 1831 (WPR/19/7/6/24/24)

Kendal June 3rd 1831

To the Overseers of the Poor of Kirby Lonsdale

Gentl^{mn}.

I am no wanting 1 year's Rent of W^{m}. Garnett & has his family seems to be in great distress from Illness & other causes, it would be great charity of you, if you would pay it for them, if you do not, I shall be under the necessity, which it will greive me much to do, of distraining for the rent, as they are now going into the third half year, hopeing you will do something for them.

I Remain Gentl^{mn}.

Yours Respectfully

Robert Boyd

161 William Gild[a]rd in Kendal to the Overseer of Kirkby Lonsdale, 16 April 1833 (WPR/19/7/6/26/54)

<Ke>ndal [*page torn*] 16th April 1833

Sir

At the request of Ellen Garnet Wife of Thos Garnet Shoemaker I Write you, desiring you will have the goodness upon receipt of this to send her on Saturday at the longest by the bearer something for herself and Children to live upon, as he is gone into Lancashire to seek work and has nothing to subsist upon but what is given to her, or getting a little upon Credit untill you relieve her, and I assure you her and the Children are in great Distress I am Sir your very

Obedient Servt

William Gilderd

To the Overseer of

Kirkby Lonsdale

162 W[illia]m Gildard in Kendal to Stephen Garnett in Kirkby Lonsdale, 11 May 1833 (WPR/19/7/6/26/49)

Kendal 11th May 1833

M^{r}. Stephen Garnett

Sir

Thos Garnitt Family being refused releif from you they have this week had some support from the Township of Strickland Kittle, and should you determine not to relieve them hereafter they will be removed to Kirkby Lonsdale imediately, half years rent will be due at Whitsuntide I am yours Respectf^{ly}

Wm Gildard

163 Thomas Garnet[t] in Pr[e]ston to the Parish of Kirkby Lonsdale, 29 May [1]833 (WPR/19/7/6/26/39)

Priston May 29th 833

Sir i wright acording to the agreemen^t^ i had with Mr Ball and your self When last i was at Kirkby Respecting the Ogmentation of my pentention Sir i find that i cannot Stop hear uneless i be well supported i Cannot do With Less than 3^{s} pr Week as i am in no Regular Work nor is i Likley Ever to Be a gain i lost my work sence i Was at Kirkby the Reayson was that i was not Abel to do it as well As theay wanted it doing my Eyesight has faild me verey muct Leatley so the work is Better done then i Can do it i went to everey Shop in preston yesterday and Could get nothing But Some Litle Shoes to Make so you may Se the nessety of my Aplection

Sir i have a wife and 5 ~~Cildr~~ Childer so i hope that you will acording to your promes take notice of my Letter Now if the meeting Should or Should not Grant my Request i Should feel verey much oblidge if you would Let me know as soon as possible so that i may Show my Landlord how he to get is Rent otherwise i Shall Be Brock up verey Shortley and then I shall Be foerst to be Removed from preston Witch i Cencearley hope you will prevente

So no more from your verey humbel

Applcant Thomas Garnet

Please to drect for me

hammons Row No. 12 Church Street

Preston

Circumtext: *In different hand [SG]*: 'Granted 2/6 P week'

164 William Garnett in Pr[e]ston to the Parish of Kirkby Lonsdale, 30 May [1833] (WPR/19/7/6/26/42)

Priston May 30

Sir

I thought it My dutey to Inform you that I have got My wife and famley at priston Acpte My thanks for your kind attention to My Wife when at your place I hope you will not forget to send Acording to your agreemen^t^ I hope you will Excuse Me writting as I thought it My duty to let you Know that we where hear

I remain your humbel Servent
William Garnett

Notes: *Although there is no year recorded on this letter, its place in the sequence strongly suggests that it was sent in 1833.*

165 W[illia]m Garnett in Preston to [Stephen] Garnett in Kirkby Lonsdale, 1 April [1836] (WPR/19/7/6/29/18)

Preston April 1

to Mr Garnett
Sir
I am given to understand By Robt Story that my Allounce is to Be Reduced I hope you will not Be offended if I Requst you to Contuney it as you have don for I am sure But for your Kind Assistance I should not have ^ben^ able to suport my famley as I Contuany to Be subject to Much Affliction Both in my self and famley I was last spring one ^Wole^ Month under the docter hands and I am now strugglen hard aganst grate Weeknes of Body to do a littel Work and Keep on my feet I have a lad wich I had put to work and Would have Been of a littel Assistance to me But he has not Been abel to work above three weeks this nine Months past on account of a Complaint in his Eyes and he is at present unabel to Work ~~[****]~~ My Request is that you will do the Best you Can for Me as you have other too don

I Remain your humbel Servent
Wm Garnett
No 40 Back Paull Squair

Notes: *Although there is no year recorded on this letter, its place in the sequence strongly suggests that it was sent in 1836.*

6.

6. GILL, letters 166–179

166 Margaret Gill in Beverley to Stephen Garnet[t] in Kirkby Lonsdale, 5 June 1827 (WPR/19/7/6/20/9)

June 5 1827 Beverley

Margret Sorah which is now the wife of John Gill   Dear frend i now take up my pen to right theis fuw lines to you to inform you how Beverlay parish has behaved to me sens i came too them it is throw having the Child with me that dos not bellong to them they will neither take me into the house nor giv me nothing ought nor they will not let him go too seech work and i am viry neear hungrid to death and can get no suport in the world i have not been ought of bed for too days and if you Would be so cind as to send me the money for the Child that i can have sumthing to eat for /an/ i can not liv for i expect to be confined every day Dear frend pitty my case in the time of need for for /wim/ starving for he has not had a but one weeks Worke sins we left Kendale and he has tramped a bove six hundred miles sins we seed you at Kirkby Lonsdale Dear frend if you would send them a s<h>arp [*page torn*] lettr i think it would doo them some good for they will not doo any thing for hus my husband was theare on monday night last and they told him they would not doo any thing so long as we ke<p>t [*page torn*] this Child and what can i doo with <the> [*obscured by wax seal*] poor little thing i took the burding [****]ry [*obscured by wax seal*] fit a hundrid and fifty miles my self but i doo not expect to live long for their is a viry trien time coming on for me in my situa^tion^ i am so poorley Dear frend i hope you will thin^k^ when you reed this few lines pleas to giv my cind love to my father William Sorah the ostler at the red Dragon in Kirkby Lonsdal^e^ and i hope he will think on my poor little sistrs so long as he doos live tell him that i doo not think that ever he will see me a live again in this world for i hav been for three days withought meat and the money would be of viry great servtis <to> [*page torn*] me pleas to send it as soon as posable if you can

When you right Direct
for John Gill Hattr /Mr/
John Wilson hattr Market
place Beverley Yorkshire

and so i remain your hum
ble sirvent
Margaret
Gill
Bevrley
Mr Stephen Garne^t^
if in office

167 Marg[a]ret Gill in Beverley to the Parish of Kirkby Lonsdale, 24 September 1827 (WPR/19/7/6/20/49)

Beverley Yorkshire Margret Gill ~~Sep. No.4~~ [*overwritten by*]^1827^ Septmb the 24
Dear frend this comes with with our cind Love to you hoping to find you in good health as it leaves me at present thank god for it we hav been viry ill of but i hope we shall be bettr of than before my husband has got work i hope for the winter to sirv the walers pleas to giv ~~in~~ our cind love to my father and sisters and tell th<em> [*obscured by ink blo*t] that i have got a littl Daughter 10 weeks old pleas when you right let me know how they all ar if not too much trouble ~~the~~ When you direct for John Gill ~~ne^e^r~~ hattr neer the Black Bull back street Bevrley
Yorkshire i remain your
humble sirvent

Circumtext: *Address of recipient*: To the overseer of Kirkby Lonsdale Westmorland with speed

168 Marg[a]ret Gill in Beverley to [Stephen] Garnet[t] in Kirkby Lonsdale, 6 October [1827] (WPR/19/7/6/20/47)

Margret Gill Bevrley Octo 61

D. Mr. Garnet i right this fieu lines wishing to Know the reason why the childs money has not com^d^ this cawarter it is noon Ɛ weeks sins it was dew on thou^r^sday we reci^ved^ the last on the 2o7 of June last <and> [*obscured by ink blot*] it is now the 16 of october Dear frend pleas to send it as soon as posable for it will be the means of his been excludid ought of his cloub the first of next Month if it dos not come for we hav dependid upon i^t^ for that purpous and it will be viry heard to los 7 years pay and i am shoure that we can not rais the money to pay it with for it is 11 and 6 this time and we have but 8 shilins a week to liv on for 4 of us and winter time coming on their is fire

and candles to find ought of it and as for me and my dear little Babys We are naked for close for Bevrley parrish has done no thing for me sins i went to them but five shilins for when i lay in i was as neer clamed to death and all throu having this poor inisent child with me many a hungry belly and a full heart hav i had sins i so you but i hope the lord will be my suporter in distress pleas to send the money as soon as posable for if he coms to be sck he will hav nothing to live on when you right direct for John Gill neer the
Black Bull Back street
Bevrley Yorkshire

Notes: *The date should read '16, but the numerals have been transposed, and the numeral '3' in the second line of this letter is also reversed in the original.*

Although the year is missing from the date of this letter, its place in the sequence strongly suggests that it was sent in 1827.

169 Marg[a]ret Gill in Beverley to the Parish of Kirkby Lonsdale, 13 April 1828 (WPR/19/7/6/21/15)

Margret Gill Bevrley April 13 1828
Dear
frend i take leav to right this fieu lins to you to know the reason whey the money has not com this cwarter it is a~~n~~ fortnight or three weeks sins it was Dieu i would av sent for it but throw having so little work this winter we stand in viry great need of it i had not money for to pay the postig of the lettr you sent word aboug^t^ the post paing of lettrs it costs hus eighting pens every lettr that we reciv from your hands you must take the *[posg]* for if it be to much for you to loos pleas could not we Draw the money from the overcier of bevrley wons a cwarter and you settl with them ons a year and then ther their would be no trouble av sending it the money that we pay for lettrs would find the Child with shos pleas to send me word if you can order it so it would be a great deal more convie both for you and for me i could not tell the reason whey you did not send the money i did not know whether you was gon ought of office or not you thought of living it the last spring when we so you last so we thoug thought wisdom to right to you one dos not know what hapnes in three months death might tak plase or many things in that time pleas to let me know if my poor old father be living at the red dragon in yet i wish to right to him pleas to let me know how poor little sisters is it is a year or more sins i seed them or heard from them pleas to send it as son as posable

so no mor
i am yours
Margret Gill

Direct for John Gill near the Blac^k^ bull Back street Bevrley

170 John Gill in Beverley to the Parish of Kirkby Lonsdale, 24 August 1828 (WPR/19/7/6/21/29)

~~G~~ [*overwritten by*] John Gill Bevrley August 24 1828

Dear frend i take up my pen With the greatist of pleasure int Hops to find you in good health As it leav's me only indifrent at present i wish to know the reason Why you have not sent they money this cwarter ~~it~~ i will ashoure you it is a viry un convenians to hus for the Child is viry near bar foot for shoes and for clos she is not well of for for his wagis is so small that i rely can not get them and him close for sirving the Walers is such a slavish bisnes for close for they Giv but twelve shilings a Week and eviry thing is so deer in our plase as for buttr is 15 pens a pound potatos is 1 shiling a stone flou^r^ ~~2~~ 3s 2 and thripans a stone 1 */p/* pound to the stone 10 for a viry fue coles i will ashore you a little money is soon spent in a famely it was diew the 2 of last month now this is the 24 of this month that is not so far of six months sins it was dew i rought to my ^father^ 2 monthes sins and he never ansired my lettr to send my youngist sister <to> [*page torn*] me she would av ~~b~~ been of viry great sirvis to me for i could av had a Work at both sp[**] [*page torn*] pay wirk and harvist but childr is so expensif to put them ought to nurs i thought if you would av let hir com to me but he has viry likly not mentined it to you a rought hir of you would of alow a littl a week With hir she would be of viry great sirvis to me you might send the half year money as it is s near the time it is not a bov a month till the time of a nother cwarter mony you think much at my righting but i can not help it for we hav all been viry ill a littl back it has hourt hus viry ill indeed

if you can send the the haf year~~ly~~ mony it would save me one shiling and 6 of postg my husband is so cros a bought it i can not liv in peas on acount of your not sending it

Notes: *Although the name at the head of this letter is that of John Gill, it appears to have been written in the same hand as those signed by Margaret Gill, and in addition is written from her perspective. In fact, all of the Gills' letters are written in the same hand, whether written from the perspective of (and/or signed by) Margaret or John.*

171 Marg[a]ret Gill in Beverley to the Parish of Kirkby Lonsdale, 8 July 1828 (WPR/19/7/6/22/49)

Magret Gill Bevrley July 8 1829

Dear

Frend this coms with our cind Love to you Hoping to find you in good health as it levith me in difernt at present it would be a viry great cind nis to if you would be so cind as to send my litt^l^ money for i do stand in need at this time above all times for i do not know my own day of been confined and i want a fiew of nessirys wich it dos not lay in my powr to get them ought of his littl arnings 10 shillings a week is not much to find all nessirys with i would thank you cindly to grant me that favour as soon as you possible you can at this time i shall not i shall not be again paing for the lettr at this time i would not hav sent for it but nessety compells me to do it ples to remembr me to my dear father and sisters i am yours Magret Gill Bevrley

172 Marg[a]ret Gill in Beverley to the Parish of Kirkby Lonsdale, 28 November 1[8]29 (WPR/19/7/6/22/23)

Margret Gill Bevrley November 28 129

Dear frend i take up my pen with greas^t^is of pleasure to right to you if you would be so cind as to send me my little money for i doe stand in great need of it for wagis is so Very small and work so scars that we can not get meat i thought you ware phraps gon ought of ofice as it did not come please to send it as soon as possable you can for we ar viry ~~very~~ hard put to it and we ar neked for shoes all of hus att this time please to giv my cind love to my father sistrs and i have got a nother littl Doughtr 2 Monthes old i hav 3 of them nou to do for a considr my famely

i am yours Margret
Gill
Bevrly
john Gill near the
Black Bull Back
Street
Bevrley
Yorkshire

173 John Gill in Beverley to [Stephen] Garnett in Kirkby Lonsdale, 19 December 1831 (WPR/19/7/6/24/42)

Beverley   Decmbr 19 1831

John Gill I right these fewe Lines to you hopeing they finde you well as it Leaves us only indifrent at preasent I would bee verry mutch ablight to you Mr Garrnett the over seer as thee Child money is a month Dew of the 2 quater and if you Will bee so kind Mr Garrnett to Send the half year monney Witch i hope it Will not ^bee^ aney disavantag to you, and it Will doe us a greet kindeness at this time and been the owl of Winter and been the dedist ^time^ off the year and they is a nother great favour that i have to beeg of you Mr Garnett and iff ^you^ would have the goodness as to get a Check of the money at your poste offic the postsman tell us itt will Come for Less money Consider 2^{s} 3^{d} is a geat deal of money for us to pay out of it and if you send the 2 pound you Cann stop it out of another quarter Consider the times is verry hard for the poor and Work is verry scarse speshley at ths time of yeyr and please to send it as soon ass you Cann and please to Rember us to our father and to inquiringe frends if not to much troble and wee should bee ^glad^ to see them all if the times would mend Wee praps Could geet over and please to Let mee know if my fathe bee at the old place yet and What ass bee Come of my sister Jane and Ann and may the Lorde bless you all and pleas to direct ass beefore

Sir I Remane your
humble Sersent
John Gill

174 John Gill in Beverley to the Parish of Kirkby Lonsdale, 11 October 1832 (WPR/19/7/6/25/56)

[*Top of letter missing*] your last
Beverley October 11 1832
Leter safe
Dear frend I Receved your Last Letter safe and you Roght to Know the age of the Childe she was born in the year 25 May 29 and I have the oder safe by me Dear frend I hope you are not goinge to take pay of the Childe yet and if you do we shall bee foste to send her to you to Keep your selves for this parrish will not Let her stay hear and it is not in my pour to keep her without aney thing as she is a very weake pourley Childe and is seldom weell and a great deal under Doctors hands and the Child is allmoste naked for Clothing as it is not in my pour to get neserys things for her and i ham ordred to Ask you for to send some more money to Clorth the Childe as our Gentlemen ~~that~~ say that the 1^{s} 6^{s} is to small for her as you Could never open your hartes to give us a sixpece above the 1^{s} 6^{d} per weake and handles that they is 1^{s} 6^{d} to pay for every *[*quater*]* money Coming witch is a great shame as one of our parson is a Justis and hee ass seen the order and so Mr Wilson and Mr Gibson Justiss and if you wonte grant the Re*[*q*]*ust of this Letter they in tend to Right to your Justis to Let them Know the Condishon of the Childe as i told them i had ask you before for some more money and got no answer

I ham yours
John Gill

175 John Gill in Beverley to Steph[e]n Garne[t]t in Kirkby Lonsdale, 20 January 1833 (WPR/19/7/6/26/11)

Beverley January 20 1833

Mr Stephn Garneet the overseer

Dear sir I would Be verry mutch a Blight to you to send mee the Childs money as it is all moste five months Due to mee and if you Could send mee the half year money as it is advance so for into the next quater you would greatley ablight mee as i ham in very Low Sirkumstanc at preasen and been out of Work at the Ded season of the year you would doo mee a Great Kindness at this Time and if you please to favour mee Sir this time as I hope you are a poor mans ^frend^ in the time of want and please to send as soon as you cann

I ham Yours

John Gill

176 John Gill in Beverley to [Stephen] Garnett in Kirkby Lonsdale, 10 November 1833 (WPR/19/7/6/26/19)

Beverley November 10th 1833

Mr Garnett Sir I Would ^be^ mutch A blight to you to send mee the Child money ass Soon ass you Cann and If you please to send the half year money 5 months tond due and if you so do you Will favour mee verry mutch it is for Margaret Sorah Childe know the Wife of John Gill And if you have seen aney of our frends and please to send us words how theay are and pleas to excuse mee for not paying the posteg of the Letter i had Not the money I ham yours

John Gill

177 John Gill in Beverley to [Stephen] Garnett in Kirkby Lonsdale, 25 March 1835 (WPR/19/7/6/28/1)

Beverley March 25 1835

Mr Garnett Sir I ham Reputed to Ask you to see if you will send me some more money for Margaret Sorah Childe your Pay Will not find her with meat Let a Larne shous and Clorth the money is not above 1s 4 ½d per weeke when the Letters is Paid for and if you cannot send mee something ^more^ to get her some clorthe and shose I shall bee forste to send her to you to see if you Can Meat Cloth Shous and to do all for 1s 4 ½d Per weeke you know Mr Garnett that I neaver had aney thing more than the Bare alouance for all this time and the Reason that i ask you for some thing more for my parresh Will not do aney thing for mee bee corse I have this Childe of yours and they say I have to Little for this Childe to keep her on And if I bee 3 months out of work they will not give mee not one penny becorse I have this Childe I have Kept the Child for 1^{s} 4 ½^{d} per week I Cannot do aney Longer Without an avance of money to get her Clorth my Children robed to save your parrish

I ham yours
John Gill

178 John Gill in Beverley to the Parish of Kirkby Lonsdale, 28 June 1835 (WPR/19/7/6/28/39)

Beverley June 28 1835

Dear Sir I Right this Letter to you to Ask you to send my wife Child money as it is Due the next weak and to ask you to send mee some more money to get her some Clorthing and shous I hame not able to suporte her out of the 1^{s} 4 ½^{d} per weake I have done it this eight years and Robed my own famley I Cannot doo aney Longer I have been very ill my self ^been^ and under Docters hands and not able to work and our parrish wonte suporte us on acount of having this ^Child^ of yours they say if i Cann a forde to keep another parrish Child I Cann aforde to keep my own they say they Could not keep her for that money that you alow mee for her it is not sofishent to get Bred let alone Clothing and Dear Sir if you cannot a low mee some thing more for to Clorth her and I shall be forste to send her to Kerby to you my harte good to keep her but what Cann I Do when I ham so mutch opresht and so ill ussed with our parrish and it would allmoste mak a man hang himself and what is it all for becose I have this Child of yours and sir I have a Small famley of my own and small wages and it is more then i Can Doo and if you will alow mee som thing more to asiste mee in getting her Clorth and shous it will try to keep her in spite of our parrish

I ham yours
Humble Servent
John Gill

179 Marg[a]ret Gill in Beverley to the Parish of Kirkby Lonsdale, 28 April [1836] (WPR/19/7/6/29/32)

Beverley April 28

Dear Sir if you please to send my little money for i am viry needfull of it at this time for we have had a viry hard winter for work and it is not a fortinight sins i Was confined of a son and i am very poorly of at this time for my husband has never had but one fortnight of work sins befor sins before Cristmas if have nevr hav had any thing from my parish of all this time please to send it as soon as you can

and Sir i remain your
~~your~~ humble servant
Margret Gill

Notes: *Although the year is missing from the date of this letter, its place in the sequence strongly suggests that it was sent in 1836.*

7.

GRIME, letters 180–232

180 Christopher Grime in Stainforth to [Stephen] Garne[tt] in Kirkby Lonsdale, 29 May 1817 (WPR/19/7/6/10/21)

1817 Stainforth   May 29th
Sir as our Rent is due som Time a go and I Biged of my Landlord for Redemety Till I have Rote to you opeing you Will Be so good as to pay my rent as I is not Able to payite My self have^ing^ such smale famley oure Rents is due at Mrtlemas and May day if not paid of Tusday ~~I~~ he will make disstress for the same pleas to send By Ropers Coach on Monday you */*l*/*ave me
Christoper Grime

Circumtext: *Below, In different hand [SG]:* Granted same as Past
Address of recipient: Mr Steven Garner Oversear of the poor of Kirby Lonsdale With speed

181 Christopher Grim[e] in Stainforth to the Parish of Kirkby Lonsdale, 13 November 1817 (WPR/19/7/6/10/45)

Stainforth   Dated the 13th Novemb 1817
Sir   I have sent you a few lines hoping you will be so Kind as to send by the Coac<h> [*page torn*] on Monday the 17th instant 2 pound as it is our rent Day for the times are so hard I Can not raise it my self being my self and five small Children so I hope you'll send it with out fail but if you do not send the money please to send me an answer before the time and in doing this you'll much oblige yours &c Christopher Grim
Direct to C grim stainforth

Circumtext: *Below, in different hand*: *[SG]:* Granted

Notes: *This appears to be in a different hand than the previous letter from Grime.*

182 Christopher Grime in Langcliff to the Parish of Kirkby Lonsdale, 6 May 1818 (WPR/19/7/6/11/11)

Gentlemen) Langcliff May 6th 1818

Desires you will be so kind as send me 2£ for my rent against monday without fail as it will be the rent day;

Christopher Grime

Direct for Christopher Grime Langcliff Near Settle.
Desires you will send me a steel belt or money to get one with.

Circumtext: *Below, in different hand [SG]*: Granted

Notes: *This is clearly in a different hand to both of the previous letters signed by Grime.*

183 Christopher Grime and Tho[ma]s Hartley in Langcliff to [Stephen] Garnett in Kirkby Lonsdale, 10 August 1818 (WPR/19/7/6/11/23)

Langcliff Augst. 10th 1818

Mr Garnett

Sir,

I have taken the oppertunity of writing to you I am sorry to inform you that I am not able to mentain my family myself without some help I hope you will have the kindness to send me something, ~~to~~ as my wife is laying in being my wife & myself & six small children I ^am^ quite unable to mentaine them without you will send me some mony, as the times are so very hard, if you will not agree to send me something I shall be forc'd to come to you, and I hope at the same time you will have the goodness to send me the belt we mention'd before as I have been verry unable to work without it, Please to send it on Wednesday next, direct for

Christopher Grime
Langcliff
near
Settle

P.S. Sir I believe the pauper to be in very great disstress at the present and has been all this spring & summer as far as is past I think it is your duty to send him some money, as I am well assured that he will do his best endeavour to mentain his family, and will not trouble you if he can help it: be asured it is hard work to ^be^ for two or three ^days^ in week with~~ou~~ one meal a day or hardly, I know it to be true myself therefore begs you will have mercy & not sacrifice.

I am Sir Yours
Speaking in sincerity
truth
Thos. Hartley
Overseer of Malham
Moors

Notes: *The postscript from Hartley is written and signed in the same hand as the letter from Grime.*

184 Richard Porter in Langcliff to the Parish of Kirkby Lonsdale, 3 September 1818 (WPR/19/7/6/11/24)

September 3^d^ 1818 Langcliff

Sir)
This is to Inform you that Christopher Grimes fameley is very Mich Destresed I have relieved this morning I Desire you to Let me Know what I must doo for them If you send them aney Money you had Better send it to me and I shall give it them as i see they stand need

I Remain yours Richard Porter
overseer

It is imposable for them to do without Relief his wife has Been nuly confined
Please to send by Return of Post

Circumtext: *In different hand [SG]:*

Granted out of Rates	5	0
Do. out of Donation Money	5	–
	10	0

185 Christopher Grime in Langcliff to the Parish of Kirkby Lonsdale, 17 November 1818 (WPR/19/7/6/11/31)

Langcliff Novr. 17th 1818

Sir,
I will esteem it as a favour if you'll have the goodness as to send me two pounds for my Rent as it is to be paid on Saturday being the 21st Instant without fail and in doing this you'll much Oblige your humble Ser^t^.
Christopher Grime

Please to send me a little more for the maintainance of my wife and Children as I have six Children and the times very dear I am not able to maintain them myself if you do not send as above mentioned I shall be under the necessity of coming to you with my family as they are almost naked they want clothing so very ill –

Circumtext: *In different hand [SG]*: Rent Granted

186 Richard Foster in Langcliff to the Parish of Kirkby Lonsdale, 19 May 1819 (WPR/19/7/6/12/9)

May 19th 1819 Langcliff
Sir) Cristopher Grime Desires me to Lett you know that his Landlord is Coming on Saterday to Receive his rent Please to send it this week With out fail as he is Unable to pay aney thing towards it himself
Please to Derect for Cristopher Grime
Langcliff
Richard Foster overseer

187 R[ichard] Foster in Langcliff to the Parish of Kirkby Lonsdale, 2 September 1[819] (WPR/19/7/6/13/23)

September 2d 1<819> [*obscured by wax seal*] Langcliff

Gentlemen)
Chistopher Grime desires me to Inform you that his famly is very ~~I~~ much destresed for Cloaths espeshely for sumthing To their feet And he is unable to Get them ~~on~~ him self If you will be so Cind as to send him sumthing It Will be Thankfuly Received
I Remain yours & R. Foster

Circumtext: *In different hand [SG]*: Granted 15s/

188 Richard Foster in Langcliff to the Parish of Kirkby Lonsdale, 3 September 18[19] (WPR/19/7/6/12/18)

September 3d 18<19> [*obscured by wax seal*] Langcliffe

Sir)

Cristopher Grime wife Requests Me to Inform you that the is Much Destresed, as her Husband has Been a Long time from home and has sent her no money she Desirs you to send her ten or twelve shilings as soone as posable

I Remaine ~~y~~ yours &
Richard Foster overseer

Circumtext: *In different hand [SG]*: Granted 5s/

189 Christopher Grime in Langcliff to the Parish of Kirkby Lonsdale, 1 November [1819] (WPR/19/7/6/12/34)

November the 1

Sir
I have roght these fue lines to informe you that i am in great destres at presant i have bene of work nerley a weck i have urt my selfe and i hope you will send me som relife as i is no<t> [*obscured by wax seal*] Able to mentane my selfe at presant And i have six smaule childer so you Cannot think that i am well of

Derect to Cristopher Grime
Langcliffe near Settle

Circumtext: *In different hand [SG]*: Granted 7^{s}/-

Notes: *Although this letter does not have a year, its place in the sequence strongly suggests it was written in 1819.*

190 Richard Foster in Langcliff to the Parish of Kirkby Lonsdale, 29 November 1819 (WPR/19/7/6/12/29)

November 29th Langcliffe 1819
Sir) Cristopher Grime Reqestes me to Inform you that his Lanlord has Been over And Demanded his Rent for his house He Desires you to send It as soon as Posable $^{£}$2.0^{s}.0^{d}. I Remain yours &
Richard Foster overseer

Circumtext: *In different hand [SG]:* Rent Granted

191 Richard Foster in Langcliff to the Parish of Kirkby Lonsdale, 28 December 1820 (WPR/19/7/6/13/43)

December 28th <u>1820</u>   Langcliff

Jentlmen)   Christopher Grime Residing in our town Disires you to be so Cind as to send him half years Rent which is £2.0.0 the first opertun^aty^ he desires you at the same time to send him ~~to~~ twelve or fifteen shilings for coals as h<is> [*page torn*] famely is very small

I Remain yours & Richard Foster

Circumtext: *In different hand [SG]:* Rent Granted

192 Christopher Grime in Langcliff to the Parish of Kirkby Lonsdale, 31 January 1821 (WPR/19/7/6/14/4)

1821

Langcliff Juanury 31

dear sir I am under the nessety of Trubli^n^g you for a Little asistance as my Children is in great Want of Clothing and as it is winter time I am noot able to get them my self

sir pleas to faivour me with this request

I M Yours

Christopher grime

Circumtext: *In different hand [SG]:* Granted 10^{s}/

193 Chr[i]s[tophe]r Grime in Langcliff to the Parish of Kirkby Lonsdale, 1 April 1821 (WPR/19/7/6/14/16)

Langcliff April 1st 1821

Gentlemen/

I will thank you to send me something to redeem myself, as I am run^{xd} rather behind, my wife is very poorly and has been for five weeks, and gets no better but rather worse, I myself have been of work a week or better, I hope you will be kind enough to send me some help, besides my family is very small, will thank you to send it on monday,

I rem^{n}.
your humble servant
Chrs^{r}. Grime

Circumtext: *In different hand [SG]:* Granted 5^{s}/ out of Rates 2^{s}/ from Donation money

194 W[illia]m King in Langcliff to the Parish of Kirkby Lonsdale, 31 May 1821 (WPR/19/7/6/14/21)

Gentlemen if you be so good as to allow Chr. Grime Rent which was due on the 12th of May it will verrey much

Oblige yours
Langcliff Wm King Overseer
May 31: 1821 and Agent for
His House

N.B. The rent is $^{£}$2.0^{s}.0^{d}

Circumtext: *In different hand [SG]:* Granted

195 Christ[oph]er Grime in Langcliff to the Parish of Kirkby Lonsdale, 1 August 1821 (WPR/19/7/6/14/31)

Aaugust 1st Lanckli<ff> [*page torn*] 1821
Sir please to seend me som Money if you Can for I ham in Great disstress at present My wife as got her Beed and My Children is in the Meseales and haveing ~~A it~~ Wife and Children down it destress me very ill please to be so kind as to send Me som Relife for them ~~have~~
Haveing 7 Children very small is more than I dow for My self
Christhoper Grime

Circumtext: *In different hand [SG]:* Granted $^{£}$1.0^{s}.0^{d}

196 Chris[tophe]r Grime in Langcliff to the Parish of Kirkby Lonsdale, 3 October 1821 (WPR/19/7/6/14/37)

Sir)

I am under the nessity of wrighting to Inform you that my Family ^is in want of^ Cothing If you would be so kind as to send $^{£}$1.10^{s}.0^{d} to assist me to get them shirts Clogs and other Cloths it would be thankfully received as winter is Setting Inn I remain

Langcliffe Humble Beggar
October 3: 1821 Chris^{r}: Grime

Cirumtext: *Appears to be in the Same hand*:

NB. Sir the Person that Claims your assistants hath 7 Children and they ^are^ in great want of Clothing as well as his Wife
W^{m}. King overseer

In different hand [SG]: Granted £1.0s.0d

197 Christopher Grime in Langcliff to the Parish of Kirkby Lonsdale, 30 November 1821 (WPR/19/7/6/14/45)

November the 30th 1821 Lancliff
Gentlemen I am under the nesesety of calling upon you concerning my Rent the sum of two pound plese to send it on monday next as I is not able to pay it myself and I hope that when you deside your poor money you will be so kind as to remember me as I have A wife and 7 Children Christopher Grime

Circumtext: *In different hand [SG]:* Granted

198 Christopher Grime in Langcliff to the Parish of Kirkby Lonsdale, 1 February 1822 (WPR/19/7/6/15/3)

Langcliff febury 1 1822
Sir
I am under the nessety of apling to you for your Kind assistance for my family being booath large an small thee are nearly naked pleas to send me sum assistans as soone as Possable pleas to present my Case to your and my frends
I M yours
Christopher Grime

Circumtext: *In different hand [SG]:* To write to Mr Hartley to Make Inquiry Respecting this famaly

199 W[illia]m King in Langcliff to the Parish of Kirkby Lonsdale, 4 May 1822 (WPR/19/7/6/15/8)

Sir)
I Desire you would be so Kind To Pay Chr^{s} Grime his Rent as soon as Conveant as J.G. Paley Esqr. will up to rec^{d} his Rents in a few Days
I Rem yours Resp^{y}
W^{m}. King Overseer
and Steward to J G Paley Esqr.

Langcliffe
May 4th 1822

Circumtext: *In different hand [SG]*: Granted $^{£}$1.0^{s}.0^{d}
Below, in pencil: $^{£}$2.0^{s}.0^{d}

200 C[hristophe]r Grime in Langcliff to Stephen Garne[tt] in Kirkby Lonsdale, 31 October 1822 (WPR/19/7/6/15/35)

Langcliff 31st Octr. 1822

Mr. Stephen Garner
Sir)

I am under the necessity of troubling you for my rent which is £2. – besides 10^{s}. that was left on last half year I hope you will be so good as to send it as my family is so great I have been out of work for this two months but have now started again with my old master which I hope I shall be able to do without troubling you any further I am your most [****] [*illegible*]

C^{r}. Grime

Gent^{n}.
Unless I have it granted I shall be like to leave my work and come to you and bring my family with me

Circumtext: *In different hand [SG]:* Granted $^{£}$2.0.0

201 C[hristopher] Grime in Langcliff to Stephen Garne[tt] in Kirkby Lonsdale, 27 February 1823 (WPR/19/7/6/16/16)

Langcliff 27th Feby. 1823

Mr Stephen Garner
Sir

I am under the necessity of troubling you it being winter time and I have been 8 weeks of my wo~~o~~rk and my family is in very great destress being myself and wife and 7 small Children please to be as good as send me £1 – as I am not able to support them.

I am your mo. obt. humble S^{t}.

C. Grime

Gent^{n}./

I hope you will favour me with this or I shall be obliged to come over on Tuesday as I shall expect it on Monday by return of post I am sorry that I should have troubled at this time but my family is in great destress

Circumtext: *In different hand [SG]:* Not Granted

202 Christopher Grime in Langcliff to the Parish of Kirkby Lonsdale, 2 May 1823 (WPR/19/7/6/16/29)

May the 2nd 1823 Langcliff

Gentlemen I desire that you would be so kind as to send me my House Rent For I have 6 very small Children and I have had very little work all the winter

Christopher Grime Langcliff

203 Christo[phe]r Grime in [La]n[g]cliff to the Parish of Kirkby Lonsdale, 22 May 1823 (WPR/19/7/6/16/35)

May the 22nd 1823 <La>ncliff [*obscured by wax seal*]

Gentlemen I wonder that you should object paying my Rent as the winter and My famelly being so verey large for I am shure that I cannot pay it my self and the Rent day was on saterday But I have beged to be excused til your vestrey Meting and if it be not settld at your Meting we must be sould up and Come to you by a removing order Gentlemen if you think peroper that it will be any better for us to Come to you and throw Me and My Children out of work we are very willing to Come

Christofur Grime

plese to send it by return it by return of Post

204 J. & W. Hartley in Settle to the Parish of Kirkby Lonsdale, 2 June 1823 (WPR/19/7/6/16/38)

Settle 2nd June
1823

Sir,

We take leave to address you on behalf of Christ^{r}. Grime of Langcliffe a Pauper belonging to your parish who is at present in great trouble in consequence of his few articles of Furniture being Distrained by his Landlord Mr. Paley for his May Day Rent. Grime States that you have hitherto paid him his House Rent but that having now applied to you, he is refused that relief without any previous warning of its being withdrawn.

This Man has been for a considerable Time imployed as a labourer for us & we take upon us therefore to say that a more Industrious hard working sober Man does not live in any County – nor one more anxious to rear & support a sickly Wife & Seven Children; five of whom are dependent upon his Hard labour for their daily Bread – and you may depend upon it ^he^ is not a Man who will trouble you when he has the means of helping himself. As his employment is entirely that of an Out Door Labourer – you may suppose the last has been a bad Winter for him, as we know it has, & we cannot but wonder how he has managed to maintain his large Family without much further relief than what he now *[receives]* at your Hands; & we think you will judge very unwisely to suffer him to be removed from Langcliff, which must be the consequence of this Distress, if it is proceeded in. We are no advocates for paying House Rents – because we do think, taken in the abstract, it is a bad system – but there are doubtless exceptions – and we tell you very honestly we think this Case of Grimes is one of the exceptions. If any Man can live by his labour this man ought to live – and you may take our Word for it he will not trouble you needlessly. We recommend therefore that you pay him his present May Day Rent – intimating that he must provide for his Martinmas ^Rent^ himself, which we think he would be able to do: - but you will be obliged to assist him ag^{n}. in paying his latter half years Rent coming due at May Day. This trifling assistance for a year or two longer we doubt not will entirely clear you of him, as his Family are getting up & will be able to contribute to their Support – and it is an Indulgence greatly due to his Industry.

You will be pleased to let this have your immediate attention & drop a line either to us or the Overseer of Langcliff. We are, Sir,

Y^{r}. Obed^{t}. Servt.
J. & W. Hartley

205 Samuel Grundy in Settle to [Stephen] Garnett in Kirkby Lonsdale, 5 June 1823 (WPR/19/7/6/16/40)

Settle June 5th 1823

Mr Garnett
Sir/

This morning Brother John & myself walked up to Mr. Clayton's mill, in order to enquire into the earnings of Christopher Grimes Children, the clerk was extremely civil, he gave us a written copy of their average earnings – which is as follows – The oldest Girl 8/6 pr Week, the second Girl 8/- and two Boys 3/6 each, total 23/6 p^{r} Week, besides this, the Father is now earning under the employ of Mr. Clayton as a labourer 15/- pr Week. This fellow deserves punishing for such a rascally application to his Parish

And remain yours very respectfully

Samuel Grundy

N.B. The above statement was taken from the Books as an average for the last two months and being under their exact earnings, as the first mention'd was 8/10½ the others in proportion.

206 J. G. Paley in Langcliff to the Overseer of Kirkby Lonsdale, 2 December 1823 (WPR/19/7/6/16/54)

To the Overseer of the Poor
of Kirkby Lonsdale

Sir/

Christ^{r}. Grime now occupying a house of mine; he informs me he belongs to your town. I have to state to you that he is now half a year's rent in arrear viz. $^{£}$1.11^{s}.0 and if the same is not paid into my Agents hands (Wm King of Langcliff) I shall give directions for the recovery of it by distress upon his effects in a fortnight from the date hereof. He desires I will say to you that if you pay this arrear he will endeavour to pay his rent in future himself. I assure you I have reasoned strongly with him at present to do without assistance as I think all should do unless under particular hard circumstances but he alleges having a huge Family and otherways unable at present to do without help.

I remain yours &c.

J.G. Paley

Langcliff Decr. 2nd 1823

207 Christ[opher] Grime in Langcliff to the Parish of Kirkby Lonsdale, 22 December 1823 (WPR/19/7/6/16/28)

Langcliff Decem^{b}. 22nd 1823

Gentlemen, I your poor Poper would take the liberty, and embrace the present oppurtunity to drop a few lines to your notice and serious consideration.

The subject of my short address is, to let you know that I shall be very thankful to you if you would be so kind as to reme^m^ber me, when you distribute what we commonly call the Poor Money. I think you have been very inconsidirate towards me neither to visit me with the above mentioned money, nor to pay me my Rent. With respect to the account you sent to Mr. Paley, it was a very incorect one, you mentioned more in your statement by 10ˢ per Week than our earnings are. With respect to Labourers work it is very scarce with us and Wages are very low. So that I hope you will be so kind as to take my case in to consideration ^and^ make amend for your former negligence towards me.

I Remain Yours Humbly Chrisᵗ. Grime

Notes: *Possibly written in yet another hand, despite being signed by Grime. Note the reference at the end of the letter to making amends for the parish's 'former negligence' towards Grime.*

208 Unsigned, Undated Memorandum Giving C[hristopher] Grimes' Children's Earnings (WPR/19/7/6/16/66)

The Earnings of C. Grimes Children

The oldest girl about	8/6 p Week
The second Do.	8/- Do.
2 Boys each	3/6 Do.

With Wᵐ Clayton & Son

Notes: *Although this memorandum is undated, its place in the sequence of letters suggests that it was sent in 1823.*

209 W. Harrison in Settle to the Overseer of Kirkby Lonsdale, 22 May 1824 (WPR/19/7/6/17/24)

Settle May 22ⁿᵈ 1824

Overseer of Kby Lonsdale

Sir/

Christʳ. Grime of Langcliff desired me to acquaint you that he has got a bill from Dʳ. Robinson of Settle of £2.15ˢ.6ᵈ If you would discharge the above he would feel verry much obliged. he as got a large Family and is at present out of work so there is no possibility of him paying it at present without distressing the Family which would be of great consequence to you afterwards.

From yours &c.
W. Harrison

210 Christopher Grime in [Lang]cliff to the Parish of Kirkby Lonsdale, 9 January 1825 (WPR/19/7/6/18/1)

January 9th 1825 <Lang>cliff [*obscured by wax seal*]

Gentlemen I am at this time ob<lige>d [*obscured by wax seal*] to Call upon you hoping that you will be so kind as to send me one pound as this Winter has been so verey bad that I Cannot that get to any work that I can in any case maintain more than myself and I have A Wife and 7 Children and as you have been dealing your Poor money I hope at this ^time^ you will Remember me as I am ~~very~~ verey poorly of at this time as I have not troubled you for this 12 months so no more at present

from Christopher Grime

be so kind as to send it by the Coach

Circumtext: *In margin*: 1825

211 Christopher Grime in Langc[lif]f to the Parish of Kirkby Lonsdale, 25 November 1825 (WPR/19/7/6/18/34)

1825 Novbr 25 Langcilfe

Sr I hope you Will Be so kind as to send Me som Relife as I Cannot work I ham lining under docter I have had a sore Misforton by a flag Cath My leeg And I thank God that my Leeg was Not snatch of with it I ham Condfind to my roum and Cannot help My self and My young Childeren under ~~9~~ 9 years of age Are of work know I ham sore destrest at present And the landlord is ^wants^ Rent and I ham Not able to pay it therefore if you wood [~~****~~] [*over-written by*] ther kindness to help at present as whe are in Great distress for som Relif

Christopher Grime

212 W[illia]m King in Langcliff to the Parish of Kirkby Lonsdale, 8 December 1825 (WPR/19/7/6/18/35)

Sir)

Chr^{s} Grime which Belongs to your Town hath had a Misfortune to Lame his Leg hath not been able to work this Forthnight Back hath Laid under the Doct^{r}. is likely to Continue Some time Please to assist him at Presant it will be of Great Service to him

Langcliffe I remain Yours &c

Decr 8th 1825 Wm. King Overseer

213 William Bateson in Langcliff to the Parish of Kirkby Lonsdale, 26 January 1827 (WPR/19/7/6/20/36)

janugrey 26 <18>27 [*obscured by wax seal*] Langcliff

Gentlemen I am sorey to inform you that Christopher Grime is in A verey poor state at this time he has been out of work 3 weeaks and 2 days and I believe he has not had one day work since and I believe at this time his fammiley is ^in^ A verey distressed state for I believe they are both clamed and starved but I intend to let him have work again as soon as I can but it will be A Good while before I can employ him but there is one thing that I will say he is as good A servant as ever I had in my employ and I believe that he endeavers as hard for A familey as any man can doo so I hope that at this time you will be so kind as to relieve him at this time while he is out of work his famely has 10^{s} 3^{d} per week

William Bateson Mason settle

214 Matt[he]w Lofthouse in Langc[lif]f to the Parish of Kirkby Lonsdale, 28 May 1827 (WPR/19/7/6/20/16)

~~S~~ Sir I Recived your leter Consening Grime Rent and I under stand that you want to know the Rent Due know is £2.5s.6d Due this May Day and I think you should send the Rent and som thing for them thay har very poorly of I will ashure you Grime is a worikng Man thimes is hard and Wages smaller is Children is starved for want of ~~Coat~~ Clothing if you pleas to send me the Rent and Sumthing for Clothing for the Children I will Lay~~ing~~ it out at Best for them lease remit an answer as soon as you Can 28 May 1827

Langcillfe I am yours and so forth

Matt^{w} Lofthouse

Circumtext: *In different hand [SG]*: Granted £1. 5s. 0d

215 Matt[he]w Lofthouse in Langcliff to the Parish of Kirkby Lonsdale, 2 November 1827 (WPR/19/7/6/20/43)

Langcliffe Novbr 2th 1827

Sir I sent you a fue lines Conserning C Grime Rent as the time is near and I want one pound of last half year May day Rent to £2.5s.6d I Recive from you one pound five shilens for May Day Rent and now the Rent this Martlemas two pound five shilens Grime is not Able to pay aney Rent is famely is very small and wages is low and I hope you will be so Kind as to pay is Rents till he get is famely a Lettle Older and perhaps he migh be Able to dow som thing hem self as your vestry me<eting> [*page torn*] is on sunday next I thought it proper to leet you now pleas to inform the Gentlemen I shal want now for Rents £3.5s.0d

I am yours Respectfully

Mattw Lofthouse

Circumtext: *In different hand [SG]:* Granted £2.0s.0d

216 Matt[he]w Lofthouse in Langcliff to the Parish of Kirkby Lonsdale, 21 December 1827 (WPR/19/7/6/20/52)

Langcliffe 21 decmb^{r} 1827

Sir I Riteing you a fue Lines Consirng ~~if~~ the Remander of Grime Rent he is Not Abl to peay Haney thing is Children is small and he is Giting them som litle Clothing for thay are starveing the Man is Very industery there for I hope you will ^be^ so good as to send Me the a Bou Wich is $^{£}$1 5^{s} –^{d} Due Martlemas last was 3-5 – and I Received from you 2 – –

I think if you Can Com of with pa$_{v}$y$_{v}$ing ^is rent^ with paing as the times is it is More than whe Can with such a famely

I remain your and so forth

Matt^{w}. ~~L~~ Lofthouse

217 Matt[he]w Lofthouse in Langcliff to the Parish of Kirkby Lonsdale, 29 February 1828 (WPR/19/7/6/21/4)

Sir I am Much so prices that you have not Answered My Last Letter Consarning the ^remainder of^ the Grime Rent wich is $^{£}$1.5^{s}.0^{d}. due Last Martlemas and I have spoke to Grime Consirning it and he told me that he cold Not pay it for the winter has been hard And he as got sum litle Cloying for his Children and he wished me to Rite to you Consirning it ~~I~~ I ham not fond of having Reares left on therefor I hope you will Consider to pay is Rents when due I think your Gentlemen may think will of it with is fameley Grime is a working Man but is Children is two ~~M~~ small to Do with ^out^ reilf please to seend me answer ^wat^ I Must Dow for I Can hav tenant for the hous the will pay up half year */*bey*/* I hope if Grime stop on you ~~it~~ will Dow the same

Langcliffe Feb 29 1828

Mattw Lothouse

218 Matt[he]w Lofthouse in Langcliff to the Parish of Kirkby Lonsdale, 28 March 1828 (WPR/19/7/6/21/12)

Langcliffe 28 March 1828

Sir I went to the Bookkeeper on Monday Last and he told me he was not to Disclose no peresons wagesis he told me that if thay was not Content they had Liberty to ^go^ Elsware wages is told of and the pople is not so well of as thay was wanes and whe now it too well I spoke to Grime to see if he Cold do somthing and he tole me know that the Winter had be so hard that he Could not there for I leave it to you what must be don please to Rite to me as soon as you Can to leet me now how you Order so no at present

Matt^{w}. Lofthouse

219 Christopher Grime in Langcliff to the Parish of Kirkby Lonsdale, 2 May 1828 (WPR/19/7/6/21/11)

Gentlemen

It is with humility that I would present a few Lines to your perrusal and kind consideration.

The subject of my short address is to inform you that I am under the necessity of imploreing a little of your aid and assistance you know May Day is drawing on and I am sorry to inform you that I shall not able to pay <the> [*obscured by wax seal*] rent, so that I shall feel verry much abligh'd to you gentlemen if you would have the goodness to interpose between me and my distress, I had 25 shillings in arrears for the last year which I was not able to pay, and the 8 shillings which you sent me I gave towards it so that there now remains due 17 shillings, and if you would have the goodness to send me the above mentioned 17 shillings along with the present ½ Year's Rent which is $^{£}$2 5^{s} I shall be verry thankfull to you as I am not able to do anything towards it myself owing to the lowness of wages, the sca^r^city of Work, together with the largeness of my Family which consists of myself and Wife along with 7 Children. N.B. Mr. Clayton's Book keeper informed me that my Land-Lord had been to enquire after our Wages and the Master would not allow any thing of that sort to be devulged to any Township I hope you will be so good as to comply with my request at this time and I will do my best to pay the next ½ Year's Rent myself as a better time of the year is coming on

From your Humble Servant

Langcliff May 2nd Christopher Grime

(1828)

Circumtext: *In different hand [SG]:* Granted £2.0s.0d

Notes: *This letter is clearly in a different, and far more confident, hand than others in the sequence, despite being signed in Grime's name.*

220 Will[ia]m King in Langcliff to the Parish of Kirkby Lonsdale, 20 May 1828 (WPR/19/7/6/21/10)

Sir Chris^r Grime which Belongs to your Town hath the Misfortoune of having his Boddy Broke Down and Surgeons woh attended him yesterd says it Nessery to have a New Truss to prevent a further accident if you will pay for one Doc^r. Robinson will furnish him with one

Your answer by the return of Post Will Much Oblige

Yours Willm King Overseer

Langcliffe May 20 1828

Circumtext: *In different hand*: the above is correct Tho Robinson Surgeon

221 T R to [Stephen] Garnet[t] in Kirkby Lonsdale, 20 May [1828] (WPR/19/7/6/21/31)

Mr Garnet

May 20	Mr. Robinson	
	Truss for [Luke] Grime	s. d.
	Lancliff	10 0
Taxis for strangulated		10 6
	Hernia	
	Medicine &c. &c.	______
		1.0.6

the above by Post will oblige yours &

T R

Notes: *Although the year is missing from the date of this letter, its place in the sequence strongly suggests that it was sent in 1828.*

222 Matt[he]w Lofthouse in Langcliff to the Parish of Kirkby Lonsdale, 3 November 1828 (WPR/19/7/6/21/18)

Gentlemen I ham under the Nesety of ~~Ritin~~ Riting to you consirning C Grime Rent Due this Martlemas wich is $^{£}$2.5^{s}.0^{d} C Grime has paid the years of ~~at~~ wich as Been for Two Last years and he Cannot pay this Rent Therefor Gentlemen he hope you will be so Good as to seend the above work is very poor And wages small Grime thinks he be forset to Come to work with you this Winter

please to send Me ansewer as soon as you can

Matt^{w}. Lofthouse

3th Novbr 1828 Langcliffe

Circumtext: *In different hand [SG]:* Granted £1.10s.0

223 Matt[he]w Lofthouse in Langcliff to the Parish of Kirkby Lonsdale, 20 May 1829 (WPR/19/7/6/22/40)

Langcliffe 20 May 1829

Sir I fell sorry to inform you that C Grime Cannot pay is Rent this May day and I hope you Will have the Caindness to inform the Gentlemen a bout it therefor I hope thay will have the Goodness to send me the Rent due to Mee this Mayday is $^{£}$2.5^{s}.0^{d} if so you will ablige me with the above here is very poor times at prese^nt^ ~~thare~~ there for I hope the gentlemen will be so Kind as to do it ~~I~~ I remane youres and so *[forth]*

Mattw. Lofthouse

Circumtext: *In different hand [SG]:* Granted not more than 30^{s}/

224 Christopher Grime in Langcliff to the Parish of Kirkby Lonsdale, 30 November 1829 (WPR/19/7/6/22/18)

Langcliff November 30th 1829

Gentlemen

I am very sorry to inform you that my Landlord will make distress if the rent be Not paid he is going to mark my goods for The times are so very bad I cannot pay myself or else I should be glad to do it for I have been very poorly of work and it has done very badly for me arrears Left on for the last half year 14s. and this is £2.5s.0d which the whole sum will be £3.0s.0d. so if you ~~will~~ Gentlemen will be so kind as to pay it

And not let my goods be sold you will Much oblige me at this time
I remain your well wisher
Christopher Grime

Circumtext: *Below, in different hand [SG]:* Granted £2.0s.0d

225 Christopher Grime in Lan[g]cliff to the Parish of Kirkby Lonsdale, 15 December 1829 (WPR/19/7/6/22/51)

December 15th 1829

Gentlemen

I am sorry to inform you that my Landlord is determined of having his rent between and next monday 21st 1829 or he will strean of my goods for I am not able to pay one shilling Therefore if are not willing to pay it I am quite willing come to you my Landlord has informed that you want a statement of me and my Childrens Wages Mr. Clayton will not give a statement of never a a workmans wages about His place if they are not satsified with what they get They are at Liberty to go elsewhere so I shall give you a statement of my self as near truth as fasible I can The wages we earn is in a general way about one pound three or four in week there is ~~9~~ 9 of us to keep out if it and my oldest daughter has been poorly for some time and I my self by ripture of my body I have Lost a deal of work and I have had a new belt made at Settle for two months and has never had a shilling to pay for With I forgot to remind you of our fireing Coals is very Dear I have 10s. 9d. to pay for every Cartfull of Coals

Gentlemen

I have given you a true account of every thing as Possible I can Therefore if Consider me and my family less incumberance with you than where we are I am quite Willing to Come, and ~~work at any~~ Gentlemen I am informed that Henry Yeaden has been informing You that my earnings Was but I will give a reason for that, becase I have left Their shop Through their bad behaviour not plueral to mention at present, but again Gentlemen I am quite astonished That you should hearken to any ones tales only Look at my family And not trobleing you for nothing but my rent, Gentlemen I am sorry, because I thought you would have had the Influence to have payd it without any */asi-station/* at all

G. you have a statement of the rent and rears in the other Letter
I remain your Servant
Christopher Grime
Lancliff

Notes: *This letter is clearly in a different, and far more confident, hand than others in the sequence, despite being signed in Grime's name.*

226 Christopher Grime in Langcliff to the Parish of Kirkby Lonsdale, 2 January 1830 (WPR/19/7/6/23/54)

January 2nd Langcliff 1830

Gentlemen

I write this to let you know that my Landlord Is quite weary of waiting for an answer from you About the Rent and is going to mark my goods as it is Now 2 Months since the Rent day and is determined To Write no more to you about it, he came in and told Me that it was your Meeting on Sunday 3rd and if Neither me nor my Wife would come He would certainly Mark on monday and have the sale the first Oppertunity Therefore Gentlemen I hope youl have The goodness to do to my Wife as if I was their myself For I have been working at the steam Engin it being Very hot I have got a bad Cold and am rather lame of a knee

Therefore I thought my Wife would be abler Than I at present to Come Therefore Gentlemen I wish you To settle yourselves about it ^and^ do not put me to any more Troble about it, I am quite astonished at you, me troubling You for nothing but it, I thought you would have supplyd my Request without all this, my Landlord desires you, if you intend to pay the Rent, Constant as I am not Able to pay it myself without some alteration of the trade Briskning or something falls out differant to expectation at present, ~~I~~ he desires you to give her a few Lines back With her and he will be much Oblidged to you so I
Remain your ^well^ wisher
Christopher Grime Langcliff

227 Matt[he]w Lofthouse in Langcliff to the Parish of Kirkby Lonsdale, 6 February 1830 (WPR/19/7/6/23/52)

Langcliffe 6 Febry 1830

Sir I ham Much suprised that you have not seen'd me Cristpar Grime Rent for Martlmas wich I wants and rears was due then I have *[sent]* to sume time

Cence and have had now Ancer fom you ther for I wish you to send me ancer what you mean to dow Grime Cannot pay if you seend them 12^{s} and thay giv it to me to wards Rears wich I wanted and Rint and reares due to Martlemas was $^{£}$3.15^{s}.0^{d} I recived of Grime 12^{s} 0^{d}

Wich is know Balance to Martlemas $^{£}$3.3^{s}.0^{d} Leet me now waht you mean to ^do^ if you send me answer I shall now wat to dow

I dow not wish to have so much Truble about it so I wish you to make your mind up what you do and leet me know and I shall what to dow so I hope ~~yy~~ you fale not to *[selt]* me now so no more ~~f~~ from it preset

Yours Ma^{ttw} Lofthouse

228 Christopher Grime in Langcliff to Stephen Garnett in Kirkby Lonsdale, 6 May 1830 (WPR/19/7/6/23/11)

May 6th 1830

Mr. Stephen Garnett

Dear sir I write these Few lines to you to let you know that I have your ^received^ Letter, I write to let you know that I have been at Mr. Robinson surgeon about a belt And he says that he Cannot aford me one under $^{£}$1.0^{s}.0^{d} theirfore if you will be so kind as to send me 10^{s} I will indeavour to make the Remainder out Meyself I am sorry that you have not Consider to send me something towards my Rent as the Rent Day is Near again and I am a long way Behind of the last and I am afraid I shall be sold up the winter as been hard and I have had bad turns In ^my^ body several times the past winter and I have been Y Very bad Now for this last week or more through my belt being bad and I Cannot Get a truss Covered ^and made^ under 14^{s} or 14.9 Therefore If you will be so Kind as to send me 10^{s} as Mr Robinson is so high, as I think I Can Get it Made where I work as my master is very good to me please to send it back By return of post and And by so by so doing yousl much Oblige your weel wisher

Christopher Grime

Langcliff

229 Christopher Grime in Langcliff to the Parish of Kirkby Lonsdale, 17 May 1830 (WPR/19/7/6/23/9)

May 17th Langcliff 1830

Dear Sir

I write these Few lines to you To let you know that if you do not Consider To send me my Request that is 10^{s} I shall be Obliged to give up my work and Come to you ~~And~~ I can get one For about 14^{s} 9^{d} therefore if ^you^ Consider to ~~S~~ send me 10^{s} you'l much Oblige me If you will send it as soon possible you can

For I remain
yours
Comp
Christopher
Grime

230 Mary Grime in Langcliff to the Parish of Kirkby Lonsdale, 6 October 1832 (WPR/19/7/6/25/55)

Langcliffe october the 6th 1832

Sir this comes to inform you that my Husband Christopher Grime has ^gone^ away to get work 9 weeaks sin<ce> [*page torn*] and I do not no where he is and I am left here with the children and what to do I no not what to do for the wagess is very little and I have both house rent and fire beside victuals to find and we can not do it so I hope that at this time you you will help us with some thing if you please as soon as you can or I shall be obliged to come over to Kirkby so I remayne yours Mary Grime

231 Christopher Grime in Langcliff to the Parish of Kirkby Lonsdale, 27 March 1834 (WPR/19/7/6/27/56)

Langcliffe March 27th 1834

Gentlemen

I write these lines to you to let you Know That I am Great Need of a belt for my body the Winter has been so bad that I am not able to get one myself, Gentlemen as this is the time of desiding the poor money, I hope you will Remember me With a little, and by so doing you will much

Oblige yours
Christopher Grime
Langcliffe

232 Mary Grime in Langcliff to the Parish of Kirkby Lonsdale, 17 May 1835 (WPR/19/7/6/28/11)

Langcliffe May 17th 1835

Sir

I write to inform you that my husband Christopher Grime has left ~~my~~ me and son and where he is I do not Know I write to let you Know that I am not able to do any thing towards a maintainance for myself and as for my son he is a very delicate boy he is scarcely ever well, I wish to know whether you will consider to allow me Somthing towards maintaining me and my son or you will send a Cart for me as I am not able to come of myself you will please to be as quick as possible As I have nothing to take or otherwise I shall be Obliged to apply to the Overseer of Langcliffe for Releife

Gentlemen I leave this to your
Candid Consideration and remain yours
Mary Grime

Circumtext: *In different hand [SG]:* Sent 5/s

8.

HALL, letters 233–247

233 William Fisher in Kendal, to John Hall in Kirkby Lonsdale, 15 September 1809 (WPR/19/7/6/2/29)

Mr John Hall Kendal 15th September 1809

Sir I am trubling you again on account of harreat hall Consirning hir house rent which was Due at whisentide Last and she Cann ~~[not] nowise~~ in now way make shift to pay hir rent I have given her till now and she is Stinted to 14^d^ p week at present by hir master on account of trade being bad and the emergency embargoe being fixed again it is two to one most of the weavers will be totley without Soone I know Mr Hall you are out of plase have the goodness to give this to one Mr Garnett I think that is his name or to whome it may Consirn She hinted to me she had goods in the house but I Said you will Still want goods and I think without parting with Somthing she will hardley be able to pay pleas Sirs to Judge of hir ^Setuation^ as you think proper and a Line from you will oblige your Hl. St.

William Fisher
highgate Kendal

Circumtext: *Address of recipient:* To Mr John Hall Kirkby Lonsdale

234 Harriet Hall in Kendal to the Parish of Kirkby Lonsdale, 2 January 18[10] (WPR/19/7/6/3/2)

Kendal Jany 2 180010

Sir

Acording to your orders I ham Righting to inform you the Adges of my Children the oldes is ten years old and the Rest younger and my oldest brings me one Shillin a Week and I can only Eann two shillins that with my Pention is only Nine shillins a week for five pepple and every thing Is so Dear that it is imposable for me to Gett Neseryes for my children and this is the first time that I troubled you for aney thing to Gett Necseryes so I hope that the gentelmen will have the Goodness to send me a Lettel Money for I can a shour you that I ham very Badly of I will be verey Much Oblidge to you if you will Lay my Ceace before the Gentelmen at the Meeting

Sir, I remain your Humble servant

Harriet Hall

Circumtext: *In different hand [SG]:* Granted 7s/

235 Ja[me]s Hall in Kendal to the Parish of Kirkby Lonsdale, 2[1] February 1812 (WPR/19/7/6/5/3)

Kendal Feby 2<1 18>12 [*page torn*]

Sir I am under the necesaty of trubling you with Line for I am sick and Very bad at this time and I put my Shoulder out on the <16> [*page torn*] of Jany and has not been able to Do any thing since nor ~~ha~~ has not Drawn only but 3^{s}.0 since for work and only the wife $1^{s}.10^{d}$ since the first week in November so you May judge of my Condtion at present I Sent by Edward *[Poole]* to you but I never Rec^{d} any thing I Could not have put on till now but for the Money you gave me at Christenmas which I was Oblidge'd to make use of and a small matter Concerning the Combers turnout but that is now over and I shall not Have a Halfpeny in the world left for support so Please to send me something on Sathirday by *[Poole]* or who you Please Otherwise I must Hunger till something Come as I have no Work at present and if I had I am not able to work

from yours Jas. Hall

236 Ja[me]s Hall in Kendal to the Parish of Kirkby Lonsdale, 4 March 1812 (WPR/19/7/6/5/4)

March 4th 1812

Kendal

Sir I am under the Obligation to Trouble you again as I am no better of my Complaint and has Nothing to Doo if I was able nor Wife <I> [*page torn*] should have come Over this week but Could <not> [*page torn*] Get any Help on the Road but Shall Come as soon as I Can Get it has left a complaint in by Back and left Side so as I am not able to Stir from Home at present so please to send something by M^{r}. Poole it will Oblidge yours Ja^{s}. Hall

237 Ja[me]s Hall in Kendal to [Stephen] Garnet[t] in Kirkby Lonsdale, 23 February 1813 (WPR/19/7/6/6/5)

Mr Garnet

Sir I am oblige'd trouble you again as I have been so bad for this Mounth past that I have not been able to do any thing but thank god I am a rather better my Disorder is the Rupter and if it do not return I shall be able to do something in a week or tow my wife still continues Very bad she was as ill last week as she has been since she begun she has not been Twenty yards from door since Martinmas we shoud have been very trouble some but for my friends at Kirkby they have been very kind money gos but a very little way when tow old folks is both Bad and cannot help themselfs but has to hire so please to return something by the bearer it will very much Oblidge yours

Ja^{s} Hall

I would have comed Over but I am not able
Feby 23 – 1813 Kendal

Circumtext: *Address of recipient:* For Mr Stephen Garnet Seedsman and Grocer Kirbylonsdale

238 Harriet Hall in Kendal to [Stephen] Garnett in Kirkby Lonsdale, 2 October 1813 (WPR/19/7/6/6/16)

Kendal Oct 2 1813

Sir

I ham sorey that I ham under the Nessety of troubleing you with these few lines for at this time all my Children are allmost Naked through my want of w[****] [***]d [*page torn*] Ill Health for I ham never well a <day> [*page torn*] to Geather and have only One Child that can by any Asstance to me for the too youngst is not able to do any thing and the Eldest is a Apprentice and have been for soom time and I how to my Landlord a years Rent the next Month and it is Imposable for me to pay him the whole years Rent so I ham Writeing to Beg the favour that you will pay half a years Rent for me at this time and I will indevour to pay it my self in futere if not the La<nd>lord [*obscured by wax seal*] will sell up my Goods and I shall be Oblidge to come to you so I hope you will have the Goodness to consider my Distrest situation and send the half years Rent which is five and twenty shillins Sir I
remain your Humble servent

Harriet Hall

Circumtext; *Address of recipient:* For Mr Garnett Overseer Kirkby Lonsdale
Below, in different hand [SG]: Granted 24^{s}/

239 Harriet Hall in Kendal to the Parish of Kirkby Lonsdale, 1 November [1816] (WPR/19/7/6/9/14)

Kendal Nov 1th

Sir

I hope that you will have the Goodness to excuse me troubling you with these Lines it is to Request the favour of ^~~you~~ to^ Assist me with a half years Rent as I have a Whole ~~years~~ years Rent Due and it is impsable for me to pay any at this time for I have only had two shillins worth of work a week all this summer and we are in a Manner ~~a~~ allmost strved but I will Endover to put on if posable if you will be so kind as to pay one half years Rent if not the Landlord will sell my Goods for it which the half year is one pound five shillins I will be thankfull if you will Answer this as soon as posable sir I Remain your Humble

servent Harriet Hall

Circumtext: *In different hand [SG]*: Granted 15s/

Notes: *Although the year is missing from the date of this letter, its place in the sequence strongly suggests that it was sent in 1816.*

240 John Jackson in Kendal to the Overseer of the Poor of Kirkby Lonsdale, 14 December 1816 (WPR/19/7/6/9/21)

Overseer of the Poor of Kirkby Lonsdale

To the Churchwardens and Overseers of Kendal, Dr.

Relief Given to	*From*	*To*	*Weeks*	*Per Wk.*	*£*	*s.*	*d.*
Widow Hall	5 Apl 1816	13 Decr	36	@ 4/	7	4	
William Garnett	Do	28 June	12	@ 2/	1	4	
					£8	8	0

The above is our Account against your Township, which I trust you will find correct; by favouring us with an early remittance, you will oblige the Churchwardens and Oveseers of Kendal.

I am your obedient Servant,

14 Decr 1816 John Jackson *OVERSEER.*

NB) Will thank you to advance James Metcalf Pension 1/ P Week

Circumtext: *Address of recipient:* Overseer of the Poor of Kirkby Lonsdale

Notes: *This is a printed proforma invoice. The content of the invoice in italics (outwith brackets) represents the printed text*

241 Harriet Hall in Kendal to [Stephen] Garnett in Kirkby Lonsdale, 30 May [1817] (WPR/19/7/6/10/22)

Kendal May 30

Sir

I ham sorey that I ham under the Nessity of troubleing you a gain as it is through Ill Health and the Ha<rdne>ss [*page torn*] of times for I have been very poorly th<is> *[ther]* [*page torn*] Mounth under the Doctor and I beleive it is Chifely from want and I have no Child to Earn any thing for they Cannot Gett any Employment so that I ham in the Greatest Destress and ham unable to pay my Rent which is a Whole years Rent which is too pounds ten shillings and my Landlord intends Selling me up the next Week which I think very heard as I have Endaverd so many years for my famely with your kind Assistance so I hope that you will have the Good<ness> [*obscured by wax seal*] to Consider my Destress an send me half <years> [*obscured by wax seal*] Rent for th<is> [*obscured by wax seal*] time and if it pleasess the Almighity to send me my Health a Gain I hope not to trouble you any more for my Rent I hope you will Answer this as soon as posable sir I Remain your Humble servent

Harriet Hall

Circumtext: *Address of recipient:* Mr Garnett Overseer Kirby Lonsdale
In different hand [SG]: Granted 20s/

Notes: *Although the year is missing from the date of this letter, its place in the sequence strongly suggests that it was sent in 1817.*

242 W[illia]m Crosthwaite in Kendal to the Overseer of the Poor of Kirkby Lonsdale [1822] (WPR/19/7/6/15/46)

Overseer of the Poor <of> [*page torn*] Ky Lonsdale

To the Churchwardens and Overseers of Kendal, Dr.

Relief Given to	*From*	*To*	*Weeks*	*Per Wk.*	*£*	*s.*	*d.*
Widdow Hall	March 30th 1821	Augst 24	21	3/-	3	3	
Do	Augst 24th 1821	Dec 28th	18	1/6	1	~~5~~7	
William Garnett	-31 do	Octr 5	5		1	19	
other expenses on Garnett						8	6
					£6	17	6

The above is our Account against your Township, which I trust you will find correct; by favouring us with an early remittance, you will oblige the Churchwardens and Overseers of Kendal.

I am your obedient Servant
Wm Crosthwaite
Overseer

Circumtext: *Address of recipient: The Overseer of the Poor of* Kirkby Lonsdale

Notes: *This is a printed proforma invoice. The content of the invoice in italics (outwith brackets) represents the printed text*

Although the year is missing from the date of this letter, its place in the sequence strongly suggests that it was sent in 1822.

243 Harriet Hall in Kendal to [Stephen] Garnett in Kirkby Lonsdale, 22 March [1823] (WPR/19/7/6/16/22)

Kendal Mar 22th

Mr Garnett
Sir

I ham sorey that I ham Oblidge to trouble you a Gain but the Old man that takes my penton for I have not been able to Go for it this winter told me that Mr Crosswaite sayd that I ham not to have it any more but it is Imposable for me to do with out it for I ham in such a bad state of Health that I ham not able to wash my self a shift for I can Carce walk a bout and as my Eldest son Leaves me next week I was thinking of wrteing for six pence more a week so I hope you will Consider and Continue my penton and Lett me or Mr Crosthwaite know by Ned Bland on wednesday Mr Buttler saw me this week and was quiet shockt to see me in such a poor state of Health

Harriett Hall

Notes: *Although the year is missing from the date of this letter, its place in the sequence strongly suggests that it was sent in 1823.*

244 Darnton Greenwood, 4 [April] 1823 (WPR/19/7/6/16/24)

This Certifies that H. Hall is a patient of the Dispensary and at present unfit for much labour –

Darnton Greenwood

Surgeon

Alp. 4th 1823

Notes: *An enclosure sent with letter 245.*

245 H Crossthwaite in Kendal to the Parish in Kirkby Lonsdale, 6 April 1823 (WPR/19/7/6/16/25)

Kendal April 6th 1823

Sir)

The inclosed is a certificate from our dispensary respecting H Hall who is not able to maintain herself she requests you to allow her 2/- per week as 1/6 is not sufficient at present on acct. of her health. If the above be not allow'd she will be oblig'd to come to you – Your answer by return will oblige

Sir/

Your Hbl. St

H Crossthwaite

Circumtext: *In different hand [SG]:* Granted 1s/6d P week

Notes: *Includes enclosure printed as letter 244.*

246 Harriet Hall to the Parish of Kirkby Lonsdale, 29 October [1824] (WPR/19/7/6/17/39)

Oct 29

Sir

I ham very sorey that I ham Oblidge to trouble you with these Lines but I ham in such a Bad state of Health that I cannot wait of my self and ham all [****] [*page torn*] unable to Write but my Destress is so Great that I ham Oblidged to Beg the favour of you to state my situation at the next Monthly meeting to Beg for only sixpence a week more for this Winter if I should Live for it is imposable for me to do without more Reliefe so I hope you will have the

Goodness to Answer this to Mr Crostwate or Lett me Know for I ashour you that my Destress is Great I Remain your Humble servent

Harriet Hall

Circumtext: *In different hand [SG]:* Granted 6^{d} a week adition

Notes: *Although the year is missing from the date of this letter, its place in the sequence strongly suggests that it was sent in 1824.*

247 W[illia]m Crosthwaite in Kendal to Overseer of the Poor of Kirkby Lonsdale [1824] (WPR/19/7/6/17/48)

Overseer of Poor KY Lonsdale

TO THE CHURCHWARDENS AND OVERSEERS OF KENDAL, Dr.

Relief Given to	*From*	*To*	*Weeks*	*Per Wk.*	*£*	*s.*	*d.*
1824							
Widow Hall	March 26th	Sept 24th	26	1/6	1	19	–

The above is our Account against your Township, which I trust you will find correct; by favouring us with an early remittance, you will oblige the Churchwardens and Overseers of Kendal.

I am Your obedient Servant

Wm Crosthwaite

Overseer

Notes: *This is a printed proforma invoice. The content of the invoice in italics (outwith brackets) represents the printed text*

Although the year is missing from the date of this letter, its place in the sequence strongly suggests that it was sent in 1824.

9.

HODGSON, letters 248–277

248 Jane Hodgson in Blackburn to [Stephen] Garne[tt] in Kirkby Lonsdale, 5 December 1803 (WPR/19/7/6/1/2)

Blackburn Dec[r] 5 1803

Mr Garner

I am induced to Write to you to Request the favour of a little Relife I am in a very bad state of health and not able to get aney thing and my Children can but get verey little trade is so verey bad and with out some Relife it wil be imposible for mee to put on and I shal be thankful for somethi ˬnˬ at this time as i am in greate Distress and to give me an Answer as soon as you can and Derect for Jane Hodgson to be left at W[m] Beckils Safford Blackburn

from your Hum[l] Serv[t]

Jane Hodgson

Circumtext: *Address of recipient:* To The Overseers of the Poor Kirkby Lonsdale Westmoreland

Postmarked: Blackburn 212

Notes: *There is some confusion about when this letter was sent, or possibly who the intended recipient was. We know that Stephen Garnett was not in office in 1803, so the assumption has been made that the date at the head of the letter is incorrect. However, as there is no indication elsewhere in the text or circumtext of a more likely date, it has been left to stand at the very beginning of the sequence of letters sent by Jane Hodgson.*

249 Jane Hod[g]son to the Parish of Kirkby Lonsdale, 15 April 18[12] (WPR/19/7/6/5/11)

Apral 15 18012

Sir I am suprised that you have taken the pay of the Childer that is Lift without ever father or Mother ^and^ I have Recived a letter this Day from My son that he is not able to suport them and I have had No suport from ^My^ husband this sixten Munths and it is verey hard that you should take the pay of the Childer and I have been hear this six weeks Mysilf and it will be 6 Months before My husband getts home I am suprised how ^you^ think My son Can suport hus aney longgar he has suported hus all Wenter and we have been all of hus Run in the fever and as things is so Deare and times is so hard My son

Can not Do aney more nor suport the house aney Longer I am suprised how you think if a famaly Can live on 3 shilings a week and now taken from them and both Me and My husband in the Castle of lancaster you have pleasd the overseear of blackburn verey will to stop the pay be Course he Dos not wish them to be bound in blackburn and I beg you wo^u^ld prived places for five of them now Derictly and I Desire you will Rite to Me ~~and~~ pleas the Childer Must Come to in lancaster and bring some thing to take them in Litt Me know Whear the Childer Must Come to Meet you for My son is bringing them in the *[*pacet*]* next week there is 3 on them under 6 years of age pleas to write by Return of post and if you Mean to give aneything a week litt Me know and Rite to blackburn to stope My son for bringing them he Cannot Do for five on them under 5 shilings a week and thay are living with him and he Can Do no more for them I have ^sold^ what is belonging to Me so no More from Me Jane Hodson $_{v}$and James$_{v}$ this is the 2 letter

250 James Hodgson in Lancaster Cast[le] to the Parish of Kirkby Lonsdale, May [1812] (WPR/19/7/6/5/37)

Sir
I have Receved a letter from My son and he informs me that you onley Alow them three Shillings a week He Cannot make shift with that he will not Keep them under five Shillings a week besides the Children is Naced and the are not able to work so it is impossible for him to keep them for that money as times is so bad out of doors
from James Hodgson
at Lancaster Castell

Circumtext: *Address of recipient:* For the Overseair at Cerby Lonsdin
Postmarked: My [**] 18[**]
In different hand [SG]: Granted 5s/

Notes: *Although there is no date on this letter, its place in the sequence suggests it was sent between April and September 1812.*

251 Jonas Bradley in Blackburn to the Parish of Kirkby Lonsdale, 21 March 1815 (WPR/19/7/6/8/3)

Blackburn March 21 1815

Sir

Jane Hodgeson has been at Mr Dewhurst the Overseer and hee wil not pay <her> [*page torn*] aney more and was Sawcey with her and tould her you owed them Money and hee wo^d^ have no more to doe with it and shee applyed to mee and Requested mee to advance hir the money every Week which I promesed hir to doe if you wil send the money that is Due and it Oblige mee as as have advanc'd hir the money for the family shes in greate need of it from youre

Hbl St
Jonas Bradley

I Desire you to give mee an Anser by Return of Poste Derect for Jonas Bradley Salford Blackb<urn> [*page torn*]

252 R[ichar]d Brookes in Blackburn to the Overseer of Kirkby Lonsdale, 24 July 1816 (WPR/19/7/6/9/7)

This is to Certify that ~~Jno.~~ ^Jas.^ Hodgson a pauper belonging to your Town is not a fit subject to be removd. therefore requires relief from the Parish –

I remain
R^{d}. Brookes
Surgeon

Blackburn July 24th
1816

An answer for attendance will Obge R.B.

Circumtext: *Address of recipient:* Overseer of Kirby Lonsdale Westmorland

253 Jane Hodgson in Blackburn to Parish of Kirkby Lonsdale, 20 August 1817 (WPR/19/7/6/10/35)

Blackburn Augt 20 1817

Sir

I am under the Nesesety of Writing to Request the favour of youre Remiting me 2 Poundes for the Landlord has taken all my goods for Rente and not Left me eather Bed or Stool or aney thing at all and the the things wil be sold on Saturday if the Rent bee not paid and I Desire you to send mee 2 Pounds and stop it out of my pay or I shall bee Obliged to Com with my family Jonas Bradley wil have no more to do with my pay I have been very Ill thees ten Weeks and I am quite Down with Distress or I should not have trubled you at this time

from Your
Jane Hodgson

Derect for James Brinand Shopkeepere
Salford Blackburn

254 William Hod[g]son in Blackburn to the Parish of Kirkby Lonsdale, 2 October 1817 (WPR/19/7/6/10/38)

Blackburn Octbr 2nd 1817

Sir my mother

Wrote a letter to concerning my brother and you never returned a answer to it so I have taken it upon me to write to you there fore if you intend me to have Im you must write by the return of Post I will take him upon the conditions that I sent you and no other so you have your Choice for I can get plenty hear and get a good fee besids I shall wait a week upon you and no longer

So I remain your Humbel
Servant
William Hodson
Salford Blackburn

255 Jane Hodgson in Blackburn to [Stephen] Garnett in Kirkby Lonsdale, 23 November 1818 (WPR/19/7/6/11/32)

Blackburn Novr 23 1818

Mr Garnett

I Shall bee greately Obliged to you if you will be so good as to Let mee have a few Weeks pay in advance I am very cumfortley setteled and my Children and my Selfe have got into Worke but Wee Want a few Necerey Articels which I am not ^~~able to get~~^ for a house which I am not able to get and shall be for Ever Thankful if you wil Assist mee at this time to get a few Necesaeare articles which wee Want and Derect to Jonas Bradley

~~S~~ Salford Blackburn
from Your &^{c}
Jane Hodgson

256 Jane Hodgson in Blackburn to the Parish of Kirkby Lonsdale, 8 March 1821 (WPR/19/7/6/14/11)

Blackburn March 8 1821

Sir

I am under the nessecity of Writing to you to inform you that Jonas Bradley is verey Backwards at paying mee my money he has sent Two letters to you and has Recived no Answ<er> [*obscured by wax seal*] and he could be glad to Recive wh<at> [*obscured by wax seal*] he has paid and i beg you wil be so good as to Write to him as soon as you can as I am in a poor state of health and the Children is the same and wee are verey poorly of and must be so til you Write

from
Jane Hodgson

257 Jonas Bradley in Blackburn to the Parish of Kirkby Lonsdale, 1 November 1821 (WPR/19/7/6/14/40)

Blackburn Novr. 1st 1821

Sir)

There being due to me for Jane Hodgsons Pention Thirty Weeks from the 28th of March to the 24th of Oct^{r}, at 2^{s} P Week is 3 Pounds which Please to remit as soon as Posiable it is Convenient and it will

Oblige Sir your Obt Servt.
Jonas Bradley

258 John Gravestons in Kendal to [Stephen] Garnett in Kirkby Lonsdale, 1 December 1821 (WPR/19/7/6/14/46)

Friend Garnett

I Hope you will excuse the Liberty I have taken in troubling you with this note, But being aquainted with the Bearer Lawrence Hodgson many years I am sorry for him in his situation permit me to Inform you he was out of Work for 12 or 14 weeks this Last summer & Broke his arm, which has verry much Reduced him, so that he is at this time Behind, with his Rent £4.10.0, & am sorry to say I have Scheduled his goods for the same which I must be Obligd to sell on Monday if you cannot Relieve him, but Being now in good Imploy he thinks he could Redeem himself by Whitsuntide by paying 4/ p^{r}. Week but his Landlord will not agree to his proposal, but he insists I must sell him up, or he will Imploy some Other, on Monday, he has a verry Good Corner Cuppboard worth 35^{s} or 40^{s}/ a verry good oak snap Table worth 12^{s} or 14^{s}/ with other goods which he can spare but I am affraid if I was to sill them By auction ~~at present~~ they would not make so much at present; goods sell's in *[ill]*, But if I had a Respectable sale I could put them in for him & make the most of them, he says he will make the money good to you again as soon as possible if you would please to advance it for him, I would willingly have done it for him if I could but at present I cannot for I believe him to be Honest, he served with me in the Volunteers of Local Militia many years & I allways Respected ^him^ as a good soldier, & steady man, so if you can assist him at this time I hope ^he^ will in a short time be Better situated, hope you will Excuse this Liberty, & Believe me yours Respectfully

John Walker

Kendal Decr. 1st
1821 John Gravestons
near
Lowther Arms
Wildeman Street

259 Jonas Bradley in Black[bur]n to Stephen Garnett in Kirkby Lonsdale, 12 October 1822 (WPR/19/7/6/15/31)

Black^{n}. Oct 12th 1822

Mr Stephen Garnett

Sir) Please to Remit me the Money due on Account for Jane Hodgson which is from March 13th to Oct 9th which is 30 Weeks at 2^{s} P Week is $^{£}$3.0^{s}.0^{d} ^from^ your Ob^{t}. Servt. Jonas Bradley

260 Jane Hodgson in Blackburn to the Parish of Kirkby Lonsdale, 4 December 1822 (WPR/19/7/6/15/40)

Blackburn Decr. 4 1822

Sir Jonas Bradley has Informed that you have stopt my Relife which is a verey Distressing thing to mee at this time my youngest Daughter has been Sick thirteen Weeks and her disorder has fallen into her Leggs and she can doe no Worke ~~is~~ not being able to stand and i am in sutch a poor state of Health as not to be able to doe aney thing for a long time back but as soon as my Daughter is Able i wil bring hir to Kirkby Lons^don^ that you may see her

from your Hum^{l} Servt
Jane Hodgson

261 Jane Ho[dgson] in Blackburn to the Parish of Kirkby Lonsdale, 30 May 1825 (WPR/19/7/6/18/17)

Blackburn May the 30 1825

Sir I send you those fue lings to let you ~~k~~ know that I have reacavd 12 shilings wich I return you Maney thanks for the same but I trust that you will take it in to Consider^shoun^ to send me a trifal more at this time as I can ashure you I ham in great want at present ad it not been for good frends I should of trubled you before now but thank god my daughter as got a grate dale better then she was and I trust if [******] [*illegible*] permit I shall not trubel $_{v}$you$_{v}$ Much longer, but at this time I hope you will not fale to send and in so doing you will Much ablige your
humbul sirvent

Jane hoggen

Please to dract for Me to bee left at William Becket Shop Ceeper Salfort

Notes: *Despite the very different orthography here when compared with Jane Hodgson's earlier letters, the handwriting is quite feasibly the same.*

262 Jane Ho[dgson] in Blackburn to the Parish of Kirkby Lonsdale, 23 August 1825 (WPR/19/7/6/18/21)

Blackburn Augst the 23 18$_{v}$25$_{v}$
sir it is with paneful feelin$_{v}$g$_{v}$ I wright to you at this time I ham truley sorry to trubel you my goods is Marked this day and will be sould on the <3> [*obscure*] day from this unles I Can pay the det and that I Cannot now I trust that you will not let me bee turned out of hous and harber in My old days for the sum of one pound the det is a gre$_{v}$at$_{v}$ deal more but if you will have the goodnes to send a Me one pound the rest I Can get of a frend Sir I beg as the last favour that you will send as my goods and all will be sould and wat will becom of me then this is not my fault it is sickness and want of work and not /met/ but you will please to let me know by return of post as qui$_{v}$ck$_{v}$ as posubel and drect for me to the Care of Mr William Becket Shop Ceeper Salfart blackburn and in so doing you Will much ublige your hum$_{v}$bel$_{v}$ sirvent Jane
hodgem

263 Jane Ho[dgson] in Blackburn to the Parish of Kirkby Lonsdale, 1 March 1826 (WPR/19/7/6/19/10)

Blackburn March the 1
1826

Sir it is with paneful feel$_{v}$ing$_{v}$ that I wright to you at this time it is not my princabel to truble you but at this time I ham compeld for the factory is wely stopt and for som time back we have had only alf time but now there is none a tole deare Sir it would pitty the hart of a stone to see blackburn in the dist-tress I ham not by my self and the shop that get my meats at will trust no more and wat to do I do not know but I trust in god that the will be better times and then I Can do again I hope and trust that you will send my a trifel to ceep us from starven

I reaseved 7 shilings that you sent som time back wich return you Maney thanks for the same and at the same time am sorry to trubel you I know that you are hard lead hom I trust you will not fale to send for I ham complatly fost and in so doing you will

Much ablige your humbel
Servent Jane Hogdem

Circumtext: *In different hand [SG]*: Granted out of Donation money 5^{s}/ out of Rates 5^{s}/

264 [Jane] Hodg[s]on in Blackburn to the Parish of Kirkby Lonsdale, 23 March 1827 (WPR/19/7/6/20/30)

1827
Blackburn March 23^{d}

Sir
I Rite to inform you we are in Great distress as we have sufferd a Great deal for want of work and sickness in our family Renders us Miserabel and Compels me to Crave some Relieff from you at the Recept of this I humbelly Beg you will have the Goodness to send me some Money if it is but small I shall be very thankful for it I would not have troubeld you if I Could have helped it but distress Compels me to ask this favour from you I Must inform you we have neither work nor meat and is in a state of starvation I Beg you will send me a trifel of Money as soon as posibel I am yours distressd servent
Jenny Hodgon

Notes: *It is unclear whether this is meant to be from Jane Hodgson, or is from another family member. It is certainly in a very different hand to previous letters signed by Jane Hodgson.*

265 J Burton in Kendal to Stephen Garnett in Kirkby Lonsdale, 9 January 1830 (WPR/19/7/6/23/25)

Kendal 9th January 1830

Gent,

I am requested to write you on behalf of the family of Lawrince Hodgson who is at present confined in the House of Correction on account of Arrears of an old Bastardy Order. The family are in extreme want – the landlord has scheduled their remaining furniture and ~~they~~ without your assistance they have no other prospect than that of being remd. to your Township –

Will you have the goodness to take their case into your consideration & say as early as possible what we must do for them –

I am Most Respy
J Burton
A.O.

Circumtext: *Address of recipient:* Mr Stephen Garnett Overseer Kirby Lonsdale
Below address: Clithro13 Jany 1830

266 Tho[ma]s Harrison to the Parish of Kirkby Lonsdale, 2 July 1831 (WPR/19/7/6/24/14)

Sir

I annex you a certificate from Mr Forrest respecting an accident wish occurred the other day to Lawrence Hodgson who belongs to your Township, as he will require relief from you during his confinement I hope you will take his Case into your immediate consideration & I shall be happy to hear from you as early as possible ~~with~~ stating what you wish to be done for him;

Waiting for your reply
I am
Yours respectfully
Thos. Harrison
Asst. Overseer

2nd July 1831

Circumtext: *Overleaf, different hand:*

I hereby certify that Lawrence Hodgson is now confined to Bed in consequence of an accident which he met with on Thursday last by which he had his Leg broken near the ancle joint – The Fracture is also accompanied with a deep wound which makes it more serious – the man is going on favourably but will be prevented from following any employment for a considerable time

Geo. Forrest
Surgeon

Kendal
2 July –
1831

Facing page, in a further hand [SG]: Granted 3[s]/ a week

267 J[ohn] Mann in Kendal to Stephen Garnett in Kirkby Lonsdale, 22 October 1831 (WPR/19/7/6/24/55)

Mr. Stephen Garnett
Sir

Yours of the 13th inst. duly came to hand – There *[was]* a mistake our account, We have not Charged you with the Pension Paid per your order of 5/- per WK to Laurance Hodgson, this account was Kept by Mr. Tho[s]. Harrison our Assistant Overseer who has resigned his situation and at present out of Town, when he returns we shall rectify our account indeed if it had not been for some unpleasant business your account would not have been sent you in manner it was. We have wrote to all Townships to the same affect –

I am Sir
Your Mo Obd[t]. Ser[t].
Jn[o]. Mann
Gov: of the Workhouse
Kendal

Kendal, Town's Office
22nd October 1831

268 J[oh]n Mann in Kendal to Stephen Garnett in Kirkby Lonsdale, 11 November 1831 (WPR/19/7/6/24/47)

The Overseer of the Poor of Ky Lonsdale
To the Churchwardens and Overseers of the Poor of Kendal, Dr.

RELIEF GIVEN TO	*FROM*	*TO*	*WEEKS*	*Per Week*	*£*	*s.*	*D.*
			1830				
L Hodgson	July 8	Octo 7	14	5/	3	10	
15th October /31 To Acct. rendered up to							
	40th September 1831				4	2	0
Crs							
	1830	1831			£7	12	0
Eleanor Chapman	Decr. 15	Septr. 28	41	3/-	6	3	0
				due	£1	9	0

Kendal, Town's Office
11th November 1831

Mr. Stephen Garnett
Sir,

The above is our account, Carrd. with your Township, the trust you will find correct by you remitting the above in Course of the ensuing Week, you will greatly Oblige the Churchwardens & Overseers of the Poor of Kendal, as they are about to wind up Mr. Harrison's accounts

I am, Sir, Your Most Obt. Servt.

P.S. L. Hodsgon is still very lame Jno. Mann
and unable to do any work

Circumtext: *Overleaf, in different hand*:

(Copy)
Ky Lonsdale 4th July 31

Mr Harrison,
Sir,

In reply to yours respecting Lawrence Hodgson we wish you to be so good as pay him 5/- P Week so long as you think it necessary & place it to our account,

I am Sir,
Yrs. Respy
Stepn. Garnett

Facing, in different hand:

Kendal 11th Nov 1831

Sir,

Will you have the Kindness to remitt the amount of the annexed a/c to Mr Mann Govr of the Workhouse as early as possible.

I am
Yr Obt St.
Thos. Harrison
late Overseer

Notes: *This is a printed proforma invoice with correspondence added. The content of the invoice in italics (outwith brackets) represents the printed text.*

269 Geo[rge] Forrest in Kendal to the Parish of Kirkby Lonsdale, 17 December 1831 (WPR/19/7/6/24/39)

I hereby certify that Lawrence Hodgson is not able to follow his usual employment –

His wife is daily expecting to be confined and it appears to me impossible for them to be supported without an additional allowance during his wife's confinement, although they have medical attendance gratis –

Geo Forrest
Surgeon

Kendal
17 December 1831

Notes: *Enclosed with Letter 271.*

270 Geo[rge] Forrest in Kendal to the Parish of Kirkby Lonsdale, 7 January 1832 (WPR/19/7/6/25/1)

Lawrence Hodgson is still unfit to follow his usual employment –
Geo Forrest

Kendal
7 Jany. 1832

Notes: *Enclosed with Letter 271.*

271 J[oh]n Mann in Kendal to Stephen Garnett in Kirkby Lonsdale, 10 January 1832 (WPR/19/7/6/25/3)

Town's Office
Kendal, 10th Jan. 1832

Mr. Stephen Garnett
Sir

Inclosed you have two Certificates respecting your pauper Law^{r}. Hodgson, Since I last saw you one of Hodgson Children broke its leg, and his wife has been confined of another Child, in my opinion he aught to have the pension of 5^{s}/- per WK continued a few Weeks longer

I am Sir your's respectfy
Jno. Mann

Notes: *Enclosures transcribed as Letters 269 and 270.*

272 James Tebay in Kendal to the Overseer of Kirkby Lonsdale, 14 March 1832 (WPR/19/7/6/25/16)

The Overseer of the Poor of Kirkby Lonsdale

To the Churchwardens and Overseers of the Poor of Kendal, Dr.

RELIEF GIVEN TO	*FROM*	*TO*	*WEEKS*	*Per Week*	*£*	*s.*	*D.*
Harriet Hall	Sepr. 30	Decr. 30	13	2/	1	6	
Do.	Decr. 30	Mar 23	12	2/	1	4	
Lawrence Hodgson	Octr 14	Decr 30	12	5/	3		
Do.	Decr. 30	Feb 10	6	5/	1	10	
					£7		

Gent^n^.

Your favouring us with the above Amount will oblige

Yours most respectf^y^

James Tebay

Ass^t^ Overseer

Town's Office

March 14. 1832

Notes: *This is a printed proforma invoice with correspondence added. The content of the invoice in italics (outwith brackets) represents the printed text.*

273 James Tebay in Kendal to the Overseer of Kirkby Lonsdale, 5 May 1832 (WPR/19/7/6/25/11)

Town's Office

Kendal May 5th 1832

Sir/

Laurence Hodgson is making application here, at present being short of employment, he wishes you to pay him his rent amounting to £2.10.0 as he has no means whatever of paying it himself & he says that unless you comply he and family will be under the necessity of being removed, on the other side you will see Mr. Forrest's acc^t^

I am

Yours respectfully

James Tebay

Ass^t^. Overseer

P.S. Your early answer will oblige

J.T.

Circumtext: *Facing page, in different hand [SG]*: Granted for Rent $^{£}$1.1^{s}.0^{d}
Overleaf:

The Overseer of Kirby Lonsdale
To Geo. Forrest
Reducing a Fracture
Medicines &c in June
July and August 1831
for Lawrence Hodgson £2.15.6
Pauper

Kendal
March 13st 1832

274 M Gawthorp in Kendal to the Parish of Kirkby Lonsdale, 3 November 1832 (WPR/19/7/6/25/61)

Kendal Novr. 3rd 1832

Laurence Hodgson having been unemployed for some time desires me to state to his Township the circumstances, with a hope they will take into consideration the difficulties arising therefrom; if they would discharge his half years rent it would materially <re>lieve [*page torn*] him and [**] as he is anxious not to trouble the township further; he thinks he has in prospect constant employment with a good livelihood in the establishment of a retail Coal yard, but he requires a guarantee for the first Coals and if the parish would come forward for that purpose he would pay the receipts regularly to any person whom they might appoint. My knowledge of him would prompt me to say in his behalf he has proved himself calculated for such an office and that he has endeavoured hard for a livelihood –

Yours &c.
M Gawthorp
Surgeon

Circumtext: *In different hand*:

Town's Office
Kendal 3^{d} Nov 1832

Sir

Lawrence Hodgson desires me to forward the above to you hoping you will consider his situation

I am Sir
James Tebay
Assistant Overseer

275 Lawrence and Abraham Hodgson in Lancaster to S[tephen] Garnett in Kirkby Lonsdale, 3 July 1833 (WPR/19/7/6/26/32)

Queen Street Lancaster 3^{d} July 1833

Mr. S. Garnett

Sir

An Action was brought against me by a Person of the name of Brockbank a Shoemaker of this Town in the Hundred Court of Lonsdale for Shoes Amounting to 10^{s}/2^{d} at the same time he stood in debted to me in the sum of 10^{s}/- for Coals – Immediately on being served with the Process I waited on Mr. Ellithorne is attorney and shewed him my account when I conceived there being so trifling a Balance as 2^{d}. nothing further would be done but greatly to my surprise Ellithorne the Attorney carried the Proceedings on through the Wapentake Court as an undefended Cause and obtained Judgement and Execution for £2.12^{s}.4^{d}. and on the 22^{d} seized my Household Furniture of every description and sold the same on the 29th day of June last past for £3.3^{s}.7^{d} and from information I have received they are not satisfied yet but intend seizing any other Property I may become possessed of.

I am now destitute of every necessary of Household Furniture and in the greatest distress for necessaries for myself Wife and Family.

The Rent of the Dwelling house in which I reside is not satisfied Amounting to about £2 due to Mr. Fisher of this Town late Coal dealer and I am about to leave the same and remove to another and he will of course be anxious to have is rent satisfied before I leave otherwise he will be Proceeding at Law against me in the Borough Court of Lancaster and Attaching my Body and in that Case I can earn nothing for the support of myself and Family when in Prison, he being a very earnest Man after Money Matters.

I have to request of you that you will lay my Case before the Vestry on Sunday next and I hope and trust they will under all the circumstances render me a little assistance at this time by an advance of a trifle of Money to relieve my pressing necessities

I am
Sir
Your Ob^{t}. Servt.
Lawrence Hodgson

Circumtext:

I Abraham Hodgson of Lancaster in the of Lancaster Auctioneer do hereby Certify that I did sell by Public Auction on Saturday the 29th day of June last past the Goods and Chattles of Lawrence Hodgson of Lancaster Coaldealer under an Execution issued out of the Wapentake Court of the Hundred of Lonsdale at the Suit of Isaac Brockbank for the sum of £3.3^{s}.7^{d} and I do further Certify that I was employed to attend such Sale by Mr. Abraham Ellithorne of Lancaster aforesaid Attorney at Law who received the money arising from such sale. As Witness my Hand the 4 day of July 1833

Abraham Hodgson

Notes: *The body of the circumtext above is in the same hand as the letter, but the signature is in a different hand.*

276 Lawrence Hodgson in Lan[cas]ter to the Parish of Kirkby Lonsdale, 6 December 1834 (WPR/19/7/6/27/11)

Lanester Dem^{er}. 6th 1834

Sir I ham abliged to Play for Relif as I am But ill of at Present I have Run be hind and weth M^{rs}. Davis and it is Martmes and I would be vere Glad if you would a sist Me at thes time I have thre Chrieldren and My wife has Never ben hable to Dow her own turnes Since She has ben Confind ihave No Regler Imploy But what I mak with taken out Coals with Bages I would be vere Glad if you would Send Me Sumthing to Pay My Rent as I am afrad of Bing Destrest Know I would be verey Glad if you would Show this at youar Meten

Plese to Right to
M^{r}. John Davis
or Me

Youar of Severent
Lawrence Hodgson

Circumtext: *In different hand [SG]*: Not Granted.
Below, in further hand:

I believe the above to be true, that relief would be properly applied in this case to Keep him from being more burthensome

John Davis, Coal Dealer

277 Jane Hodg[s]on in Preston to the Parish of Kirkby Lonsdale, 9 February 1834 (WPR/19/7/6/27/49)

Sir/

Am sorry to troble you but Necessity obliges me so to do for sickness and old age as brought me to a state so as not to be able to work for my living but must submit to gods will I have been living at Stely Bridge the other side of Manchester for the last nine years and have latly Buried my son who as been the means of my suport for a long time and the loss of him obliges me to troble you the two Daughters I had with me when I came to you last are boath married but I cant expect them Keeping me though the aught so to do I have got on my jorney as far as Preston to come to you but am not able to get any further without some asistance which I hope your goodness will consither to do I am at presant with my Daughter at Preston ware I can stop for a few days and hope you will have the goodness to let me have your ansure how I ham to do if your goodness can alow me any thing weekly will return back to Stely Bridge if not shall be obliged to get Preston Overseers to remove me to your place waiting your ansure I am your umble serv[t].

Jane Hodgon

Preston 9th Feby 1834

may Direct Jane Hodgon John Lawes ^No12^ Hope Street Preston Lancashire

10.

KITCHEN, letters 278–289

278 John Kitchen in Preston to [Stephen] Garn[ett] in Kirkby Lonsdale, 31 March 1820 (WPR/19/7/6/13/4)

Preston Mar 31th 1820
Mr Garnit

Sir thes is to Enform you that I am very porley & has Bene for a Long Time I have Bene of work a Bout 9 months & am Now verey Badely of for our Celowes & all is Run out for we have Nothing Cuming in & we are 68 yeres of age Sow you may think that we are Badely of & Cannot dow aney Longer with out Sum Relefe which I hop you will *[geret]* us I Should not have Trubled you But it is Realle Nesesity & unless you Canseder to Send Me Sum thing I shall Be Obeleged to a pely to the Oversere of Prestone & Be Removed from her to Kirby lonsdale for we have Dun as Long as We Can for I Expected getting Better But I am Worst Now than I have Bene for sum Time & Canot get propr Nurishement your Spedy ansur will Much Obelege your humbell Servant &c

John Kitchen

Derect John Kitchen
Number 13 Snow Hill
Pereston

Circumtext: *Facing page, in different hand [SG]*: To be Examined as touching a settlement and a Copy sent to this Township

279 Grimshaw and Palmer in Preston to the Parish of Kirkby Lonsdale, 15 April 1820 (WPR/19/7/6/13/8)

The Borough of Preston in Lancashire to wit

The Examination of John Kitching of the Borough aforesaid

Labourer taken upon Oath before me Hugh Dewhurst Esquire Mayor one of his Majestys Justices of the Peace in and for the said Borough this 15th Day of April in the year of our Lord 1820 touching his last legal Settlement –

Who saith that about twenty years ago he took a House in Kirkby Lonsdale of M^{rs}. Bramwell at seven pounds and a close of Land near the same Town of the same Person at three Guineas a year and occupied these for a few years – At May Day, and whilst he was in the occupation of the House and Land aforesaid he rented a Shop in Kirkby Lonsdale aforesaid under Mr Birch at three Guineas a year and occupied the whole for About two years And has done no Act since to gain a Settlement to his knowledge or Belief –

John Kitchen

Sworn before me
Hu: Dewhurst
Mayor

Circumtext: *Facing page*:

Sir/

At the request of the overseer of Preston we send copy of an Examination of John Kitchen which was sworn to and the original is in our possession

Yours respectfully
Grimshaw & Palmer

Preston 15th
April 1820

280 John Kitchen in Preston to [Stephen] Garnet[t] in Kirkby Lonsdale, 13 September 1821 (WPR/19/7/6/14/35)

Preston Sep 13th 1821

Mr Garnet

Sir I would Tak it as a faver if you would Send me Sumthing as I am Verey Badeley of & we ar Much desterss^d^ & in a Bade stat of helth my Brother James when I wass over promesed to dow Sumthing for me but he has not bene <a>s [*page torn*] good of his word if you will Send me Sumthing it will much obileg your Ever humbell Servent & Well

Wisher John Kitchen

281 Edw[ard] Briggs in Preston to S[tephen] Garnett in Kirkby Lonsdale, 1 October 1822 (WPR/19/7/6/15/27)

To Mr S. Garnett

Sir

This is to Certify that the Wife of John Kitchen living at Snow Hill Preston is now under my care labouring under [*******] ^Typhous fever^ they are at present I believe standing in need of some relief

Edw Briggs Surgeon

Fishergate Preston

Octo^r^. 1st 1822

282 John Fallowfield in Preston to the Parish of Kirkby Lonsdale, 2 November 1822 (WPR/19/7/6/15/36)

Preston Nov 2 1822

Sir/

You will pardon me in this addressing you it is in behalf of old John Kitchen & his wife who belong to Kirby Lonsdale they are in a very helpless state the Overseer sent them 10/ about three weeks ago – which is now expended, if they would allow the poor Creatures three or four Shillings weekly ^it^ would do them more service, you might perhaps get your Brother the doctor to see them & indeed he might pay the money for the Parish as long as thought they stood in need of it, your kind attention to the request would confer an obligation

On Sir

Yours most respectfully

John Fallowfield Junr.

Circumtext: *Below, in pencil*: Dringiot

283 John Fallowfield in Preston to the Parish of Kirkby Lonsdale, 6 December 1823 (WPR/19/7/6/16/57)

Preston Decr. 6th 1823

Sir/

You will excuse ^me^ I hope in again addressing [****] [*overwritten by*] you upon the case of John Kitchen who belongs to your Parish, I beg to inform you that he is now dead & the Family are desirous ^that^ some trifle should be sent towards his Funeral expences, they having supported him the last 3 year without any parochial relief, if the Officers of the Parish should think proper to assist Them you may remit the amount to Mr. Bugg, Surgeon of this place he being a person you will know & who will be able to inform you of the propriety of such a relief

I am
Sir
Yours Respectfully
John Fallowfield Jun[r].

284 Ruth Kitchen in Preston to the Parish of Kirkby Lonsdale, 2 March 1826 (WPR/19/7/6/19/11)

Preston 2nd March 1826

Sir

As the overseer of the Parish unto which I belong I am under the Painful necessity of Trubling you with these few liens for the Purpose of desiring from you Some relief or assistance as my advanced years is now arived to that State when I am Sinking under old age and infirmity and am now Gotten Past doing any thing Towards my Support and Trade and other things is now in a deploreable Situation this may Perhaps be Some things better but I shall never be younger but shall Continue to Worsten and as men and Christians I think you will Easily Suppose that Persons at 75 years are Past doing much and I hope and Trust I shall be assisted in a reasonable manner I am now in real and Great Distress without one to assist me and I hope you will not delay so you may have an oppertunity of sending any ~~week~~ [*overwritten by*] Fortnight by John Taylor the Carrier who is Coming from your Town next Tuesday and longer then that you will not I hope Put me off as I am now Distitute of all the Comforts of life I need not tell you you that I shall require Weekly relief as I have now nothing to depend to you and I hope you will not fail sending in Hopes of receiving your assistance and Some Settled relief I shall leave matters with you and remain

Sir your obed. Humble
Servant
Ruth Kitchen

No11 Snow Hill
Preston Lancashire

Circumtext: *In different hand [SG]*: To Come to Kirkby Lonsdale

285 Ruth Kitchen in Preston to [Stephen] Garnet[t] in Kirkby Lonsdale, 11 February 1830 (WPR/19/7/6/23/30)

Preston Febuary the 11th 1830

Mr. Garnet Sir
I am under the nessety of wrighting these fue lines to you hoping you will take It in to Consideration and adapt me a little more mony weekly for I am in gr<ea>t [*page torn*] distress at present throu sickness and I Can get nothing to doo to wards a living the times is so bad and if I Could get ever so much to doo I Cannot doo It through my bad helth and sir all I desire from you is to advance me sixpence per week more to my allouence to wards my house rent as I Cannot pay my rent any other way so I desire you will be kind enough to grant me my request

So I remain
your humble Servant
Ruth Kitchen

286 Ruth Kitchen in Preston to [Stephen] Garnet[t] in Kirkby Lonsdale, 30 July 1830 (WPR/19/7/6/23/57)

Preston July 30th 1830

Mr Garnet
Sir) The reason of my troubling you at this time is to aquaint you that it is impossibl for me to subsist myself on One Shilling and Sixpence P. Week and as I am in my Eighteth year it is a long Jorney to come over to Ky Lonsdale at my age hoping you ^will^ lay my case before the Vestry Meeting and send me somthing more or I shall be Obliged to be removed to the Workhouse

I am yours &c
Ruth Kitchen

287 Ruth Kitchen in Preston to [Stephen] Garnet[t] in Kirkby Lonsdale 16 December 1830 (WPR/19/7/6/23/31)

Preston Decr. 16th 1830

Mr Garnet)

Dr Sir I take ^the^ liberty of adressing you at this time as Winter is Approaching and Am very poorly myself and having House rent and firing to provid and not able to do any thing towards a subsistance I hope you will have the goodness to make my situation Known at the Monthly Meeting as I shall be Eighty years of Age the third of next March hoping they will have the goodness to Alow me A trifel more in Addition to my present Allowance

I rem^{n}. Your Humb^{l}.
Parishioner Ruth Kitchen

Circumtext: *In different hand [SG]*: Granted 6^{d} a week more

288 Ruth Kitchen in Preston to [Stephen] Garnet[t] in Kirkby Lonsdale 26 July 1833 (WPR/19/7/6/26/28)

Preston July 26th 1833

Mr Garnet
Dear Sir)

I am very sorey to trouble you but I am greatly in Nessity for shoes shifts and bed Gowns as I it is the first time that I have made any application for wearing apparel since my Husband Died & hope you will have the Goodness to State my case at your Meeting in hopes that you will send me some thing

I rem^{n}. your
Hum^{bl}. Servt.
Ruth Kitchen

Circumtext: *In different hand [SG]*: Granted 7^{s}/

289 Ruth Kitchen in Preston to the Parish of Kirkby Lonsdale, 3 October 1834 (WPR/19/7/6/27/22)

Preston Oct[r]. 3rd 1834

Dear Sir/

I am sorey to trouble you at this time but Winter is comming on and I am in want of almost all things that is Nessary to cover me and my weekly subsistance is little enough to keep me alive I shoud be very much Obliged to ^you^ if you woud send me a trifel to Inable me to get something to cover me with In so doing you will Oblige

Your Hum[bl] Serv[t]
Ruth Kitchin

Circumtext: *In different hand [SG]*: Granted 5s/

11.

LANGHORN, letters 290–320

290 Thomas Darwen in Lancaster to the Overseers of the Poor in Kirkby Lonsdale, 21 May 1812 (WPR/19/7/6/5/17)

Lancaster 21st May 1812

Gentlemen/

William Langhorn whom you lately relieved, has a Child Dead and he is unable to pay the Funeral Expences, what with a Sick Family, little work and provisions dear, makes him an Object of your attention, be so good as to send him something or give me orders what you wish to be done for him, your answer will Oblige

Gentlemen
Your Obd Hble Srt
Thomas Darwen
Overseer

Circumtext: *Address of recipient:* The Overseers Of the Poor Kirby Lonsdale
Postmarked: Lancaster 23 MY 23 1812, 289

291 W[illia]m Langhorn in Lanc[a]ster to the Parish of Kirkby Lonsdale, 6 December 1815 (WPR/19/7/6/8/12)

Sir/

I am sorry to be so troublsom but nessety Cumpels me to it my Master hath redused my wadges to 12 shillings pr Week so that it is impasable for me to surporte my self and Famly withoute asstence had you thought proper to have paid me 1 half year's Rent I have trubled you no more or if you will do it now I can get a House but I desire you will write and tell me what you intend to do and pleas to send me soom Mony otherwise I will be Oblidged to send my Wife and Famley to you as it is not likly an Old Man lick me can Expect to get as mutch mony as a Stoute young Man as I am not able to Work for it I must Agane desire you will send mee soom money otherwise they must Cum to you immedatly

I am yours
Lancester Respectfully
December 6th 1815 ~~Mr <Rotherington>~~ [*almost scrubbed out*]
Wm Langhorn

Notes: *The first signature was scrubbed out before Langhorn's was added. It is likely that 'Rotherington' was the actual author of the letter, and mistakenly signed it in his name even though it was written from the first person perspective of William Langhorn.*

292 B[etty] Langhorn in Lanc[a]ster to the Parish of Kirkby Lonsdale, 26 December 1816 (WPR/19/7/6/9/23)

Sir/

I hope you will agane pardon me given you this truble but I hope you will Rember me agane this Christmacl as well as the last for time's are so very hard with me that I cannot do with what I have without you assest me with a little more what you ware so good as give me at Cirby did not half pay my Rent besid's my Chelldern are nearly Nacked for want of Clow's my youngest Child gro's wors in place of better – I have no work at present so I beg you will be so good as send me a lettel Relif with [~~*****~~] [*overwritten by*] Jeffrey Mackey on Satturday and ^you^ will mutch relive my desstres
Lancaster Decem I am with Great $Resp^{t}$
th 26 1816 Your's
B Langhorn

Circumtext: *In different hand [SG]*: Granted 7/6

293 B[etty] Langhorn in Lanc[a]ster to the Parish of Kirkby Lonsdale, 30 [January] 1817 (WPR/19/7/6/10/4)

Sir/

I am sorry to be so trublesom but Nes^s^ety compels me to it I resived your cind donation of $7^{s}.6^{d}$ which is all the mony I have had this 3 weeks as I can get no work so you may think how I am satuated you may bilive me me and my Poor Children are nearly Clamed you know oute of the 5 shilling's I resive from Mr Darwen I leve 2 in his hands ~~for~~ for my Rent my Children are ~~near~~ almost starved for want Close and it is very hard I can get them none it is not in my pour to dow with what I have so I beg you will either write to Mr Darwin and pay my Rent while tims are so harde or send me soom Relife with Jas <Mackey> and you will mutch relive my Destress for I ashoure you I would not truble you if I could any way Avoide it

Lancester Jen 30th 1817

I am with great
Resp^t^ B Langhorn

Circumtext: *In different hand [SG]*: Granted 1^s^/ P week more till the end of April

294 Churchwardens and Overseers of Lancaster to the Overseers of the Poor in Kirkby Lonsdale, 21 April 1817 (WPR/19/7/6/9/10)

The Overseers of Kirby Lonsdale
To the Churchwardens and Overseers of Lancaster, Dr.

Relief given to	*From*	*To*	*Weeks*	*Per Week*	*£*	*s.*	*d.*
Widow Langhorn	27th Sepr 1816	31st Jany 1817	18	5/-	4	10	
Do.	31st Jany 1817	28th March	8	6/-	2	8	
Wm Addison	14th Feb^y^.					10	
					£7	8	

Circumtext: *Address of recipient:* The Overseers of the Poor Kirby Lonsdale
Postmarked: Lancaster 21AP21 1817, 239

Notes: *This is a printed proforma invoice. The content of the invoice in italics (outwith brackets) represents the printed text.*

295 Churchwardens and Overseers of Lancaster to the Overseers of Kirkby Lonsdale, [September 1817] (WPR/19/7/6/10/51)

Overseers of the Poor of Kirkby Lonsdale

To the Churchwardens and Overseers of Lancaster, Dr.

Relief given to	*From*	*To*	*Weeks*	*Per Week*	*£*	*s.*	*d.*
Wid: Langhorn	30th May 1817	26th S[ep]r 1817	17	6/-	5	2	

Notes: *This is a printed proforma invoice. The content of the invoice in italics (outwith brackets) represents the printed text.*

Although there is no date on this letter, its place in the sequence, and the invoice dates, strongly suggest it was sent shortly after September 1817.

296 Thomas Darwen in Lancaster to the Parish of Kirkby Lonsdale, 2 January 1818 (WPR/19/7/6/11/2)

Lancaster 2^{d} Jany. 1818

Sir,

I have paid Langhorn to the 26th Ult: and I am sorry to say I do not wish to pay her any longer, any other person I have no objections to pay, and should be glad to serve you in any thing but this

I am Sir
Yours truly
Thomas Darwen

297 J. John Robinson in Preston to the Parish of Kirkby Lonsdale, 12 January 181[8] (WPR/19/7/6/11/1)

Preston
Jany 12 181*[8]*

Gents

It is respecting Betty Langhorn I write you, her Goods are now seized for Rent and will be sold on Saturday if not paid the Purport of this is to ~~enquire~~ request you to send her $^{£}1.12^{s}.0$ which is what she owes with Expences, or a note to the Landlord purporting the same it will do – She says you may reduce her weekly pay 4^{s}/ until it be paid Your early ans^{r} to her will oblige

J. John Robinson Overseer

Notes: *Although the final digit from the year is missing on this letter, its place in the sequence strongly suggest it was sent early in 1818.*

298 Thomas Darwen in Lancaster to the Parish of Kirkby Lonsdale, 21 March 1818 (WPR/19/7/6/11/8)

The Overseers of Kirby Lonsdale
To the Overseers of Lancaster Dr.

Relief given to	From	To	Weeks	Per Week	
Widow Langhorn	30th May 1817	26th Decr 1817	30	6/-	9
$Marg^{t}$. Addison	24th October	27th March 1818	22	2/-	2 4
					£11 4

Sir,

I beg leave to hand your Account requesting yours in return, and as I quit the situation of Overseer at the expiration of the present Overseers year should wish our Accounts Balanced

I am Sir
your Ob[t]. Hble Sr[t].
21st March 1818 Thomas Darwen
acting Overseer

Notes: *This is a hand-written proforma.*

299 Stephen Stockdale in Lancaster to Stephen Garnett in Kirkby Lonsdale, 21 July 1818 (WPR/19/7/6/11/20)

Mr. Stephen Garnett

To Stephen Stockdale Dr.

To Cash paid Eliz[th]. Langeron from 1st Jan[y]. 1818 to July 1st 1818

	£	s	d
To 10 Weeks @ 5/ P Week	2	10	0
To 16 Weeks @ 6/- P Week	4	16	0
	7	6	0

Sir,

Agreeable to your Order I have paid E. Langeron as above, I have to request you will Remit the Money as above-mentioned by the Bearer.

I am
Y[r]. Ob[dt]. Ser[t].
Lancaster Stephen Stockdale
21st July 1818

Notes: *This is a hand-written proforma.*

300 Stephen Stockdale in Lancaster to the Parish of Kirkby Lonsdale, 11 December 1818 (WPR/19/7/6/11/36)

Lancaster Dec[r]. 11th 1818

Sir,

I have inclosed E Langhorn's Acc[t]. for whom I have paid as under.

	£	s	d
From July 1st to Decr. 9th 1818 23 weeks at 6/ P Week	6	18	0

I am
Your Ob^dt^. Servt.
Stephen Stockdale

Circumtext:

6	18	0
2	4	0
9	2	0
1	0	
10	2	0

301 Betty Langhorn in Preston to the Parish of Kirkby Lonsdale, 29 [April] 1819 (WPR/19/7/6/12/4)

Preston Apreal the 29 1819
Jentleman I desire you will take it in to considerion to let me have the sum of 2 shillins per week ^with my yongst Child^ as for my ouldest Gerl she arns me 3 and 6 pence per week but you was in formed that she had 4 and 6 but if you right to Mr Swainson he will let you know all about it Jentlemen I hope you will Consider to let me have this 2 shillings and let me know wear I must recive it if you pleas jentalmen 3 and 6 is but very little for me and tow childer to liv on if you Do not let me have it I shal be obliged to Go to sum Justis so I Desire you will send me an ancer as sone as posable you can heare is no work and we canot starve so im your umbale servent Beetty Langhorn
Drect to Mr Yeats Grocer
Church street

Circumtext: *In different hand [SG]*: Granted 2s/ P week

302 Elizabeth Langhorn in Preston to Stephen Garnet[t] in Kirkby Lonsdale, 10 May 1819 (WPR/19/7/6/12/7)

Preston May the 10th 1819

Mr Stephen Garnet
this Comes to let you know that the faviour is Returned and I have been Down again five Days I writ to Mr Stephen Stockle disiring him to Let me have a quarters pay he sent word back that he was not to let me have any thing but once a month My youngest Child is very ill and I am quite Distresst youl

please to write to Mr Stephen Stockly imadiately to let me know what I am to have and if you think you Can Mantain Mantain us for less till 2^{s}. per week I am willing to Come and in short I will be Removd for I Cannot nor will not be quite Lost – while I have a parish to flee two – I will send Mr Stephen Stockly this week to know what I am to have Mr Stephen Stockly will let me have Rilife and soon if you send a line to him

So no more at Present from yours

Elizabeth Lang Horn

303 Betty [Langhorn] in Preston to the Parish of Kirkby Lonsdale, 30 June 1819 (WPR/19/7/6/12/15)

Sir Preston June 30th 1819

I have taken the liberty of writing again to you I Rote Some time Since and has got No answer but I hope you Will have the goodness to Rite by Return of Post and let me know whether you Will Relieve us or Not as we Cannot Stop hear to be famished I have My youngest Child in the typhus Fever and has been a Week and I have done While I can do No longer I went to the overseer of this Town he orderd me to Rite to you to see what you Intended to do for us We are both Naked and lost for want of Food We have had Nothing to take too this Week but What the Neibours has been Pleased to Give us I went to Mr Swainson were My oldest Girl Works to see if he would take her in to work again if we should be Removed and Come back but he will Not and the Will Not Relieve part of our family but all togather So dont delay Writing with Speed for we Cannot stop hear to be Entirely lost I hardly know Wich way I Must get for I Cannot bear Shakeing in a Cart Nor to Walk I am Not Able but some Way I am like to Come if you Will Not do Something for us I am distrest as ill as I Can be What with bad health and Sickness among the Children I have Neither Nothing to Put on our backs Nor Can get Nothing to suport the Children with if you could send me something to Get something to our back and help us while We Get better We Will try and do some Way I h<ave> [*page torn*] Not been able to do any thing since I had the typhus Fever indeed if I was able Nobody Would like to Employ Me While I have the Fever in the house. Please to Rite by Return of Post Sir I am your Obedient Servent

Betty Longhall

[*In margin*] if you send any thing send by John Taylor and We will Meet him at the New Cock on Tuesday

Circumtext: *In different hand*:

P.S. I believe the bearer is distress you do something for them
Yours
John Robinson
Overseer

In further hand [SG]: Granted £1.0.0

Notes: *Even though this letter is signed with the surname Longhall, it is written in the same hand as Betty Langhorn's previous letters. This could be because she had a friend or scribe to write for her, and they mistranscribed her name.*

304 Betty [Langhorn] in Preston to the Parish of Kirkby Lonsdale, 1 September 18[19] (WPR/19/7/6/12/17)

Sir Preston September 1st 18019
I take the liberty of Writing this to you as I Rote to Mr Stephen Stockdale Desiring he Would have the Goodness to Send Me Six and twenty Shillings to lose My Cloaths wich was Been out in Pledge the Cost Me above 5 pound but he would Not do it he Sent Me word you ordered him only to pay Me once a Month Wich I think is Very hard My Money Costs Me 2 shillings Every time it Comes My oldest Girl is Now under doctor Brigs with a bad knee wich Will I am afraid will be of bad Consequence he orderd her to bathe She has twice but has done her No good therefore you Must Send Me Some keep by John Taylor for I Cannot do any longer I owe twelve Shillings for My Rent Wich I Must pay Imeadeatly or Else what few things I have Must be Sold I have Nothing that is worth any thing but one bed wich Mr Swainson Gave Me When My goods were Sold if you Will Not Realeave Me I shall be like to Go to this ovesear of this town and get Realeaf and then the May Remove us for I Cannot bear to see My Children punished as the have been and Now My daughter Now laying on My hands it is impossable for Me to do I am like to have My Money different to What I have We are <a>ll [*page torn*] Naked and it is Not in My power to get any thing for them So you Must Either do Something More for us or we Must Come to you times is So bad there is No Work and what to do I Cant [*****] [*page torn*] if you Cant believe Me you Must Some of you Come and see our distress for 2 shillings a Week Will Not do So I hope you will Send by John Taylor and Get Mr Stockdale to let Me have My Money different Sir I am your Obedient
Betty Longhall

Cirumtext: *In margin, different hand [SG]*: Not Granted if she cannot do she may come to the Workhouse

Notes: *Even though this letter is signed in the surname Longhall, it is written in the same hand as Betty Langhorn's previous letters.*

305 Betty L[a]nghorn in Preston to the Parish of Kirkby Lonsdale, 26 December 1819 (WPR/19/7/6/12/32)

Preston December the 26
1819

Jentelmen this is to in forme you that I have my rint to pay sence I was at Kirby that is one quarter and I have been very porley ever sence I was over so I desire you will be so kind as to send me the sum of 2 pound that will pay my rent and put me on for awile I have my youngest Child is very porely at present under the Docter and I am in Distres at presant so I hope you will consider my sittwaton and send by John Taylor and I will met im on tusday next but oneless you do not send to me I sertenly myst com to you I wish to know whear I must resev my weekly pay for my youngest child I am your umble servent Betty Longhorne

I could wish to be paid by Mr Stockdale on if you please

Circumtext: *In different hand [SG]*: Granted 7^{s}/ and to write to her Informing her that her Rent will not be paid

306 Stephen Stockdale in Lancaster to [Stephen] Garnett in Kirkby Lonsdale, 28 March 1820 (WPR/19/7/6/13/3)

Mr Garnett

	£.	s.	d
To Stephen Stockdale Dr.			
To 4 Weeks Cash @ 4/ P Week paid E Langhorn	0	16	0
To 48 Weeks D°. @ 2/ P Week D°.	4	16	0
	5	12	0

Sir,

I have paid her up to the 29th Ins^{t}. at which Time the Year ends and as I intend declining having any thing more to do in this Business, I hope you will Order some other Person to pay her in my stead she is so very Clamarous, I am

Sir Yours most truly

Lancaster Stephen Stockdale

28th March 1820

Notes: *This is a hand-written proforma.*

307 William Davis in Preston to S[tephen] Garnett in Kirkby Lonsdale, 3 May 1820 (WPR/19/7/6/13/10)

Preston May 3rd 1820

Mr. S. Garnett

Dr Sir,

The bearer – Langhorn has applied to me for money to assist her to remove to Manchester, which of course I refused according to my father's instructions. Her little girl has been dismissed from our Mill, on account (as I understand from the Manager) of her refusing to do the work assigned to her by her task-master, and particularly in consequence of an improper interference on her own part. – I cannot pretend to say what her prospects in Manchester are, but if she were less disposed to travel than she seems to be, I think she might obtain a situation for her daughter in Preston.- If you continue to encourage her claims, it is not improbable that she will ere long become very troublesome to you. Her pention is paid to the present date.

I remain yours respectfully

William Davis

308 Eliz[abe]th L[a]nghorn in Manchester to Stephen Garnett in Kirkby Lonsdale, 1 August 1820 (WPR/19/7/6/13/18)

Manchester August 1st 1820

Mr Stephen Garnett

Sir/

I take the liberty of writing to you to inform you of my situation when I came first to Manchester I was 3 weeks and 3 days before I could get a days work for either my self or or the oldest Girl I wished my self back again many a time but thank God I have plenty of work for my self but the Factory are a many of them Stopt and I cannot get the Girl any work but I have got her a very good Place as Nurse if I can get her some decent Clothes. She is at Mr Fords Tin Man Cateaton Street so if you will be so kind as to allow me 20

Shilling to Clothe her and Send me Two Pound more to buy me a Bed and some nessary things that I am in great want of I will stop the Two Pounds in my Pencion as there will be due 6/- on the 9th of August. your compliance with this will greatly Oblidge Sir your Most Ob^{t} Hb^{l} Servt

Elizth. Longhorne

No.5 Scholes Buildings back Water Street

Manchester

NB Please to write as soon as possible

Notes: *The handwriting and orthography of this letter are very different from Langhorn's previous correspondence. The fact that, once again, her name is misspelt might suggest that the writer is not overly familiar with her.*

309 Elizabeth Langhorn in Manchester to the Parish of Kirkby Lonsdale, 17 August 1820 (WPR/19/7/6/13/20)

1820

Honoured Sir, Manchester 17th Aug

I am under the nessesity of adressing you I wrote to you before but have Got no Answer which both Suprises and hurts me I have now ten Shilling, which will be due to me from you on Wednesday next and I beg you would have the Goodness to advance me two pounds and and I agree to Stop my Weekly pay untill the money be run less for I am truly distressd having no Bed for my Children or my Self to Lay upon I can earn Victuals by my own Industrey as I have plenty of Work but I Can Spare nothing towards puting nessesarys into my place therefore I beg you Will Condescend to Comply with this request and I have a very Good Lady who I work for Will take my Girl intirely ^of my hands^ as a Servent if you will have the Goodness to Give her two Suits of Cloths throughout So I humbly beg you will have the Goodness to Cloth her and then She will be provided for I trust you will not think me unreasonable I wish to trouble you As little as possible but if you Cant at this time Send me the Sum I so much want I beg you will Send to me Imeadiately after the first Sunday – please to direct for me at no5 Schoales Street near Young Street Back Water Street Manchester

from your truely Obliged

and very humble Sevent

Elizabeth Langhorn

Circumtext: *Address of recipient:* Mr Stephen Garnett Kirby Lonsdale near Whittington on the Other side Lancaster

Postmarked: Lancaster 19AU19, 23[*]

Notes: *This letter is in yet another hand.*

310 Elizabeth Langhorn in Salford to the Parish of Kirkby Lonsdale, 1 November 1820 (WPR/19/7/6/13/29)

Salford Novemr ^the^ 1 1820

Gentleman

I take the Liberty of Wrightiting a few Lines to inform you of my Presant Situation I was oblig'd to Remove from the Plase where I Lived when I Wrote to you on a Count of Getting my Living by Washing I am Removed more in the Countrey now Gentlemen their is ten Shillings Due to me if you will have the Goodness to Send me thirty Shillings to the ten will be two Pounds I shall Esteem it a Particklar favour and Likewise One Pound to Cloth my Oldest Girl as Mr Ford is willing to take her Provideing I Can Get her two Shutes of Close to Change her in She then will be took of your hands I have her at home with me and I am not able to maintain her myself I have no Bed to Lay on But a Bit of Straw and nothing to Cover us the Wether Gets very Could we shall be all Perrished I did not wish to trouble you until I had Sumthing Due to me Gentlemen I hope you will Consider me at this time for I have done to the utmost of my Power be so kind if you Plase to Send me the Sum of three Pounds by Return of Post I have thank God Plenty of Work But very much Put about for a few using nesescarys Gentlemen if you Complay with my Request I will not trouble you any More until the money is Run up my Youngest Girl as been very Poorly with very Bad Eyes I belive it to be with Laying on the floor Gentlemen if I was to Come Over I Should Loose all my Work and it will be very Expencive I Could not wish to Put no more Expencis ^in^ Wrighting than I Possible Could help I hope you will not fail to Send by Return of Post you will Much oblig you^r^ hum^l^ Servt

Elizabeth Langhorn

Plase to Direct for me
Back George Street Tamlingsons
Place No1 Bottom of Burrow
Street Salford Near
Manchester

Notes: *This letter is in yet another hand.*

311 Elizabeth Langhorn in Salford to [Stephen] Garnet[t] in Kirkby Lonsdale, 1 March 1821 (WPR/19/7/6/14/9)

Salford March 1th 1821

Mr Garnet Sir

I Wright to inform you I Receivd the Last money you sent me Safe I shall Esteem it a Perticklar favour if you will have the Goodness to send me the sum of three Pounds and I hope this Sumer I shall be able to Bring myself Round this Christmass I was a month very Poorly and not able to do anything and I have had the Misfortune to have some Cloes Stole to the a Mount of five Pounds the Cloes belong to Mrs Richards the have been very Good the Bare half of the Expence it as been a heavy Loss to me and as Caused me to be six weeks Rent behind at 2^{s} 6^{d} Per Week and a Load of Coals as the Winter as been very Bad for Drying Cloes I have Got Plenty of Good Work if I have my health I hope I shall not trouble you for so much at a time I have had my Daughter in the Infirmery with her Eyes and I belive she Would a Lost her Sight Entirely if I had not a took to the Oldfield Lane Doctor I have her Medisines to Pay for as I Get them my Children as not been able to Get me a Penny Since I Came their as been so many Factorys Standing still the Ladies as behaved very well to me Espesiley Mrs Barker I have all her Work and Others she as Got me I keep Getting More Every Week I hope I shall do very well in a Bit of time I hope you will Consider me and Send me a small trifle to what you alow me wile the Children is so Poorly and Pay yourself for the Letters Out of the money I hope I shall not need to Wright to you any More until the Money is Run up I hope you will send as soon as Possible you Can for my Landlord is very uneasey about ^it^ with me being a stranger I am sorry to trouble you for so Much at a time But I hope [***] [*overwritten by*] it will be the Last time

I Remain your Hum^{l}
Servt Elizabeth Langhorn

P to Direct for me No.3 Brewery
Street Salford Near Manchester

Circumtext: *In different hand [SG]*: Granted $^{£}$1.0^{s}.0^{d} in advance of pension

312 Betty Langhorn in Manchester to [Stephen] Garnett in Kirkby Lonsdale, 1 June 1821 (WPR/19/7/6/14/22)

Manchester June 1th 1821

Mr Garnett
Sir
I hope you will Excuse me for troubling with these few Lines as I am under the nessesiety at Presant as my Money is Run up and their is 7 Weeks Due to me on tuseday Next I shall Esteem it as a Great favour if you will have the Goodness to send me ^two Pounds^ Notes as I stand Greatley in need through a bad Bout of Sickness I have not been able to do my Work I am */Benn/* behind with my Rent and the Landlord is very sharp I whent to Mr Hodkinson the Overseer of Salford he desired me to Wright to you and if you did not answer my Letter Mr Hodkinson will Wright to you himself Besseys Eyes Continues to Get no better she as nearly Lost One Eye if you wish to know her age if you will Go to Mr Manleys in Lankerster you will Get her Regester she was Six years Old in Febury Last, I hope sir you will Send to me as soon as Possible you Can as the Landlord whants his Rent, I Realy believe Bessey will never be able to do anything Ellin has been with Mrs Forden a four weeks she would a took her for Good if I Could a Cloath he to make her Decent Both the Children is quite Naked I dont know what to do with them I hope Plase God to spear me with Health I shall be able to do without troubling ^you^ for my Money before it is Due if you will ablige me this time I hope I shall not need to trouble any More until my Money is Due I hope you will not fail to answer this as soon as you Can you will Much ablige

Your Humb Sert
Betty Langhorn

Direct for me No3 Brewery Street
Salford
Manchester

313 Elizabeth Langhorn in Salford to S[tephen] Garnet[t] in Kirkby Lonsdale, 28 June 1821 (WPR/19/7/6/14/26)

Salford June 28th 1821

Mr S Garnet
Sir I hope you will Excuse me for Wrighting to you as I wrote to you and Got no answer I Could not think the Reason I do not wish to trouble ^you^ before my Money was Due my youngest Child Continues to be very Bad and

no hopes of her Getting Better it is now Six Weeks Since she begun to be so Bad and I am at this time very ill Put about I hope you will have the Goodness to Let me have the sum of two Pound as I hope it will be in my Power not to trouble you any more until my Money is Due and this Run up if you Cannot advance me the sum of two Pound I hope you will have the Goodness to Let me have what you Plase I hope you will not fail to Wright as soon as Posiable you can you will Much

ablige your hum[l] Ser[t]

No3 Brewery Street Salford   Elizabeth Langhorn

314 Elizabeth Langhorn in Salford to S[tephe]n Garnet[t] in Kirkby Lonsdale, 30 August 1821 (WPR/19/7/6/14/33)

Salford Aug[t] 30th 1821

Mr S[n] Garnet

Sir

I hope you will Excuse me for troubling you with these few Lines in hopes you will not be affended I have had a very Bad Illness I have been under the Doctor three Weeks But I am now Got a Little Better I shall not be able Long to Get my Living by Washing I have Great incoragement from the People I Work for to Get a Mangle in this town it will be a Good Liveing for me their is a very Good Mangle to be sold in the Nabourhoo^d^ th ask Eight Pounds for it the whant two Pounds in hand and the Rest of the money the will take Weekly if I Can Raise this Mangle I shall be able to Get a Liveing in a very short time without troubling you I hope Sir you will Consider and help me this time their is One Pound 4 Shillings Due to me now if you will have the Goodness to Let me have three Pounds as soon as Posiable you Can as their as been another Person about it But the have Promised to not Let it Go to any One Els until Next Thursday to See if I Can Raise the Money I am very sorry to inform you that Besseys Eyes Continues to be very Bad She Cannot Look at Day Light I hope Sir you will Complay with my Request as I will not trouble you any More until the Money is Run up and if the Mangle answers my Expectation I hope I shall not need to trouble you any More

until then I Remain
Your hum[l] Ser[t]
Elizabeth Langhorn
No.3 Brewery Street
Salford
Manchester

315 Elizabeth Langhorn in Salford to S[tephen] Garnet[t] in Kirkby Lonsdale, 29 November 1821 (WPR/19/7/6/14/44)

Salford Novr 29th 1821

Mr S Garnet
Sir

I hope you will Excuse me For troubling with Wrighting in hopes you will have the Goodness to Answer this as Soon as Posiable you Can as my Money was Due on the 26 of this Month I have Ellen very Poorly at home the Children is very Badley off for Cloes I should be very Much abligd to you if you Posiabley ^Could^ Relieve me with a Little More this Winter quarter as I am very Poorly in Health myself I will not trouble you any More until it is Run up Plase to Wright by Return of Post you will Much ablige your hum^l Servt

Elizabeth
No.3 Brewery Street Langhorn
Salford

316 Elizabeth Langhorn in Bradford to the Parish of Kirkby Lonsdale, 23 February 1823 (WPR/19/7/6/16/12)

Bradford Feb 23rd 1823
Sir I write to inform you that I have not received any thing since I received the one Poun note you ^sent^ in november Last I have wrote three letters to you and I ~~no~~ never got Answer yit I left Manchester on the 21st of November I laid ill 23 weeks before I left my Daughter was ablige to come to me for I was all most lost for I was not able to do any thing for my Self So She Brought me to Bradford I desire you ^will^ write by the return of Post and if you dont write and send me my money I shall be ablige to Come with the Carrier

So I remain your Humbell
Servant Elizabeth Lang~~man~~^horn^

Direct for me Coal pit Lane to the Care of Petter dean East Bradford Yorkshire

Circumtext: *In different hand [SG]*: 1823 March 8th sent her 1 pound note

Notes: *This letter is in a different hand.*

317 Peter Dean in Bradford to the Parish of Kirkby Lonsdale, 30 June 1823 (WPR/19/7/6/16/43)

Bradford June 30 1823

Sir/

I send this to say I am surprized that you have not answered the Letter my Mother in Law Elizabeth Langhorn sent you some time ago she would have been with you some time since but since she wrote she has been confined to her bed by a severe fit of sickness and she has a very bad Leg which disables her from earning her own living she would have come but she is unable to walk and she cannot bear shaking by the Carrier or Waggon and Coach fare she can't afford to pay I have been to the Overseer at Brad ford and he has advised me to write again and if it is not answered to Apply to him and he will remove her as it is not in my Power to mentain her and her Daughter as I have three Small Children of my own any thing I can do I will very Willingly but I cannot do more if she is any better if you do not write you may expect her in a fortnight and if she is not you may expect her as soon as she is able to be removed and her Daughter hoping that you will be so good as to ~~an~~ answer this as soon as possible without any further trouble. I Remain Sir your

hble Servant

Peter Dean

Direct for Elizabeth Langhorn to the care of Peter Dean Woolcomber Pit Lane Barker end Bradford yorkshire

318 Elizabeth Langhorn in Bradford to Stephen Garnett in Kirkby Lonsdale, 27 December 1823 (WPR/19/7/6/16/61)

Bradford December 27th 1823

Mr Stephen Garnett

Sir/ I am v<ery s> orry [*obscured by wax seal*] to trespass on you^r^ Goodness but at <this> [*obscured by wax seal*] time I am forced by Nescessity to do it the times are very bad here at present my Son has been out of work this last Seven weeks indeed here is scarcely a Woolcomber in work at this time in this town he has been on tramp ever since he fell out of work and now he thinks of going to place so that I shall have nothing but the two Girls wages which at present is very small as the Mills are Stinted to 3 days work in a week as for my part I had not been able to earn 5 shillings ~~a week~~ since I came back from Kirkby Lonsdale as here is no work to be got except going out a Washin^g^ and I am not able to do it I had a Master at me yesterday from Rochdale that wished me to engage with him for a year he will find both the Girls and me in work he will let me have a Reel into my own house so that I think by the blessings the Almighty we should be able to do very well if we could once get there but with work being so very slack we have not been able to pay our last half years rent which is £2-10^{s} the Landlord threatens to sell the few Goods I have but he has consented to wait till I have wrote to you and had an answer back again ~~so~~ the Master has likewise agreed to wait for an answer till this day fortnight when if you will be so good as to send me my rent they will fetch us and allow us to pay the expences at so much per week out of our Wages if you will not the Girls mean to go themselves and I shall be abliged to come to you entirely as they are not able to find another home they are very good Children and if they had had plenty of work I would have been sorry to have applyed to you at this time or if the Master would have lent me as much & have taken it out of thier wages I would not but they would not you must be be so good as to let me have an answer before this day fortnight as they are coming at that time for two or three families out of this Neighbourhood hoping you will do as well for me as you can I Remain Sir your obliged

Servant
Elizabeth Langhorne

Direct for John Millar Coalpit Lane Barker End
Bradford Yorkshire

Circumtext: *In different hand [SG]:* Not Granted

319 Elizab[e]th L[a]nghorn in Rochdale to the Parish of Kirkby Lonsdale, 29 January 1824 (WPR/19/7/6/17/3)

Rochdale January 29th 1824

Ser I am sorey to trubel you aney more but I Canot avoid it at ~~per~~ present ser I desire you will send me a ~~L~~ littel of money and I should be very thankful for it for I am very ill of at present and we are Just shiften to Rochdale and we ware forsed to sell all the Goods and we want more for we have noe so no more it present derect for John Miller hemer hall Nere

Rochdale
Elizabath Longhorn

Notes: *This letter is in yet another hand.*

320 Elizabeth Langhorn in Rochdale to the Parish of Kirkby Lonsdale, 26 July 1824 (WPR/19/7/6/17/33)

July 26 1824
Sir I take this oppertunity of writing to you hoping it will find you in Good helth as it Leaves My ~~mate~~ ^mother^ Verey poorley at present she has Been under Docter Wood 2 Month and she is not Able to do aney thing yet I am forsed to Let my Sister stay at home with her and there is Nothing But Me and by Litel Sister Wageses to all and it is more than I am Able to do for there is Boath Docter and Clothing firing Vitls and all other for I have Done My Verey Best to keep from trubling you therefor if you will send Me 2 pound I will do my Best to take Care of her and if you will not I will throw ^her^ on this town and thay as thay will With her for I Will do ~~no~~ no More

if you do not send me sum Money for I shall have all sould at the door verey Shortley if I have no Asistance as for My lital ^sester^ she Lise Me in More than she ~~E~~ Earnes and if you Could Get her A plase it Wood Be Boath for Me and her for she Wood Learn Sum thin More than Been in A mill so I desire you will Wright back and Let Me no how you are for Doen Whether you will Send Sum Money or no for if you do not I Must throw her on this town emedetly for I Can do no Longer Derect for Elizabeth Langhorn to the Care of John Miller Wool Corner hamer hall Nere Roachdale

12.

LOWRY, letters 321–336

N.B. Although it is unclear what relationship Lowry has to the children in his charge who are the subject of his letters, it appears that he has entered into a long-term arrangement with the township of Kirkby Lonsdale to take guardianship of them in return for maintenance payments (he refers to it as their 'pension'). It may be that they are the illegitimate children of his wife, or perhaps she was widowed before she married him. Alternatively, they could be the orphaned children of his own son or daughter.

321 Rob[er]t Cragg in Kendal to [Stephen] Garnett in Kirkby Lonsdale, 2 March 1822 (WPR/19/7/6/15/5)

Mr. Garnett Kendal March 2nd 1822

Ser

I was requested by Wm Lawrey to inform you that he has god a Violent inflamation in his Leg, and ~~he~~ is not able to suport his famaley he request that you will relieve him, as they are in the Greatest nesesaty he has a Child very Badley and not likely to get better,

I am Sir Your's Truly
Robt. Cragg
Surgeon

Circumtext: *In different hand [SG]:* Granted $^{£}$1.15^{s}.0^{d}

322 W[illia]m Lowry in Clitheroe to Stephen Garn[e]tt in Kirkby Lonsdale, 11 December 1822 (WPR/19/7/6/15/43)

Mr Stephen Garnitt
Sir) As to what we talked off when I left Ky. Lonsdale the month will ^be^ up this Day and if you will Kindness to send with the Bearer, (Fawcett) it would much Oblige me As the weather has been Extremly Bad since I cane

and by so doing I will ever
Remain

Yours Ob^{t}.
Clithero W^{m}. Lowry
Decr. 11 – 1822

NB Direct for
Mr Strickland Grocer Clithero

323 William Lowry in Clitheroe to the Parish of Kirkby Lonsdale, 19 March 1823 (WPR/19/7/6/16/20)

Sir) As you have sent me word Respecting the pension you have allowed my wife that you will take something of –

I now Sir humbly thank you and the Gentlemen of Ky, Lonsdale for every favour I have had But at the same time I never could think myself so much under Obligation for to Mentain and Cloth three Children for one shilling & Eight pence a week each –and I dont Mean to take any less with them untill such like time as they can Do something for themselfs for my own part I never wanted one shilling of the publicks mony of the Township of Kirky Lonsdale for my own use in no Respect whatever

Sir if you or any of the Gentlemen thinks proper and can keep them for any less you are at your Pleasure to take ~~them~~ them any time

I Cannot hear Sir pretend to state in this small Epistle the Cost of Nesseseareys of Clothing and other things out of the money I have Rec^{d}. to keep them from the Clemency of the season

But I know very well I am out of pocked ~~wt~~ By them as yet –

I have done my Duty so far as I thought without one word ever Before of dissatisfaction and as I was willing to bear little Burden I Cannot thinking of Bearing to much, ~~as yet~~ when I Look Back to Such a winter as I have had in a strange Place

I doubt Sir I have Trespassd upon your Goodness in ^time^, writing so much on the subject for which I would be Extremly sorry

But Excuse for this time
and I will always have the
Pleauser when ever Required
to be Truly Sir
Yours most
Clithero Ob^{t}. Hum^{ble} Servt.
March 19 1823 William Lowry

Notes: *From* 'Yours most Ob^{t}...' *onwards, the handwriting is different to that of the rest of the letter*

324 W[illia]m Lowry in Blackburn to the Parish of Kirkby Lonsdale, 3 December 1823 (WPR/19/7/6/16/55)

Blackburn Dec. 3^{d} 1823

Sir

I would have brought the Boy Charles Marsden home on Sunday but for the want of money he went on Tuesday the 14 of Novr. and his Expences will be nine shilling per week Boarding & two shilling ^a week^ for Doctoring for as many weeks as any person stops he cost me one pound two for him and taking him thear

~~Its~~ So it is not in my power to loose him from thear without your kind & Benevolent assistance on the Occasion

The amount of Expences from the time aforsaid up to the 14 of Ins^{t}. will £2.9.6 Besides the $^{£}$1.2^{s} it has cost me and the further Expence of Bringing him home he will be under the Necessity of stoping till I hear further from you

I am Truly yours &c.

NB If by post Wm Lowry
Direct to W Lowry
No8 Syke Street Blackburn

[*Overleaf*] The month will be up this Date the 3 but, cannot think of taking what you said Sir in your former letter Since this has happened to Charles

I am
W Lowry

Circumtext: *In margin, in different hand [SG]:* Granted $^{£}$3.0^{s}.0^{d}

325 W[illiam] Lowry in Blackburn to the Parish of Kirkby Lonsdale, 12 May 1824 (WPR/19/7/6/17/23)

1824
Blackburn May 12

Sir)

You have the goodness to send the Children pensions money ~~avis~~ with William Fawcett or by post and the arears of last account as I was paid short with £1-4- for seven weeks and from the 3 of December till the 28 Jan^{y}, Recd ~~£4-4~~ £1-12, making a Balance of Nineteen shilling from the 3^{d} Decr till the 17 of March and now 8 weeks due this Day will be two pound

I could wish you would send me the according to what was agreed once a month for I cannot want it any longer the Boy will always have Lame hand as he never can move his fingers
I hope will send the money immedatly as I am in want of it
NB if by post I am yours most
No.8 Syke Street Respectfully
W Lowry

Sir
I dont mean to be put off any longer for the Children ~~If~~ If ^not^ considered
Immedatly I must be under the Needcesty of appling to the Township of Blackburn for the Recovery thereof as they ^are^ so opprisive upon me for the Nessecary of Life and Clothing
I am &c. WL

326 William Lowry in Blackburn to [Stephen] Garnett in Kirkby Lonsdale, 10 November 1824 (WPR/19/7/6/17/41)

Blackburn Novr. 10 1824

Mr Garnett Sir
I would be much oblige to you to send the Children Money by the Bearer or by post Immedeately as I am in want of it Now – I always Expected it coming before this time Sir you will find the 4 of Augt till the present date to be Fourteen weeks – which will be £2.2s – and by so doing I will ever Remain
Your Humble Sert
William Lowry

NB if by post
No 8 Sike Street

327 William Lowry in Blackburn to [Stephen] Garnett in Kirkby Lonsdale, 22 February 1826 (WPR/19/7/6/19/8)

Mr Garnett Blackburn Feby 22d 1826
Sir)
I am under the painfull Needcesty of writing to acquaint you that you must Inform the Gentlemen of the vestry at the first meeting they must take it into their Consideration for further Relief to the Children for they are

in a state of Starvation for want of Employment for their is no work to be had for None of us which I am sorry to say and not a shilling to Earned by none I need hardly enter into any Detail of the present state of the Country to which all of you already knows For Tounge can hardly express in the Limits of this Epistle the famine and Distruction of the pressure of the times that has Befallen upon all the working Class of people

I hope Sir for any answer as soon as posable for to Relive the mind and any further Information will always be thankfully

Recived and answered by your

Humble Servant

William Lowry

Circumtext: *In different hand [SG]:* Granted 1s/ P week

328 William Lowry in Blackburn to [Stephen] Garnett in Kirkby Lonsdale, 7 February 1827 (WPR/19/7/6/20/32)

Mr Garnett Blackburn Feby 7 1827

Sir I am under the needcesty of Troubling you with a Letter by post as William Fawcett so Seldom comes to Kirby and Never see's you if you would have the Kindness to request Mr Fawcett to pay the Childrens pensions when I am in want of it I would be Much Oblige to you for the Great Destress that always pervails in this Country is Shocking to the feelings of human Nature & like to be no Better all out of Employment Day after day & week after week I dont know what will be the Consequence but has a Gloomey appearance at present I will Sir take as a favour if you will ~~be~~ send the Money by the post or by Wm Fawcett Next week You will find I was paid up to the 29 of Novr How it is with Wm Fawcett I cannot tell but you will know Sir

and by Doing you will much

Oblige your H^{ble} Sr^{t}

William Lowry

Before I close I think it my Duty to Inform you, They are Making the Country pay 1^{s} 3^{d} in the pound for the power Loom's that was Broken in the late Riot of April Last upon a Day's Notice otherwise a cart will come to the Door Carry away the Goods for the Recovery thereof &c.

The above Collections is taken from the Rate Book the poor Rate is 2^{s} in the pound

329 William Lowry in Blackburn to [Stephen] Garnett in Kirkby Lonsdale, 7 May 1827 (WPR/19/7/6/20/14)

Blackburn May 7 1827

Mr Garnett Sir

I am Sorry to Trouble you with a Letter but the 12 of this month is fast Aproching and Landlords has no money for their Rents, William Fawcett is not been Regular in coming this while back, you have paid me up to the 28 of March which I am Oblige to you for your kindness Sir) I think proper to mention if you Could Appiont a person to pay me hear it would save every letter Cost 1^{s}/4^{d} £1 and with 2£, 2^{s} which makes it heavey, Thear has a Great many familys gone from this Town to America within this 2 months past and more a going nothing but Emegration is talked off hear for all that can get away

In the Bills of Mortalitey of Deaths thear has above one Hundred Children Died in the Workhouse in Six weeks past many familys as lost all thear Children 4 and 5 in number some Calls it the Black fever

I hope you will Excuse my freedom in writing the above

and for which I will ever Remain

Yours Humble Sr^{t} William Lowry

Direct as before No.4 Old Square

If I should Change my situation
in any Respect I would let you know Sir

330 William Lowry in Blackburn to Stephen Garnett in Kirkby Lonsdale, 25 June 1827 (WPR/19/7/6/20/6)

Blackburn June 25 1827

Mr Stephen Garnett

Sir If you would please to send the Childrens pension by the post, I would be much oblige to you Sir,

I Recevied from Mr. Fawcett £1.^{s}.^{d} which would pay me from the 30th March till the 2^{d} of May Which I hope Sir you will find Correct for any thing as I know

I will ever
Remain your Truly
Hu^{bl} S^{t}
William Lowry

N.B. ^Sir)^ I would be sorry to offend ^you^ of the Trouble and Expence of paying postage of Letters For which I will pay them so from hear and back again – As Mr Fawcett has ~~been~~ not been regular of coming this while Back
to Kirkby Lonsdale

331 William Lowry in Blackburn to [Stephen] Garnett in Kirkby Lonsdale, 13 December 1827 (WPR/19/7/6/20/40)

Blackburn Decr 13 1827

Mr Garnett
Sir
I would be much oblige to you send the Children Pension ^by Return of post^ I am Sorry to Inform you Sir that my wife still continues so Poorly and has lost the use of her Limbs at Present ^and^ her Complaint is like to Return on her again (the Doctors Calls it the Purples or Spotted fever) – I will assure you Sir our house has been in Great Distress since I Last saw you and they threating if I come Troublesome hear to Remove me to you as I cannot swear to my place as being born in Scotland and never Gaining any Settlement – but Sir I hope you will give your Opinion in this Case as any person may feel for my present situation at this time and in this season of the year if any thing can be done Rather than my house Broke up as my wife is not able to be moved from her Bed

and by doing you will much Oblige
your H^ble S^t
William Lowry

332 William Lowry in Blackburn to [Stephen] Garnett in Kirkby Lonsdale, 19 February 1828 (WPR/19/7/6/21/5)

Mr Garnett Blackburn feby 19 1828

Sir I am highly Oblige to you for your Opinion on the subject in Last Letter which Satisfied me on that purpose but thank God I hope I will be able to come Round again although my wife still Continues in a helpless state she can only go a cross the floor by the assistance of Crotches and we have Lost our youngest Child Died about a three weeks since

you will have the goodness Sir to send the Children pension you thought of a Reduction in your Last Sir But I hope you will Consider Different when you look into our situation at this time for the Children is in want of Clothing and I will Depend upon your Great felling and Kind Generosty upon which Sir I have always found you to be a friend

I am Truly you Obdent Serv[t]

William Lowry

Circumtext: *In different hand [SG]:* This Payment in full then to be reduced to 2[s]/

333 William Lowry in Blackburn to the Parish of Kirkby Lonsdale, 3 June 1829 (WPR/19/7/6/22/1)

Blackburn June 3[d] 1829

Sir)

I am told by Mr Parker the Courier that the Gentlemen of the township of Kirkby Lonsdale Iintends Reducing the Children pension Admiting of the Great Goodness they have Behaved to them Still I am afraid that the Boy will be Pauper upon your Respective Township

I have done all in my power to get him a Trade ~~a~~ he was taken from the Cotton Mill about 12 months Since on account of bad health he could only serve thear as Job Lad for a Small wage after that I got Situation at Mr Parkinson Tallow Chandler he promised me to take him of he answerd after he had about 5 month of Trial he sent him home and now he is at home Doing very Little which I am Sorry to think he will never be able to work for his Living for he can be no Trade, not even a Miller Mr Clarke Refused him on that account I have done every thing its well known in my power, and Still for more is Required and I hope you will Consider not to take any of thear pension of as I Consider very Little to high price of provision and all other of necessary of Clothing Besides I have penny every week to pay for school wages and they are ~~only~~ getting only small wages from the factory

So I will Leave the Case to your
Kind and feelling Consideratin
and Remain your humble
Serv[t]
William Lowry

Circumtext: *In different hand [SG]*: Alowed 1s/ P week

334 William Lowry in Blackburn to the Parish of Kirkby Lonsdale, 5 November 1831 (WPR/19/7/6/24/48)

Blackburn No^{v} 5 1831

Gentlemen

I Return you my most sincere thanks for the kindness you have always shown to the Fatherless Child<re>n [*page torn*] and Great has been the support they have Receved from your Respective Township with every attention of Pleasure of your Regular Punctleness altho I must observe much has been paid still if you Could Consider the Charge that I have you would Continue the small pension on for the Boy He is now Arrived to 18 years of age he is not and I am sorry to say never will be able to Work for his Liven to the full Amount of a another man on account of his Hand he only does Job work for a Child wage and I can do no Better with him on that account (and he is fine sturdy Boy and always willing to do his Best the Gentlemen I hope further Consider his Cercumstance and allow him the small pension he has had from you

An answer from your Respective Meeting will Greatly oblige your Humble Sr^{t}

NB By return of post William Lowry

Direct No4 Old Square

335 William Lowry in Blackburn to the Parish of Kirkby Lonsdale, 3 December [18]31 (WPR/19/7/6/24/40)

Blackburn Decr 3^{d}. 31

Sir In my last I did not state to you The Boy wages I told you his Earning was unregular his work is done by piece he makes when he has full time from 4^{s}/6 to 4^{s}/8^{d} and as low as 3^{s}/4^{d} in full time But half time about 2/6

and they say Going to stop for a while altogether if Trade does not mend soon not been a piece sold in Manchester these 3 weeks Back Mr Rodgers factory is stoped on that account and Wensley fold is about stoping too. The Manufactors of this town Goes to Manchester every Tuesday and if they have Bad Market they do Grinded from the face of the Worke People the next day or week – if the Boy had been capeable he ought to Bring in 8^{s} or 10^{s} a week But I dout but he will have to trouble further after a than I Require of you now for I could not keep him in Meat and Clothes if I had not the assistance of the other Children

your answer
will much oblige
William Lowry

Circumtext: *In different hand [SG]:* Continue the 1^{s}/ a week through the Winter

336 William Lowry in Blackburn to the Parish of Kirkby Lonsdale, 27 June [18]32 (WPR/19/7/6/25/34)

Blackburn June 27th 32

Sir I will be much oblige to you to send the pension as it is Due this day –
I thought once of writing sooner as the youngest Girl Betty is only Delicate of her Health and like to be and often of her employ^ment^ and as I stated to you once in a former Letter the Boy's wages is Still the same very Low that I hope you will ~~need so~~ have the goodness to send it with the Bearer

I Remain your Truly &c
William Lowry

Thear is now four Candidates in the field to Represent this Newly made ~~Boro~~ Borough Mr Fielding a Gentleman of this Neighbourhood and one that has given much Employment to many hundreds of hands is one and a Mr Bowring of London ~~and~~ a man I know nothing of But by his Political Conduct and Mr Hindle a Magestrate of Woodfold Park whear H. Sudell Esq. formerly Resided
and Mr William Turner of Shrigley Hall in Cheshire But Carreys on Extensive print ~~worl~~ work in this place the other the Squbs that is going from Day to Day The walls is plasterd with them is astonishing the various Reports about all thear Characters and of all thear Tyranny not one of them is *[Colieyed]* together every one upon his own Bottom

Excuse me W Lowry

Circumtext: *In margin:* This Borough has 700 voters 656 full votes the Rest Widow Women

13.

MOORE, letters 337–358

337 W[illia]m Worthington in Ribbleton to the Parish of Kirkby Lonsdale, 7 October 1816 (WPR/19/7/6/9/11)

Dear Sir)

Their is Edward Moor a poor person belonging to your Town his famally is in grate want and distress In so much that they have been Obligd to apply to me For relief diferant times and if you Cannot provide Something to their better support I shall be obligd to remove Them to your Town they have four small Childern and Herself Just at down leying and no work to be got ~~this~~ For her this two months back still they think with a little Support wile she gets up again they Can Come round He still works at the Old Shop at high Brockhall But the famally lives in the Township of Ribbleton I hope you will aquant the heads of your Town and Consider something for them by the return of post –

By so doing you will Oblige yours &c Wm Worthington

Overseer

Ribbleton 7th Octr 1816

NB Plais to Derect to me at the old dog, Preston

Circumtext: *In different hand [SG]:* Granted out of Donation Money 10^{s}/

338 Will[ia]m Worthington in Ribbleton to the Parish of Kirkby Lonsdale, 25 November 1816 (WPR/19/7/6/9/17)

Sir)

I receivd yours on the 10th Instant in Behalf of Edward Moor I was obligd to Relive him last night his wages is redust To six shilling a week if you do not instantly Allow him 4^{s} a week he will be removd to your Town hes applied to me to publish a Sale of his Goods to pay his debts that will take place In the Corse of a week therefore you may expect Them the later end of next week except you Comply with the above and it must be By return of post I remain yours

Willm Worthington

Ribbleton Novr 25th 1816 Overseer

Plase to derect as before

Circumtext: *In different hand [SG]:* Granted 3s/ P week

339 W[illia]m Worthington in Ribbleton to the Overseer of the Poor of Kirkby Lonsdale, 23 February 1817 (WPR/19/7/6/10/9)

Overseer of the Poor of Kby Lonsdale
To the Overseer of Ribbleton

Sir) As it is our annual Meeting on thursday next you will be obligd to Settle upon or befor that day Then we will not trouble you any morer untill the Expiration of six months Edward Moor wife got Her bed the same week you sent the last time Though good friends and neighbours she is got well up Again and the Child died soon after I have relivd Them up to the 26 Instant wich will be 12 times that Will be £1.16 – you may send £2.0.0 if you Plais I request your early remittance will much Oblige yours obedient servant Wm Worthington

PS) if you want mee to make any Alteration with them you may Let Mee know at the same time
Overseer
Ribbleton
Plais to Derect to Mee Old dog Preston 23 Feby 1817

340 Ja[me]s Parkinson in Brockholes to the Parish of Kirkby Lonsdale, 15 August 1817 (WPR/19/7/6/10/33)

Brockholes august 15th 1817

Sir/ If you Will be so kind as to Send Edwards Moors Wikley Pay from the 14th of last May to the 13th of august which will be $^{£}$2-1^{s}-0^{d} and Direct to Jas Parkinson Brockholes To be left at the old Dog Preston Pleas to Send By return of Poast and you Will Much oblige yours, ~~Fro~~

Jas Parkinson Edwards Master

341 James Parkinson in Brockholes to St[e]phen Garnett in Kirkby Lonsdale, 3 July 1818 (WPR/19/7/6/11/19)

Brockholes July 3th 1818

Mr Stiphen Garnett

Sir/ Pleas to send Edward Moors Pension due from 31th of december last Derict to ould dog Church Street Preston and youl Oblige yours &c
James Parkinson

342 Ja[me]s Parkinson in Brockholes to [Stephen] Garnett in Kirkby Lonsdale, 29 December 1818 (WPR/19/7/6/11/39)

Brockholes December 29th 1818

Mr Garnett
Sir/ Pleas to send Edward Moors Pention July 1 is the first Payment and 2^{s} in my hand I hope you find right Pleas to derict to Be left at the ould dog Preston and youl ~~mu~~ much Oblige yours Respectfuly
Jas Parkinson

343 James Parkinson in Brockholes to Stephen Garnett in Kirkby Lonsdale, 8 October 1819 (WPR/19/7/6/12/23)

Brockholes October 8th 1819
Mr Stephen Garnett

Sir,
Be so Cind as to Send Edward Moors Pension due from the 6th of Jenury last as I am in want of Cash Edward has <Been> [*obscured by wax seal*] Sick ^and^ of his work 8 weeks since I rote Last But is Got to work again Pleas to send to the ould dog Church Street Preston
I am yours Respectfully
James Parkinson

Circumtext: *In different hand [SG]:* Octr. 29th Remitted 7-0-0 which pays Edward Moor for the 1st Decr. 1819

344 Ja[me]s Parkinson in Brockholes to St[e]phen Garnett in Kirkby Lonsdale, 3 November 1820 (WPR/19/7/6/13/31)

Brockholes November 3th 1820

Mr Stiphen Garnett
Sir)
If you will be so kind as to send Edward Moors Pension due from the 1th of last December be so Cind to Derict it to be left at the ould dog Preston youl Much oblige yours Respettfully
Jas Parkinson

345 Ja[me]s Parkinson in Brockholes to St[e]phen Garnett in Kirkby Lonsdale, 22 November 1820 (WPR/19/7/6/13/34)

Brockhole November 22th 1820

Mr Stiphen Garnett

Sir)

yours I receivd on the 18th with Moors Pension $^{£}$7.10^{s}.0^{d} and as to his wages he has 7^{s}.6^{d} Per week and vitels as to his Famely he has 5 Children the ouldest 14 years the yongest about 3 years ould he has 2 Pair of looms going his Second Son is lame of his knee If you make any ~~alterateon~~ ~~alteriet~~ Defirance Be so Cind as to let me know By Return of Post and youl much oblige

Yours Jas Parkinson

346 Ja[me]s Parkinson in Brockholes to St[e]phen Garnett in Kirkby Lonsdale, 8 December 1820 (WPR/19/7/6/13/39)

Brockholes Dec 8th 1820

Mr Stiphen Garnett

Sir

What I laid down for Edward Moor since you send is 6 shilings before I got your letter Moor returns you many thanks for your kindness to him and will Strive to do if you will have the goodness to send him a little Charity money now and then as is 2 son is lame and if you do to send it to the ould place yours Obdint

Servant

Jas Parkinson

Overseer

347 Ja[me]s Parkinson in Brockholes to the Overseer of Kirkby Lonsdale, 30 December 1821 (WPR/19/7/6/14/48)

Brockholes Dec 30th 1821

To the Overseer of Kirby Lonsdale

Sir

Edward Moor is Brought to low Sercumstanses on account of bad health with is Wife and Children is Son has still a Bad knee and Wm Cross Esq will Pleas the Dockter but he must be borded at Preston and Moor is not able without helps and I have Done what I shall do with^out^ some security is wife is il doing and if is Son Must Come the whole Famaly will Come together yours Respectfully

Jas Parkinson overseer

Circumtext: *In different hand [SG]:* Agreed for his son to come & the Work House

348 John Gorton of Farington Hall, near Preston, to the Parish of Kirkby Lonsdale, 28 January 1822 (WPR/19/7/6/15/2)

Farington Hall 28th Jany 1822

Sir,

In reply to yours of the 7th the said Edwd. Moore has had the best Medical advise in this neighbourhood respecting his Sons disease and they seem all to agree that there is no chance for his recovery, and in consequence he is not agreeable for him to come to your place without the rest of the Family who are at this time in a state of starvation both food and raiment and has in a great measure been supported by the benevolent good Neighbours during there late Sickness which has not yet terminated as his Wife is at this time almost in a helpless state He therefore humbly begs that you would be something towards Clothing his naked Family and a little present and occasional relief <a>s [*page torn*] his necessities may call, and he will do all that his in his power to keep from you as much as possible, I think it much advisable for you to grant him his request, if you do not, he will be under the painful Obligation of bringing his Family to you which ~~you~~ will be very expensive to the Parish, he has already given his Master Notice that he will leave him in the course of a fortnight unless he can find some means of sustenance and he his Master seems to be very sorry at parting with a faithful and good servant.

Have the goodness to Write as soon as convenient and direct to John Gorton Farington Hall near Preston to be left at the Old Dog in Preston Lancashire

If you do ^not^ consider to do something for him you ^need^ not to Write as it will be only putting him to the expence of Postage

Circumtext: *In different hand [SG]:* Granted £1.0s.0d and the same for the boy as he would Cost in the Workhouse

349 John Gorton in Farington Hall, near Preston to the Parish of Kirkby Lonsdale, 4 April 182[2] (WPR/19/7/6/15/6)

Farington Hall 4th Apl. 182<2> [*edge of page frayed*]

Sir,

Yours of the 5th Feby came safe to hand with the £1 note inclosed, which my neighbour E. Moor gladly received, and has applyed it to useful and necessary purposes such as Clothing his Son &c who remains in the same State of health only the Doctor says that he has a greater waste, and has further to inform you that the said E Moor Wife was this day ^been^ deliverd of a dead Child and was three days previous to her delivery so indisposed as to require the assistance of a Doctor, which as involved him into a state of great want, he therefore humbly begs that you will take into consideration his present circumstance, and Write as speedily as convenient and say what your House stands you in Per head per week so that by application to the Overseer of Preston he may receive the Money by your authorizing him to Pay it –

Which will greatly Favour your Most Obet Humble Servt

John Gorton

Direct as before to J Gorton Farington Hall N^{r}. Preston to be left at Preston Post Office

350 John Gorton in Farington Hall to the Parish of Kirkby Lonsdale, 6 May 1822 (WPR/19/7/6/15/9)

Farington Hall 6th May 1822

Sir,

I am much surprised that you have made no reply to mine of the 4th Apl acknowlidging the receipt of the £1 Note, if you doubt the truth of my assertion respecting the distressed state of Moor's Family you had better send a person over to see them he tells me that he is owing £2 for Rent and other debts which is out of his power to discharge, and that his Wife is lying Sick and cannot be removed and therefore unless you consider to do something for him, he will be under the necessity of applying to the Parish Overseer for relief, as he cannot do any longer without some help, he therefore desires that you would Write by return of Post and consider to do something for him

Which will greatly ^Oblige^ yrs &c John Gorton

PS direct as before

351 John Gorton in Farington Hall, near Preston to the Parish of Kirkby Lonsdale, 28 October 1822 (WPR/19/7/6/15/33)

Farington Hall 28th Octr 1822

Dear Sir,

Yours of the 10th May with the two pound inclosed came safe to hand which was gratefully received by my neighbour E Moore, and with respect to the State of his Sons health, he is no better, his wound having a great waste of matter &c and hopes that you will have the goodness to transmit to me his weekly pay as early as convenient

Which will much oblige yrs. &c.

John Gorton

PS Direct to Farington Hall Farm
near Preston

352 J[ohn] Gorton in Brockholes to the Parish of Kirkby Lonsdale, 8 May 1823 (WPR/19/7/6/16/30)

Brockholes 8th May 1823

Dear Sir,

Yours with three Pounds inclosed arrived safe, and has to request you to transmit me E Moore sons weekly pay as early as possible. he remains in his usual state of health, and his Mother has laboured under a long and severe indisposition which will in all probability terminate in a decline, which causes the said E Moore to have a distressed House I do assure you

I am your Most Obedt Servt

Jno Gorton

Direct to Brockholes Moor
Near Preston

353 Will[ia]m Worthington in Ribbleton to the Parish of Kirkby Lonsdale, 10 November [18]23 (WPR/19/7/6/16/52)

Ribbleton 10th Novr 23

Sir)

As Mr John Gorton have *[flit]* Edward Moor aplide to relive him Wich I have done ever since the 4th of June As the money is wanted I expect you will remit it by return of post and direct it to mee at Peter Warden's, Ginbo entry Preston Wich I shall bee reddy to repeat again By so doing you will Oblig Yours &C

Willm Worthington

NB Edward Moors wife is Verry likely to die And is son remanes verry bad Upon the walle the are in a miserable ^state^

354 W[illiam] Worthington in Ribbleton to [Stephen] Garnett in Kirkby Lonsdale, 6 May 1824 (WPR/19/7/6/17/20)

Ribbleton May 6th 1824

Mr Garnett

Sir I recevd yours inclosed £2.10.0 Wich was right up to the 23 of Novr 1823 I extect you will remit the same as I have Given him some in advance plais to send By retirne and derect to Peter Wardens Ginbo Entry By so doing youl Oblige

Yours &c. W Worthington

NB Edward Moors wife is not Expected To see this month over she is verry bad and his son remanes verry lame

355 Tho[ma]s Edge in Ribbleton to the Parish of Kirkby Lonsdale, 4 June 1824 (WPR/19/7/6/17/30)

Ribbelton June the 4th 1824

Sir

Edward Moore is in arrears for rent £2.10^{s}.6^{d} and a great deal more for different articles and if his rent is not paid I shall put in for the whole sum he owes me If you agree to pay me the rent I shall forgive him the rest If not I shall take what there is and you may expect that they will be removed to there own parish very soon I should wish you to write as soon as possible and let me know what you want to do
so no more from yours &.

Thos Edge

Please to direct for Thos Edge to be at John Fowlers Old Cock Church Street Preston Lancashire

356 Edward and Mary Moore in Rib[b]leton to [Stephen] Garnett in Kirkby Lonsdale, 4 April 1825 (WPR/19/7/6/18/36)

Ribleton Ap<ril>l [*page torn*] the 4th 1825

Mr Garnett

We are sorry to Trouble you on this subject but our Preasant Necessitty Causes us to doo it My wife is still as helpless as a Child she Cannot neither Get to bed nor up without help nor walke over the floor neither Can she doo any thing after the family So you May Reasonabl think we are in a poore State we are Run three pounds in dept ~~into~~ to George Abbot and we beg and desire as you will Send us some Money as Soon as posable or I dont know what will become of us Georg Abbot begs that you will as he knows its imposable for us to Pay it if it Please the Lord My wife Gits her Health I hope we shall not be Troublsom but while things are so bad on our sides we Cannot Help it if you will be so Good to a Low us what you a Low people weekly we shall take it as a Great Faviour so no more at present from yours

Edward Mary Moore

Please to send it by the Garrison derected to us to be Left at Peter Wardens

Jinbo Entry

357 Isabella Wilkinson in Rib[b]leton to the Parish of Kirkby Lonsdale, 21 January 1826 (WPR/19/7/6/19/2)

Ribleton Jenurey the 21 1826

Gentlemen

I wish to inform you that Edward Moore and his wife and two Children are all down in a voilent faviour and thro that your Certain they Must be in a sad Condition therefore they wished Me to send a few Lines to inform you of it and they beg youl send ~~ge~~ them speedy Releife for its not posable they Can doo without your assistance I am a nighbour to them and Can see dayley there distriss so you Must not fail to send some Money derectly as its hard they should be Lost for want of something to Get them up a Gain and Send it to Peter Wardens in the Ginbo Entry and as soon as you Can after you Recive this for they are in Great distress yours Isabella Wilkinson

X the mark of Edward Moore

358 Edward Mo[o]re in Preston to the Parish of Kirkby Lonsdale, 2 February 1826 (WPR/19/7/6/19/3)

Preston Feburay the 2d = 1826

Sir

We Recivd your Letter and the Check for £1 and Return you our Sincere thanks For it as we was very badly of at that time and at Presant I have to inform you that My oldest son nineteen years is dead he departed this Life this morning and its not posable That we Can Get him interd without your asistance so we beg youl delay no time in sending us as Much as will Bury him as we are orderd to Bury him as Soon as we Posably Can the Faviour Rages so bad in this Place I am Giting better and so is the Rest of My family that is Living I hope it will be Long before we shall need to trouble you a Gain and now we Cannot help it I hope as things has happened So you will not fail Sending with Speed and Derect to Me to be left at William Wardins Jinbo Entry I am yours

Edward More

14.

NELSON, letters 359–448

N.B. The relationship between John and Joseph Nelson and their families is complex. John Nelson is Joseph Nelson's son, and is married to Ruth. After John's death, Ruth is also known as Widow Nelson Junr. Grace Nelson is Joseph Nelson's wife, later widow, also known as Widow Nelson Senr. The complexity is compounded by the fact that Jeremiah Haley, Overseer, advocates on behalf of John and Ruth, whereas John Haley advocates on behalf of Joseph and Grace. The exact relationship between John and Jeremiah Haley is unknown, but they are clearly acquainted.

359 John Jenkinson of Clayton to the Overseer of Kirkby Lonsdale, 18 July 1809 (WPR/19/7/6/2/20)

The Overseer of Poor Kerby lonsdale Dr.					
to Overseer of Clayton by pay to			£	s	d
Joseph Nelson 3rd November 1807				7	
18th		Do.		3	
26	Do.			3	
1st December 1807				3	
7		Do.		3	
19		Do.		3	
23		Do.		3	
27		Do.		3	
Jany. 2nd 1808				3	
7	Do.			3	
14	Do.			3	
21	Do.			3	
28	Do.			3	
Feby 4				5	
			£2	8	
		Recd in part	1		
		dew	£1	8	

Sir)

I am threatend with a summons for Reelif by Jo Nelson if I am compel'd to relive shal at the same tim take out remuval orders as I think I am badly ewused by you

Clayton 18th July 1809 John Jenkinson

Circumtext: *Overleaf:*

Answer to the Other Side August 11th 1809

Sir)

Yours I Recd. and by it I observe what as you Have allowed Joseph Nelson appears like a weekly pension on Conversing with the late Overseer he Informes me he never authorised you to Give him a pension we have paid his House Rent Regularly but not doughting what ~~was~~ as you have advanced him was done from motives of Humanity and I Concive it a very Necessary thing for one Overseer to place a sort of discretionary pour or Confidence in another and on that account I wish you to Relive Joseph Nelson as in your Judgement seems most proper not doughting but that you will do the same as if you was doing for your own Township I would wish you to keep of a weekly pension if possible –

Inclosed you have a one pound note which I hope you will Recive safe and will Remit as you ~~as you~~ wish

I am Sir your Obdt Servt
Stephn Garnett Overseer

Address of recipient: Overseer of Poor Kirkby lonsdale

360 John Jenkinson in Clayton to the Parish of Kirkby Lonsdale, 14 August 1809 (WPR/19/7/6/2/24)

Clayton 14th August 1809

Sir)

I receivd youers with a one pound noat and am at a los how to account for youer conduct it is strange to me to ^have^ a count with you since 1807 ^and in^ August 1809 onley pay part would it not have loked better to have paid som thing over postig of youer Letter cost 1/4½ and 8/ left on – it is a pleasuer to me to asist an Overseer but I expect to be reimbust with out all this truble

Your Hble Servt
John Jenkinson

PS I have had Jo Nelson Wife this morning very big with child but have given her nothing til i have settled with they'l be a great expence whether you belive it or not

Circumtext: *Address of recipient:* Overseer of Poor Kirkby Lonsdale
Postmarked: Bradford 216

361 Joseph Priestley in Clayton Heights to the Parish of Kirkby Lonsdale, 7 [***] 1809 (WPR/19/7/6/2/51)

Clayton heights [*****] [*page torn*] th 7 1809

Sir
Your letter I Rec<eived> [*page torn*] In due time it Inclosed one pound note wich I placed to Jo nelson acount towards his Rent I have taken all the pains possobel to get him to raise somthing himself but all to no porpos he not Abel to pay one shilling I should have made destress before this time with out troubel you Again but his sittuation his so pittey full it Enough to break the hardest heart to see them – hes between 60 and 70 years of age and very poorly he one small child and wife very big Again

NB Therefore I desire you to Remit mee one pound if you pleas if not there no chance but they must be brought with order
your most obedn servant
Joseph priestly

Notes: *Although the month of writing is missing from this letter, its place in the sequence strongly suggests that it was written between letters 360 and 362.*

362 Joseph Priestley in Clayton Heights to the Parish of Kirkby Lonsdale, 5 May 1810 (WPR/19/7/6/3/10)

Clayton heights May ^{t}h 5 1810

Sir
I have one more favour to beg of you, that <you> [*page torn*] Remitt mee two pounds for Josph Nelson Rent Due may day 1810
Pleas to Remitt Immedelly for there no way but you to pay me thay must come to Kerbey londale your obd servant
Joseph Priestley

363 John Jenkinson in Clayton to the Parish of Kirkby Lonsdale, 14 November 1810 (WPR/19/7/6/3/30)

Clayton 14th Novmb^{r} 1810

Sir

The Overseer of Kirby Lonsdale to the Overseer of Clayton by pay to Joseph Nelson from 10 April to 29 Octob^{r} 1/ pr Week 1 6 0

from Do. to 26th Novb^{r} 4 Weeks at 2/ pw 8

1 14 0

NB I think they canot Dow with les then 3 Shilings per Week this Winter the old Man is nearly past Work hath a young Wife that hath little mainegment in hir and 2 small Children pleas to send me som money emeadetly as I am very poor

youer Hlb Ser^{t}
John Jenkinson Overseer

364 Joseph Priestley in Clayton Heights to the Overseer of Kirkby Lonsdale, 10 April 1811 (WPR/19/7/6/4/10)

Clayton Heights Apiril th 10 1811

Sir
I have one favour more to beg of you that is to Remit mee Joseph Nelson Rent wich is two pound if you pleas
Pleas to ~~Rite~~ write between and may day if it Agreabel
NB There no way to be done but you to pay or them to be brought to your township

Your Obedet
Joseph Priestley

Circumtext: *Address of recipient:* For Overseer poor Kirkby Lonsdale Westmorland *Postmarked*: Bradford

365 Mary Bentley in Paradice to the Parish of Kirkby Lonsdale, 9 June 1811 (WPR/19/7/6/4/4)

Paradice Jun 9 1811

Sir

This is to inform you that John Nellson who belongs to you is destressed for relief for him self and Family non of them has any work but him self and the house Rent must be paid there is near a years Rent due and if it is not paid soon the owner will sell them up his Wife has had one Child since he troubled you and will soon have a nother the Rent must be paid the 17st or the furniter will be sould therefore be so good as send them Monie to discharge the Rent and as much more as you pleas they are real objects of Charity the Rent is $^{£}$1 13^{s} pleas to derect for him to

Mary Bentley
Paradice near
Bradford
Yorkshire

Mary Bentley

Cirumtext: *In different hand [SG]:* Rec^{d} this on 15th June 1811

366 John Jenkinson in Clayton to the Parish of Kirkby Lonsdale, 22 August 1811 (WPR/19/7/6/4/18)

Clayton 22nd Augus 1811

Sir) I sum time since sent you a noat for Money paid to Joseph
Nelson famaley 3. 0.0
to 22 July but have not recived it eat have since paid to 28th August 0.14.0
plese to send the sum of 3.14.0
the famaley canot subsist without more as work is very scase hear
you must athureise me to pay more

Your Hbb^{l} Ser^{t}
John Jenkinson Overseer

Pleas to Direct to be left at
John Nicholsons Stationer Bradford

367 Jere[miah] Haley in Horton to the Parish of Kirkby Lonsdale, 24 October 1811 (WPR/19/7/6/4/21)

Horton 24th Octb^{r} 1811

Gen^{n}./

I Rec^{d} yours covering a Guinea note for John Nellson whic<c> [*page torn*] I have Relieved them with, and I can asure you the family is in great want they are all almost naked besides haveing $^{£}$1.18^{s}.0^{d} on for Rent which I am perswarded they cannot pay, from the bad state of traid hear they cannot have constant employment and one of their Children is constant sick – if you would have the goodness to pay their Rent and alow them a little weekly untill Times mend perhaps they would get on if not I see no possability that they can but I shall be under the necessaty of bringing them to you I beg your answer by Return of post and Remain your Hbl^{e}. Servt.

Jere. Haley
Overseer

368 John Jenkinson in Clayton to Stephen Garnett in Kirkby Lonsdale, 25 November 1811 (WPR/19/7/6/4/25)

Clayton 25th Novemb^{r} 1811

Mr Stephen Garnett

Sir)

at the request of Jo Nelson I desiear you to send won pound rent dew to Joseph Priestly on Satardy last Destriess would have ben made to Day but I requested time to rite to you and the Day is fixed on Monday the 9th of Decmb^{r} nex youer emedeat answer will greatly ablige youer

Hlb Ser^{t} John Jenkinson Overseer

369 Jere[miah] Haley in Horton to the Parish of Kirkby Lonsdale, 20 March 1812 (WPR/19/7/6/5/7)

Horton 20 March 1812

Gen^{n}/.

I have Relieved John Nellson with one pound Twelve Shilling at 2^{s}/- per week for <16> [*page torn*] weeks Besides he will have Two years Rent Due at May Day, at $^{£}$1.13.0 per year his Landlord is for making Distress for the same but in consideration that I would write to you he has defered it untill I Receive your answer wheather you will pay or not I beg you will Remitt the money I have paid him and if you will not Remitt the Rent his goods will be sold and of course him and Family must be removed to you as there is no possability of him paying it nor of getting on for the future without Relief your answer by return of post will much Oblige your Hbl^{e} Servt.

Jere. Haley Overseer
of Horton n^{r}. Bradford

To the Overseers
of the Poor of Kerby Lonsdale

370 John Jenkinson in Clayton to the Parish of Kirkby Lonsdale, 1 April 1812 (WPR/19/7/6/5/9)

Sir)
pleas send Me 26 Week pay for Joseph Nelson from 14th October 1811 to 13 April 1812 at 2/ Shillings £2.12.0 and if you think proper to send the Rent up to 1st May nex half a year you will greatly Ablige youer Hlb Sert
John Jenkinson Overseer of Poor
Clayton 1st April 1812

Pleas dericte to be left at John Nicholson's Stationer Bradford

Circumtext: *Below, different hand [SG]*: Rent Granted

371 Jere[miah] Haley in Horton to the Parish of Kirkby Lonsdale, 6 May 1812 (WPR/19/7/6/5/14)

Horton 6th May 1812

Genm/.

I Sent you an amount of money paid to John Nellson about 5 weeks back Requesting a Remittance but have herd nothing from you since the Sum then due was one pound Twelve Shillings Since that time the man has been sick and is So Still I have Relieved him for the last 5 weeks with one pound which makes the whole sum I want £2.12s.02d – he has now 2 years Rent due and his Landlord is about to Sell the few things he has the Rent is £3.6s.0d –

I beg your answer by Return of post saying wheather you will Remitt or not if not if the Man is gotten so far Better I shall Remove the Family to you if not I shall put them under Suspended Orders untill he is Better –

From yours &c.
Jere: Haley Overseer

372 John Jenkinson in Clayton to the Parish of Kirkby Lonsdale, 2 October 1812 (WPR/19/7/6/5/29)

Sir)

Pease to send by return of Poast £2.2.0 money paid to Joseph Nelson on youer acount from 11th May 5th October 21 Weeks at 2/ Pr and you will greatly Oblige

Youer Hlb Servant
John Jenkinson
Clayton 2nd October 1812

373 John Jenkinson in Clayton to the Parish of Kirkby Lonsdale, 23 November 1812 (WPR/19/7/6/5/33)

Sir) Clayton 23 Novembr 1812

I som time since sent you a Bill for Money paid to Joseph Nelson which is not com to hand this morning I had Nelson Landlord for his Rent who saith he will Waite no longer pleas send som money by return of Poast to beleft at John Nicholson Statinoner Bradford I am Sir youer Hlb Se^{t}

John Jenkinson Overseer

374 Jere[miah] Haley in Horton to the Overseer of Kirkby Lonsdale, 30 December 1812 (WPR/19/7/6/5/35)

The Overseer of the Poor of Kerby lonsdale

To the Overseers of Horton D^{r}

To 42 weeks pay to the Family of Jno. Nellson

from the 12th Marh to 30th Decem^{r}. 1812 @ 2^{s}/ Per £4.4.0

Gen^{n}./ I will thank you to Remitt the above sum by Return of post – I have to Inform you that I have had Nelsons Landlord makeing application for his Rent he informs me that there is Due this Christmas $^{£}$2.11^{s}.0^{d} which he sais he will imedietly make Distress for if not paid and Nellson saies he cannot pay it –

I wished the Landlord to waite untill I wrote to you I beg therefore you will answer this soon as possable which will much Oblige yours &c

Jere. Haley Overseer

Horton 30th Decem^{r}. 1812

375 Jere[miah] Haley in Horton to Steph[e]n Garnett in Kirkby Lonsdale, 20 January 1813 (WPR/19/7/6/6/1)

Mr. Steph^{n}. Garnett Horton 20th Jany 1813

Sir/.

Yours of the 5th Ins^{t}. is come to hand I can but thank you for the contents which has given me an oppertunity of correting my errer I find your ac^{t}. Credited for $^{£}$3.0.0. in May I have looked over all the payments to Nellsons Family and find that the $^{£}$3.0.0 Remitted in May paid up to the 3^{d} June 1812 – my errer I sopose Originated in takeing the Date of the first ~~date of the~~ Acc^{t}. I sent which I see Stands in a memorandam Book the 12th March your acc^{t}.

Stands ^when corected^ there from the 3^{d}. June to the 30th Decem^{r}. 1812 30 weeks @ 2^{s}/ per $^{£}$3.0^{s}.0^{d} which I make no doubt you will find right and Remitt –

John Nellson has Three Children whose ages are as follows the Oldest 8 years the next 4, the youngest 1 ½ years old –

I Remain yours with all Due Respect
Jere. Haley
Overseer

376 John Jenkinson in Clayton to the Parish of Kirkby Lonsdale, 25 January 1813 (WPR/19/7/6/6/2)

Sir)

Youer Pauper Joseph Nelson is very bad his Wife came on Thursday last for sum adisinol relife I gave hir 2/ the next morning she came for som more and I refused to alow hir eney then she somaned me to apear ~~who~~ before a Majestrate to shew cause why I refused to Day and he hath ordred me to give eight Shillings per Week during his ilness I have thought proper to aquent you

Thear is a half year Rent dew at Martilmes last youer answear will greatly ablige Sir youer Hlb Se^{t}

John Jenkinson

PS Sum money would be verey exseptable
Clayton 25 Jany 1813

377 John Jenkinson in Clayton to Stephen Garnett in Kirkby Lonsdale, 3 February 1813 (WPR/19/7/6/6/4)

Clayton 3d Feby 1813

Mr Stephen Garnett
Sir)

I rece^{d} youers to Day and hasten to inform you concerning Jo Nelson Famaley they have two Children one 4 years and the other two a young Wife him self a bought 70 years a reant dew 1.0.0 he is ^in^ a Club receves 5/ per Week I have Given 3/ to make 8/ from 5th October 1812 to 18th Jany 1813

15 Weeks at 2/ Pr.	1 10 0
15 Jany	2
to 1 Feby	3
to 11th	3
	1 18 0

I am Sir) youer Hlb Sert
John Jenkinson

Circumtext: *In different hand [SG]*: No rent Granted

378 John Jenkinson in Clayton to the Parish of Kirkby Lonsdale, 14 May 1813 (WPR/19/7/6/6/11)

Sir)

We have this Day sold Joseph Nelson Househould Forniture that hath produced one pound seven shillings and sixpence in part of 1.18.0 Rent expences 2/6

Ballance dew to Landlord	0.13.0
dew to me	3.17.0
	4.10.0

plas to send the Ballance emedatly as I am in great straits for money and I must make up my acounts emeadtley

I am Sir youer Hlb Serv[t]

Clayton John Jenkinson Overseer

14th May 1813

Circumtext: *Below, in different hand [SG]*:

7 weeks @ 2[s]/	14.0
1 Do. @ 3[s]/	3.0
	17.0
over paid last paym[t]	2.0
	15.0
Expenses say	2. 0.0
	2.15.0

379 Jere[miah] Haley in Horton to the Overseers of Kirkby Lonsdale, 14 April 1814 (WPR/19/7/6/7/5)

Horton 14th April 1814

The Overseers of the Poor of Kerby lonsdale
to the Overseers of Horton D[r]

To 40 weeks pay to John Nellson from	£ s d
28th July 1813 to 4th May 1814 @ 2[s]/- pr	4 0 0

Gentlemen

I will thank you to Remitt me the Above sum by Return of Post which will greatly Oblige your Hble Servt.

Jere. Haley
Overseer of the Poor
Horton nr Bradford

Circumtext: *In different hand:* x^{d}

380 John Haley in Great Horton to Stephen Garnet[t] in Kirkby Lonsdale, 6 July 1814 (WPR/19/7/6/7/9)

Mr Stephen Garnet   Great Horton July 6th 1814

Sir My Neighbour Joseph Nelsin a poor man says he belongs to your Township of Kerby Lonsdal<e> [*edge of page cut*] and that about 30 weeks Since himself wife & fameley was at Kerby they Came away and now Lives at a place Caled Parradice in Horton and their Circumsta^nce^ at Presant is Such they Canot do without Relief any Longer Joseph does his best as far as his age will permit but it will not do, for thir mayday Rent is yet unpayd and the Landlord will not wate any Longer and if their goods be Sold there is no way but one for them, and his wife is Verrey big with Child and Expects her bed in a few days therefore they Pray you to help them at this time Imeadietley as they wrote to you before Mayday and have not herd any thing since they are Surprised as you promised them you would answer them whenever they wrote but you must Answer now I Believe or they will be Obleged to Come to you now their Rent is one pound and you must Send 10 weeks pay that will be one pound that is 2 pounds in the whole and pleas not fail Imeadietley to Send it and Shall Remain yours Respectively

John Haley

you may Either Direct to Joseph Nelson or to me
if you Direct to me or to him Either say
John Haley Paradice Great Horton
near Bradford Yorkshire

Sir I have written nothing but the Truth as far as I am able to Judge John Upton of Sedburgh knows me

Circumtext: *Address of Recipient [SG]:* Mr Stephen Garnett, Oversear of Kerby lonsdale near Kendal

381 John Haley in Paradice near Horton to the Parish of Kirkby Lonsdale, 7 November 1814 (WPR/19/7/6/7/11)

Paradice near Horton
Sir/ Novr 7th 1814

Joseph Nelson <a> [*page torn*] pauper Belonging to your Township Desires me to Write to you Desiring you to Relieveing him as you Promised when he & wife was at Kerby. at presant Joseph & wife and 3 Childering are in Verry poore sircumstances their youngest Child was born just at the Time your Last Letter Came and is alive and Old Joseph begins to fail and tis not possable that he Can mantain his famaley his <st>rength [*page torn*] fails and he Canot Earn what they need and you must Send him Sumthing hansum or both him and familey must Come to Kerby by Sum means or Other for [****] [*overwritten by*] Indeed they are nearley fast at all points and their Rent of 30 Shilling is nearly Due and you must send him one pound beside the Penteon you Agreed to give him – the pound is to pay his Rent with youl please to answer this Letter Imeadietley Either to Joseph or to me John Haley Paradice Horton near Bradford Yorkshire yours Respectively John Haley

382 John Haley in Horton to Stephen Garnett in Kirkby Lonsdale, 26 November 1814 (WPR/19/7/6/7/14)

Mr Garnett Horton 26th Novr 1814

Sir/ Yours with a pound Note Came Duly to Hand for wich Joseph Nelson Returns his thanks to you for the same and Likwise for your Advance of his pention to 2/6 per Week But Old Joseph Desires Me to write to you again for him as follows Namley Old Joseph is Verry porley and has given over work three weeks since will be next thursday and he is Realey Verry Short of Breath and spits a great Deal whether he will be Better or not I Canot tell but I think he is almost done now the Pound Note you sent is gone for Rent & 10s/ is still behind & Sumway must be done for his Subsisting or he Canot Live he therefore Desires you to Advance him one pound in Advance of his pention if you will not do no way Else and you must do it Imeadietly or he will be Obliged to throw himself on Horton but he will wate if possable till your Letter Comes to aquaint him what he must do he is so badley that he Canot be Removed at presant and 2/6 per week he never Can Subsist on 5 a fam<ely> [*edge of page cut off*] I Canot tell what must Come of them
turn over

[*overleaf*] I think you had better help him hansomly at this time till we See whether he gets better or not but this I Leave to do as you think proper But I have written the truth as I Can and I am an eye wittness John Haley

Circumtext: *Address of Recipient:* [*******] Mr Stephen Garnett, Oversear ^nr^ Red Lion, Kerby Lonsdale, near Kendal in Craven
In Margin: Direct as Before for Joseph has Nothing to Loose a Letter with

383 John Haley in Horton to Stephen Garnett in Kirkby Lonsdale, 18 December 1814 (WPR/19/7/6/7/15)

Mr Garnett Horton Decr 18th 1814

Sir/ this Morning Joseph Nelson Died about 4 OClock how he is to get Buried I Canot tell But either me or Sumbody Else must Learn Sum Money till you send sum to Burry him with. now the Last Note that you Sent is all done a week or more since and I should have wrote sooner but I put them off and now he is Dead and there is the Widow and 3 Children all girles the Eldest is turned of 7 years and the youngest is 22 weeks Old – and the Widdow is not Capable to Earn but a Verry Little been only a Worstet Spinner and not much work to be had I think She ^and her Childeren^ Canot live on less than 5 Shillings per week and She must have it Weekley paid by sum person whome you may Appoint or the fameley will have to Come to Kerby Imeadietly for at presant I think I never saw a porer fameley without meat as they Should have and Clothing and Bedding you may Write back Imeadietly and you must at this time send something hansom to Bury him with and Support them till winter is a Little over and you Consider whether to Relieve then or take them to Kerby turn over

[*overleaf*] Every Duble Letter from you is 1^s^/8^d^ I think you had better send 4 or 5 pounds at this time and appoint me or Any Other person how to pay it to her and I will Obey your Orders now Consider this Letter over and I Leave you to do as you think proper for I write free of favour to any one John Haley

Circumtext: *Address of Recipient:* Mr Stephen Garnett Oversear near the Red Lyon Kerby Lonsdale ~~in Craven~~
In margin: Direct as before

384 John Haley in Bradford to Stephen Garnett in Kirkby Lonsdale, 2 March 1815 (WPR/19/7/6/8/2)

Sir March 2[d] 1815

yours of the 23 Decr Inclosing 4 pounds I Recieved 2 pounds for the funeral Expences of Joseph Nelson and 2 pounds to be paid to the widow in weekley payments of 5[s]/ each to begin the 21 of Decembr I have therefore paid her 5[s]/ Each week Ever Since ~~but in~~ now when I wrote to you Last I did not now of aneything that nelsons widow Could get to Burey him with But a Old Combers Club of which he was a Member alowed her a small matter as he was an Old member So that one pound helped her to Bury him then I had 3 pounds Left out of which I have paid as above She and the Childrin are in great want of Nessareys but I have holden hard as yet tho shee is Verrey porley and how she Lives I Canot tell but I think Verrey Meanley I wish you to Send me Sum Money and Order me how to go on I Shall not pay Much Longer without and she Canot do without and I think not able to Come till better I will be fathfull in what you Order and trust me with Send by Returns of post her Rent will be twenty five shillings at may day

Direct your Letter for me to be Left at Stephen Parkinsons
Bradford

I am yours Most Respectfully

John Haley

Circumtext: *Address of Recipient:* Mr Stephen Garnett Oversear Kerby Lonsdale
Postmarked: Bradford
In Margin: I paid 2[s]/5 for the last Letter

385 John Haley in Horton to Stephen Garnet[t] in Kirkby Lonsdale, 23 March 1815 (WPR/19/7/6/8/4)

Sir/ Horton March 23[d] 1815

yours of the 13th Instant I Recieved Including two pound Notes and my Instructions but I have to Aquaint you with a Disteresing Case on the 9th of this Month the Eldest Daughter of Widdow Nelson Cloths Caught fire and She was Dreadfully burnt Before the flame got Extingwished She was so Dreadfuly burnt that her life was Despared of and a Doctor was Caled in who did not Like to meddle with her but on the Neighbours Begging of him and promising him pay from me or you he Undertook the Case which has been Verry trublesom and Chargeable so farr after the fire was got out nearlay then he Ordered pultises of white Bread and Swine Same that Cost from 1/4 to 1/6 a Day and Last Sunday thought a Mortification was About to take place but on her being Clean washed all her Sores there was not so bad but their is now Sum hopes of her Recoverey with Length of time in all this youl se that a Little money is wanted I think one pound will not be Enough tho the Doctor says he will Charge as Low as possablle I have been obliged to advance Duble these 2 Last weeke I Could not help it for Shame on me if I had turn over

[*overleaf*] you must answer me this Letter Imeadietly and help me with sum Money and your Instructions for I am teased for money Dayley and the Circumstance is so Verry Destressing I Canot help but Relieve. Direct as Before yours Most Respectively John Haley

Circumtext: *Address of Recipient:* Mr Stephen Garnet Overseer Kerby Lonsdale Craven

386 Jere[miah] Haley in Horton to the Overseers of Kirkby Lonsdale, 22 May 1815 (WPR/19/7/6/8/6)

The Overseers of the Poor of Kerby Lonsdale
To the Overseers of Horton D^r^

To 52 weeks pay to Jno Nellson	
from 4th May 1814 to 4th May 1815 @ 2^s^/ pr	£ 5.4.0
To extra pay during sickness	1.2.0
	6.6.0

Gentlemen

I will thank you to Remitt me the above sum by Return of post – John Nellson is very Badly and has been so for upwards of Two months so that he Cannot work I have viewed him and think he will never get better – the money they had left in my hand for the Rent they have drawn besides the £1.2s.0d extra pay and the Rent is to pay –

I wish for your Direction for the future as the family must be a great expence there being five persons to maintaine your speedy answer will greatly Oblige

your Very Hum^l^. Servt.

Jere. Haley Overseer

Horton 22^d^ May 1815

387 Jere[miah] Haley in Horton to the Parish of Kirkby Lonsdale, 6 June 1815 (WPR/19/7/6/8/7)

Horton 6th June 1815

Gentlemen,

I Sent you my Bill pr. post for money Paid to John Nellson up to 4th May last - £6.6.0

To Do. May	8th		.4.0
To Do.	15		.4.0
To Do.	19		.2.0
To Do.	22		.4.0
To Do.	26		.2.0
To Do.	27		.2.0
To Do.	29 To Bury Do.		2.0.0
To Do.	Do.		.4.0
To Do. June	2d		.2.0
To Do.	5		.4.0
			9.14.0

I have to inform you that the Poor man is dead, the pay and the expences of the funeral have been Rather heavy but they have Indeed been in a most Distressed Situation haveing 4 Small Children and the Oldist of them has ^had^ the misfortune to break his arm –

I am informed that Nellsons Widow is come To you if so you will Settle with her about Their future pay if they should stop here –

I beg you will have the goodness to Remitt me the above ~~su~~ sum by return of Post with Orders for their future pay –

I imploid a Doctor for him but hav not got his bill but expect it will not be much –

I Remain yours &c.
Jere. Haley Overseer

388 Jere[miah] Haley in Horton to the Overseers of Kirkby Lonsdale, 22 September 1815 (WPR/19/7/6/8/10)

The Overseers of the Poor of Kerby lonsdale
To the Overseers of Horton Dr

	£ s d
To arrears of pay Left on @ Last Bill	3 8 0
To 17 weeks pay To Widow Nellson from	5 2 0
5 June To 2d October 1815 @ 6s/- Pr	8 10 0

Gentlemen/

I will thank you to Remitt me the above sum by Return of Post which ^wil^ much Oblige your Very Hbl^{e} Servt.

Jere. Haley Overseer

Horton 22nd Septem^{r}. 1815

389 Jere[miah] Haley in Horton to the Overseers of Kirkby Lonsdale, 18 November 1815 (WPR/19/7/6/8/11)

Horton 18th Novm^{r} 1815

The Overseers of the Poor of Kerby lonsdale

To the Overseers of Horton D^{r}

	£ s d
To pay for Widow Nellson as p^{r}. Bill sent by Post up to 2^{d} October last	8 10 0
To 7 weeks pay To D^{o} from 2^{d} Octob^{r} to 20th Novr 1815 @ 6^{s}/- pr.	2 2 0
	10 12 0

Gentlemen/.

I will take it as a kindness if you will have the goodness to Remitt me the above Sum by Return of Post pray fail not

and you'l Oblige your most Obd^{t}. &c

Jere. Haley Overseer

390 Jere[miah] Haley in Horton to the Parish of Kirkby Lonsdale, 23 December 1815 (WPR/19/7/6/8/15)

Horton 23^{d} Decem^{r} 1815

Gentlemen/

I Sent you my account P^{r}. Post some Time back for money Paid on your account To Widow Nellson the amount of which up to 20th Novm^{r}. Last was

from 20th Novm^{r}. to 25th Decem^{r}. 1815	£10 12 0
5 weeks @ 6^{s}/- P^{r}.	1 10 0
	12 2 0

I once more beg you will have the goodness to Remitt me the above sum so that I may Receive it by this Day Week Whi^c^h will do me a great Kindnes and will much Oblige your Hbl^{e} Servt.

Jere. Haley Overseer

391 John Haley to [Stephen] Garnett in Kirkby Lonsdale, N.D. (WPR/19/7/6/8/16)

Mr Garnett
Sir/ Widdow Nelsons pay was up you know on the 5th of this Month and thro the Affliction in the Fameley I am in Advance Ten Shillings and with all that I have done the Famely are Verry Porley don to the youngist Child has been Verry Ill Several weeks And now it Restes Verry Little Either Day or Night the Eldest Daughter that was burnt is getting better there will be 15 Shillings to pay for Rent at Mayday the Doctor Charged 18 Shillings I payed the post and gave the Widdow the Rest you promised to write before now if you have not before this arrives do Imeadeitly and Send Sumthing at once as the post is so Chargable and the Fameley is not fit to Come at presant Yours &c

John Haley

Direct as before

Notes: *Although this letter is undated, its place in the sequence suggests it comes between letters 390 and 392.*

392 Jere[miah] Haley in Horton to the Overseers of Kirkby Lonsdale, 9 March 1816 (WPR/19/7/6/9/2)

The Overseers of the Poor of Kerby lonsdale
To the Overseers of Horton Dr

	£
To Bill Sent p_r. Post up to 25th $Decm_r$ 1815	12 2 0
To 13 weeks pay to Widow Nellson from 25th Decemr. 1815 to 1st April 1816 @ 6s/- pr.	3 18 0
To a Doctor Bill for Medicin and attendance for Jno. Nellson during his Indisposition	1 3 6
	17 3 6

Gentlemen,

I Request you will have the goodness to Remitt me the above sum by Return of Post without faile, as it is now becom a Searious Sum and I am much Straitned for money – you will see I have made out the note to 1st April the time our new Overseers begins to pay – besides I have Lent the Poor Woman £3.10s.0 to buy a Pair of Loomes with for her Oldest Son to Weave in which she promises to pay by Installments –

Pray Disapoint me not at this time and you'l Oblige

Yours Most Respectfully –

Jere. Haley <u>Overseer</u>

Horton 9th March 1816 –

393 Jere[miah] Haley in Horton to the Parish of Kirkby Lonsdale, 18 February 1817 (WPR/19/7/6/10/8)

Gentlemen, Horton 18th Feby. 1817

I have to Inform you that Widow Nellson Junr. and Family are quiet out of Work, She has Sommoned me before Two Magistrates for more Relief, and they made an Order upon me to alow her nine Shillings a week which I have Paid her for 3 weeks, I wish for your direction what to do in this case her Oldest Child is a Boy and fitt to put out an Aprentice and he is her greatest Charge ^he^ being with her –

I Sent you My Bill for Monies Paid to her	£
up to 17th December Last	9.18.0
from 17th Decr. 1816 to 18th Feby. 1817 - 9 weeks @ 6s/	2.14.0
To 3 weeks additional Pay @ 3s/- pr.	9. 0
	13.1.0

I beg you will favour me with a Remittance of the amount ^by Return of Post^ with your Directions how to act with Respect to the above family

From yours Respectfully

PS) if I Hear nothing from you Shall Remove them

Jere. Haley Overseer –

[*overleaf*] 1817
Feby. 21st

The Guardian of the Poor to apply to the Overseer of Great Horton to know the number ^and ages^ of Widow Nelsons Family and to enquire what employment she generally follows and in the mean time to order her to be relieved with nine shillings a week –

394 Jere[miah] Haley in Horton to Step[he]n Garnett in Kirkby Lonsdale, 4 March 1817 (WPR/19/7/6/10/10)

Mr Stepn. Garnett Horton 4th March 1817

Sir/. in Reply to yours of 18th Ult. I have herewith sent you the names & ages of Widow Nellson's Children –

Joseph aged 13 years an half

Sarah	Do.	8	Do.
Thomas	Do.	5	Years
Daniel	Do.	3	Do.

the employment which the Mother has been accustomed to was Winding Worsted and Cotton Bobbins for Warpin and weaving, her Oldest Son Can weave Callico but has neither work nor Loomes to weave in and I se no possability of him Obtaining either –

waiting your answer I Remain
Your Most Respectfully
Jere. Haley –

395 John Haley in Horton to Stephen Garnett in Kirkby Lonsdale, 21 March 1817 (WPR/19/7/6/10/12)

Mr Stephen Garnet Horton 21 March 1817

yours of Sepr 7th 1816 Inclosing a Crown Note Value £10 that paid me for Widdow Nelson to the 2d Octr and now I have been paying her Ever since ~~at~~ the Same pention of 5^{s}/- per Week and I shall be in Great want of it on the first Day of April Next as I have a payment then to make therefore I desire you will send it me Without fail against that Day and if you please to pay up to Mayday it will be much Better as it will be all Included in one Letter as to widdow ^Nelson^ and her familey they are in Verrey pore Circumstances I Verreley Believe they have not half meat her Eldest Daugter has been ~~V~~ Verey porley sum time she lookes like a goost and she has nothing to help her With her youngist Child Canot Still goo She must have more pention or her and familey Canot Subsist I have holden her of all I Can with her old pention But if you will not think proper to alow her Sum more She will apply to our Oversear Jerey Haley and to a Justis Order and if She does they will Grant her 3^{s}/ a week more in her presant Cercumstances you will not fail Writting Imeadietly as the Case Call for itt and Let me Know how I am to do in this Case and I will Obey your order

Yours &c John Haley

Direct as Before

Circumtext: *In different hand [SG]:* If 1^{s}/ ^a week^ in advance will satisfy she may remain if not to come to this Township

Address of Recipient: Mr Stephen Garnett Overseer Kerby Lonsdale near Kendal Craven

396 Jere[miah] Haley in Horton to the Overseers of Kirkby Lonsdale, 23 October 1817 (WPR/19/7/6/10/41)

The Overseers of the Poor of Kerby lonsdale
To the Oveseers of Horton D^{r}

To 33 weeks Pay to Widow Nellson Junr.	£ s d
from 11th March to 28th Octb^{r}.1817 @9^{s}/- p^{r}	14 17 0

Gentlemen/

the above is our acc^{t}. against you which I will thank you to Remitt by Return of Post which will much Oblige your very Hbl^{e} Servt.

Jere. Haley Overseer

Horton 23^{d} Octob^{r}. 1817

397 Jere[miah] Haley in Horton to the Overseers of Kirkby Lonsdale, 24 July 1818 (WPR/19/7/6/11/21)

The Overseers of the <po>or [*obscured by wax seal*] of Kerby lonsdale

To the Overseers of Horton D^{r}

	£ s d
To 21 weeks Pay to Widow Nellson Junr	9 9 0
from 25th Feby. to 23rd July 1818 @ 9^{s}/- p^{r}	
To 21 weeks Pay to Widow Nellson Senr.	6 6 0
from 25 Feby. to 23d July 1818 @ 6^{s}/- p^{r}	15 15 0

Gentlemen,

I beg you will not fail Sending me the above Sum by Return of Post as our Committee Insist of Remittances being made for out Standing Pay every 3 months or Discontinueing payment

I am yours Respectfully
Jere. Haley
Overseer

Horton 24 July 1818

398 Jere[miah] Haley in Horton to Step[he]n Garnett in Kirkby Lonsdale, 2 March 1819 (WPR/19/7/6/12/3)

Horton 2^d March 1819

The Overseers of Kirby lonsdale
To the Overseers of Horton D^r

	£ s d
To Ballance Left on us to 31st Augs^t. 1818	0 5 0
To 27 weeks pay to Widow Nellson Junr. from 31st Aug 1818 to 8th March 1819 @ 9^s/ P^r	12 3 0
To 27 weeks Pay to Widow Nellson Senr from 31st Augt 1818 to 8th March 1819 @ 6^s/ P^r	8 2 0
	20 10 0

Mr Step^n. Garnett
Sir,

I beg you will have the goodness to Remitt me the above sum in the course of a week as I am going out of Office this month and must have my out Standing Pay Collected before I can make up my accounts on which account it makes me more urgeant at this time and I hope you will not disapoint me –

I have viewed the Nellsons and think the younger may do with a Shilling p^r. week less althow she is but ill off for a Little work the Old Wooman can do with no Less as Shee is very badly off and has to fetch a Pound of Wool to Spin at Least 6 Miles

I Remaine Yours Respectfully Jere Haley
Overseer

399 Will[ia]m Marshall in Horton to the Overseers of Kirkby Lonsdale, 7 October 1819 (WPR/19/7/6/12/22)

Horton 7th October 1819

The Overseers of Kirby Lonsdale
To the Overseers of Horton D^rs.

	£ s d
To Acc^t. sent by Post up to 4th Octr. 1819	19 7 0
Octr. 4 To cash p'd Widow Nelson Senr. & Wid^w Nelson Junr 2 Weeks each 12/ & 16/	1 8 0
	20 15 0

Gentlemen

The above Account I trust you will find correct an early Remittance is requ^i^red, as the positive Orders of our Overseers & Committee are, "to discontinue Payment for those Towns who do not pay immediate attention to the settlement of their Accounts".

I am, Gentlemen
Your Obd[t]. Servt.
Will[m]. Marshall

400 Will[ia]m Marshall in Horton to [Stephen] Garnett in Kirkby Lonsdale, 23 October 1819 (WPR/19/7/6/12/24)

Horton 23[rd] Oct[r]. 1819

Mr. Garnett

Sir/

I reciv'd yours of the 18[th] Instant enclosing a Bill value twenty Pounds having a Balance due to this Township fifteen shillings, both the Families being paid up to the 17th Instant – At your Request I have examin'd them and herein send you the Statement as given to me.

Ruth the Widow of John Nelson says she can only earn about one Shilling a Week – Her son 16 years of age weaves 1 Callico Piece Per Week for which he receives One Shilling and six Pence. Her Daughter 10 years of age nurses a Child for which she receives One Shilling & 6[d]. weekly. She has 2 ^other^ Boys 1 – 8 years old & the other 5 years old who earn nothing

Grace the Widow of Joseph Nelson spins Worset & earns about two Shillings a Week – Her Daughter 13 years old nurses a Child for her meat and has no Wages – another Daug[r]. nurses a Child for which she has One Shilling a Week & another Daug[r]. 5 years old who earns nothing.

From the above Statement I am of Opinion that if you have any Employment at all for them they would do better with you than here and as I have positive Orders from the Committee to discontinue advancing Money for other Townships you will please to say by return of Post Whether you are willing to fetch them yourself or you are willing to pay my Expences for removing them to you without an Order to remove. Or that I must apply to the Magistrates for removal Orders according to the Statute in that Case made & provided or that you will send three Months pay in advance.

I expect by this Time you have heard from another Quarter that we have discontinued to relieve them, as such they are now in distress and an early Answer is particularly required

I remain
Sir
Your Obe[t]. Hbl[e] Ser[t].
Will[m]. Marshall
Overseer &c

401 John Haley in Par[adice] to [Stephen] Garnett in Kirkby Lonsdale, 27 November 1819 (WPR/19/7/6/12/28)

Mr Garnett, Sir/ Nov[r] 27th 1819

By the desire of Ruth & Grace Nelson I Write once more to inform you that According to your Orders they Sould all they few things they Had in Housald furniter and Paid of thir Rent and Sum Small Debts they Had Contracted and yesterday they all went down to Come by the Waggon But he said he Could not take them and they Expected our Oversear metting them at Brad ford and giving them the Money you Ordered him to give them Come With and he did not so they all Came back and I have letten them go into their ould Habitations again and this Day they have Desired me to write as follows as to Ruth and her familey their is a young Man Offered to take her Eldist son and Learn him to Weave Worsted and will give 3s/ per Week for him till May & then More if he Deserves it the Rest are Earning as you have writin Before and So if you Pleas Ruth & famley will Stop and Strive to do with seven Shillings per Week if you Pleas to alow it But if you Still wish her and famaley to Com they Will as to Grace Nelson & familey her Eldist Daughter has been Out two years & she has given one Shilling per Week all the time with her and now the Man Offers to keep her for Nothing and Learn her to weave if youl let her stop the Next Dauter Earns one Shilling per Week the other Nout her self 1[s]/6[d] Still she is Willing to try with 5[s]/- per Week and Stop at Home if you pleas and if not will Come as you have Ordered pleas to give an Answer to theas Proposals Without fail as it is Such a Searious Consequence and send it by the Waggoner he Says he will see you and we will meet him – on thursday Next at Bradford for your Letter

Frend Garnett in My Opinion I think you had Better Allow them as they have proposed a little Longer perhaps Sum of the Childering may get out of your Care and their Parents two I have Stated the truth as near as I Can and so you may do as you pleas Shall Remain yours &c

John Haley

Paridise Nov[r] 27/ 1819

Cirucumtext: *Address of Recipient:* Mr Stephen Garnett Ovesear Kerby Lonsdale near Kendal

Postmarked: Bradford 210

402 Will[ia]m Marshall in Horton to the Overseers of Kirkby Lonsdale, N.D. (WPR/19/7/6/12/33)

78)

The Overseers of <Kirby> [*page torn*] Lonsdale

To the Overseers of Horton D^{r}.

	£	s	d
To a former Acc^{t}. delivered	21	5	0
To Cash paid Widow Nelson Junr. 22nd March 1819		8	
To D^{o}. paid Widow Nelson Senr. same day		6	
To D^{o}. paid D^{o}. Junr. 29th March		8	
To D^{o}. paid D^{o}. Senr. same day		6	
	22	13	0
March 13th C^{r}. by Bill & Note	21	10	0
	1	3	0
For Monies paid Wid^{w}. Ne^l^son Junr & Senr. from 5th April to 4th Octr. 1819 being 26 Weeks at 14/ Pr Week	18	4	0
	£19	7	0

Gentlemen

By Order of the Committee I have to request you will remit the above by return of Post as we are at present very much straitned for Money and please to say whether or no you wish me to pay forward

I am

Gent^{n}. Your Obd^{t}. Servt

Willm. Marshall

Overseer & Govr. of the

Workhouse

Notes: *Although this letter is undated, its place in the sequence suggests it comes between letters 401 and 403.*

403 Will[ia]m Marshall in Horton to [Stephen] Garnett in Kirkby Lonsdale, 10 July 1820 (WPR/19/7/6/13/16)

Horton 10th July 1820

The Overseers of Kir<by Lo> nsdale [*obscured by wax seal*]
To the Overseers of Horton D$^{\underline{rs}}$

	£ s d
To Acc^{t}. sent by Post up to the 18th Octr. 1819	20 15 0
C. by Bill & Notes	20 0 0
	15 0

	£ s d
1819	
Oct. 18 To Cash p'd Wid^{w}. Nelson Senr. & Junr.	1 8 0
Novr. 1 To D^{o}. £1.8.0 15th To D^{o}. £1.8.0 29th to D^{o}. 14/-	3 10 0
Decr. 6 To D^{o}. 10.0 13th to D^{o}. 1.0.0 27 To D^{o}. 1.0.0	2 10 0
1820	
Jany. 10 To D^{o}. 1.0.0 24th To D^{o}. 1.0.0	2 0 0
Feby. 7 To D^{o}. 1.0.0 21st To D^{o}.1.0.0	2 0 0
Mar 6 To D^{o}. 1.0.0 20th To D^{o}. 1.0.0	2 0 0
April 3 To D^{o}. 1.0.0 17th To D^{o}. 1.0.0	2 0 0
May 1 To D^{o}. 1.0.0 15th To D^{o}. 1.0.0 29th To D^{o}. 1.0.0	3 0 0
June 12 To D^{o}. 1.0.0 26 To D^{o}. 1.0.0	2 0 0
July 10 To D^{o}. 1.0.0	1 0 0
	22 3 0

		£ s d	
C^{r}.	By Notes Octr. 30th 1819	7 0 0	
	By D^{o}. Jany. 13th 1820	5 0 0	22 0 0
	By D^{o}. June 30th 1820	10 0 0	
	Balance due to Horton		£0 3 0

Mr Garnett

Above is the Particulars of your Account which I trust you will find correct, and I remain

Sir
your Obd^{t}. Servt.
Willm Marshall
Overseer &c

404 Will[ia]m Marshall in Horton to the Overseers of Kirkby Lonsdale, 7 December 1820 (WPR/19/7/6/13/38)

The Overseers of Kirby Lonsdale
To the Overseers of Horton D[rs]

	£ s d
To a former Account sent by Post	6 3 0
To Cash paid Ruth & Grace Nelson	
from 16[th] Otober to 11[th] Dec[r]. 1820	4 0 0
being 8 Weeks @ 10/- Per Week	
	£10 3 0

Gentlemen

Above is your Account with this Township I doubt not but you will find correct and I am not a little surprised you have not remitted me the last Account before this Time for it is the positive Orders of the Committee to discontinue paying for those Townships who do not pay immediate attention to the settlement of their Acco^u^nts as such I could wish you to send me the above by return of Post if you wish me to continue to relieve them as above

I remain Your Obd[t]. Servt.

Horton 7[th] Dec[r].
1820

Will[m]. Marshall
Overseer &c

405 Will[ia]m Marshall in Horton to the Overseers of Kirkby Lonsdale, N.D. (WPR/19/7/6/13/45)

The Overseers of Kirby Lonsdale
To the Overseers of Horton, Dr.

Relief given to	From	To	Weeks	Per Week	£	s	d
Grace Nelson	25 July 1800	16[th] Oct[r]. 1820	12	4/-	2	8	0
Ruth Nelson	D[o].	D[o].	12	6/-	3	12	0
	Balance of former [Acct].				£6	3	0

Above is our account against your Township which I trust you will find correct. By favouring us with an early Remittance you will oblige

Yours respectfully
Will[m] Marshall

Notes: *Although this letter is undated, its place in the sequence suggests it comes between letters 404 and 406.*

406 Will[ia]m Marshall in Horton to the Overseers of Kirkby Lonsdale, 20 March 1821 (WPR/19/7/6/14/14)

The Overseers of Kir<by Lo>nsdale [*obscured by sealing wax*]
To the Overseers of Horton D<u>rs</u>

	£ s d
For Monies paid to Grace Nelson and Ruth Nelson on your Acc^{t}. from 11th Decr. 1820 to 2nd April 1821 being 16 Weeks at 10/ Per Week	8 0 0
To Balance of former Account	<u>0 3 0</u>
	£<u>8 3 0</u>

Gent^{n}/

On the 29th Instant new Overseers are to be appointed shall therefore esteem it a Favour if you will remit the above as soon as possible for the year's accounts must be made up immediately after such appointment

I remain
Your Obd^{t} Hble Servt
Willm Marshall

Horton 20th March
<u>1821</u>

407 Will[ia]m Marshall in Horton to the Overseers of Kirkby Lonsdale, 3 July 1821 (WPR/19/7/6/14/27)

Horton 3rd July 1821

The Overseers of Kirby Lonsdale
To the Overseers of Horton D^{rs}.

		£ s d
To account rendered		8 3 0
C^{r}. by Notes from S. Garnett		<u>7 10 0</u>
1821		13 0
April	2nd To Cash paid Wid^{w}, Nelson Senr. & D^{o}. Junr. 2 Wks	1 0 0
	16 To D^{o}.	1 0 0
	30 To D^{o}.	1 0 0
May	14 To D^{o}.	1 0 0
	28 To D^{o}.	1 0 0
June	11 To D^{o}.	1 0 0
	25 To D^{o}.	<u>1 0 0</u>
		<u>£7 13 0</u>

Gent[n].

Above is our acc[t]. with your Township and an early Remittance is required, as it is the Determination of our Committee to discontinue from paying for other Townships; as such I can advance no more Money until I hear from you

I remain
Yours &c
Will[m] Marshall
Overseer &c

408 John Haley in Paradice to [Stephen] Garnett in Kirkby Lonsdale, 20 July 1821 (WPR/19/7/6/14/29)

Paradice
Horton July 20th 1821

M[r] Garnett

Ruth and Grace Nelson had their pay Stopt on the Ninth of July the Oversear James Marshall and the Comittey said they woald Pay no more till they had a Remittance from you Marshall said he had Written and got no answer Since then he says he has gotten a Letter and Sum Money But he says you have Sent one Pound three Shillings Short of what he has Laid down and Still Both him and the Comittey will not Pay till you Write to them again Concerning this affair Our Comitey Pays Ruth and Grace Everey fortnit and it will be a Month Next Monday Since they had any Money of Marshall and their Credit being Small they are Reduced to trying Circumstances and Unless we Supported a Little they would be Verry Ill of hope on Recipt of this you will write Imeadietly to Marshall for they Canott do without Pay Much Longer at any Rate I Should not have Written But Both Marshall and the Comitey Sent me Word to Write to you twice and they Desired I would hope you will write soon and not faill and Reconsill all partes your Verey Respected Frend &c

John Haley

409 John Haley in Horton to [Stephen] Garnett in Kirkby Lonsdale, 1 August 1821 (WPR/19/7/6/14/30)

Mr Garnett/ Horton August 1th 1821

I Recieved your Letter Inclosing a two Pound Note which I have divided Betwixt them in Preportion as was their share as to their Childering Ruths as follows her Eldest son She has gotten out to Learn to Weave and his master finds him meat and part Cloths and She finds part and washes for him her Next a Doughter is Out also and they find her meat but Ruth has to find all her Clothes her next a Boy is of a Weakly Habit of Body and oft Short of Breath therefore he is still with her at Home doing Nothing her next a fine Boy But two young to Set to any Work here, Ruth is of Small Earnings herself she is hard put to it at maney times. Grace Childering her Eldest Daughter gotten Out to Learn to Weave and her time will be out by Martinmas and then She Should do for herself if She Could ^get her^ a pare of Looms. her Next Girl goes Out to Wind Small Bobins at 1/6 per Week the Next a Girl She has been much afflicted Both in her Body and Eys but as She grows Elder I think her Eye Rather Strengthes but She ~~[****] [***]~~ [*overwritten by*] has a good appetite and Old Grace Can Earn Very Little by Spinning that is her Employment. the Girl that is at 1/6 per week She has to find her all meat and Cloths and youl Recolect Both the Nelsons has to pay their Rentt and find their fire out of their Earnings and pentions

as to their pentions they Could do with it Every Week Verrey Well. they will Still be more so every fortnit and a Month will be Still Longer I wish you Could find Means to send to Bradford Every fortnit without Posting it is so Chargable for them to Pay. But for the firs time if you Can find no Other way you may Remit at a Month and I will help them till it Comes. I still

Remain yours
Respectively
John Haley

410 John Haley in Horton to [Stephen] Garnett in Kirkby Lonsdale, 10 September 1821 (WPR/19/7/6/14/34)

M^{r}.

Garnett I Answered your Letter Imeadietly I am Surprised you do not Write Again Before this time you promised to Remitt Either every fortnit or Month but you have not So maney weeks have Elapsed and no Letter or Remittance the poor Nelsons are in Greeat Destress all their little Credit is at an End and my Affairs are such that at presant I Canot help them any Longer therefore you must Remit Imeadietly and if you please to send a little Over I will be answerable for it and pay them in proper time do fail not to Remit Imeadietly at this time and your Obleg yours &c

John Haley

Horton Paradice Sepr 10th 1821

411 John Haley in Horton to [Stephen] Garnett in Kirkby Lonsdale, 7 January 1822 (WPR/19/7/6/15/1)

Mr Garnett
Respected Friend Horton Jan^ry 7th 1822

the Nelsons was Paid up to the Twelft Decmber Last and now two Months have Elapsed since and no Letter or Remittance have Com'd and they are at the far end Realy and Cannot tell how to get on from Day to Day till your Remittance Come therefore I hope you will not Delay to Send Imeadietly on the Recept of this and I will attend at the Post Office Next Satturday and Sunday Morning therefore please not to fail and youl Oblege yours Most Respectively

John Haley

412 John Haley in Horton to [Stephen] Garnett in Kirkby Lonsdale, 20 May 1822 (WPR/19/7/6/15/11)

Mr Garnett Horton May 20th 1822
not fully knowing whether you be in Office or not I am Under the Nessaty of Writing to you again Concerning the Nelsons Pentions Eight weeks Will be due next Wedensday to them and now they begin to be in Strate Circumstances Notwithstanding my little help I hope you will Remitt on Receipt of this Imeadietly and if youl send a five Poun Bank of England Note it will be in their favour and I will take Care it pay for ten Weeke. Last Letter was Charged threble and this is the Reason for me desiring you to send a five Pound Note if you happen to be out of office I hope youl inform your Successor and not Delay and in your Next Inform me how I may Direct Next time and in so dong youl Oblege youre Most Obedient Ser^vt John Haley

NB Shall be at the Post Office Next Friday and Saturday Mornings adue and may the Blessing of God be with you and Familey in time and to all Eternity

413 John Haley in Horton to Stephen Garnett in Kirkby Lonsdale, 8 October 1822 (WPR/19/7/6/15/30)

October 8th 1822

Mr Stephen Garnett
Sir)
tomorrow Eight Weeks pention will be Due for the Nelsons and as they are now very much Stratned I hope you will Remitt a five Pound Note as Usal to Come by next Friday or Saturday at the farthest and youl Oblege yours
Most Respectively
John Haley
Horton Paradise October 8th 1822

NB the Last Came safe to hand

414 John Haley in Horton to [Stephen] Garnett in Kirkby Lonsdale, 10 December 1822 (WPR/19/7/6/15/42)

Horton December 10th 1822

Frien Garnett
I once more Write to Informe you that 8 Weeks will be Due tomorrow of the Nelsons Pention and they hope you will be kinde Enough to Remitt as Usal for ten weeks and that it may Come by Satturdays Post as now they are Verrey Stratned in Curmstances I think if you Continue their Pention this Winter it Would be as well and se how Provisions are and them in Helth in the Spring and then you may do as you think proper yours Respectively
John Haley

Paradice Decr 10 1822

415 John Haley in Horton to [Stephen] Garnett in Kirkby Lonsdale, 19 February 1823 (WPR/19/7/6/16/10)

Friend Garnett/ Horton Feby 19th 1823
This Day two Months Pention will be Due and the Nelsons are Nearly at the End for Subsisteance Old Grace has been Verrey porley and Could not work they tell me that both her and her two Childeren are all in the Itch hope you will Remit Soon as Usall

From yours Most Respectively
John Haley
Paradice Feb[y] 19th 1823

416 John Haley in Horton to [Stephen] Garnett in Kirkby Lonsdale, 21 May 1823 (WPR/19/7/6/16/34)

Frend Garnett/ Horton May 21th 1823

This Day makes 10 Weeks pention Due to the Nelsons that will be £3.10.0 According to your Last Statement and if you send Exactly this sum by Post the Expence will hurt them Very Much therefore if you think proper may send a five pound Note as Usal and I will take Care it be Rited and Equaly paid in proper Time as to the Mistake I Cannot find it out but you are Mistaken in a Week for all your Letters to me Corraspond one with another hope you will Write soon as they are in great need

Yours Respectively &c
John Haley

Paradice May 21

417 John Haley in Horton to [Stephen] Garnett in Kirkby Lonsdale, 13 August 1823 (WPR/19/7/6/16/47)

Mr Garnett/ Horton August 13th 1823

I am Obleged to Write sooner than Usual on account of Ruth Johns Widdow been Verrey porley Shee has been so Sum time and has been Obleged to Call in a Docter and Still she gettes no better and Canot bide to Work to Earn anything she Must have helps Imeadietly you Must therefore send Imeadietly all their pentions that is due and you should order Ruth a 5 or 10 shillings Extra at this time as her Case is Verrey Distressing and her Circumstances Verry low I have Stated the Case as near as I Can and Shall Leave it to you to do as you think proper but her Case Requires help youl please to send soon as In so doing youl Oblege Yours &c.

John Haley

418 John Haley in Horton to Stephen Garnett in Kirkby Lonsdale, 26 December 1823 (WPR/19/7/6/16/60)

Mr Stephen Garnett Horton Decr 26th 1823
Sir/

Yours of the 22 August Came safe to hand with its Contents Wich I paid the Nelsons According to Order and now it being 3 Months since they are now in Great want of a further Remittance Which I hope you will send as soon as you Receive this Letter and please to send a five pound Note on account of poastage you did Verrey Well Last time in sending by Thomas – the Gard as it Cost them Nought for which they Return you thanks Shall Conclude hoping this will find you in good Helth

yours Most Respectivly John Haley

Paradice 26 Decr 1823

419 A. Thomas in Great Horton to the Overseers of Kirkby Lonsdale, 10 February 1824 (WPR/19/7/6/17/7)

To the Over<u>seers of the Towns</u>hip of Kirby Lons^dale^

Gentlemen/

I take the liberty of writing to you respecting the case of Grace Nelson a poor person belonging to your township, who has been indisposed for the last 9 weeks, and still continues much worse having three children, the resources of her friends being spent, and utterly incompetent to afford herself necessary assistance, humbly solicits the further pecuniary aid of the Town, in order that her distresses may in some measure be alleviated, which has solely arisen from long and tedious affliction.

Great Horton A: Thomas Surgeon
Feby. 10th 1824

420 John Haley in Horton to [Stephen] Garnett in Kirkby Lonsdale, 3 March 1824 (WPR/19/7/6/17/11)

Horton March 3rd 1824

M^r. Garnett/ Sir

I have to write at this time to you of the Case of Old Grace Nelson as follows Before the Last Remittance Came she was not Able to work nor has She

Earned any thing since but kept Declining and now She nearly lies all in Bed She is Greatly Afflicted Indeed and to all Apperance will not live Long. All her frends and Neighbours who sees her thinks so several of our Badgers have let her have to Subsist on till your Remittance Came Before time and now also but they begin to tire and at presant there is two of hir youngist Childeren with her and they all three are to keep the Elder water on her the Case is Deplorable Inded. your Last Remittance paid up to 31 Decr and now 9 weeks is Due you must Remit Imeadietly and sumthing Extra to to her weekley pay you must send at this time as there is 3 to keep and Coles. I Canot see that 5^{s}/ per week will Subsist them but I Leave it to you to do as you think proper and as wee all think she will not Live Long I Shall soon have to write again yours Most Respectively John Haley

if you send by Thomas the Coach man it would be as well and please to Direct for me to be Left at Stephen Parkinsons Broad Stones
Bradford
as I shall then get it sooner

421 John Haley in Horton to Stephen Garnett in Kirkby Lonsdale, 19 March 1824 (WPR/19/7/6/17/13)

Mr. Stephen Garnett Horton March 19th 1824
Sir/
yours of 15 Instant Came to hand with the Contents all safe. Next Morning I went and Divided the Money to them and Old Grace Shair was paid Imeadietly for Rent, Coles, and for what she had gotten to subsist on till till the Money Came from you. as she was so porley it was thought proper to Remove her to Ruths. so she was Removed a fortnit since and there she Died on the 18 Instant with Ruth and Now she is to Burey and her Relations will not have any thing to do with the funeral Ruth will be Obleged to get sum frends to help her to Burey her till you remit Sumthing to pay them with. as to her Housald furneter there is Nothin to be made of it I would not have anything given there will be the Coffin the Horse Litter the Dues the Grave and the Winding and Ruth is Such Cirmstanced as not to do aney thing I think not Less than two pound or 2 Gunes will do if that will do as to her Eldest Daughter She has gotten a Home and if she Has Helth will do for her *[*self*]* and a pore man Has ta<ke>n [*page torn*] her Middle Daughtr for 5 years and will find Her Mea<t a>nd [*page torn*] Cloths and Lern Her to Weave her youngest Daughter is with Ruth and she ^is^ willing to try a Month or 2 with her if you Allow her two Shillings per week. if not you Must Order

sum way for her to get to Kerby this Letter you will be pleased to Answer Imeadietly as it is on Death I hope you will and in so Doing you will Oblege yours &c

John Haley

422 John Haley in Great Horton to [Stephen] Garnett in Kirkby Lonsdale, 2 June 1824 (WPR/19/7/6/17/29)

Great Horton

Mr Garnett June 2 1824

Sir/

yours of the 22 March with two pounds for the funeral Came Duley to hand and now 10 weeks will be Due tomorrow at 6^{s}/ per week hope you will be so kind at to Remitt Imeadietly as Ruth has Driven to the Last shift and Cannot do any Longer Betty the youngist Child is nearley ten years of Age and Ruth gets Nine pence per week for her at presant to Nurse a Child She is a Gaunless Girl so you may Order Concerning her as you plese the 2 pounds that you sent to Defray the Expences of Grace Nelsons funeral was all paid and by the help of a few Frends all was paid of

So Remain yours Respectively

John Haley

Horton June 2^{d} 1824

423 John Haley in Horton to [Stephen] Garnett in Kirkby Lonsdale, 13 August 1824 (WPR/19/7/6/17/34)

Horton August 13th 1824

Friend Garnett/

it Being now 10 weeks Since Ruth Remittance Came and she being Verrey Much Stratned as Both Worstet and Cotton are Verrey Low at presant therefore youl please to Remitt as soon as possable and pleas to Allow her the same pention as Before as the Earnings of Both Herself and Children are so Verrey Small and the Trade is so bad with us she Canot tell how to Carrey on with any thing taken of

Joseph her Eldest son is 21 at one Shilling and Vitules Sarah her Daughter is 15 Learning to weave Mother finds Cloths Tomey her son is 15 Learning to weave Mother finds Cloths Dan her son is 10 she has one Shilling per week for him and she has to Both meat him and Cloth him as to Ruth shee winds a few weavers Bobins when she Can get them this Statement is as near the truth as I Can tell how to write ~~of~~ I think Betty is a Charge to her. youl Consider these things and do as you think proper.

I am yours Most Respectively

Paradice John Haley

Augst 13. 1824

424 John Haley in Horton to [Stephen] Garnett in Kirkby Lonsdale, 9 September 1824 (WPR/19/7/6/17/36)

Mr Garnett Horton Sepr 9th 1824

Sir/ About a Month since I wrote to you and Sent you all the perticulers that you Desired me to send and now 14 weeks pention is Due and no Remittance I am Verrey Much Surprised you do not Write Ruth Canott do much Longer her friends Begin to tire of Letting her have to Subsist on therefore I hope you will Write Imeadietly and not fail and as Letters are so Chargable if you Could make it Convenient to send a £5 note and if there is any thing over I will see it writed you Must consider that Betty is a Charge to Ruth she Cannot keep her with meat & Clothes washing & Login I think with anything Less then three shillngs per week Yours Most Respectively

John Haley

Paradice 9 Sepr 1824

425 John Haley in Horton to Stephen Garnett in Kirkby Lonsdale, 3 December 1824 (WPR/19/7/6/17/45)

Horton Decembr 3rd 1824

Mr Stephen Garnett/

yours of Sepr 8 Came Duley to Hand and now 10 Weeks being Elapsed of Ruth pencion and Shee begins to be much Stratned how to get on. She is not well of at presant not Verrey well in Health Hope you will not fail to send Imeadietly on Reciept of this as to Grace Nelsons Child that you Alow Ruth 2^s/ per week with She Cannot Keep her with it you must allow her Sumthing per week more or please to say She must Come to Kerby and How and How you think will be the best way for her to Come to you Ruth is Hurt with her

I am Sir yours Respectively
John Haley

Paradice
Decr 3 1824

426 John Haley in Horton to Stephen Garnett in Kirkby Lonsdale, 14 August 1827 (WPR/19/7/6/20/21)

Horton Augst 14 1827

Mr Stephen Garnett
Sir/ yours of 26th March Inclosing five Pounds paying the Nelsons for the 28 same Month Came Safe to Hand and now the time being up for you to Remitt Again hope you will send Imeadietly as Her Rent is unpaid and Her Daughter is Verrey porley and Has been so Sum time so that Ruth is in Verrey Stratned Circumstance therefore hope you will not fail to send and youl Oblege

yours &c John Haley

Horton Aug 14th 1827
Paradice Mancion

427 John Haley in Horton to Stephen Garnett in Kirkby Lonsdale, 5 June 1828 (WPR/19/7/6/21/39)

Mr Stephen Garnett Horton June 5th 1828
Sir)
as to the Nelsons first Ruth famaley is a young Girll and Coming to be a Woman but she has Verry poor Health and Canot do Intierley for herself and if she does not get Right will Decline away the Next is a Boy and Learned to Weave and I think may do for himself the Next is a Boy Short and thick But he is Learning to weave But Canot do for himself as yet. Ruth their Mother has got Each of them a pair of Loomes part of thee price is Paid for them and the Remainder is to pay as to Grace Nelson famaley she Left 3 Girles two of them does for themselves But one the youngist about1 4 years Old is Verrey Deficient in Memorey and sence and Can see not weell on one Eye a Verrey Simple foolish Creator and Cannot Learn hardley any thing

her Uncle thook her when her Mother Died But he will not have her any Longer with two Shillings per Week so Ruth has Taken her and if you please will Try with her this Next 20 Weeks and if you think Otherwise you will have her to Kerby please to ^send^ Word how she may come

So I Remain yours Most Respectively & &c

Horton June 5 John Haley

428 John Haley in Horton to [Stephen] Garnett in Kirkby Lonsdale, 24 October 1828 (WPR/19/7/6/21/22)

Mr Garnett/ Sir Horton Octr 24th 1828

your Remittance not Coming at the time appointed have Caused me to Write once more Ruths famaley have been Visited with the Typus fever and 2 of her Children have been Verry Ill Indeed and a Doctor have been Called in they have been ill a Month or better but they are getting better theyir Circumstance was so that they must have Reliefe on Sumbody therefore we have Advanced above half the money that you will send at this time and Other friends have helped and youl Remember Betty of the Other famaley has been to keep all this 22 weeks with meat and Cloths and for anything that she Can do I would not have her in the House for it if she wants to bring <her> [*page torn*] meat with her she Canot see verry well & bad memorey tis Impossable to Learn her anything she is so short of witt memory and Understanding I Cannot tell what must Cum of her as she is going of 15 years, I think if Ruth getts this Winter over and all well in Health Shee might do Without pention but we are short sighted Creatures Canot tell what a Day may bring forth. I hope youl not fail to Remit on Recipt of this and Direct for me to left at Stephen Parkinsons Broad stones Bradford and in so doing youl Oblege yours &
John Haley

[*overleaf*] my Daughter pites Bett and Rather than she should Com to you this Winter she will take a Trial of her this next 20 weeks with you allowing the 2 shillings per Week as usal youl please to send your mind about it

429 John Haley in Horton to [Stephen] Garnett in Kirkby Lonsdale, 23 February 1829 (WPR/19/7/6/22/5)

Mr. S<tephen> [*page torn*] Garnett Horton Febu^{ry} 23/ 1829

Sir/

the 20 weeks being up Next Wedensday I thought to Write to you to Aquaint you of the Sircumstances of Both the famaleys as to Ruths her Eldest a Man now is gone out to place in farming her next a Girl is 20 years old Learned to Weave Well her next a Boy gooing of 18 years he Can Weave Well her next a Boy 15 years this [*page torn*] Month Should Wind Bobins if these Children be well and Would Work and not be Idle they need not be any Charge to you Ruth herself goes out Weekley a Washing and brings in 5 or 6 Shillings a Week and Good mends I think she may do Without after this time if they Continue Well but do as you please if you Entierly Cut her of She may Cum Over to plead for her self and if she does I would not have you tell her now of me Writing ~~in~~ in this manner or would I have you take aney Notice of it in your Remitance to me as to Betty of the other famaley that my Daughter has kept these Last 20 Weeks I Canot but give her a bad Caracter she is a dirty slothful Nasty Idle Creator and a Verey great Liear I think She Can See Verry porley she Canot Learn anything dull Stuped Sleepy Verry little sence or Ever will have I think Ruth wuill not have her or her Uncle or her sisters with the allowance any More But my Daughter thinks She will try Other 20 Weeks with her at the same pention and then the Wether will be Warmer for her to Come for I think she will have to Come in thee End But if you think to take her now Send word how she may Come I have Cleared my Concience Direct for me to Stephen Parkinsons
Broad stones Bradford Yours &c

John Haley

Paradice Mantion 23 Feb

430 John Haley in Horton to Stephen Garnett in Kirkby Lonsdale, 13 August 1829 (WPR/19/7/6/22/48)

Horton Augst 13 1829

M^{r}. Stephen Garnett
Sir/ I fully Expected you Writing and Remiting Before now. in your Last you Wrote that Betty might stop a Little longer and now 24 Weeks is gone and no Letter or Remittance have Come and my Daughter is Entierly Satisfied With her and wishes that she may be taken away Imeadietly for Betty Cannot Be

Learned to do anything as she Should. She grows more Stuped more Unthoutfull and Unsensable an Idle nasty Slovenly Girll But always forward at meat and will eat as much as 3 Girls of her age Should do and this Dayley with greedness Steal more if it be near that she Can get it But you will see for your self when you gett her. Therefore I Desire you would Remit what is Due as soon as possable and Order how and what way She may Come Over to you and when that we may now whear to liverer her. and Indeed I think you had Better take hir now than let her stop any Longer as she is now turned of 15 years and she Requiers Care to be taken of for she is a Verrey Great Lier and not fit to Come in a Neighbour House. But if you take her to the Workhouse She may Grow Better with Care. I Shall now Conclude hoping you will Remitt on Receipt of this

yours Most Respectively
John Haley

Paradice Mantion
aug. 13. 1829

431 John Haley in Horton to the Parish of Kirkby Lonsdale, 24 September 1829 (WPR/19/7/6/22/29)

Sir/ Horton Sepr 24th 1829

your Letter of the 4th March Inclosing me a £5 Note that payed the Nelsons to the 25 Febuary then Ruths pention was Discontinued since then Bets is Continued at 2/s per Week so from the 25th Febury to the 23rd Sepr is 30 Weeks that is £3 that is Due. that I have Laid down Which I hope you will Remit on Recipt of this. you wrote that if Betty Came to you she Must Walk it by Herself But she Realy is not Capable to do it by herself and she Cryed and promised to be a Better Girl. on this we Agreed to try her a little longer and that is the Reason of me not writing sooner But about a fortnit since She Runaway to Ruths But my Daughter fetched her Back that Night, and she Behaved pretty well till yesterday, and as She was with the Boy in the field playing she all on a sudon left him Crying Verrey Hard till he was Black in the face and we know Nothing of it till a saw him and Brought him Home and said Bett was gone to Ruths again and as yet she is not Comed. Ruth keeps a Verry Disorderly House for you people to Come to and her Children is Verrey Idle and Naughty and she does not Restrain them as she Oought. I think she will not be longe or she Com to See you for Money But She deserves none as now they are weell and in Work and Able to Work if they were not Idle Ruth is for Bringing Bet to Kerby But I Believe it is all to get money from you for herself shall now Concluge Desiring you to Direct for me to be left at Stephen Parkinsons Broadstones Bradford

Yours &c John Haley

432 John Haley in Horton to the Parish of Kirkby Lonsdale, 15 October 1829 (WPR/19/7/6/22/27)

Horton Octr 15th 1829

Sir)

yours with 3 Skipton Notes Came duly to hand I wrote you Last that Bet had left us she tryed 2 Days to get to live with any one But all in Vane no one would have anything to do with her then she got to Ruths and Begged of Ruth to take her in or I would Send her to Kerby so Ruth Came over and said she Cold do Nothing with her she had Nothing for to do and What might Com on her she Could not tell and Desired I would take her in again till you had ordred sum way About her so I perswaded my Daughter to try her Again a little longer and ^Bet^ Cryed and said she would Behave and do Better than Before But my Daughter will not keep her Unless she Be paid the 2 Shillings per week so I was Obleged to fall in as Usal as there is Nothing But Loss at that and greef and Truble with her sumti<mes> [*page torn*] I think she Borders on Idoitesm and she Can Never Come of herself therefore please to write me Whether you will Continue to alow the 2 shillings per week as Usal a little longer or not and What I must do with her youl please to write me an Answer to these perticulars and in so doing
youl Oblege yours &c. John Haley

NB youl please to Direct for Parkinsons as before

Paradise Mancion House
Octr 15th 1829

433 John Haley in Horton to [Stephen] Garnett in Kirkby Lonsdale, 14 December 1829 (WPR/19/7/6/22/22)

Mr Garnett Horton Decr 14th 1829

Sir/ I have to Aquaint you that Last Wedensday in the forenoon as Betty was Washing up after Breakfast she Broak a Large pot Bowl Nothing was said to her but that she might gather up the Scars and Carrey them into the Lane She did so and then she Runaway and made of Ruth and her Sister and us have sought her several miles Round but Could hear Nothing of her till this Morning that a man Informed me that he met her on the high Road at a place <C>aled [*page torn*] Cottingley more and she Asked him the way to Kerby and pased on this was on Wedensday afternoon so we think she is on the Road or perhaps may have Reached you Before this Letter Comes to hand as we Wish her well at the fare End. Since your Last Remittance there is Eleven Weeks Rund on at two Shillings per Week Which I hope you will Remit as soon as you Can Conveniently as we hope to have Nothing to do with her any more I hope you will Write us Word in a few Days wether She be Comd to you or not or if you have herd of her as we Shall be Uneasey About her till we here of her I hope you will not fail and Believe me to Remain your Most Respectively frend and Well wisher &c

John Haley

Paradice
Mantion 14 Dec^{r}

434 John Haley in Horton to [Stephen] Garnett in Kirkby Lonsdale, 26 October 1830 (WPR/19/7/6/23/40)

Mr Garnett Horton October 26th 1830

Sir/ By the Desire of Hanah Nelson I Write to you once more she Says that 12~~0~~ Weeks of her Weekley Pay will be Due tomorrow and She Desires you to Remit it and she Desires you to be so kind as to send her Pay for a Quarter to Come at this time as She wants to purchas a Pair of Loomes to Weave in as she has none of her own. She had Borrowed a pair but they now want them for their own use and if you will be so kind as Grant the favour to her at this ^time^ she will not truble you Again of six Months if all is Well and at presant she and the Child is Verry Well she Desires you to send word how her sister Betty is you Must Direct the Old way John Haley Great Horton &c or by aney way you think proper to Convey the Money

John Haley Paradice G H Octr 26th 1830

435 John Haley in Horton to [Stephen] Garnett in Kirkby Lonsdale, 9 December 1830 (WPR/19/7/6/23/36)

Mr Garnett Sir/ Horton Decr 9th 1830

yours I Duley Recieved and in Answer I have to say that I met James the Gard of the Coach on 15 Novr According to Appointment But he said he had no Money from you I met him Every time that Week and Twice Since and have been twice since but Can hereof no Money and the Last time Woods was Verry sausey so Hannah Desired me to Wright Again and say that the Loomes she had Borrowed was taken from her and that now she has none to Weave in and that if you do not help her at this time She will be Obleged to Come to you Directley

turn over

[*overleaf*] as she Cannot subsist Without Weaving she would Endever to Mantain herself ^and ~~Child~~^ Child with the Eighten pence weekley pention if she had lomes and Health. as to Edward Flather he is at Home in the same place where Hodgshon found him before his Mother says he Must pay no more and as far as I Can Learn he does not Intend till he be made Sum way, or if you send for him he Might pay if he would and I think he will Before he serve, so you may do as you think proper I have sent you the Best ~~inf~~ information I Can get I Disire you not to Let Hannah or any person Know what I have wrote of Flather as I think his mother is not to good

I hope you will write Imeadietly yours &c

Respectively

John Haley

Paradice Mantion
Decr 9th 1830

Notes: *In the correspondence that follows, it emerges that the Flather mentioned in this letter is the father of Hannah Nelson's illegitimate child (Hannah is the adult daughter of Grace Nelson).*

436 John Haley in Horton to [Stephen] Garnett in Kirkby Lonsdale, 10 January 1831 (WPR/19/7/6/24/57)

Mr Garnett Horton Jany 10th 1831

Sir/ with Regard to Hannah She and Child is well and I got her Money and Paid it to her but it was a full Month before. but there is an Other misforton happned. Ruth Daughter Sarah is with Child about twenty or 21 weeke gone. There was Every Liklehod of her been Married. But the man has turned his mind and now will not the mans name is David Haley he is a Collier by Trade. Our Towns people has found Sarah out and they are not willing that she Should stay in the Town any longer then a few Days so of Consequence they took her yesterday Before a Magestrate to make Oath of her Settlement and Bring her with an Order in the Corse 8 or 10 Days therefore I thought fit to let you know if you think proper to Order sum Other way they say that there is a Way that one Town Can Indemnify an oher Town so that the Child will not belong the town it is born in but Still Belong as its Mother there is a Case of this happened Latley In our Nabourhod and it is done so and Ruth Could wish her Daughter to Stop and lying with her at home if you please and Can do so therefore you must not fail to ~~let~~ ^~~let~~^ ~~me~~ send me word how you will do or they will bring her with an Order verry soon

Yours Respectively

Paradice Mantion John Haley
Jan 10th 1831

Notes: *Intriguingly, Haley writes that Ruth's daughter, Sarah, has been 'found out' by the townspeople of Horton having got herself with child outside marriage, and that they 'are not willing she should stay in the Town any longer than a few days'. However, it also seems that, in fact, this is an entirely pragmatic threat from the vestry, in order to indemnify itself against any future responsibility for the child.*

437 Ab[raha]m Baker in Horton to the Parish of Kirkby Lonsdale, 2 April 1831 (WPR/19/7/6/24/34)

Horton April 2 1831

Sir/

Hannah Nelson one of your Poor with us has requested me to write to you for her Childs Pay now due 22/6 she says as she is much <in> [*page torn*] want of it your remitance by return of Post will be very acceptable

For Han^{h} Nelson
Abm Baker Overseer

438 John Hirst in Great Horton to the Parish of Kirkby Lonsdale, 26 May 1831 (WPR/19/7/6/24/25)

Great Horton ^May^ 26th 1831

Sir

I write to you concerning Hannah Nelsons child pay of Great Horton as Hannah and ~~I~~ me was married at Bradford Church the 5th day of May in the year of our lord 1831 I now think it is my duty to write to you to hear which way you are for taking, weather you are for sending me the money that is due or that I must send the child to you by an order and I think that Edward Flather only wants sharply looking after for he is in very good work if you do not return me a very speedy answer I shall send the child without fail

I remain yours
John Hirst

Direct
John Hirst
Great Horton Bank Bottom
Near Bradford

439 Ruth Nelson in Horton to the Parish of Kirkby Lonsdale, 28 July 1831 (WPR/19/7/6/24/12)

Gen[t]
I rite to inform you that my Daughter was Brought to Bed yesterday and in Consequence she is in want of things Nessasary for those times it not being in my power to help her you will please to send her releif the father of the Child has never Brought her any mony she will come as soon as she is able to Affilatate you Complaince
will Oblidge your Ob[t]
Servant
Ruth Nelson
Direct for me Horton Bank
Bottom Horton Near Bradford
July 28 – 1831

440 John Hirst in Great Horton to the Parish of Kirkby Lonsdale, 8 October 1831 (WPR/19/7/6/24/2)

Great Horton Oct[r] 8th 1831
Sir
I take this oppertunity of writing to you concerning Hannah Nelsons Childs pay and I hope you will send the Money that is due as before, I recived your letter the 16th day of July please be so kind to send me word how my Sister Betty is
from your
John Hirst
Derect
John Hirst
Wool comber
Bank bottom Great Horton
Near
Bradford

441 John Hirst and Sarah Nelson to the Parish of Kirkby Lonsdale, 20 February 1832 (WPR/19/7/6/25/9)

Feberury 20 1832
Sir i take the liberty of writing these few lines unto you giving you to understand that you promised to pay me the money Quarterly concernin^g^

Hannah Nelson Child i wish to Know the reason why you do not fullfill your promis i shall expect the full amount for i will not keep it for less than the deemed pay   i remain yours

John Hirst

NB please Sir you promised to send me some money at Christmas and you hav^e^ send none yet i am very ill and Stand in great need of in

i remain Sar^a^h Nelson

Yorrs

Notes: *The handwriting in this and the following letter are the same, whether signed by John Hirst or Sarah Nelson. The fact that there is a note added to each by Sarah may seem curious, as Hirst earlier claimed (Letter 438) that he had married Hannah Nelson and had taken parental responsibility for her illegitimate child. However, in Letter 444 it appears that Hannah and Sarah are living in the same household, presumably with John Hirst.*

442 John Hirst and Sarah Nelson to the Parish of Kirkby Lonsdale, 3 March 1832 (WPR/19/7/6/25/18)

March 3 1832

Sir

i take the liberty of writing to you concerning hannah Nelson Child pay i expected it at the time if i do not receve an answer in a week from this letter the Child will be sent by an order form the poorhouse we are both out of employ and the town will not keep other town poor i shall expect it along with a answer to this teller due 24 ^shilling^ feberuay ^28^   John Hirst

N B we have waited with patiance and i think you are a man of on Concideration as you would have sent it before now i shall expect it along with the other

Sarah Nelson

443 John Hirst to the Parish of Kirkby Lonsdale, 19 May 1832 (WPR/19/7/6/25/27)

May 19 1832

Sir i now it is my duty to send to you another time Concerning hannah Nelsons Child pay i do not intend to friten you with my letters the Child is not mine and i Cannot keep him for less then the oder if you do not Think proper to pay me according to the order i hope you will be so good as to fetch the

Child if not i shall send him i beg you will answer this once it now stands goad to me £6 May 16 according to the order i recived your last letter safe March 12 hoping you will oblidge me this once

i am yours

John Hirst

i hope you will answer ~~L~~ me this time ether with mony or without

444 Ruth Nelson in Horton to the Parish of Kirkby Lonsdale, 4 July 1832 (WPR/19/7/6/25/37)

Horton July 4 1832

Gen^{t}

You will be so kind as to send the mony Due Next monday Fortnight to sarah Nelson and Hannah Hirst for their Children as soon as possible and be so kind as to send it in One Letter as it will save Expence Gen^{t} I hope you will take it into Consideration and <s>end [*page torn*] them ~~[**]~~ something more as I am Growing Old and it is Impossible for me to Assist them

hoping you will
Comply I Remain
Your Parishoner
Ruth Nelson

445 John Hirst to the Parish of Kirkby Lonsdale, 25 December 1832 (WPR/19/7/6/25/73)

December 25 1832

Sir i take liberty of writing to you Concerning Hannah Nelsons Child pay giving you to understand that the Father of the Child is both able to pay and will pay if looked after i think it is high time to have my money payed according to the order due unto me $^{£}$2.8^{s}.6^{d} on the 26 if you will not look after the Father Send me the money or i shall be constrained to try other means

John Hirst

446 Ruth Nelson in Horton to the Parish of Kirkby Lonsdale, 4 May 1833 (WPR/19/7/6/26/50)

Horton May 4 1833

Gent

You will be so kind as to send my pay by the 13th May as it is my Rent Day your Compliance will Oblige your Parishoner

Ruth Nelson

447 Ruth Nelson in Horton to the Parish of Kirkby Lonsdale, 8 March 1834 (WPR/19/7/6/27/4)

Horton Mar^{h} 8 1834

Gent

I rec^{d} your letter of the 27 Feby and mony for wich I return you my thanks the Children are both Liveing David Haley and E^{d}. Fladden ~~have~~ are both married and Each a Child and in my Opinion they are both able to pay if you think proper to make them I hope you will allow them something more per Week trade being so bad at present that it is impossible for them to maintain there Childrens with only 11^{d} pr Week Each when postage is Deducted if not they will be Compeld to apply to Horton

Yours

Ruth Nelson

448 Ruth Nelson in Great Horton to the Parish of Kirkby Lonsdale, 6 September 1835 (WPR/19/7/6/28/31)

Great Horton Septr 6 1835

Sir

At your request I send you this Letter to inform you that my Daughtr is not married nor Likely the father of her Child is Married and has a Wife and 1 Child his Trade a Collier is bad in sumer I think if you was to seek after it you would get something. be so kind as to send Sarah and Hannah in One Letter as it would save Expence it will be Due on the 9th

Your Obt S

Ruth Nelson

15.

PEARSON, letters 449–481

449 Rob[er]t Pearson in Whitehaven to John Hall in Kirkby Lonsdale, 29 [****] 1809 (WPR/19/7/6/2/8)

Whitehaven [****] [*page torn]* the 29th 1809

Mr Hall/ I desi<re y>ou [*page torn*] will send me my Pention in due time and Lett me know the day that I am Payd up to as it was 2 weeks past the time acording to my Recking the last time which it dos very Badly for me that way so I desire you will send it in tim

So I Remain Yours
Robt Pearson
To be left at Frederick Mooneys
Pranks Lane George Street
Whitehaven

Circumtext: *Address of Recipient:* Mr John Hall Shop Keeper Kirby Lonsdale Westmoreland
Postmarked: Whitehave<n>

Note: *Even though there is no indication in which month this letter was sent, the fact that it was sent to John Hall suggests it predates the rest of Pearson's correspondence in the collection (we know that Hall was the overseer before Stephen Garnett, who took office sometime in 1809 – see Letter 233).*

450 Rob[er]t Pearson in Whitehaven to Step[he]n Garnett in Kirkby Lonsdale, 15 August 1809 (WPR/19/7/6/2/25)

Whitehaven Aug<ust> [*obscured by wax seal*] the 15th 1809

Mr Garnett/

I desire you will send me my Pention which is due on the 16th and more over I am in great want of Cloths Espesley Briches Stockins and a hanker-chief which I hope you will be so kind as to Send them and not to delay in sending my Pention but you will Please to See about getting it advansed or other wise I must aply here I was at a Magestrate and told me he would give me an order to the overseer here so I hope you will see about it but do not fail in sending it at this time besides it Costs me 1^{s} 4^{d} Eath time Pleas to derect for me to be left at the Post office till Called for

I am yours Robt Pearson

Circumtext: *Address of recipient:* For Step^{n} Garnett Over seer Kirby Lonsdale Westmoreland

In margin in different hand [SG]: Granted 1/ more Pention

451 Rob[er]t Pearson in Whitehaven to Stephen Ga[rnet]t in Kirkby Lonsdale, 28 September 1809 (WPR/19/7/6/2/30)

Whitehaven Septr the 28th 1809

Mr. Garrnet/

I am under the Nessesity of writing to you again for Cloathing again for I am quite Naked for boath Coat Westcoat and Briches and Stockings which I hope you will not delay in sending them and besides you must Send me more suport for it Cannot be Expected that 2^{S}/ P Week will keep life in at the price that Provitions is at and I am not able to earn aney thing to help it so I need not say aney more about it

So I Remain Yours
Robt Pearson

Derect for me at
The Gins [****] <Whi>tehaven [*obscured by wax seal*]

Circumtext: *Address of Recipient:* For Stephen Garrnet Overseer Kirby Lonsdale Westmoreland

452 G[eorge] Gibson to Revd Mr Knipe in Kirkby Lonsdale, [19 June/July 1811] (WPR/19/7/6/4/29)

[*letter torn or cut*] Agreeable to your request I call'd upon Robt Pearson and found him a very poor and feeble old man 81 years of age there is no removeing him but in the <c>oach [*page torn*] and I think it would be a wild Scheme to do it, he would be content with 3/ P week one of which he pays for his lodging, and I am sure the other two is little enough to keep life in, he is badly off for Shirts not having more than two these 4 years indeed my wife had compassion and gave him 2 old shirts – if the Overseers would give me an order to get him two coarse shirts and a pair of common stocking and also to pay him 3/ P week I should do it with pleasure as Old age and poverty presses heavy upon him wait yr command, believe me yrs

G Gibson

Circumtext: *Address of Recipient:* Rev^{d} Mr Knipe Middleton Kirkby Lonsdale

Notes: *The first half of this letter has been cut or torn off, which means that there is no date. However, its place in the original sequence of letters and the incomplete remains of the postmark suggest that it might have been sent in June or July 1811.*

453 John Pearson in Whitehaven to [Stephen] Garnett in Kirkby Lonsdale, 25 January 1812 (WPR/19/7/6/5/1)

Whitehaven January the 25th 1812

Mr Garnett,

I John Pearson the son of Robt Pearson as a parishoner I am sorry that I am under the Nessety of applying to you for Relief as I have a wife and 3 Small Children and my wife being Sick this 24 weeks and I having a person to find meat and waige to has thrown me to great distriss and it has Caused me not to be able to answer my hous Rent so that My Landlord his going to distriss me for it which if he do it will Cause me to apply for a Removel so if you would be so kind as to Send me the length of $^{£}$2 pound to pay that with I hope in God I would be able to sustain my fameley in some degree or other but the waiges for weaving is viry low indeed here and work is not Plenty and Provitions his high, if you grant me this aplication I hope with the asistance of the Almighty it will prolong me from becomming a burthin upon you alltogether

So I Remain Yours
John Pearson

Please Direct for me
Weaver at Ginns Near Whitehaven

Notes: *The handwriting in John's letter is clearly the same as that in his father, Robert's, correspondence.*

454 John Pearson in Whitehaven to [Stephen] Garnet[t] in Kirkby Lonsdale, 16 February 1812 (WPR/19/7/6/5/2)

Whitehaven Feberuary the 16th 1812

Mr Garnet

Sir I am Sorry that I am under the Nessesity of troubling you with another Letter Consirning the application I maid before for that Relief which I mentioned before and I have Now only beged of my Landlord to wait till I gett a answer from you which I hope you will take it into a Consideration to asist me in my present Situation which by the afliction of my wife has brought me to this I Cannot by aney means lay aney blame to my Landlord for going to distris me for it is the Case here that the Landlord will have his rint at the day Now if it is the ~~that~~ Case that I am not Suported Now he will proved and I must Make applycation here for I Can do No other which I would be sorry to apply for a weekely suport but in the present situation I Cannot avoid it he will wait the Coars of a week for your answer if not then I must apply here so I Remain

Yours
John Pearson
turn over

[*overleaf*] Pleas to Derect for Me
Weaver Ginns Near
Whitehaven

455 John Pearson in Whitehaven to [Stephen] Garnet[t] in Kirkby Lonsdale, 4 February 1813 (WPR/19/7/6/6/3)

Whitehaven February the 4 1813

Mr Garnet

Sir I am sorry that I am under the Nessesity of aplying to you for some Relief as My Wife is lying Bad and three helples Childer which I am not able to Suport them and I have no other place to Clame a Settlement My Father being a Parishoner and I Never was under aney Endenter Nor Never Payd aney ~~J S~~ */*Sisments*/* of aney Kind Imeadate Relief is Required for My Wife is not able to Be Removed for she has to be Lifted into bed and out

I am yours John Pearson

Circumtext: *In different hands*:

John Morrow
Francis Twedale
Thomas Wood
Thomas Earle

Joshua Dixon
M.D.

456 John Pearson in Whitehaven to Stephen Garnet[t] in Kirkby Lonsdale, 25 April 1813 (WPR/19/7/6/6/10)

Whitehaven Apriel the 25th 1813

Mr Garnet

I wrote to you before ~~stating to you~~ stating to you the situation I have been in so Long and the situation of my fameley at present and Beging sum more Relief which I have Never Rec^{d} aney acount from you if you would be so kind as to send me a little more Relief to asist me with till I see whether I gett the work that Mr Burrly has promised me but that will be after Whitsuntide and how long after I Cannot tell for it depends then how the yarn Come in from Bleaching as for the work that I have at present and the situation of my Wife I am not able to suport my fameley or I would be Viry sorry to trouble you but if I do not gett some suport I Cannot put on till the time above mentioned but I will be obliged to Come to you which I am Shewer will be a greater expence to you than alowing me a Little here for what ever you was to a low me it would be viry thankfully Rec^{d} for distris is bad to bide

I am yours John Pearson

Circumtext: *Address of Recipient:* For Mr Stephen Garrnet Over seir Kirkby Lonsdale Westmoreland

Postmarked: Whitehaven 26 AP 26 1813 326

457 Rob[er]t Pearson in Whitehave[n] to Stephen Garnet[t] in Kirkby Lonsdale, 3 October 1813 (WPR/19/7/6/6/17)

Whitehaven October the 3^{d} 1813

Mr Garnet/ I am under the Nessesity of writing to you and in great want of all Kind of Nesecerys I have Nothing Neither to keep me Warm nor yeat Clean and Mr Gilson does not wish to do aney thing of that kind without orders from you and it is Viry Little wearing aparrel that I have Even gott so that I am intirley out of all sorts so I desire you will Either send or other wise Write to Mr Gilson and Impower him to Act in the same

I am Yours
Robt Pearson

Circumtext: *Address of Recipient*: For Mr Stephen Garnet Over Seer Kirkby Lonsdale Westmoreland

Postmark: Whitehave<n>

458 Geo[rge] Gibson in Whitehaven to Stephen Garnett in Kirkby Lonsdale, 24 March 1814 (WPR/19/7/6/7/3)

W[t]haven 24 Mar
Dear Sir 1814

I was favor'd with yours this morning, a few hours after I received it R. Pearsons son came to tell me he was dead, I went and made enquiry what was commonly allowed on such cases which I found to be generally two Guineas, in course I immediately gave them two Guineas they are very poor – James Grundy paid me to 30th march Inst, I have 3/ in hand the Balance will be £1.19.10 which Grundy can settle I am Sir yrs respectfully Geo. Gibson

Circumtext: *Address of Recipient:* Mr Stephen Garnett Guardian of Poor Kirby-Lonsdale

Postmarked: Whitehaven 25MAR25 1814 326

459 John Pearson in Whitehaven to the Parish of Kirkby Lonsdale, 20 October 1816 (WPR/19/7/6/9/12)

Whitehaven October the 20th 1816

Sir

I am Sorry that I under the disagreable Nessesaty of aplying to you for some Relief towards my Rent as it is out of my Power to make it up and the most of the Landlords here has but viry little money so that if I have not some asistance it will be a means of bringing us a burthen upon you

We are six of a fameley and wages is but Viry low and work Viry scarse here which I supose it is the same with you and I Cannot say whether I shall be able to suport my fameley or not but with some asistance of what I have mentioned I shall indevour all I Can I would not wish to become a burthen if possible I Could avoid it

So I hope Sir you will not fail in granting me some asistance

I am yours
John Pearson

Derect for
John Pearson Weaver
Ginns Near Whitehaven

Circumtext: *In different hand [SG]:* If needful give him 10/

In further hand, in pencil: No[v] 14th gave him 5/ J Grundy

460 John Pearson in Whitehaven to the Parish of Kirkby Lonsdale, 23 October 1818 (WPR/19/7/6/11/29)

Whitehaven Octr. the 23d 1818

Sir I am sorry that I am under the necessity of applying to you for some Relief we are 7 of a familey and as I have had the sickness that is the Typus feavour in our hous this 13 weeks and I have been Short of work all summer onley about 4 days work in the week and now I have onley two days work and then I do not know when I shall gett aney more so that I have don as long as I Can and my wife and oldest Daughter is a loosing for want of Relief so that without your asistance as soon as Possible I shall be forced to apply here

I am yours John Pearson

Circumtext: *In different hands:* Joshua Dixon, M.D.
Jonas Walker Overseer
In further hand[SG]: Granted out of Rates 15/ out of Donation Money 5/ ~~Granted $^{£}$1 0^{s} 0^{s}~~

461 John Pearson in Whitehaven to the Parish of Kirkby Lonsdale, 29 November 1818 (WPR/19/7/6/11/33)

Whitehaven November the 29th 1818

Sir I am Very Sory that I am under the nesesity of applying to you again from the Situation of our work and the situation of my famely nesesity forces me to apply as for my wife she his aparently no hopes of hir Recovery She his in it the third time and as for my work when I had it I have onley made 16s.8d per week this Considreable time back and my hous Rint Now is 2s. pir week and 1s. for fire having to keep it Night and day so you may judge whether nesesity Calls me or not which I am viry sorry it should but I hope you will not neglect me at this time

I am yours John Pearson

Circumtext: *In different hand [SG]:* Granted out of Donation Money 5^{s} out of Rates 15^{s}/

462 John Pearson in Whitehaven to the Parish of Kirkby Lonsdale, 13 December 1818 (WPR/19/7/6/11/38)

Whitehaven Decr the 13th 1818

Sir I am sorrey that I am under the necesity of troubling you with another application as nessesity forcies me to it but I supose as the Doctor and overseers name was not to it you supose it to be fals but I ashewer you we have had 5 out of the 7 Lying it is Either 18 or 19 weeks since the Sikness first begin in our hous and it Returning on my wife has brout hir so week that it is not known what way it is going to be with hir and the situation of my Earning I Cannot do without Relief which I know I Can gett here by applying I put of troubling you so long as ever I Could do so I desire your answer as soon as possible that I may know what to do in it for the Situation my famely is in there is no time to delay had I applyed here at the first they would have aloud me Relief and hired a woman in to the hous to look after my fameley I do not know how you think I am to suport 7 of us with 10s 8d per week takings 3s of it for hous rint and fire and there is no prospect of it being aney better this winter

I am yours John Pearson

463 John Pearson in Whitehaven to the Parish of Kirkby Lonsdale, 1 December 1819 (WPR/19/7/6/12/31)

Whitehaven December the 1th 1819

Sir I am sorry that I am under the nessesity of troubling you for some Relief as I am viry badly of for work this while back but I still indevoured to put on as well as I Could but I a shuer you it was but viry poorly and it is getting wors for this last 7 days I had only 5s and 4d so you may judge what that will do for 7 of us and I applyed to one of the Masters for some other kind of work to help out with but he told me that they wanted no work doing for they Could sell nothing so I have but poor hopes of being aney better so that I was thinking of getting my family moved but if you grant me some little Relief I might pirhaps put on a while to see if orders would Come in and then there would be an alteration

I beg you will not delay in sending for it is greatly wanted

I am yours

John Pearson

Circumtext: *In different hand [SG]*: Granted 1.0.0

464 John Pearson in Whitehaven to the Parish of Kirkby Lonsdale, 3 August 1820 (WPR/19/7/6/13/19)

Whitehaven August the 3 1820
Sir I am sorry that I am under the Nesesity of applying for some Relief for I have been viry pooly of for Work all this Summer onley 4 days work in the week and Now my Wife is brought to bed of a nother Child and my Work is Reduced again it is onley 9s Shillings pir Week now so that it is impiss^i^ble for me to suport my famely on it before now I have been allmost fainting at work but I was still hoping for better but it is wors so without Your asistance I Cannot Continue here, I am Yours
John Pearson

Circumtext: *In different hand [SG]*: Granted 20s/

465 John Pearson in Whitehaven to the Parish of Kirkby Lonsdale, 4 January 1821 (WPR/19/7/6/14/1)

Whitehaven january the 4th 1821
Sir I am sorry that I am under great Necesity of applying to you for Relief which I should be very sory to do if I Could avoid it but our Masters has stinted Every man to 10^{s} per week taking 2^{s} from that ^for hous rint^ leaves viry little for my fameley you may judge What 1s pir head will do and we have no hopes of mends for this allways was the time for Canvas going of but they have Sutch a stock on hand that we do not Expect aney alteration before next winter it is not in my power to gett as mutch as will bring me over to lay my Case before you so I hope the Gentelmen from this will take it into Consideration and settle somthing weekley on me as I have sent you a Corect account of what we have aloud weekley and what remain for my fameley so that your asistance is greatly wanted Necesity Calls for it as soon as possible
I Remain yours
John Pearson

Circumtext: *In different hand [SG]*: Not Granted at present

466 John Pearson in Whitehaven to [Stephen] Garnett in Kirkby Lonsdale, 2 May 1821 (WPR/19/7/6/15/7)

Whitehaven May the 2 1821
Mr Garnett I am Sorrey that I am under the disagreable nesesity of making aplication to you if you please to asist me with my Rint as it is not in my

power to raise it from the want of health for I have this winter all a long been in Sutch a poor Stat of health as I never Expearenced we have been maney a time very pinced to gett vitules

I hope the Gentelmen will take it into Consideration to asist me at this time

I Remain Yours
John Pearson

Circumtext: *In different hand [SG]*: Granted £2.0.0
In pencil: £2.10s.02

467 John Pearson in Whitehaven to [Stephen] Garnet[t] in Kirkby Lonsdale, 31 October 1821 (WPR/19/7/6/14/39)

Whitehaven Octr. the 31st 1821

Mr Garnet I am Sorry that I am under the Nesesity of applying to you to asist me with my Rent as it is not in my power to Rays it up I told you the situation of my work which insted of being better it has been wors Ever Since for I have sometims work and sometimes non so that I have been Viry pinshed to gett Vitules for my fameley and likewise I have been troubled with a good deal of sickness my self and likewise my fameley and at the present there is two of them sick but I blame the Shortness of victules for it for I was in general indued with good health I have been so far beat that I have been allmost Ready to give up and apply for a Removal Still a fresh hope Struck my mind but Now all hopes of aney amendment for this winter is over the masters themselves as [******] [*page torn*] now for they are putting hands of and we do not know Every week who is to be the Next so that I am in a viry Critecal Situation betwixt my Landlord and what little work I have I hope from this Corect acount that the Gentelmen will Consider my situation and asist me throw it or otherwise I am don

I Remain yours
John Pearson

Circumtext: *In different hand [SG]*: Granted Rent

468 John Pearson in Whitehaven to the Parish of Kirkby Lonsdale, 30 October 1822 (WPR/19/7/6/15/34)

Whitehaven Octr the 30th 1822
Sir I am sorry that I under the painfull necsity of applying to you for Relefe of my House rent which I was in great hopes I should not have had ocation but I think I am born to Crisis and hard fortune for I have been lying this 5 weeks of a lame Leg which I had but viry bad hopes of it at one time and I am not able to work mutch with it yeat when I take a Serous thought of my hard fortune it trouble me till I Call again to Recolection that the Lords will must be don and I must submitt to it all and I am viry mutch afraid of my bad health again this winter as there is a pain still lays in my Side ever since winter last I hop the Gintilmen will have no objections in asisting me which if I had been able to work I would not have troubled them I am yours
John Pearson
the derections is
Temple Laine No.4

Circumtext: *In different hand [SG]*: Granted same as last year if necessary

469 John Pearson in Whitehaven to [Stephen] Garnett in Kirkby Lonsdale, 14 January 1823 (WPR/19/7/6/16/3)

Whitehaven January 14th 1823
Mr Garnett I am Now laying in a Deplorable Situation I took on the Night of the Sixt a very strong shiviring fit which made the bed Crack under me and it shot from head to foot throw my Whole frame and I have been Racked with pain day and Night ever since I have never been out of my bed nor no sines of Relief I hope sir you will not fail in Reliefing me at this time I am fetched viry Low and viry weake
John Pearson

Circumtext: *In different hand [SG]:* Tempel Catharine Street

470 John Pearson in Whitehaven to [Stephen] Garnet[t] in Kirkby Lonsdale, 8 February 1823 (WPR/19/7/6/16/7)

Whitehaven Feby the 8 1823
Mr Garnet I am sory that I am under the painfull Necesity of applying to you again for Relief as I am Now 5 weeks Confined and I am onley like a young Child learning to walk a Cross the floor I am afraid it will be some time before

I be able for my work if Ever I be I am Sorly afraid I shall not as the disorder has fell down into one of my legs and it apers as if as if it were going to be left week and the Cinies is drawn quite stif which gives me a great Concirn I hope Sir you will not Neglect me at this time as you may be Shewer my want is great in my Condition

I am yours
John Pearson

471 John Pearson in Whitehaven to [Stephen] Garnet[t] in Kirkby Lonsdale, 25 February 1823 (WPR/19/7/6/16/14)

Whitehaven Feby the 25th 1823
Mr Garnet I wrote to you before but Recd no answer which inducies me to think that you supose me to be imposing but I shall now lett you know my situation it is 20 weeks now and I have not been able to make a full weeks work only two weeks out of all that and now I am going in 8 weeks not able to do aney thing the first month I was not Expected life and since that the disorder is fallen into my leg which it has been twice opned and no aperance yeat of me getting soon to work but I am viry mutch afraid that it will leave my leg weake and I shall not be able to work now Sir you may judg of my situation whether I am in Necesity or not but I have don as long as I Can so that without your asistance I must be obliged to apply to this township for Relief which I should be very sory to do if it was not Real necesity but I hope you will not put me to that

I am yours John Pearson

Circumtext: *In different hand [SG]*: Granted £1.0s.0d

472 Joseph Hodgson in Whitehaven to the Parish of Kirkby Lonsdale, 26 February 1823 (WPR/19/7/6/16/15)

I hereby certify, that John Pearson of this place has been ill since the 14th of last Month: and that for the last month four weeks he has not been able to leave his house

Joseph Hodgson
Apothecary

Whitehaven Dispensary
Feby. 26th 1823

473 John Pearson in Whitehaven to [Stephen] Garnet[t] in Kirkby Lonsdale, 21 March 1823 (WPR/19/7/6/16/21)

Whitehaven Martch the 21th 1823

Mr Garnet I am sorry that Nesity urges me to trouble you with a third letter for some Relief or otherwise your orders to apply here which I am very unwilling to do without your orders alltho I have been strongly advised by people that sees my situation I was 10 weeks and never brought one penny into the hous and Now my wife is lying and not able to turn hir self in bed and has been now going in three weeks she may survive till you Recd. this and she may not for the Doctor now Can Recomend nothing but Nurishment for hir and it is not in my Power to gett it for hir for me laying so long of you may judge wheither I am in distres or not I do ashuer you that your asistance is greatly wanted or otherwise your orders to apply here or otherwise to lett me know if you wish me to be Removed when she is able for to suffer sutch distris it would be mutch better for me to be nyer hand and you Could se my situation alltho there is nothing there that I Could make so well out for my fameley

Sir I hope you will
Relief my distris at this time
I am yours
John Pearson

474 J[ohn] Pearson in Whitehaven to [Stephen] Garnet[t] in Kirkby Lonsdale, 1 May [1823] (WPR/19/7/6/16/59)

Whitehaven May the 1th

Mr Garnet I am sorry that I am under the painfull necesity of making aplication for asistance with my hous rent as it is not in my power to Raise it from the aflicted state I have been in and is yeat all tho I have got to work it is not a great deal I am able to do for I have one leg Still in a bad state and in deed all one side is bad I Can say with a Clear Conshions that I have not been able to work a full weeks work only two this 7 months and my wife is but in an indifferent state yeat am viry mutch afraid that I shall not gett strength of my leg to indevour for my famely I am yours Jno

Pearson

Circumtext: *In different hand [SG]:* Rent Granted

Notes: *Although there is no year by which to date this letter, its place in the sequence strongly suggests that it was sent in 1823.*

475 John Pearson in Whitehaven to [Stephen] Garnett in Kirkby Lonsdale, 11 December 1823 (WPR/19/7/6/16/58)

Whitehaven Decr the 11th 1823

Mr Garnett I am sorry that I am under the necesity of applying to you for helps for my Rint as I have used Every indevour and all that I Can raise is but 11s shillings for from the week State of my body and the disorder which remains in my leg and beside I gott my back hurt Laitley so that it is [******] [*illegible*] that I am able to do what I am doing as my work is viry bad and I am not able to persavear it Causes me to sitt 16 or 19 hours every day and onley makes 9 shillings pir week and that only when I have work for we have a great delay waiting for work So you may judge my situation is not very good so without your help we must be sold up and besides I find that I Cannot hould out so maney hours as I have don from my wack state now Sir I have laid my situation in short before you and I hope the Gentlemen will take it into Consideration to asist me as nature Can do no more than it can bide

So I Conclude and Remains
Yours John Pearson

476 [Alice?] Pearson in Whitehaven to the Parish of Kirkby Lonsdale, 28 February 1824 (WPR/19/7/6/17/9)

Whitheaven Feb 28th 1824

Sir
I am under the nessety of wright^ing^ to you as my husbant was under the nessety of goin away to seek work and I have only my son doing aney thing at Present and that will Be only this week and is ernings Can only Be small of a boy of 12 years of age so If you would Be so kind as to send me sum small Rilief as my Quarter rent is due and you know that it is hard doing for a woman with 6 Children and Littel or nothing Cuming in

From Your humbel Servant
Alias Pearson

Circumtext: *Address of Return Recipient [SG]:* Mr. John Gibson Tea Dealer 61 Draper Street Whiteheaven Granted 10^{s}/

477 [Alice] Pe[a]rson in White[h]aven to the Parish of Kirkby Lonsdale, April [1824] (WPR/19/7/6/17/17)

Apral Whiteaven

Sir ^i^ Beg leave to let you know that Me and my Children as ben sick sinse Mr Grundey was at my house and ^and one of my^ young Wimane as had the scarlet fever And i was oute of work 6 days so that i was abliged to borow 6 Shillings and as for my husbant sending Aney thing for hour Coming for he had One pound hads for the goods Going be Sids they are sadley broken so that he had them ^re^ payre ^them^ Sir i rot this the Last month and my husbant he Sent me relief so that it stoped of writing til now and we have had no work since las tusday And we dont Expect aney this weak Comi^n^g so you may Be sch^ou^re that Betwen sicknes and want of work you May be schour of my want that I was forst to get 4 shilings more ^so that it well be 1 poound 5 shillings^ at my Bread shop so that mr Grundey ^and you^ will Concloude a bout our Coming so that we may not be long here I had 26 Power Rate 15 Lamp and paiing tax I went to the Cares and they would not In Gage such a large and the one man Charged Ɛ pound to Cndle so that I tok the other man at 2 pound 5 shilings to Cndle ^m^y Land Loard will a bate nothing of the ful Rent mr Grundey knows ~~w~~ wat my Bil was at the shop and I hve it not in my Power for aney perigens on the Road and all for want of work which I am sorey for it But I hope it will be the lat trouble for you the man must be payed hear as Senley inge to Candle

So no more at present from your
Humble sirvent Alies Person
Ples send as so To as posebl

Mr Brone wanted to write But I tolde him I could write My self

Notes: *Although the content of this letter does not indicate in what year it was written or sent, its place in the sequence suggests that it was sent in 1824*

Note also that the writer (Alice(?) Pearson) states that she had someone on hand who would write for her ('Mr Brone' [Brown?]) but that she wanted to write herself, despite her imperfect command of written English.

478 John Pearson in Holm to [Stephen] Garnet[t] in Kirkby Lonsdale, 6 May [1824] (WPR/19/7/6/17/21)

Holm May the 6
Mr Garnet as the time draws near for the moving of my famely I thought proper to write to you to know as I purpose writing to Whitehaven on ~~on~~

Sunday whether there is aney arraingment maid or not or wheither I must send them word to apply to the Overseer at Whitehaven but I am allmost Certain that if there be no word of aney araingment maide they will have applyed before my litter reaches there as they will want to be a way

I am yours John Pearson

Notes: *Although the content of this letter does not indicate in what year it was written or sent, its place in the sequence suggests that it was sent in 1824.*

479 Tho[ma]s Atkinson in Hulme to the Churchwardens and Overseers of Kirkby Lonsdale, 22 April [1833] (WPR/19/7/6/26/52)

To
The Churchwardens & Overseers of the Poor of the Township of
Kirkby Lonsdale

Gentn/

John Pearson a Pauper belonging yr Township hath not only been in a Bad State of Health the last 15 Days and quite unable to follow His Employment but Continues so – the Doctor whose Certificate is here with attached hath attended & done what He can for him – He now stands need of Relief and without your Assistance I Really dont see how the Man is to be got to his Employment again

Hoping for your Kind & Immediate Attention which will Oblige Yrs Respctfly

Thos Atkinson
Guardian

Circumtext: *Facing page, in different hand*:

This is to certify that John Pearson of Clawthorpe has for the last fortnight been affected with a Violent pain in his head and general debility of the body and in consequence thereoff he has been incapable of following his usual occupation

Wm Hacking
Surgeon

Hulme
April 22^d^

Notes: *Although the content of this letter does not indicate in what year it was written or sent, its place in the sequence suggests that it was sent in 1833.*

480 Rev. [A William Shaw] in Hulme to the Churchwardens and Overseers of Kirkby Lonsdale, 3 May 1833 (WPR/19/7/6/26/45)

To the Churchwardens & Overseers of the Township of K Lonsdale –

Gentn John Pearson a Pauper belonging to your Township late in Our Employ – from Sickness & a sort of general Dibillity hath not been able to earn a Sixpence during the last month & tho He is now I hope coming Round again unfortunately now his ^Wife^ fallen Sick and from as much the same sort of Complaint with which he hath been Afflicted – Do suffer me to State to your Vestry that those people really do Stand great need of some Releif to restore them to some little Strength again –

In hopes that you will take their Case into Consideration & if you will Drop us a Line with your order We will do the Needfull on Yr Ac
Waiting Yr. Ans^{r} We are Gentn Yrs.
With Due Respect
Hulme May 3 1833 Rev. <A. William Shaw> [*not clearly legible*]

Circumtext: *Address of Recipient:* To the Churchwardens & Overseers of the Poor of the Township of Kirkby Lonsdale

In different hand [SG]: Granted 6s/

481 Tho[ma]s Atkinson in Hulme to the Overseer of the Poor in Kirkby Lonsdale, 3 July 1835 (WPR/19/7/6/28/41)

To the Overseer of the Poor of the Township of Ky Lonsdale/

Sir/ As Guardian & Overseer for this Township I beg to acquaint you that Jno Pearson who belongs Yr Township is & hath been most Sorely afflicted in both his Legs so much so that He is not only unable to follow Any Employment but under the Necessity of laying his Legs up under Poultices &c this affliction having Continued now some time hath put him into great Distress – I consider this a Case of Relief & the Townships duty to Render it this for Yr Consideration & Yr Attention

Hulme Will Oblidge Yrs
July 3 1835 Thos Atkinson
Overseer

16.

ROBINSON, letters 482–509

482 Tho[ma]s Robinson in Preston to the Parish of Kirkby Lonsdale, 12 February 1824 (WPR/19/7/6/17/6)

Preston 12th Febry. 1824

Sir

I am very sorry that I should be under the necessity of addressing you on the subject of relief but having been upwards of four Months out of employment I find myself compelled to it my Father Joseph Robinson was a Mercer & Draper at Kirby Lonsdale and died about 1793 or four leaving my Mother with myself and two sisters which are since dead I was born in April 1790 I have a wife and 3 Children my wife is a very unhealthy person and has been under the Doctors for a long time which has been very expensive and we are ~~we are~~ in daily expectation of receiving a bill from one which will not be less than 2£ and which we are unable to pay I was Brought up a Cotton Spinner with my Uncle Robinson at Halton near Lancaster who is dead about 10 Months since and I have been since that time a Preston Their are several new Factories Building at Preston so that I expect work will be plentifull this next summer but at present their are a deal of spinners out of work I get a day or two when I other spinners are off but it is only very little that I can earn by that means I am therefore under the necessity of asking for relief till I can get into work which I shall do as soon as possible

Mr John Miller of Halton Park can testify to the truth of what I have stated

I remain your humble Servt.
Thos Robinson

Three tun yard
North Road
Preston

483 Tho[ma]s Robinson in Preston to the Parish of Kirkby Lonsdale, 13 March 1824 (WPR/19/7/6/17/12)

Preston 13th March 1824

Sir

Having received no answer to my former letter I am under the necessity of writing again to you on the same subject I have not had any employment since I wrote before and have been compelled to dispose of several things out of the house to support my family but having nothing more to sell I cannot tell how it will be possible for us to live without some relief I expect to be at work in a fortnight or 3 Weeks at a new Factory that is about starting and I have promise of the first wheels if you would be so kind as to send what will support us till then I hope I shall never again be troublesome as I can assure you that I am neither idle or drunken and only want employment Please to write as soon as possible and Direct to be left at Mr Prestons

[*overleaf*] Mr. Preston's three tuns North Road

I remain your Obdt Servt Thos Robinson

484 Edward Gardner in Halton to the Parish of Kirkby Lonsdale, 14 June 1824 (WPR/19/7/6/17/31)

Halton June 14th

1824

Gentlemen/

I have to acquaint you that a person of the name of Thomas Robinson applied to me respecting his settlement he said he had been at your place claiming it and you was opinion that his settlement was in our Parish I wish to state Gentlemen that in consequence of the application made to me I had him examined upon oath by the Majestrates at Lancr. on Saturday last and upon that examination it was found that his settlement was not with us,

I am Gentlemen,

Yours respectfully

Edward Gardner Overseer

P.S. I have wrote this at the request of the paupers friends

485 Tho[ma]s Robinson in Preston to the Parish of Kirkby Lonsdale, 26 August 1824 (WPR/19/7/6/17/35)

Preston 26th Augst. 1824

Sir

I had a letter from Halton some time ago saying that the overseer had been at Kirkby to see about my settlement and that you wanted to know whether after I came back from Manchester M^{r}. Robinson did not come to me and hire me for some specify'd time now I believe I said when I was at Kirkby that I never was hired for any time but only so long as it should be agreeable to both sides for me to stay and that I could either have left or been turned off at any weeks end I never was engaged on any other terms at the time I got the letter from Halton I was spinning for a man that was sick and I thought if any other work fell out when I had done there I would not give you any trouble about it but that job only lasted 3 weeks and I have had only a fortnight's work since for another sick man I have now been 3 weeks without any employment and am not able to do any longer without some assistance as I am got behind with the rent and have not any thing to get what we want to support life we could not possibly have done so long as we have done but for the assistance of our friends at Halton but as they have nothing to spare without injuring themselves we cannot <ex>pect [*page torn*] them to maintain us altogether the Overseer would tell you that it was the opinion of the Lancaster Magistrate that I belonged to Kirkby and I am almost persuaded you will think the same and if you do you will be so kind as to send us something to enable us to live till I can get some constant employment which I shall do as soon as possible but if you still think that I dont belong to Kirkby be so good as to send us word as soon as you can for we must certainly be removed some where that a settlement may be found next week as we really can do no longer please to pay the postage of your letter for I have not as much as will loose it I remain Your Humble Servant

Thos Robinson

To be left at the Three Tuns
North Road

486 Tho[ma]s Robinson in Preston to the Parish of Kirkby Lonsdale, 11 September 1826 (WPR/19/7/6/21/1)

Preston 11th Septr. 1826

Sir

I have been very much dissapointed at not receiving any thing from you this week having not had above two days work since John Taylor was here before at this present time we have not any thing in the house nor where to get any thing I cannot tell I should have wrote before now but knowing that Mr. Davis was at Kirby I thought you might perhaps wish to have some conversation with him about it and have sent it by him I have seen him this morning and he says that he just spoke to you and promised to see you again before he came away but that he had not the opportunity to call so that I yet hope you had intended to send it by him I therefore most earnestly beg you will send by return of Post as we are actually destitute of every means of support and have no other way but sell all that we have and if we have any thing left after paying what we owe to try to get back again I beg you will not consider this on the nature of a threat as you are aware we Have no other alternative at least whilst we stay at Preston I should be really very sorry to be obliged to come back and I think that I may get employment before long if I could have the means of staying here a while longer but without immediate assistance it is quite impossible

I remain your Obed^{t} Ser^{t}

Thos Robinson
No.48 Spring Gardens

487 Tho[ma]s Robinson in Preston to the Parish of Kirkby Lonsdale, 25 July 1828 (WPR/19/7/6/21/32)

Preston 25th July 1828

Sir

I suppose Mr. Robt. Davis will have informed you that I have lost the situation that I had got at Mr. Swainson's Warehouse I was engaged for a month but I did not suppose that it was for no longer but at the month end Mr. Swainson thought proper to take the same man on again without finding any fault with me that I know of but M^{r}. Davis will be able to tell you all about it I have not yet been able to get another situation ~~yet~~ and having removed my fa<mily> [*obscured by sealing wax*] hither as soon as I got into work we are redu<ced> [*obscured by sealing wax*] to the greatest distress and I am sorry that I should thus soon be obliged to apply to you for assistance as without it we shall be unable to live and we have it not in our power to get back either to Lancaster or any where else I have endeavoured all I can to get work but hitherto without success this week I shall have two weeks rent and shop to pay which is as long as I can have any credit for and therefore without your assistance I see no prospect but sell what few things we have and come back but if I could stay here I think I can perhaps get some thing to do by and by I remain your Hl. /ssmte./ Ser^{t}. Thos. Robinson

488 Tho[ma]s Robinson in Preston to the Parish of Kirkby Lonsdale, 30 August 1828 (WPR/19/7/6/21/28)

Preston 30th Augst. 1828

Sir

I am sorry to say that I have not got into any regular employment yet as work is very bad to meet with I had two days work last week at some new streets they have been making but they have dropt it at present this week I have had nothing to do nor can I say that I have any prospect just at present but I hope I shall be able to get something or other to do before long of which I will not fail to inform you as soon as it happens I have this week received 12s of John Taylor

I am Your hb^{le} Ser^{t}
Thos Robinson

489 Tho[ma]s Robinson in Preston to the Parish of Kirkby Lonsdale, 25 September 1828 (WPR/19/7/6/21/25)

Preston 25th Septr. 1828

Sir I have to acknowledge the receipt of 1 Pound by post for which I return you many thanks and should be very happy if I had no occasion to ask for more I can assure you that I have used every endeavour to get employment to support myself and family and am at present engaged for a month at Wm. Davis & Co. factory at 11s per week I am in hopes that it will be a permanent situation at least till I can get a better as their Manager who engaged me and with whom I am pretty well acquainted promised I should have a better as soon as any fell vacant but there is no prospect at present. It is not possible for 6 of us to live on 11s and pay rent and all things besides One pound or rather

19/10 is all that we have had for a Month, and we are so much in arrear as we could not pay any rent in that time our house is 2/6 per week and this is six weeks that we have not paid if you would set us strait and allow us rent till I can get a better place we would try if we could live and I have told our Landlord that I would write to you and he has promised to wait for your answer

I expected to have received something by John Taylor last Tuesday and if it had not been that I had got this place since I dont know what we must have done and the little I have to take this week end will not support us till next and we are as much behind at the Shop as they are willing to let us have I hope you will excuse my importunity for if it were possible to do without troubling you it would be great pleasure to me and I hope and trust it Will not be long before I shall be able to do so I remain your Hob^{le} Ser^{t}

Thos Robinson

490 Charles Albert in Preston to the Parish of Kirkby Lonsdale, 8 October 1828 (WPR/19/7/6/21/23)

North Road Preston 8th october 1828

Sir/ I beg leave to inform you that I am under the necesetty of addressing these lines to you hopeing you will not fail in Riteing ancer immadetly to me as I Can not stop any longer without my money from Thomas Robinson one of your parishners he hows me 8 wicks Rent at 2s.6d per wick which makes at this time – £1.0^{s}.0^{d}

I am verey Sorray for the man and is large family as I am quit Certain they have been nearly starved <f>or [*obscured by wax seal*] want of foode and som Cloase they have Strove thayer best ever Sence thay have been in my house but work being Short in Preston, Robinson Could not get any thing to do untill lately and now is wages is onely 11 shillings per wick that is but small to maintain six piple as for paying rent or Cloase out of that it is not posable – therefore I hope you will please to have the goodness as to pay me is Rent or els I most put baileys into the house as I Cannot loos the Rent I am wiling to take the Rent monthley or Quarterly if you will say that you will see me paid – poor man I am Sorray for im he is gon verey thin sence he Came to preston he apers to me to be industerus verey sober and onist inclined. Sir you may depend on the above I beg you will be please to ancer this immadetly before I take any other stops I most have my Rent from Som body as I have a large family and Can not aford to loos the Rent and as I have stated above Robinson is not able to pay me one peney nor to by imself a pair of shoes tho is feet is Constant quit wet – if you was to see them you would be sorray for im –

I am Sir yours truly
Charles Albert
North Road Preston

I beg leave to ad that Edward Tomlinson Esqr. near Kerby Lonsdale knows me well as I pay im som pounds every febuary for Ground Rent in Duke Street Preston

491 Charles Albert in Preston to the Parish of Kirkby Lonsdale, 12 October 1828 (WPR/19/7/6/21/24)

North Road Preston october 12th 1828

Sir/

Yours I Receved and the inclosed Pound Note in which I am much oblight to you for the Same but I perceve in your letter that you have not promiss me any forder pay. Therefore if you dos not I Certainly Most Make Robinson and is family quitt my house immadetly without a promiss from you or Som Sponceable person – Robinson is a strainger to me he only Came to my house last June I therefore Cannot let im have my house without any Rent as I well no it is not in is power to pay any So it apers to me if you Dont see that is Rent will be paid he most quit my house and no dout but wat he Most go to is parish for im and is family is alredy starveing poor man he Can not do More then he dos I ashore you thay lives Verey thin I ashore you that I Charges im much less for the house then any body els I ad and Could have for the house 7d per wick more then I charge im – I pay all taxes out of the 2s-6d per wick so that I only have left about 2-0 per wick – I beg leave to ad that a family like Robinsons be longing to preston parish Receves from the over seers wickly 5 or 6 Shillings a wick I many pounds in a year to the poor books as I have near 40 houses – Robinsons masters Name is Davis a Gentleman from your town and he Rents a very large house of ~~ed[***]~~ Edward Tomlinson Esqr. so that Mr. Tomlinson nows the above Gentlemen well I metchen these things so that if any defrode was ment they soon may be found out – the above Mr. Davis keeps a large facterry and Robinson works for im for a 11 Shillings per wick – & I hope I have not afended you in any thing I have Rote in this letter if I have I ask parden for the same I beg that your goodness will be please to Rite and let me no wat I have to depend on in a few days from this date – Yours Charles Albert

I paid 1-2 for your letter ~~being Duble~~

492 Tho[ma]s Robinson in Preston to the Parish of Kirkby Lonsdale, 27 June 1829 (WPR/19/7/6/22/33)

Preston 27th June 1829

Sir

It is with the greatest reluctance that I again apply to you for assistance I have for some time been engaged as a canvasser for books and have been able hitherto to support my family in some way by it but Whitsuntide being lately past and now the Races coming on people are very slack at taking in books besides to make it answer it is necessary that I should be from home a good deal and if I had what would keep my family at home and myself from home a week or two particularly till these Races are over I should then have an equal chance with others and I think there is might be a living got by it but at present I am really reduced to the greatest distress out of which I can see no way of escape but by your assistance and if you would be so kind as to send by John Taylor next week I should be very much obliged to you and will endeavour as much as possible to do without having occasion to apply to you again My oldest Daughter has been upwards of a year in service at Liverpool so that I suppose she will have got a settlement there

Mrs Parkinson call'd to see us last week I remain Sir your Obet Servt

Thos Robinson

493 Tho[ma]s Robinson in Preston to the Parish of Kirkby Lonsdale, 30 June 1829 (WPR/19/7/6/22/32)

Preston 30th June 1829

Sir

I am sorry to have to repeat my application to you but necessity compels me to it I suppose you perhaps might not receive my letter time enough to send by John Taylor as he did not bring any word at all I should not have defered writing so long but through thinking I might perhaps get some orders before the week was expired but in this I was entirely dissapointed and was therefore under the necessity of applying to you I still think that I might be able to get a living by this business if I could extend my circuit more especialy when there Races are over and I intended to go to Lancaster next week ~~till~~ and continue in that quarter till Preston was got settled there are many people that make a comfortable living but they are obliged to travel a good way and I think I might do as well as others if I had the same chance but as it is I am quite unable and am at present in the greatest distress if you would have the kindness therefore to send by the post I will not presume to mention any sum but leave it to your own judgement as I have fully stated my views and I do assure you that no exertion shall be wanting on my part to do without further assistance as soon as possible but as we are I really do not know how we are to exist till you can send to relieve us I therefore confidently but humbly rely upon your kindness without which we cannot possibly for the present exist I am with the greatest respect your Obd[t] Serv[t]

Tho[s] Robinson

Circumtext: *In different hand [SG]*: Granted £1.0s.0d

494 Tho[ma]s Robinson in Preston to the Parish of Kirkby Lonsdale, 13 May 1830 (WPR/19/7/6/23/10)

Preston 13 May 1830

Sir

My Son Thos died this morning and as I am entirely unable to defray the expences of his funeral I am obliged to apply to you hoping that you will favour me for this time I am very thankfull for all the kindness that I have experienced from you and I beg you will excuse this application but as his protracted illness has prevented me from using that exertion which is necessary in the business that I am at present engaged in I am truly at a loss to know how to get this week over I should have gone of this morning to Lancaster and tomorrow to Burton in Kendal and round that country for which I should have received what would have supported us at present but as I am prevented from undertaking this journey I beg you will send me something to support us till we get through this difficulty in addition to the funeral expences. I am very sorry to be so pressing and hope to be able after this to do without troubleing you any further

I remain your Obe[dt] Ser[t]

Tho[s] Robinson

495 Tho[ma]s Robinson in Halton to the Parish of Kirkby Lonsdale, 21 May 1830 (WPR/19/7/6/23/7)

Halton 21[st] May 1830

Sir

Having not received any answer to my application to you respecting the funeral of my Son I am induced to solicit your attention again to the subject hoping you will be so kind as to assist me Being unacquainted with the proper method of proceeding in a case like this I ordered a Coffin to be made instead of applying as I find I ought to have done to the Overseer's at first and when I had waited till Saturday in expectation of hearing from you I was obliged to apply to them and they told me they never gave any money but found a Coffin and paid the Dues and as I had got a Coffin they gave me a certificate for the payment of the Dues but they only pay 3/5 and the Church demands 5/- a friend was obliged to pay 1/7 for me I hope you will be so kind as to enable me to defray the expence I have incurred I can assure you that it is with very painfull feelings that I thus appeal to you and if I could any way avoid it I should be very happy to do so the Coffin is 13/- and if I could pay the Overseer's it would prevent any further trouble or expence

I shall be at Halton again next week and if you would be so kind as to send by J. Metcalf to be left at 9 Hutton's Halton
I remain Sir you Ob[t] Ser[t] Tho[s] Robinson

496 Tho[ma]s Robinson in Preston to Stephen Garnet[t] in Kirkby Lonsdale, 20 October 1830 (WPR/19/7/6/23/41)

Preston 20 Octr 1830

Sir

I am very sorry to have to apply to you again for assistance but necessity compels me to it My Wife who is a very delicate woman at all times is at present so poorly that I am not able to leave home this week and I should have been at Lancaster and as my means of obtaing money depends upon soliciting it I shall have nothing to take this week She is under the Dispensary Doctor's and they have sometime urged me to apply to you as they say that nothing but great care and strengthening food can restore her and at present it is wholly out off my power to get her what she should have even now at the time am writing there is nothing in the house that she can take for dinner and she is Obliged to fast I beg therefore that you be so kind, as to send us something for her sake for I can truly say that her very life depends upon it hoping to have a favourable answer in a few days I subscribe my self Your
Humble Ser[t].
48 Spring Gardens Tho[s] Robinson

Circumtext: *Address of Recipient:* Mr Stephen Garnet Overseer Kirby Lonsdale
Postmarked: Preston Oct 20 1830

497 Charles Albert in Preston to the Parish of Kirkby Lonsdale, 6 April 1831 (WPR/19/7/6/24/33)

North Road Preston 6th April 1831

Sir/

I hope no ofence in trubleing you with this letter, it is to inform you that Thomas Robinson and most all is Children are at this time down with a faver verey bad and as been for som time and is wife is afraid of haveing it as this day she ~~feel~~ feels her Self verey poorly and wat is to be Come of them I dont no for thay are actley in verey great distress indeed at this time – I belive if thay dont get Som Releef immadetly thay most die for want and indeed if is wife Should go down with the faver who then most look after them I am verey Sorry for them and always have been though always thay have been Sober quiet Clane and industerus piple ever Sence thay have been in my house – Mrs Robinson have disired me to inform you that thay are this time without any money or any thing els to take to – Sir as I no all the above to be actly truth I make bold to steate the Same to you and do trust that you will not be afended at me for Riteing this letter by Mrs. Robinson disire as her husband is not able to Rite nor Sit up in bed poor woman she Cant hardley keep on her legs I ashore you Sir, Robinsons house is at this time a verey distress house as any in preston

I am Sir your Most humble Servant
Charles Albert

498 Tho[ma]s Robinson in Preston to [Stephen] Garnet[t] in Kirkby Lonsdale, 23 April 1831 (WPR/19/7/6/24/29)

1831

Preston 23^{d} April

Mr Garnet

Sir/

I have to acknowledge with my best thanks the receipt of your letter to Mr albert <c>ontaining [*page torn*] 1£ which was a very reasonable relief as that time we had not one healthy person in our family, the Children are all ^~~well~~^ except the youngest got better and I am so far recovered as to be able to walk out a few hours for several days this last week but still so weak as not able to go out of town which is the only chance I have of making any thing; I shoud have wrote by Robt Taylor on Friday but I thought I should have been able to go to some Gentlemen about 5 Miles out of town today but before I got 1 mile I was obliged <t>o [*page torn*] give it up and was scarce able to get home, I have borrow'd 2/- which I have promised to pay next week but am afraid I shall not be able or to obtain the means of subsistence without further assistance from you which I hope you will afford me till I have recovered a little strength to enable me to resume my business as I really dare not venture from home at present and the Doctor has ordered me to carefull for a while as there is danger of a return of the complaint which was an inflamation of the Lungs and for which I was copiously bled and blister'd which I suppose may be the reason of my extreme weakness hoping you will be so kind as to send as soon as possible I remain your

Humble Serv[t]
Tho[s] Robinson

499 Tho[ma]s Robinson in Preston to the Parish of Kirkby Lonsdale, 25 February 1834 (WPR/19/7/6/27/7)

Preston 25[th] Feb 1834

Sir
I am very sorry to have to trouble you for assistance but our youngest Child has died today and I am quite unable to bury it myself, and humbly hope you will be so kind as to send us what you think may enable us to get through this difficulty and I hope I shall not have to trouble you again on a similar occasion

I remain with all respect
your hub[l] Ser[t]
Tho[s] Robinson

Circumtext: *In different hand [SG]*: Granted 15s/

500 Tho[ma]s Robinson in Lancaster to the Parish of Kirkby Lonsdale, 30 July 1834 (WPR/19/7/6/27/32)

Lancaster 30[th] July 1834

Sir

I beg to inform you that I have been living at Lancaster since the rent was paid at Preston last time which I believe is 17 weeks since this weeks end our rent is £5.10.0 a year and taxes we are intending to shift to another house next week if you would be so kind as to send the money by Rob[t] Taylor on Saturday which Mr Preston our Landlord at Preston said was to be 2/- per week; I remain hour Obe[dt] Serv[t]

Tho[s] Robinson

501 Tho[ma]s Robinson in Lancaster to the Parish of Kirkby Lonsdale, 13 August 1834 (WPR/19/7/6/27/31)

Lancaster 13th Augt 1834

Sir

I am very sorry to have to apply to again to you about the rent, I was not aware that it would make any difference my moving from Preston here and as my business lays chiefly about this district I thought it more convinient to be ^here^ expecting that I might rely upon the 2/- per week, the custom here is to pay half yearly or Quarterly and we agree'd to be at liberty to leave this house by giving a months notice if it did not suit us I gave notice five weeks since and indended to leave last week end as we have taken another house and have got leave to stay here this week out and leave at the weeks end if we pay the rent I humbly hope you will enable us to do so as it ~~is~~ ^is^ utterly impossible for us to pay it ourselves I remain your hum^{b} Servt

Thos Robinson

502 Tho[ma]s Robinson in Lancaster to the Parish of Kirkby Lonsdale, 19 November 1834 (WPR/19/7/6/27/16)

Lancaster 19th Nov 1834

Sir

Having another quarters rent now due I am again under the necessity of applying to you being totally unable to pay it myself and I humbly hope that you will once more render that kind assistance which I have hitherto experienced from you

I remain Your Obe^{dt} Ser^{t}

Thos Robinson

503 Tho[ma]s Robinson in Lancaster to the Parish of Kirkby Lonsdale, 6 December 1834 (WPR/19/7/6/27/14)

Lancaster Decr 6 1834

Sir

I take the liberty of again addressing you as I have only a few days allowed to pay my rent and I am quite unable to pay it without your assistance which I humbly hope you will afford me this time hoping to receive your answer by John Taylor on Monday <I re>main [*page torn*] your hub^{le} Ser^{t}

Thos Robinson

Circumtext: *In different hand*: Granted 1.0.0

504 T[homas] & J Robinson in Lancaster to the Parish of Kirkby Lonsdale, 7 April 1835 (WPR/19/7/6/28/50)

Lancaster April 7 1835

Sir/

I am very sorry that I am oblige'd through necessity once more to be troublesome unto you but in consequence of not being able to gain a living we are obliged though against our wish to ask your assistance, but our Rent is run up to two pounds and we find that we are unable to pay it therefore if you would be Kind enough to send it by the bearer this on saturday we should be very thankfull for it and likewise if you would ~~be~~ send us something besides to help to support us which we stand in great need off for I can assure you that we do not get more than two meals a day and if you do not consider to send us anything we shall be obliged to apply at the overseers office at Lancaster which we shall not like to do therefore let me once more humbly ask you to consider our situation and have a little pity upon our distress situation and you may be assured that if we could do without it we certainly would [*****] [*page torn*] Remain yours Obdent^{ly}

T & J Robinson

505 Tho[ma]s Robinson in Lancaster to the Parish of Kirkby Lonsdale, 16 May 1835 (WPR/19/7/6/28/9)

Lancaster 16th May 1835

Sir

The rent day is again arrived and I am quite unable to pay it without your assistance which I humbly hope I may again experiance I am owing for half a year and 3 Weeks and the Landlord is very urgent for it if you will be so kind as to send by Taylor next week I shall be extremely obliged to you I remain with all due respect

Your most Obe^{dt} Servt

Thos Robinson

506 Tho[ma]s Robinson in Lancaster to the Parish of Kirkby Lonsdale, 19 August 1835 (WPR/19/7/6/28/32)

Lancaster 19 Augst 1835

Sir

My Landlady is here again for the rent and is ditermined to be put off no longer and I am sorry that it is not in my power to do any thing towards it I gave them the £1. that you were so kind as to send but there remains £3.9s at the present and I do not really know what to do about it I have prevailed on them to wait till Saturday and I hope you will be so kind as to send by John Taylor and enable me to keep my house together I remain your Hum^{l} Ser^{t}

Thos Robinson

507 Tho[ma]s Robinson in Lancaster to the Parish of Kirkby Lonsdale, 2 December [1835] (WPR/19/7/6/28/15)

Lancaster Dec 2^{d}

Sir

Our Rent being again due I am under the necessity of applying to you as I have not been able to get into constant employment of my kind yet, my former Master whom I told you was poorly is sin<ce> [*page cut*] dead and no other person has yet be [*****] [*page cut*] here to suceed him tho I have expect<ed> [*page cut*] them every week and have been doing any thing I could get to do to put on with I believe we are owing £2.16.0 and the Landlord will be here next week for it I remain your Obd^{t} Ser^{t}

Thos Robinson

Notes: *Although the content of this letter does not indicate in what year it was written or sent, its place in the sequence suggests that it was sent in 1835.*

508 Tho[ma]s Robinson in Lancaster to the Parish of Kirkby Lonsdale, 24 February 1836 (WPR/19/7/6/29/9)

Lancaster 24 Feb 1836

Sir

Our Landlord has been for his rent and is coming again next Saturday but one and I have no means of paying it without applying to you as I have not yet got into regular employment and I hope you will have the kindness to assist me I think that it is £2.5.6 We are owing I remain Your hum^{l} Ser^{t}

Thos Robinson

509 Tho[ma]s Robinson in Lancaster to the Parish of Kirkby Lonsdale, 25 May 1836 (WPR/19/7/6/29/28)

Sir

Our Landlord will be here next week for his rent and I am obliged to apply to you for enable me to pay it as I have not yet the means of doing it for myself

I remain Sir
Your Hum^{l} Servt
Thos Robinson

Lancaster 25 May 1836

17.

SILL, letters 510–525

510 R Acton in Wigan to the Overseer of Kirkby Lonsdale, 7 January 1817 (WPR/19/7/6/10/2)

Wigan Jany 7 1817

Ed Sill a person belonging to your Township has applied at our office for relief, which I have thought proper to advise you off before the ordinary steps in these Cases are enterd into for if we are put to the trouble of a removal they will not be permitted to return our Magistrates being determin'd on that head he has a Wife that as been very poorly ever since she lay in & one Child & through the scarceness of work & lowness of Wages has not been able to earn more than 3/- per Week for this last month which makes his case very bad for Information respecting his Settlement I refer To James Sill living in your Township he having done nothing in his own right to gain a settlement since he left your Township waiting your order to relieve them

I remain yours Respt^{y}

R Acton

Overseer

Circumtext: *Address of Recipient:* To the Overseer of the Poor of the Township of Kirby Lonsdale Westmoreland

Postmarked: Wigan JA16 1817, 219

511 W[illia]m Acton and P Foden in Wigan to the Parish of Kirkby Lonsdale, 30 June 1818 (WPR/19/7/6/11/18)

Wigan 30th June 1818

Sir,

Edwd. Sill has again made application for a renewal of his former Pay of two shillings p Week, which was allow'd him about twelvemonths back, his Wife now lies dangerously ill of a weakness, verging towards Dissolution, therefore it will be necessary to allow them something, your Order shall be punctually attended to by Sir

Yours respectfully
for W[m] Acton Overseer
turn over P Foden Clerk

P.S. We have relived him

P. Foden

Circumtext: *Different hand*:

I hereby certify that Sarah Sill the Wife of the within named Edw[d]. Sill is sick & stands in need of relief

Edw[d]. Hill Minister
of Wigan

512 Rich[ar]d Bubs and William Acton in Wigan to the Parish of Kirkby Lonsdale, 10 September 1819 (WPR/19/7/6/12/20)

We Certify that Sarah Sill Wife of Edward Sill, is in a bad State of health and has been so these months Back and is now near her down lying and we think that her Husband is Not Able to get her such necessaries as she now wants and will Want when she lies in

Wigan 10th Sep[r], 1819
Be pleased to send
your answer to the
Overseers Wigan for
Edward Sill Hudsons
Croft

Rich[d]. Bubs
Surgeon
William Acton Overseer

Circumtext: *Different hand:* I believe the above statement to be correct L Hill Curate of Wigan

Further hand [SG]: Granted £1.0.0

513 Will[iam] Acton in Wigan to the Parish of Kirkby Lonsdale, 6 November 1819 (WPR/19/7/6/12/25)

Wigan 6 November 1819

Sir,
We are extremely sorry to inform you that about 3 weeks ago Edward Sills Wife was (after a most painful & very difficult Labor) delivered of twins the are both likely to live, but sorry to say the Mother is dead – The poor Man is

consequently left with 3 small Children, to Wit, The Twins and another not 3 years of age

His situation (as you must conceive is most truly pitiable, during her Sickness we sent a Doctor, and we have also given him a little more relief than what you sent, which together with the Funeral expences including the Surgeon's Charge Amounts to £2-1-6 and which we hope you will remit by return Of Post, accompanied with your Directions stating how we are to act with the Family in their present Dilema – The Man himself thinks he had better to go to your Town, having no Friends here, who can render him the least possible Assistance, his Earnings are only 8s/ wkly as weaving is so very low here, you are also aware that wherever he is the Twins are obliged to be nursed & which could not be done here under 8/- weekly, therefore we certainly are of the same Opinion so that your most early Instructions in this sad Case will highly oblige Sir

Yours respectfully
Will. Acton
Overseer

514 P Foden in Wigan to Stephen Garnett in Kirkby Lonsdale, 9 November 1819 (WPR/19/7/6/12/26)

Wigan 9 Novr 1819

Sir,

Yours of this morning we duly rec'd covering £3 and according to your request have made all the Enquiry we possibly could relative to his rent & Furniture and it appears that he has nothing in his House worth notice, being only an old Chaff Bed, 2 Chairs, an old Stool, and a few other necessaries of but little Value, the Looms that he worked on were the Landlords from whom he rented the House – and it appears also by Sill's Confession that he owe his Landlord more than they are worth – We have agreed with a Woman (a wet nurse) to accompany the twins to your Town for her Expences being borne to Kirby Lonsdale, and 2/6 Per day for Compensation, and I can assure you we had some Difficulty in procuring one, at this Season of the Year –

We have given him forty shillings to bear their Expences and which will leave a Balance in our Favor of £1.3.6 and which you can remit by the Woman at her return if You think proper, or by Post Office Order – You will please to observe that you will have the Woman to pay 2/6 P Day for her Trouble, with her Expences back also – They will start from Wigan tomorrow Evening in a Waggon for Preston & the next morning Thursday will take the Lancaster Packet Boat, and arrive at Lancaster about 4 OClock the same Evening

We consider it would be an Act of great Charity if you could contrive to meet them at Lancaster, the Infants being so very young, & perhaps, a Conveyance not just at hand, we have done all we could for you and hope it will prove satisfactory

I am Sir
Yours Respcy
P Foden

N.B. We should have waited for another answer from you before the Family set out, but he was so very anxious to start that wee thought this the best & Cheapest mode

P.F.

Circumtext: *Address of recipient:* Mr Stephen Garnett Overseer of the Poor Kirby Lonsdale

515 Edward Sill in Wigan to the Parish of Kirkby Lonsdale, 4 July 1828 (WPR/19/7/6/21/33)

Wigan July 4 1828

Ss I Take up my pen to write and I am sory to let you know that I am in a steat of Derestress for I have no work for the wavers is standing out for wages and I have no work I am sory to think we are under the necesety of send for some mony and I hope you will oblige me with the same Eather something that is proper and if not I hope you send me some mony to Cary us to you I shall be obliged to Apply to wigan and Get Removed wich I shoud sory to Do

I am yours
Edward Sill

516 P Foden in Wigan to the Parish of Kirkby Lonsdale, 18 February 183[3] (WPR/19/7/6/26/4)

183<3> [*page torn*]
Overseers' office Wigan 18 Feb^{y}
Sir,

I address you in Behalf of your old Pauper Edward Sill who is sick & under the Medical Care of one of our Surgeons consequently unable to follow his usual Employment

He requests that you will be pleased to send him a little assistance – I need not advert to his family, as you know sufficiently well –

All the earnings of the house amount to no more than 3/- waiting your early remittance I am Sir

Yours respect[y]
P Foden
Overseer

Circumtext: *Different hand:* Being under the Care of me P.J. Chadwick Surgeon

Notes: *Although the content of this letter does not indicate when it was written or sent, its place in the sequence suggests that it was sent in 1833.*

517 P F Foden in Wigan to the Parish of Kirkby Lonsdale, 20 March 1833 (WPR/19/7/6/26/59)

Overseers' Office
Wigan 20th Mar/33
Gent[m].

From the subjoined Doctors' Certificate you will perceive the distressed situation of your Pauper & his family –

It will be necessary to extend the relief For under these calamitous Circu/m/stances together with E Sills own ill health it is impossible for them to exist without your further Kindness –

Whatever you send we will deal it out as you think proper – They have had all the sovereign you sent except 3/6 -

I am Gent[m].
Yours resp[y]
For Will Acton
P F Foden

Circumtext: *Overleaf, different hand*:

Gentn

This is to certify that on Wednesday last, one of Edward Sill's sons, had the misfortune to have the forearm and upper arm fractured the former being a severe case of compound fracture, the Consequence of which was that on Sunday last amputation above the Elbow joint became indispensable Being under the care of

Wigan S.J. Chadwick
March 18th 1833

Below, further hand:

I have seen the patient referred to the Statement on the other side of this paper, and entirely concur with Mr. Chadwick
March 18th/33 Jno. Latham
Member of the London College
of Surgeons

518 P F Foden in Wigan to the Parish of Kirkby Lonsdale, 2 April 1833 (WPR/19/7/6/26/56)

1833
Overseers' office Wigan 2 April
Gent^{n}.

I am sorry, but am constrained to address you again in the Behalf of Edwd. Sill, & more particularly on his Boy's a/c who has lately had his Arm amputated above the Elbow and at present in a precarious state –

We had expected a letter & order 'ere now, but none arriving we are compelled to apply again, & do hope you will return an Order early as possible, as the family is plunged in great Distress – I am Gentlemen
Yours Respy
for Will Acton overser
P F Foden

519 P Foden in Wigan to the Parish of Kirkby Lonsdale, 11 April 1833 (WPR/19/7/6/26/55)

1833
Overseers' office Wigan 11 April
Sir,

The Bearer Edwd Sill and his Boy present themselves before you, agreeable to your letter of Instructions

We have advanced to him 12s/ to carry him to your Township and 0/8 Postage of your Letter –

You will please therefore to hand him 12/8 if you think it can be done with Safety
I am Sir
Yours respectfuly
for Will Acton
Ov
P Foden

520 From P Foden in Wigan to the Overseers of Kirkby Lonsdale, September 1833 (WPR/19/7/6/26/73)

The Overseers of the Poor of Kirkby Lonsdale
To the Churchwardens and Overseers of the Poor of Wigan, Drs.

Relief Given To	*From*	*To*	*No. of Weeks*	*As Per Week*	*£.*	*s.*	*d.*
Edwd. Sill's Boy	4 May	20 Sepr	20	2/6	2	10	

Overseers' office Wigan Sept 1833
Sir
Your early remittance of the above will highly oblige
Sir
Yours respectfully
for Will Acton / Ov
P Foden

Notes: *This is a printed proforma invoice with correspondence added. The content of the invoice in italics (outwith brackets) represents the printed text.*

521 W[illia]m Acton in Wigan to the Overseers of Kirkby Lonsdale, 8 August 1834 (WPR/19/7/6/27/33)

The Overseers of the Poor of Kirkby Lonsdale
To the Churchwardens and Overseers of the Poor of Wigan, Drs.

Relief Given To	*From*	*To*	*No. of Weeks*	*As Per Week*	*£.*	*s.*	*d.*
Edward Sill	8 July 1834	9 August 1834	26	2/6	3	5	–

GENTLEMEN,

The above is our account against your Township, which I trust you will find correct. By favouring us with an early remittance, you will oblige the Churchwardens and Overseers, who have given positive orders to discontinue payment for those Townships who do not give immediate attention to the settlement of their Accounts.

I am, Gentlemen
Wigan 8th August 1834 *Your obedient Servant,*
Wm. Acton *Overseer.*

Notes: *This is a printed proforma invoice. The content of the invoice in italics (outwith brackets) represents the printed text.*

522 W[illia]m Acton in Wigan to the Overseers of Kirkby Lonsdale, 26 February 1835 (WPR/19/7/6/28/4)

The Overseers of the Poor of Kirkby Lonsdale
To the Churchwardens and Overseers of the Poor of Wigan, Drs.

Relief Given To	*From*	*To*	*No. of Weeks*	*As Per Week*	*£.*	*s.*	*d.*
Edward Sill	10 Jany 1835	21 March 1835	10	2/6	1	5	–
To Postage of Double Letter March 7th 1834					0	1	4
					£1	6	4

Gentlemen/

You will much oblige the Overseers of the Borough if you will have the goodness to remit the above on or before the 10th of March next, as the Overseers Books must be made up by the 25th of March

I am, Gentlemen
Yours respectfully
Wm Acton

Wigan 26th Feby 1835

Notes: *This is a printed proforma invoice with correspondence added. The content of the invoice in italics (outwith brackets) represents the printed text.*

523 W[illia]m Acton in Wigan to the Overseers of Kirkby Lonsdale, 16 September 1835 (WPR/19/7/6/28/29)

The Overseers of the Poor of Kirkby Lonsdale
To the Churchwardens and Overseers of the Poor of Wigan, Drs.

Relief Given To	*From*	*To*	*No. of Weeks*	*As Per Week*	*£.*	*s.*	*d.*
Edward Sill	21 March 1835	19 Sepr 1835	26	2/6	3	5	

Sir/

I hope you will make an immediate remittance as our committee will ^not^ allow us to pay for those Townships who do not pay their accounts promptly when sent in

I am yours respectfully
Wm Acton
Overseer

Workhouse Wigan
16th September 1835

Notes: *This is a printed proforma invoice with correspondence added. The content of the invoice in italics (outwith brackets) represents the printed text.*

524 W[illia]m Acton in Wigan to the Overseers of Kirkby Lonsdale, 4 March 1836 (WPR/19/7/6/29/3)

The Overseers of the Poor of Kirkby Lonsdale
To the Churchwardens and Overseers of the Poor of Wigan, Drs.

Relief Given To	*From*	*To*	*No. of Weeks*	*As Per Week*	*£.*	*s.*	*d.*
Edward Sill	19 Sepr 1835	5 Decr 1835	11	2/6	1	7	6
Postage and Bank Commission 5 Sepr 1835						1	2
					£1	8	8

Sir/

You will perceive by the above acct that ^we^ have stopped sills pay, our reason for doing is because that lad you allowed it to has committed a Felony and was tried and found Guilty and Committed to the House of Correction for a Certain time but is just liberated from Prison again and his Father has applied again this morning to have him upon the Books but we have refused to do so until we Know your pleasure, I dont think his father is able to Keep him by his own Labour if you wish us to continue the pay you will please to Say so when when you make your remittance Which I trust you will as soon as possible your Compliance will Oblige

Workhouse Wigan Yours respectfully
4th March 1836 W^{m}. Acton
Overseer

Notes: *This is a printed proforma invoice with correspondence added. The content of the invoice in italics (outwith brackets) represents the printed text.*

525 Edward Sill to the Parish of Kirkby Lonsdale, 4 March 1836 (WPR/19/7/6/29/6)

Wigan 4th March 1836

Sir)

I have taken this opportunity of writing a few lines, & request to know the reason that the pay for my Son is stopped. I have been this morning to the Overseers Office & they acquainted me there that there was no more pay for me. If it is through the misconduct of my Son, you very well know that I cannot be answerable for his actions as I am not always in his Sight, I am extremely concern'd at his conduct upon my own account but more particularly upon his, but this I can say he never saw any thing either from myself or Wife to give him the least encouragement to do as he has done and you well know that it is out of our power to keep him with the pay ^stopped^ so that if there is not any more to be allow'd for him I shall be under the necessity of bringing him to you for I cannot maintain him for it is very hard to provide a scanty allowance for ourselves and that you know it is as the state of things are at present. I hope you will not fail to give the orders to the Overseers here for the continuance of the allowance for I do not wish to give you any more trouble I am with respect your well

wisher Edward Sill

18.

THISTLETHWAITE, letters 526–545

526 J[ohn] Thistlethwaite in Ingleton to the Parish of Kirkby Lonsdale, 29 June 1809 (WPR/19/7/6/2/17)

Sir

I send this to inform you that I is got home and I hope that you will send that a usuly and to give Thos. Chambers it for he as laid it down for you and for my Part I is not well and for her Part she is not fit to work for any thing that is got i must doe it my seff so I Could wish you to be so kind as to send it or else we Cannot do for we must Come to you and so no more at Present from your &c.

Jno. Thistlethwaite

Ingleton June 29th 1809

[*Overleaf*] for the reason of you stoping this my Wife as been verey badley off while I have been a way for we husally got ~~owe~~ all of Thos Chambers and now they will let us having nothing for we howed them some thing be fore and you stoping this is made them for letting us of having any thing so you must be so kind as to give him it and let us have as usually

527 J[ohn] Thistlethwaite in Ingleton to the Parish of Kirkby Lonsdale, 24 October 1809 (WPR/19/7/6/2/37)

Ingleton Oct 24th 1809

I send this to inform you by my brother to let you Know that I am going to be in distress for My Wife dose not know her own *[hirser]* and I is wanting all necessities for her which makes me write to you to let you know that you must do some thing for her or else I shall be forcd to bring her to you and as for paying the Doctor tis shoor that I cannot, he will not be willing to come unless he was sure of his Pay so you must rather send word with my Brother or a line to let me know and that as usully for we cannot do and so no more at present from yours

&c. Jno. Thistlethwate

528 Rich[ar]d Balderston in Ingleton to the Parish of Kirkby Lonsdale, 12 June 1810 (WPR/19/7/6/3/13)

Gent

Robert Thislewood a Poor person belonging to your Township is at present in a Poor state of Health, and Wholy unable to Earn any thing towards the maintainance of his Wife and two small Children, his Wife the bearer of this will inform you of the poor situation he is in, Which I do ashure you is very distressing, I hope you'll have the goodness to relieve her and am Gent. your most obt. Hble Servt.

Rich^{d}. Balderston
Overseer

Ingleton 12 June 1810

529 Ann Thistlethwaite in Ireby to [Stephen] Garnett in Kirkby Lonsdale, [July 1822] (WPR/19/7/6/15/19)

Ireby Sir the Time is up Wich Maks our Penchan Du and to do with out out it We canot But as the Gentlemen Gave thir Word that I shud have it then the time was out and the rent Pad we Canot dout it Bot our serkamstans is wors Since ther has Ben ^so^ Much tok it is tu to one that we Could Be trasted one Pane whear We Coude have Ben trasad a Pound Befor Bot it was on the same Ground that you Brot me from Ingleton by ranen me doun that Was in Your Ppaur I donat men to say you in pertekler Bot it sems a Great Comfert sum to do me ane Meschif they Can bot it will be a Poor Gratefekshan to Bring a Poor famle to Destrokshon as no dout Bot it will for Wer ron Vre far bad at Present and my wife has Not a Pet Coat to her Back Worth a farden our famel bids a Great deal of doen far and you Know that it is winter with us Bot I hop the Gentlemen will for give the Letel warmth I was in at the Las Meten for to tread of a worm it wil torn in Time Bot ther no flin from males of sum Peope you will Pleas to Give me sum mone as I am vre far on Bad and on trost Can get nothng your humble apler Ann Thistlethwaite

I should not have [***]t [*page torn*] this lin Bot /shrank/ and could n<ot> [*page torn*] com bot lais in want

[*Overleaf*] One weck is Penshon of 2^{s} is du to day AKorden to the Promes of the Gentlemen the first Sunday in the month of July – 1822

and we ar vre Badle of for Clothen

Circumtext: *Address of Recipient:* To Mr Garnett of Kirkby

Notes: *This letter is difficult to decipher and is an extreme example of 'oral writing', or perhaps of the cognitive struggle involved for partially literate letter writers (see note in Introduction).*

Although this letter is not dated, the content strongly suggests that it is was written in or around July 1822.

530 Anne and John Thistlethwaite in Ireby to [Stephen] Garnett in Kirkby Lonsdale, 25 March 1824 (WPR/19/7/6/17/14)

Ireby March 25/1824 for John Husththwaite

To Mr Garnett Sir I hop that you will beffriend me at this time or it is up with Me on all sides for the rent I Canot Pay one farden towards for it is out of my Pour to get meat at the rate that potatoes and meal is at for when a mel time Comes we Canot till that get to shop for a meal and I belev to speak the Truth we have got into all the Det we Can this winter for I think that 5 pound would Not Clear us at this time and my son Has N<ot> [*page torn*] Ben able to do ani thing as he is Pourle and has ben so for sum time and my wife has ben Pourle and I have ben as well but I know that ther is No Poor Person Nether in this Town No one Els that is mor sisad at this time i am for been poor for ther is No Poor famle that is in this Town nor one other Bot has got ther rent salled for a thir by Geft or by Penshon from the Town ship and for my Part I have Comed to your mitins bot to No Porpos atol bot to be Tould to Go hom and work as if I Did Not work bot that you Intirle Rapet my famle then all we Can do is quit short of Geten meat at this Dear Time of Provishons then half a Crown Per Week is Letel Enuf for potates for our famle as thir Know selen to get once a day it ma sem a deal bot Potates is all ther is no meat at this Cris of Distres as I may Kal it then our work Bringes so smal a trifel in for so much dear as at Presant and all so dear Bot I sopos that you Tould my wife that you had Got an a Count of my famles Erenen a 11 shilens in the week from Mr Bragshaw Cotton Poter out of Clapham and that you had it in Black and Wite wich makes it to the Contrare for I have a Cope of the Book wich makes it £11.a11s. from May the 10/1823 till Janure the 31/1824 and out of that [***] [*obscured by wax seal*] shilens and 2 pense for healds and charge 6s to say Not a word of the Dats bot to Tel the Truth as you must Know ther was sum Time to get our Torf in wich was last in a Great /miss/ and sum Time for shearers to Pay for the beden of thos I got hom know this store I donot dout has ansrad the Porpas of sum vrey hardanad People that is Prejadest against my famle and me Bot I have Not forgot the /posel/ brace ueseg to me Nor the impresonment I most un resonable sufrad at that Plase to Gratfe my

Enemes nor the Black Book that Come out then I wanted redres of grivances but that all got over with ll the want of Brad that I sufared at that time and abuse from sum vrey unworth Pepole and know I am to be Toul of a Tread weel Bot I hop the Pepole that wishes me this Evle will find sum thing mor to do then wish my Ruen so much Bot For Gades sake do not Jone with my enmes Anne Thistlethwaite and John

[*Overleaf*] John Longstrath demands his rent and will Not be put of ane Longer then the 12 of May Next on one Pertens that *[*avre*]* the rent is 3 Pound so I hop that you will of your Goodness Not let me Be sould up as Longer then that time will be alowed for the rent to be Pad in

Notes: *Again, this letter is very difficult to decipher at times.*

531 John Langstrath of Ireby to John Thistlethwait[e], 26 April 1824 (WPR/19/7/6/17/15)

Mr John Thistlethwait I desire you will be so good as pay my rent as Mr Martin has sent that I must pay mine rent on the 4 of May and you was to pay your rent when I pay'd mine as you know that you only pay'd me 15^{s} shilings and their remains 3 pounds & If you dont pay I shall make Destress
Ireby April Yours John Langstrath
26th 1824

532 John Thistlethwaite to the Parish of Kirkby Lonsdale, 6 May 1824 (WPR/19/7/6/17/19)

May 6th / 1824

Sir for the Lordes sak have merce on us as all the Pour restes in your hand Pray be mercful unto us and do Not so very hardle with us as to Break us up at this time for you will find Let hem that is my Enemes at Ireby or Els Whear that it is out of our Pour to help our selfves at one nat for all things is so dear that it is out of our Pour to get Bread Bot we would hop that if the Crop was of that things would be Cheaper and if we be Brok up Wear don for our hops will be balesta^d^ and a Quit recen^a^d for our Gods will Go for Northen at this Plase and it will Gratfi my Ireby frens that did me so much Ingre about this Time 2 years sence but if that Gentleman ~~wich~~ Had ben Mr Duncan it would had No Efekt for he would have ben too mach aquantad with the Ellmenin^ness^ of the Person to have minad on ward of Shears bot I Could not Pleas No Longer at that Plase with out Los to my self bot No Por Person has a Good word from that Qurter for I beleve them to be Poor heaters for Godes sak have mercey on me and Grant me my request and I shal forever Pary for you

John Thistlethwaite
Pleas to ancer this line if you will help
us if Not we are don

533 John Thistlethwaite in Ireby to the Parish of Kirkby Lonsdale, 31 May 1824 (WPR/19/7/6/17/28)

May ^the^ 31 / 1824 Ireby

Sir Mr John Langstrath has Given Me to to understand that he will be No longer Pot of for if my rent Be Not satelad for he will Pot A Balef in to our hous and sell for the rent Akorden to Law and this is the reson I troble you with this Lin hopen that you will se som of the other Gentlemen and faver me at this time with your Good will as I Canot Pot Mr L of ane Longer atol for his rent he will have other By Pament or by Destres and it is out of my Pour to Get Bread for my famle at the rat that Proveshons is at Know Meal 5^{d} and Potatess 7^{d} per ston and all in Perporshon ther was one Good Job I Did for Kirkby that was Clearen them of one of the famle for he did Not Know ane thing about it untill I instraked Her hou and that was by Brother Harlen <u>Who</u> Nou blonges unto Ingleton and I mit have Don stel mor if you would have Enabled me so to do your servant respeckfull

John Thistlethwaite

534 John Thistlethwaite in Ireby to Stephen Garn[e]tt in Kirkby Lonsdale, 20 February 1825 (WPR/19/7/6/18/5)

Sunday the 20 / 1825

To the overseer and Gentlemen of the Township of Kirkby Lonsdale Gentlemen I am sorle opresad by Mr John Langstrath Landlord of the Premases I know hauld in Part as He has sent his Brother to tak Pashion of the Garden and is vrey Ell Toingad and vrey sose Graden All up be for him and the Landlord John Langstrath will not Give one Ewear to ane thing I Can say to him for it is mone he wants and mone he will have if all the things I have in the house will Pay Pad he will be be and will Not hear one thing I Can Pay for mone I have Non Nor frens with out you the Gentlemen of the Meten will lend your assitans the Lord help me for frens I have Not one that Can befrend me for it Is moer that Mos befrend me or sum one of the

Gentlemenes word for my rent for I Canot [***]as [*obscured by sealing wax*] it that over I would Do for I have tried all my frens ovre whear and to my soray finds them all willen but Not able to do ane thing for me so I once mor most humble request your kind asstans for if I be Torned out of this hous I Canot tell whear to find a setewashon that will ancer atoll for us at the rent or Com one whear Near it for I have Tread all over bot Canot Get one in Clapham or ane whear els under 6 or 7 Pound that will ancer the samePorps for my famle and our Trad to togeader the Lord send you to Consider Not to ruin us Quit as soum People would have it Not ben our frens at this Tune at Ireby I am ashamed of sending bot that Cant do at this time for to Pay for the Children Let a lone rents for Godes sake be merceful to us for we have No whear Els to look for Merce but to you at this time and if you donat the Lord be mereful to us for wear standening about at Presant Lik No Poor People but ourselves Dasturd Cumferter or frend in destres wen Poor bsids I Canot mak you to think mor */*bld*/* the Time that our famle has had since you thay Nu would Not Pay my rent ther Has Ben nothen too bad that slander Could invent Nor Males sugast and I you to be so Good as to help me out and ther is one thing wors then all that is my Wife is Naver one Day well and I belev it to be troble for one thing that hurts Her and as you most know it is a great Let down in our famle for ther is excusase Enuf among so larg a famle as ours thing <that> [*page torn*] it mit be satled if you would give your word for me to stop again bot for me I am Quite Don for he will Not tak my word none a Count for he sees I Canot do it of my self for he axed me me if I Could find a frend the other Day as it was of No use for him to tak mine Nou I bage of you to Consider of this in as faverable a maner as you Can Do for the Lordes sak or wear ruend Quite if It Could be that I could Get a Nother house that would */*mauld*/* us I am Not able to sheft my Gods if ane ther be left for No one knoes the Tro ble of Loums but them that has them to do with In short Gentlemen I Dont know that to say to Gane your ascestans for I am at my wites end I Can say no mor so the Lord send me Help by you I am your Distresad humble servant respeckifly

John Thistlethwaite Ireby

I have one preposel to mak that is if you will Give us one and sixpans Per wee we will hearafter Pay our rent monthle that is after May day next you Sir know that a Troble the windas most have Ben Paten in and maken sutable for weven and Know to be all over in 2 years time then mad so sutable Sir do Consider our kas this Time and help us out of this Troble for I have Not the Least bot a fu words from you Mr Garnatt would Go a Great road in our faver With the Gentlemen and Pray be so Kind if Not we are ruenad Quite and Torned to the Dour I have No other hop but in you

Left

it is Quite out of my Pour to Help my self out of this Troble be Not my Enme for Godes sak bot for Give me the Troble I May Have Given you at one time for the Lordes sake

[*Overleaf*] Gentlemen this house is the Bis adapad for our Tread of ane I Can Met with and I Could Not Get one in Kirkby to ancer so well for 10 Pound as this dos at Presant since I have Pot Wendas in to it and a Great expense it has Ben to me i hop will Konsider my

Setwashon and if so I shal
be vrey thinkful and vrey
much oblegad to you
Gentlemen

Circumtext: *Below, different hand:*
To see John Longstrath
to agree with him Respecting
John Thistlethwaite Rent in the Best
manner I can

Address of Recipient: For Mr Stepham Garnatt Kirkby Lonsdale Westmorland Febure the 20

535 W Wallwer in Ingham to Stephen Garnett in Kirkby Lonsdale, 12 March 1825 (WPR/19/7/6/18/7)

Mr Stephen Garnett
Overseer

Ingham

Sir March 12th 1825

Robert Thistlethwaite, a poor man resident here, but belonging to your Township, is quite confined to the house by a pain in his breast, and an enlargement in his bowels – His wife can earn nothing, as she cannot procure worsted to spin –
They are in very necessitous circumstances, and I believe, the disorder has been much increased by from want of nourishment – I think his recovery very doubtful – I do not know what better keep, and warm weather may [*****] [*page torn*] I hope you will consider to settle a regular pension upon him, till he either recovers, or dies – They have been an industrious pair, and he has followed his [*****] [*illegible*] when he ought to have been in his bed –

They are in great distress, I am just returned from visiting them – I have desired them to send a person on purpose –

I remain
Sir,
Your obed[t]. Ser[t].
W Wallwer

536 John Thistlethwaite in Ireby to the Overseers of Kirkby Lonsdale, 3 [****] 1825 (WPR/19/7/6/18/38)

Ireby Satrday the 3 1825
Sir I had the mesforton the 19 day of Novr after leaven work to be sat By the fire and at Panful of Milk on the fire for soper wich by som over site was Not fexad in the Crane and then Boilen unlokale fel down on the fire and spelad onto my Leag will saven sum of the Children wich has mad me unable to work at my Loum and am Virey lam yeat as the fire was Not out in one week besids my Wife and Douter ane is Both of them Pourle so that ther is Nothing mad to soport so Large a famle bot I hop that you and the Gentlemen of the metin on Sunday will be so good as to relev me and the relef will be most thinkful recevad by your servent John Thistlethwaite

To the overseer and Gentlemen
Respekifly of Kirkby

Circumtext: *Different hand [SG]:* Granted 5[s]/

Notes: *Although no month is given in this letter, its place in the sequence suggests that it comes between letters 535 and 537.*

537 John Thistlethwaite to Steph[en] Garnett in Kirkby Lonsdale, N.D. (WPR/19/7/6/18/39)

That ever I do or that ever Can I do the rent is on one side my Cradeters on the other side and on there hand the Town ship Bent on my ruen but Not on mine Bot the Childrenes all so for it is vrey well Noen that the famle was Never in Helth at Kirkby nor myself I would have you and your son and Mr Grunds to Consider that you Canot distres me a Lon but the famle most sofer Likewise Wich you seem at tims to Pete you

I hop will Consider I hop Not to be so hard hartad as to be all in one mind on Sunday next your servant would be glad of sum relif for the famle as it is will be found ther in Need in the End I am sorey to say I am Nothen but a Skof for Kirkby Lonsadale meten a tendentes and has Comd 8 or 9 tims for the relif 5^s wich makes the Good people in Kirkby think i am faen with all the mone but Mr Parker or auld John Langstrath

[*Overleaf*] A litel after Martlemas 1823 that he mos Not post for the Toun would pay 3 pound and I mite pay the other my self Know Just for Godis sak think yourself Jos for my Palase for one momant and Let reasan return to his plase and then I think you Canot [th]ink I have ben farele Delt with this 2 years John Thistlethwaite

Lord God send me to find Mr [******] [*scrubbed out*]

Circumtext: *Address of Recipient:* For Mr Stepham Garnett Kirby Lonsdale groser

Written under (and perpendicular to) the text of the letter (different hand): Mr Thistlethwaite Ireby

Notes: *There appears to be text missing at the beginning of this letter, suggesting that a page has been lost or was omitted when the original was posted. There is therefore no indication of the date for this letter, but its place in the sequence suggests it belongs between letters 536 and 538.*

538 Ann Thistlethwaite in Ireby to Steph[e]n Garnett in Kirkby Lonsdale, 4 February 1826 (WPR/19/7/6/19/4)

Ireby Feby the 4 1826

to Mr stephan Garnett Sir) I Diser you will have th Goodnes to speck for me to the Gentlemen for I well know one word from you will Go ten times as far as one thing I Can say for my self For it is know favure and it is time for my Lanlord to sat his hous and Garden for he has A tenand in wating for an ancer and the time is up wich my Lanlord Gave me for to Get an ancer from the meten If you will Not Give your word pleas to be So Good as Give me 2 shilens mor per Week wich will enable me to pay my rent my self weekle I hop that the Gentlemen will be so kind as to Grant me sim thing for Clothing for my Children be it that ever it will I shal be vrey think ful for it for this Last storm has ben savele felt by hus as our Blanketes is worn out and we have ~~hav~~ No kind frend to Give us ane the onle rod We have is to Crave the Goodness of the Gentlemen the meten wich I op will Grant us sum relef wich will be most thinkfull recevad by us we and our famle has ben out of helth this winter but is Geten beter think God for it I Canot Conclud without retoring you and All the Gentlemen thinks for your Goodnes to us the Last year in Given us sum thing for the Children for we ar vrey think ful for ane thing be it ever so homle humble your servants John &

Ann Thistlethwaite

[*Overleaf*] My wife has Not ashou to her foot worth one thing
Praye God Bles me we ar all wants
Will hear in this
world ben poor
I bage your Parden for the troble at this time given
by me

Circumtext: *Different hand [SG]:* Agreed to pay his rent for the year 1826

539 John Thistle[thwaite] in Ireby to the Parish of Kirkby Lonsdale, 1 April [1828] (WPR/19/7/6/21/14)

Ireby April 1th Sunday

Sir) this comes to inform you that a hous I Canot Get for mospart is too larg in rent or too small to hould my famley as at the Least We moust have three Bades up and our Loums Besides all other things so that I Canot Get a hous that will Do under 5 or 6 Poundes Except one in the Parech of Leck Wich ^Belongs^ to Mr. Jonas Yeats and my Wife has ben to see to Taket bot he is Not for Leting it till he has seen you about the rent as he Will be shour or I most Not have it I think it Worth 3 Pounds with all the Prevlegs I spoken of to us ther is Non other to be got for us that will Do it is up at the fell side this one bot roum Weant and most pot up With Enconvences if We should be so hope as to Get it bot he is Lik all other people the ferst Word was dos the Parech Pay your rent and if I should hapen to say one thing otherwise all is over over all is over Go to Who I will ane further Conversation was all at an End it was we will be be shour of our rents I have had a Great Deal of Trobel on this a Count for people is all of one sort With me on this a count so this is the onlly one I Can have ane Chanch at all others ben taken up on a Count of my thinken them too Large rentad for a Parech to Pay Nor Dared I to [**] [*illegible*] them to pay 5 or 6 Pounds this fu lins I hop you will Not think much at my sending for I have Ben onle vrey Pourly for sum time Back and this has ben a Great hurt to us of Late I Diser that you and the Gentlemen will favor me as I Donat wish to Pot one Pone out of yours Pokets that I Can help in ane wise for if you will Not help me all is over me Geting a hous Except this I am in and it is sad in the Toune that thay will thro me out at May day in ded he Tould me he would have it at all Events so he shal Pleas God I should be so fortunat as to Get you To speak for me to Mr Tomas Yeats of Leeck as he will see you befor he will do ane further and I Could Lik to Contine on this side to Get my Childern of to Plases the ouldest too a Gerl and a Boy Dos Not Belong to you if they stop Till Witsuntide Nor shal ane of my Childern if

Pleas God I liv for I Will Get them all of as my Chanches Beter hear then in a Toun as they Get [larnad to melk] and is usad to Godes Wich is the first word [exad] their a Plas fales out if No Melker No Plas I am Nonatal Wich makes me wish my Children to Plases your vrey humble servant John Thistlewood

This here I sent as Yeats
Will Call som day on you
for Godes sak donot see me
With No hous at Mayday

Notes: *There is no year indicated in this letter, but its place in the sequence suggests that it was written in 1828.*

540 John Thistlethwaite in Leck to the Overseers of Kirkby Lonsdale, 9 June 1829 (WPR/19/7/6/22/34)

June the 9 1829

To the overseers and Gentlemen of Kirkby Lonsdale Gentlemen I Diser you will be so Good as to Pay me my rent up for it is Quite out of my Pour to Do it for my self and Mrs Yeats I have Got to understand will be No Longer Put of in Ded it is nearly out of our Pour to Keep the Dour open on ane A Count for ane thing that is to By for provishon that is for poor people is Not to be Bout with ane Erness that We Can Ernen but I Ned not to tel you you Know hou it is as well as me bot mad me rite this to you I thought it would be vrey hard for me to to be Torned out of this house after all the Laber I have had in Gating Windas in at my own Expence for it will sut Mr Yeats to a Title for he will Give me a Notis No doubt at August for the Plase Was Litle Beter than a hull then I Came to it but at ane rate it has Cost me a Great deal of Laber and Expences for Roum for our famley is not to be Got ane Whear if I had as much roum at Kirkby it would Kost 10 Pounds such as it is or I would have ben sorey to have ben ~~up~~ up hear Bot 3 or 5 Bads is Quit Litel Enuff for my famle for I have 7 Children that I Cannot Gat one thing bot A Little winding out of bot my ouldest Daughter is Gon to plase wich will Do me No Good as it Was your Wish so to be and so She is Gon for I Canot Do for myself so I most do as I Can arels she was a help to me and No hurt and my other Daughter is at hom Not ben able to Do one thing for hear self or me this month and mor Ben not Well I hop you Will Konsider my state for I Donot wish one Troble to Nather you nor me that Can be Avoidat and as so I hop you will be so Good as to Considre it for I Canat helpit or I would Not Troble you if I Could helpit With thos fu Lins bot I Could Not Quite stat all that I Could have wishad to you on Sonday last pleas to be Merceful Knid Gentlemen I remain your servent most humble so

John Thistlethwaite Leck

541 John Thistlethwaite in Leck to the Parish of Kirkby Lonsdale, 30 July [1830] (WPR/19/7/6/23/49)

Leck

July 30th Friday Night 9 Clock Sir Tomas Yats has ben over and has tould me that he will No longer be Pot of for he will have is rent or he will see for he will be Pot of Not one mor on ane A count so I have Nowhear to Go to bot to you for I am Not able to Pay one farding for meal is All I Can Gate for I have No Body to help me in the least Robt Left <m>eaten [*page torn*] with on the Coffun more is Mared arme is in Plase so that I have Nobody Nother to help Nor hurt me bot 7 Children and myself and wife ther is 15 shilens du for this haf year Rent and 20 for ould ther is no Dout but I most Los the work [*****] [**]rought [*page torn*] in the Garding wich has ben No lette<r> [*page torn*] No Propet as yeat bot a Great hurt if I [**] [*page torn*] Sorad out of Dours and work Quite for Nothing I have not this in hops that you will Tak it to Konsiderashon and befrend me For no other Frend have I bot the Gentlemen of Kirkby on Erth to rely on for one Pane that over I have had my wife Poole and Not able to do her house Work and Dear Tims I Ned Not To Tell you of for the Poor wich has No frens to help them I am shour I Canot Got Nocaceres of Life at Presant By No means Canot bot Ayre with me that all is vrey Dear and past Comen at for us inded we Can Not Got that We should have I am Given you Troble to Recd this Paper To the Gentlemen of your meting on the First Augst 1830 I Disir you will Befrend me sir)

Your servant Gentlemen
Most Respeckfuly so
John Thistlethwaite

Circumtext: *Different hand [SG]:* Agreed to pay the rent which is 1.15.0 and reduce the pension 1s/ P. week

Notes: *Although no year is given in this letter, its place in the sequence strongly suggests that it was sent in 1830.*

542 Tho[ma]s Yeats in Leck to the Parish of Kirkby Lonsdale, 4 September 1830 (WPR/19/7/6/23/44)

Leck Septr. 4th 1830

Sir I Desire to know if your Township has agreed to pay John Thistlethat is House rent arrears which will Amount to on the Twelft of May Next to five pounds he has bean Two years Last May and the first year I received three pounds and the Last year Two pounds ten Shillings and the House and Garden and ~~Stable~~ rent is Three pounds [***] [*obscured by sealing wax*] shillings per Annann Also I desire to know if you Intend to pay him his rent in full after this year as I have Given him a Proper Aquitance

I remane yours
Thos. F Yeats

543 John and Ann Thistlethwaite in Le[c]k to the Overseer of Kirkby Lonsdale, July 1831 (WPR/19/7/6/24/16)

July Satrday 1831 Leek

To ^the^ ovrcer and Gentlemen I Disir you will be so Good as to pay Tomas yeats my Rent he is Greatle put out of ~~in~~ Temper at Ben Disapointad of is rent ther is No Dout bot he intends to Give me A Notis for he unther stod as will as me that you Would pay my rent With the mone you stopad out of my penshon or Els I mite have Gon Whear I pleasad for a hous for he will have No Troble a bout it ane more that aver for I Canat pay one thing that aver over Nor Did I think of your Doing in this maner for my wife was porly all Winter & Id Kepet of you as much as posable 25s & 6d was all the adishanal relef I had in All this Long time it did Not pay a person for washen Nor Near you most be shour I am and mus be obleg to my frens for To relev me parte that over for we have don all in our pour to Keep as much of you as posable for you do Not Know hou it pot us to it to spar the shilen you stopad to pay the rent to Tomas yeats my Wife sad it most be out of the Childrens Bales it and they have letel enff bot hou aver by frens we have pot on till this Time bot if you persist in Not paying the rent it will Dish us up at once for my Wife has onle just Got to Do sum Lettle Jobs & is onle in a pourly wai sum Days Beter and sum Wors

ther is one thing mor I Could Wish to remind you of that is out of my famle you have had No Troble bot on the Contrarewise it has ben all our stode to Got them of you 3 is Got of you Nou it was your wish for them so to be Got of Not to Troble you & if I Could be Quite as I is I mite Got them

All or most of them of Township of Kerkby bot ther is all was this to do avre year Wich makes us to stink to all wich would befrend us or our Children in Placn them for We are a Bogl to all for ther is No Bod lik us of that is avre year fit to be hoistad out of Dours For rent and for me to Gat a hous it is Quite an imposable ther is all wais so much Talk hou Bad our rent is To be Got I had a Great Deal to Do to Gat this one bot I have don a Great Deal at this place to be Tornad out Know be plesad Kind Gentlemen to Consdire this paper in the Bast lite for you will find it all rite

John & Ann Thistlethwaite your humble servant Respikfully # post pad

544 John Thistlethwaite in Leck to the Parish of Kirkby Lonsdale, 5 March 1836 (WPR/19/7/6/29/7)

Sir I Diser you will have the Goodness to ^think^ of John Windle as you most think he has ben vrey Good Now as you ^no^ it should have be Pad a Cording to your Bargen at the Time that is to say 2 years and Gaen in three and you vre well know the a grement for it ^was^ to be Pad in one year Nou I hope you will Gentlemen have the goodnes to recive this Line in stead of my Comen over as I have plente of work at presant ther is No one to Ern ane thing the Girl that wove is porle and has ben this fortnat back vere poorle two she is I mit have had a Chance if this had ben onrable pad to have Got a Nother Boy of them ould enof it was the wish of the meten for me to Got my Boys of at one Time and I hope if the mone be pad you will have Don With this one Boy that is foraver I mean to the onrable Gentlemen at the meten Asemblead your Servant respekfly

the aplekashon is for one pound
one pound 15^{s} Ben pad to wards
5 pounds

John Thistlethwaite
Leck March 5th 1836

545 John Thistlethwaite to the Parish of Kirkby Lonsdale, 1 July 1836 (WPR/19/7/6/29/22)

Mr John Windle of Westhouse sends to Diser that you mr Garnett and the other Gentlemen of Kirkby Lonsdale will be so Good as to setle the remander of the prentis fee up for stepham Thistlethwaite as you know it is a Long time since it was Du acording to our bargine and as you ar satlen besnas I hope you will satle this at this Time you may all planle see I have mor to Do thin I can do seen the the redusad state of my panchon and the Cloas I have to find for hem is too much for me to do of myself so for Godes sake setle this afare

a mongest others for you will have No mor to Do for him £2.15 is pad £2.5s remans to pay I Diser you will have the Goodnes to satle this afare as ther is yeat between 3 & 4 years to find Clos this Dou and you will Not
be Trobled with it ane more as it
is bot rite and respeckfully John Thistlethwaite
Justle Du & a July 1th 1836
Cording to your
Wish I hop this will
be faverable recevad
and satled at Last

Circumtext: *Different hand [SG]:* Nothing Granted

19.

WILSON, letters 546–565

546 James Wilson in Blackburn to the Parish of Kirkby Lonsdale, 23 May 1822 (WPR/19/7/6/15/12)

Sir

I am sorrey that I am under the Nedcessaty of Troubling you for aney thing but having had boath my Legs Broaken which have kept me from work for thirteen Months and having in that time gon behind with my rent 6 pounds with no prospect at prsent of paying it I am under the nedcessaty of applying to you for some assistance to prevent my Landlord from distressing me and hope you will take my Situation into consideration without delay & have 6 Children at home three of whome are only able to do aney thing and all the can get per week is only ten shillings to support 8 of us this will convince you that had it not been great nedcessaty I Should not have troubled you for any thing I hope to be able in two or three Months to go to my work again and had it not been for my deficiency in paying my rent I should not have troubled you my Landloard being verrey urgent and but a Short time *[given]* me to pay this 6 Pounds I hope you will have the goodness to assist me as soon as possiable which can a lon preven my Family from being left destitute

I am with due respect
yours James Wilson

Direct for me
James Wilson
Shal[***][*smudged*] Dresser
Duke Street Blackburn

May 23d 1822

547 James Wilson in Blackburn to [Stephen] Garnet[t] in Kirkby Lonsdale, 27 May 1822 (WPR/19/7/6/15/13)

Mr Garnet

Blackburn May 27
1822

Sir/

Yours came to hand this day and take the liberty of Stateing that in the year 1804 I rented that Publick House the sign of the Bulls Head at the Annual rent of 14 pound which I understand intitles me to reliefe having paid one years rent and taxes

I am yours respectfully
James Wilson

Circumtext: *Different hand [SG]:* To write for his Examination to be taken upon oath before a Magistrate and sent to us

548 Benj[amin] Patterson in Blackburn to the Parish of Kirkby Lonsdale, 14 June 1822 (WPR/19/7/6/15/16)

Blackburn June 14 1822

Sir

James Wilson a poore person resident hear and belonging to your parish had the Missfortune to break boath his leggs som time since and of course rendered him unable to follow his husual Employ as a Coach Driver and having a large Famely is reduced so as to stand in need of parish relief he is in arears for rent Six Pounds and if not immediately paid he will be distressed for the amount and then of Cours have to be removed to you immediately

James Wilson got is Settlement in Kerby lonsdale by occupying the B<ulls> [*page torn*] head in your town before he came to it, it whas occupied by William Sawsit when he came to live at Kerby lonsdale he left the Sunn Inn Gargrave he Enterd upon the Bulls head March 1 1804 and left it the day before Midsummer day next after therefour of cours is settlement will be with you the rent he paid whas fourteen pounds a year

I am Yours
Benj Patterson
Overseer

549 Ja[me]s Wilson in Blackburn to [Stephen] Garnet[t] in Kirkby Lonsdale, 23 July 1822 (WPR/19/7/6/15/21)

Mr Garnet Blackburn July 23d 1822

Sir/

Yours of the 8th Inst. came duly to hand by which you inform me that a person will call on me but no one having calld as yet I am under the nedecessity

of troubling you again and hope you will lose no time in assisting me for my Landlord is determined to wait no longer and having desribed my Situation already to you – you must be convinced that mine is a Situation that requires relief had it not been for my misfortune of having boath my Legs Brock I should by no means have troubled you – in the hope you will assist me without delay
I am Sir your obedient Servt.

Jas. Wilson

550 James Wilson in Blackburn to [Stephen] Garnett in Kirkby Lonsdale, 7 August 1822 (WPR/19/7/6/15/22)

Mr Garnett
Sir/

I must trouble you with another letter and am greatly Surprised that the person you spak of has never calld nor yet have I received aney answer to my last you can not be unacquainted with my Situation after being unable to follow my employment for sixteen months with so large a Familey and so little to support them on my Landlord has been extremely kind or I should have been obliged to throw myself on the parish long since I have prevaild on him to wait untill next wednesday and if you do nothing for me the overseer will remove us and the expence of removing us will be great. I have applied to the overseer here to write you which he refused to do having already said all he can and if my few goods are sould whot can I do with my 6 small Children which I have at home we must be removed there is no other alternitive but I hope you will prevent this expence and trouble by assisting mee to pay my rent without delay for ~~nxt~~ next wednesday is the longest time I can have I would not have troubled ~~[*******]~~ [*scrubbed out*] my parish for aney thing had it not been for my misfortune and hope the Lay payers by granting this favour will have no further need of assisting mee in the hope you will assist me and prevent our removal

I am Sir yours &c
James Wilson

Blackburn
August 7th 1822

551 James Wilson in Blackburn to [Stephen] Garnett in Kirkby Lonsdale, 8 October 1822 (WPR/19/7/6/15/29)

Mr Garnett Blackburn Octr. 8th 1822

Sir/ It was my earnest wish, and fond expectation)after your late kindness for which accept my sincear thanks to you, and the lay payers(to be able to support my familey without becoming aney more Troublesom to you, but alas my hopes are again for a wile all vanished – having had the Misfortune to have my leg broke again I had onley been at my work about ten weeks and was recovering my Strength fast when on Wednesday last I was employed to take a Horse to Bolton which fell with me and falling on my Leg broke two of the Bones in the same place it wase before this is now the third time in ~~three~~ + two years and Six weeks – I would therefore beg of you to lay this my unfortunate situation before the Lay Payers, and beseach them to grant me some further Support during my confinement, for my Familey for which I shall be verry thankfull and am Dear Sir, your unfortunate Hble Servt

James Wilson

Circumtext: *Different hand:* J Lancaster Surgeon

552 J[ames] Wilson in Blackburn to [Stephen] Garnett in Kirkby Lonsdale, 20 November 1822 (WPR/19/7/6/15/39)

Blackburn Novr. 20th 1822

Mr. Garnett Sir/

I took the Liberty of writing you some time Since too inform you of my my third misfortune in two years and six weeks, which you may easily conceive have been the means of involving me and my familey in worse circumstances than ever I hope you have taken the trouble of Laying my last before the Lay payers who I hope will sympathise with me in my present distress – the Assistance you so lately Granted me saved me from some more troublesome circumstance then I was then in, for which I desire to thank you with heartfelt Gratitude – and am Sorrey I should be under the nedcessaty of again Troubling you so soon the money you sent me did not quiet Settle my arrears of rent, and it has and is now accumelating, may I hope you will take my case again into consideration and grant me further assistance untill I am recoverd by so doing you will *[ease]* a mind already overburdend and save my familey from Further Misery – would wish an answer soon to satisfy my Landlord and am with due respect your Humble Servt – J. Wilson

Circumtext: *Different hand [SG]:* Granted £1. 0. 0

553 James Wilson in Blackburn to [Stephen] Garnett in Kirkby Lonsdale, 10 December 1822 (WPR/19/7/6/15/41)

Mr Garnett Blackburn Decr 10th 1822

Sir/

having as yet had no answer to either of my applycations to you for some relief I must trouble you again and hope you will take my case into Immediate consideration my Landlord calls upon me several times every week to learn if I have heard from you untill I fear his Patience is near exausted - and you are well aware in my present Situation with so large a Familey I can not give him aney thing having Scarce half sufficient of Provisions for my Children this, Sir is an afliction to a parent which none but those who have experianced it can feel – and where my Family broke up and cast on the parish I am convinced the expence would be greater than aney relief we stand in need of at present for I trust by the Blessing of God that I shall Shortly recover altho I feel my leg mend verry slowly, owing to its having been broke in the same place before – I leave my case to your sympathy and beg of you a Speedey answer to Satisfy my Landlord otherwise I fear the worst
I remain Sir your Humble Servt. James Wilson

554 James Wilson in Blackburn to [Stephen] Garnett in Kirkby Lonsdale, 17 December 1822 (WPR/19/7/6/15/45)

Mr Garnett

Sir/

I received yours inclosed one pound and am extremely sorrey the Select Vestry will not assist me in paying my rent I assure you Sir I know not what to do nor how to keep my Landlord from selling my few Goods and turning me out of doors with my Familey I hope the will yet consider my case which is a case of real distress and if the are not agreable to pay my rent to allow me more than 2 shillings per week when you consider my Familey you may easily imagine that 4s/ per week would be little enough this sum would in some measure relieve our present wants and I hope you will grant it untill I recover which I trust will be ere long with maney thanks for your former kindness and in the hopes you will grant me 4s/ per week
I am Dear Sir your obedient Servt.

James Wilson

Blackburn Decr. 17th 1822

555 James Wilson in Blackburn to [Stephen] Garnett in Kirkby Lonsdale, 31 January 1823 (WPR/19/7/6/16/4)

Mr Garnett Blackburn Jany 31 1823

Sir/

I am again under the nedcessaty of Troubling you for my Landlord is determind to wait no longer without some prospect of getting the rent I owe him I have done all I can to keep him from distressing me in expectation that the Lay payers would ere this have done somthing more for me to enable me to pay him I have prevaild on him to give me another week untill I wrote you now Sir let me beg of you to endavour ~~to~~ either to prevail upon them to settle my rent or allow me something more per week to enable me to pay it as he will be put of ~~aney~~ ^no^ longer for you know my Familey is great and the expence of removing us would be considerable and there will be no other alternative if somthing is not done
I remain your Hlble Serv[t] James Wilson

556 James Wilson in Blackburn to [Stephen] Garnett in Kirkby Lonsdale, 4 April 1823 (WPR/19/7/6/16/23)

Mr Garnett

Sir/

I am the under the nedcessaty of again troubling you finding it impossiable as yet to suppoart my Familey my Leg continues still verrey weak and am scarce able to walk and if the Lay payers will not grant me some further relief I shall be under the nedcessaty of getting a removing order for my Familey for we Can not Starve and to work I am not yet able my Lanlord Still continues to Show pittey for my Familey but he will not Long continue to do so I fear but I hope kind Sir you will do your utmost with the Lay payers for me and prevent if possiable my present and threatend distress in the hope of some Speedey relief I am Dear Sir
Blackburn April 4th Yours &c. James Wilson
1823

557 Joseph Mullineaux in Blackburn to the Parish of Kirkby Lonsdale, 15 April 1823 (WPR/19/7/6/16/26)

Blackburn Apr. 15th
1823

Sir
I have made enquiry for James Wilson that belongs your Town and whas informed that he his but in distress I whas informed that he had nine Childeren and the youngest whas a bout 17 months Ould his ouldest son has lived at *[hedin]* in Our Town and he now his in a bad state of health at present which he whas like to Leave his situation and he now remains at home he has 3 Childeren in employ and he himself has got to take care of coach horses but he his very lame himself he tould me that if you whould have the goodness to pay the rent for him which will be £6 dew on the 12th of May next he whould do his best endeavours knot to Trouble you for aney thing more his lanlord tould him if his rent whas knot settled at May next he whould distress him
I ham yours Joseph Mullineaux

[*overleaf*] P.S. The last £2 you sent him he gave it to the Lanlord or he would have Distressed him he says all the money he has received from you has gone for the expence of Doctors and rent

Circumtext: *Different hand [SG]:* Granted £2.0s.0d.

558 James Wilson in Blackburn to [Stephen] Garnett in Kirkby Lonsdale, 19 May 1823 (WPR/19/7/6/16/33)

Mr Garnett Blackburn May 19th 1823

Sir,
I have received the two pounds you sent me and have given it to my Landlord £6.0.0 was ~~is~~ the sum owe and for rent when I gave him what you sent me he said he would give me untill next Monday to pay the remainder but no longer and in my Present Situation I find it impossiable to raise /1^{s}. of the money for to add to all my other misfortunes my oldest son has been down 7 weeks in the Typhus Fever and no prospect of his Spedey recovery and all my Familey are nearley naked for want of Clothing with no means of procuring aney for them & my Leg continues verrey weak which makes me verrey unfit for work and the little I get is not half Bread for us in Sutch circumstances what can I do I see no other alternative but getting a removing order for myself and Family which tho painfull to me yet there is no other

prospect I have applied to you to pay my rent this you inform me the Lay payers are not willing to doo I have likewise applied for a trifle per week as relief to enable me to settle ~~my~~ my rent during these seans of afliction I am not able to support them nor are the able to support themselves my Landlord I must say has been verrey kind but his Patiance is now worn out with us and there is no other alternative but being removed for we have been obliged to part with most of our Articles for meat to keep us in the Land of the Living – now Dear Sir these things I have faithfully stated to you and could wish you to Lay before the Lay payers and as my Landlord has only given me untill this day week before he proceeds against us I hope you will not fail to write me before that time and give me your advice and opinion and believe me with maney thanks for past favours

Yours &c
James Wilson

Circumtext: *Different hand [SG]:* Granted 2.0.0 by Mr. John Grundy and if Mr Jn. Grundy sees it necessary One pound more

559 James Wilson in Blackburn to the Parish of Kirkby Lonsdale, 9 April 1824 (WPR/19/7/6/17/16)

Blackburn April

Sir/ nedcessaty compells me to trouble you again and hope you will take my case into consideration we have experienced a moast deplorable Winter a great part of it two of our Children have been laid up and intirely unable to work my arrears of rent Still remain unpaid and no prospect of paying them I have struggled and starved in order to pay by the Month but with having so mutch Sickness have found it impossiable to keep Straight and had not my Landlord shown me great kindness I should have been turned out of doars but he has seen my distress and this has kept him back I hope you will Lay my situation before the Lay payers and hope they will grant me some small weekly allowence for our sufferings are great and beyond endurance doo kind Sir/ use your interest in my behalf nothing would induce me to ~~comply~~ apply but real distress which I can not avoid in my present Situation

may I beg an early answer and
in hopes of some assistance

I remain
Yours respectfully
James Wilson

Duke Street
April 9 1824

560 Tho[ma]s Forrest in Pleasington to the Overseers and Select Vestry of Kirkby Lonsdale, 5 May 1827 (WPR/19/7/6/20/15)

To the Overseer and Select Vestry of Kirkby-lonsdale Sirs) James Wilson in Blackburn a poor family belonging to your township and a tennant of mine is now owing for rent 6£ 3s. 11½d. he hast a wife and 5 children and out of employment the eldest son is lame and two of the other is adding 1s/9d a week Pr. head that is what the have to maintain themselves with but what their neighbours gives them – I wish know wither you will pay the rent or not if you dont I will distress immedately for it without any further notice

Pleasington I remain Sir's
May 5th 1827 Yours respectively
Thos. Forrest

Circumtext: *Different hand [SG]:* Granted £5.0s.0d

Further hand: You must send an answer back by return of Post to James Wilson Duke Street Blackburn

561 James Wilson in Blackburn to [Stephen] Garnett in Kirkby Lonsdale, 27 June 1827 (WPR/19/7/6/20/26)

Mr Garnett Blackburn June 27th 1827

Sir/

I have received your letter and am sorry you should charge me with giving a fals statement of my situation for if I have errd it has been by not stating our situation as bad as it really was for I am convinced that notwithstanding many have sufferd greatly in This Town yet few have sufferd more than we have you wish me to give you an account of my Family and a correct statement of our income, I have 4 sons and one daughter at home and 3 sons and one daughter from home the youngest at home is 5 years of age the second 9 – the 3 – 12 the 4 – 15 the 5 – 20 years of age the two youngest are employed at turning Weels for Rope makers the youngest of which earns 1s/6d per week the second 2s/ the 3d son Turns a Machine for flatning Wire for Reed Makers and earns 3s/6d per week my oldest son has no trade and has only had six weeks Work since last November at which time he was employd with me in taking care of Coach Horses for which we receivd 7s/ per week for boath of us, a person took our work for considerable less wages and we were dismist and since November I have been out of employment and indeed if I had work I am unable to follow it haveing had my legs broak three times in two years and six weeks which by reason of my Age and the rhumatism give me after extream pain my Wife has occasionally taken in a little sewing or

Washing but boath our earnings have not averidgd 1s/ per week since November so that we have not more than 7s/6d or 8s/ per week to mentain 7 persons Taxes and Cloathing Fire &c. our House is too mutch rent for us and we would have left it and taken a less but could not pay our arrears so that we have been compelld to remain against our will

Yours &c James Wilson

Circumtext: *In the same hand:* We the undersignd employ the 3 sons of J. Wilson at the weekly wages stated above

In different hands:

Roger Pen[?] Roper	Minister	J. Price St. Paul's
Cuthbert Cottam Reed Maker	Church Warden	Robt. Brooks

562 J Morby in Blackburn to the Overseers of Kirkby Lonsdale, 12 March 1833 (WPR/19/7/6/26/2)

This certifies that James Wilson is unfit to follow any employment in consequence of having sustained a severe injury of the hip joint

J Morby

Blackburn Surgeon

March 12 1833

Circumtext: *Below, different hand:*

To the Overseers of Kerby Lonsdale

the above statement is correct, I have this day seen the man and he walks upon two crutches, should you be disposed to relieve him here you had better wright soon

I am as Benj. Patterson

Overseer

563 James Wilson in Blackburn to the Parish of Kirkby Lonsdale, 3 July 1833 (WPR/19/7/6/26/31)

Blackburn 3d July 1833

Sir/

I am sorrow to be under the painfull needcesity of an application to you for relife through my unability to work – and not only so but my Daughter has been under the Docters hand for a twelve months – that our Sitiuation is trully deplorable – and if you dont relave – I will have a moveing order – for my family – so we must make a Vertue of needcessity – and if it had not been for friends I should been obledged to have Troubled you before – I realy cannot do with less than for shilling weekly, I have paid of Rent since I was lame weekly – but there is three Pounds in arrears – and I may have my little goods sold any ~~any~~ day – I hope you will acknowledge the receipt of this letter Immediately, as there is no time to delay I am &c James Wilson

564 James Wilson in Blackburn to the Parish of Kirkby Lonsdale, 10 July 1833 (WPR/19/7/6/26/27)

Blackburn 10th July 1833

Sir,

I have to acknowledge the receipt of your letter – and $7^s/0^d$ – and agreeable to your request I herewith send you a statement of my family, it consists of my Wife and three Childer 2 Boys and One Girl – the oldest Boy is 16 years of age and is at Present employed with a Tallow Chandler – has $6^s/0^d$ weekley – the younger Boy is 14 years of age – is an aprentice to a rope-maker – has $3^s/0^d$ weekly – the girle 11 years of age has been under the Docters hands this twelve months is quiet uncapable of doing any thing towards her Keep – as she cannot dow any thing we send her to school – our rent is $^{£}$5-10-0 yearly and it lays us One Pound more for water and taxes – I sent you word that I was about $^{£}$3-0-0 in arrears of rent, since I have been intirley unfit – out of the 9s/0d which the Boys gets us I pay $2^s/0^d$ so that only $7^s/0^d$ weekly for Vituals & all other necessaries suck as fewel soap &c. I was very thankfull for the relave you sent me I am Sir your obedient Humble S^t.

James Wilson

Circumtext: *Different hand [SG]:* Granted 2s/6d a week

565 James Wilson in Blackburn to the Parish of Kirkby Lonsdale, 9 August 1836 (WPR/19/7/6/29/15)

Blackburn 9th of Augt 1836

Sir,

I want to Know the reason you have stoped my Pension – as it is imposible for me to dow without it I am very poorly of my self, not only so but my Daughter is so lame and ill health beside, that she can render no assistance what ever, there is fower of our family, and out of the fower, there is only my son that brings inn any thing toward our subsistance, and that is only $5^s/0^d$ per week, he is an aprintice to a rope maker, and what you sent I paid my rent with it, which will be due in three weeks, my case requiers your Mature and deliberate consideration if this Pension is stoped I will have the disagreeable needcessity ^To^ apply to Blackburn Overseer for a removeing Order – therefore I hope you will have the goodness to acknowledge the receipt of this letter, that I might Know what I have to do your Complayance will obledge your Humble S[t].

James Wilson

20.

WINDER, letters 566–599

566 John Winder in Kendal to the Parish of Kirkby Lonsdale, 19 June 1810 (WPR/19/7/6/3/15)

19 June 1810 Kendal

Sir
The Reason of my not sending you a Statment of our Ernings was Because my Wife did not Percive What was written on the Back of the note till it was to Late for Gear Hall
So I have sent it you now
I have one son a Prentas Smith Wilson
he is 7 years of age – he has – 4^{s} 6^{d} Pr week
I have ^15^ one ^do^ son a Prentas with Georg Braithwaite $_{v}$Brings 4^{s} 0 week$_{v}$
I have one ^do^ son Brings in 1^{s} 6^{d}
and I have 12 shillings Pr week
I was Obliged to Borrow money for my Rent
I desire you will be so Kind as to send me some thing or Nessity will Cause me to Come to Kirkby it is Very hard to Hunger or Part With our Cloathes I shall be Obliged to do one or the other
So I am yours
John Winder

567 John Jackson in Kendal to [Stephen] Garnett in Kirkby Lonsdale, 24 June 1817 (WPR/19/7/6/10/26)

Mr Garnett
Sir,
Mary Winder to whome you allow a small pension, is now very ill and confined to her bed, wod it not be better for you to allow her something more than for us to put her under a suspended order of removal – please to give an early reply and you will much oblige
Sir,

Your most Ob^{t} Servant
John Jackson
Kendal Overseer
24 June 1817

568 Mary Winder in Kendal to [Stephen] Garnett in Kirkby Lonsdale, 6 August 1817 (WPR/19/7/6/10/32)

Mr Garnett Kendal Augt. 6th 1817

This comes to inform you that Mr Jackson as Stop Paying my Pension untill he have answer from you I hope you will favour him with answer as Soon as Posable as it is imposable for me to do with out a Pension as I am veary Poorley and week yett Mr Yelldand tould me that Mr Jackson was to containa Paying my Pension But I would rather have a answer from your Most Humb.

Ser^{t}. Marey Winder

Circumtext: *Different hand [SG]:* To see her at Kendall

569 John Jackson in Kendal to the Overseers of Kirkby Lonsdale, 6 November 1817 (WPR/19/7/6/10/43)

Overseers of the Poor of Kirkby Lonsdale

To the Churchwardens and Overseers of Kendal, Dr.

RELIEF GIVEN TO	*FROM*	*TO*	*WEEKS*	*Per Week*	*£*	*S.*	*D.*
Widow Hall	4 April 1817	24 Octr.	29	@4/-	5	16	
Mary Winder	20 June	4 July	2	@5/-		10	
Do. Do.	4 July	25 July	3	@4/-		12	
Do. Do.	25 July	29 August	5	@3/-		15	
Ann Hall	11 July	24 Octr	15	@2/6	1	17	6
~~Ann Webster~~	25 July	12 Sept	7	@5/-	1	15	
Widow Allen	22 August	3 Octr	6	@6/-	1	16	
William Garnett	19 Septr	10 Octr	3	@5/-		15	
Thos Garnett	Do.	Do.	3	@4/-		12	
					£14	8	6

The above is our Account against your Township, which I trust you will find correct; by Favouring us with an early remittance, you will oblige the Churchwardens and Overseers of Kendal.

I am your obedient Servant,
6 Nov. 1817 John Jackson *Overseer*

Notes: *This is a printed proforma invoice. The content of the invoice in italics (outwith brackets) represents the printed text*

570 John Burton in Kendal to the Parish of Kirkby Londsdale, 6 February 1826 (WPR/19/7/6/19/5)

Kendal 6th February 1826

Sir,

I have been desired to address you on behalf of Mary Winder a Widow belonging to your Township resident in Kendal – I understand she has at present 2/- Pr week from you but owing to her being in a very poor state of health and not at all able to do any thing towards her support it is necessary that an increase of pension be allowed her till she gets in some degree better – She is not able to be removed and without something is done for her very soon we shall be obliged to suspend an order of removal

I am Sir
Mo: obtly Yours
John Burton
Asst. Overseer

571 M Gawthorp to the Parish of Kirkby Lonsdale, 23 January 1827 (WPR/19/7/6/20/34)

I certify that Wm. Winders Wife is a Patient in the Dispensary & unfit to be removed

M Gawthorp
Surgeon

Jany. 23 – 1827

572 William Winder in Kendal to the Parish of Kirkby Lonsdale, 24 January 1827 (WPR/19/7/6/20/35)

Kendal Jany 24 1827

Sir
I am sorry to inform you that I am quite out of work and has been for some time and not likely to get any yet my wife has been poorly for a month and Continues much the same I shall be very much Oblidged to you if you could relieve my distressed situation a little you will see by the enclosed that my wife is not in a fit state to be removed

I am Your
Humble Servt.
William Winder

573 W[illia]m Jennings to the Overseer of Kirkby Lonsdale, 23 June 1827 (WPR/19/7/6/20/4)

To the Overseer of Kirby
Sir

Wm Winder is now so far behind with his rent, and I am sory to say that I must size upon his goods unless you come forward to help him – he is realy a very industrious man – and tho he has a large famely he would do if he could get plenty of Work – I do think it is your duty to assist him, to prevent what may be worse = but of this you must exercise your own judgement –

I remain yours respectfully
Wm Jennings

June 23d 1827

N.B. amount of Rent due £3.10s.0d.

Circumtext: *Different hand [SG]:* Not Granted

574 William Winder in Kendal to the Parish of Kirkby Lonsdale, 28 November 1827 (WPR/19/7/6/20/51)

Kendal Novr. 28 1827

Sir

I am very sorry to inform you that I have only about half week for some time back if you think you can do anything for us we shall be very much oblidged to you for a little money will be very acceptable if we have no relief from you very soon we shall be oblidged to come altogether

I am your
humble servant
William Winder

575 W[illia]m Winder in Kendal to the Parish of Kirkby Lonsdale, 5 October [1828] (WPR/19/7/6/21/26)

Kendal 5 October

Sir/

I am very sorry that necessity Obliges me at this time to apply to you for relief, I have two children very poorly and I am now in such a poor state of health myself that there is possibility of maintaing them without your assistance, if you please to enquire into my conduct you will find, that I have always done my utmost endeavour to Maintain my Family, but now when my health is failing and work so bad I have no other lawfull and honest means left than applying to you, I trust you will take my case into your consideration and send me relief without being compelled to come over as I cannot come there and back in One day and, it is attended with unnecessary expence, But if no answer returns by next market day I shall be Obliged either^r^ to come myself or be removed, I should have been very sorry to trouble you but I realy am forced,

I am Your
Obed & Humble St.
W^{m}. Winder

Circumtext: *Different hand [SG]:* Granted 5s/

Notes: *Although there is no indication in what year this letter was written, its place in the sequence strongly suggests that it was sent in 1828.*

576 W[illia]m Jennings in Kendal to [Stephen] Garnett in Kirkby Lonsdale, 29 November 1828 (WPR/19/7/6/21/19)

Mr. Garnett

Sir

Wm Winder finds himself unable to pay his rent – I have only got two five shillings from for the last year – and their now remains due £3.10^{s}.0^{d} – I believe the man is sober and industrious, but he can only have one Web in the week – which amounts to 8/ or 9/- and for their large famely it is but a small matter I do not think it prudent to let the rent go any Farther – and I must be under the necessity of selling if the Township does not agree to pay it – an early reply to this Letter is expected

I remain yours &c.

Kendal Wm Jennings

Novr. 29th 1828

Circumtext: *Different hand [SG]:* Granted £2.10s.0

577 William Winder in Kendal to [Stephen] Garnet[t] in Kirkby Lonsdale, 28 January 1829 (WPR/19/7/6/22/11)

Kendal Jany. 28 1829

Mr Garnet

Sir/

I am sorry to trouble you but I cannot do any longer my Wife is verry porly and has not been able to go out for a fortnight and I have 2 Children verry ill one is in the scarlet fever and the other is I am afraid begun and I have verry little Work and I hope you will be so kind as to send me something on Saturday with out paid I am your humble Servt.

William Winder

Circumtext: *Different hand [SG]:* Granted 5s/

578 W[illiam] Winder in Kendal to the Parish of Kirkby Lonsdale, 13 June 1829 (WPR/19/7/6/22/39)

Kendal 13th June 1829

Sir/

In consequence of the ill state of my wifes health, I am Obliged to send for immediate relief we are in a very poor state we trust you will send us something by Wednesday The Doctor has been here to day and desired us to write immediately, my Wife has been very dangerous, and without your assistance there is no possibility of recovery there is not half work to get for the any Weavers, and I am Obliged to wait on my Family, we are not able to get a nurse,

I am your humble
Sert
Wm Winder

579 M Gawthorp to the Parish of Kirkby Lonsdale, 24 June 1829 (WPR/19/7/6/22/35)

I certify that Wm. Winders Wife has been for some time a Patient in the Kendal Dispensary & requires parochial relief

M Gawthorp
Surgeon

Circumtext: *Different hand:*

June 24 1829

Gent) The above is a certificate from the surgeon of our Dispensary who has [at] tended this wife of Wm. Winder for the last fifteen weeks – W.W. Begs me to say that he cannot possibly keep his family upon the amount of his earnings – his attention is so much taken up by the cases of their present situation that he is not able to do so much as he otherwise could get through, and as work can only be obtained at certain intervals his situation is a very distressing one – There does not appear to be any likelihood of his Wife's recovery – You will be Kind to say as early as possible what we must do for you –

I am &c.
John Burton
Assis Overseer

580 W[illia]m Jennings to the Overseers of Kirkby Lonsdale, 28 October 1829 (WPR/19/7/6/22/53)

To the Overseers of the Township of Kirby
Gen)

Wm Winder wishes me to state to you that it is utterly impossible for him to pay his rent – they are 7 of a family – and he cannot make more than 8/ P. week – and had it not been for the assistance he as recieved from Kind friends, both himself and family must have had long since to have come to you altogether, at Martinmass next their will be £5.0s.0d. due for rent – He says if you do not take his case into consideration, and relieve him, he must be under the necessity of giving up House Keeping and coming to you all together –

I remain yours &c.
Wm Jennings

Oct. 28 1829

Circumtext: *Different hand [SG]:* Granted £4.0.0

581 W[illia]m Winder in Kendal to the Parish of Kirkby Lonsdale, 24 January 1830 (WPR/19/7/6/23/24)

Kendal 24th Jan 1830

Sir,

I am sorry that I have again to trouble, but I am at present not able to work, and the work I have had latterly has not been sufficient for support for me and my and my Family but at present I am very poorly and has been since last Saturday, You will be so Kind as send me a trifle as soon as possible as we are realy in great need –

I am Your humble
Srt.
Wm. Winder

582 B. Hayton in Kendal to the Parish of Kirkby Lonsdale, 3 February 1830 (WPR/19/7/6/23/53)

Kendal 3d Feby 1830

Sir

Widow Winder is very unwell and cannot subsist on what she has allowed from you I shall feel much obliged if you will send her ~~send~~ Two or three shillings More when you send the other which will much oblige

Your Obt Servt
B. Hayton
Churchwarden

583 W[illia]m Jennings in Kendal to [Stephen] Garnet[t] in Kirkby Lonsdale, N.D. (WPR/19/7/6/23/38)

Mr Garnet
Sir
We have reced no rent from Wm Winder since that you sent in December last – There is now £5.0.0 due – on the 11th of this month – they request me to write you and to say that you will be so kind as to send it, as it is intirely out of their power to pay it – please to write me as soon as convenient

Yours respectfuly
Wm Jennings

Kendal [****] [*page torn*]

N.B. They are thinking of removing this time time, and it must be settled before

Circumtext: *In different hand [SG]:* Granted

Notes: *Although this letter is undated, its place in the sequence suggests that it belongs between letters 582 and 584.*

584 W[illia]m Winder in Kendal to the Parish of Kirkby Lonsdale, 3 March 1830 (WPR/19/7/6/23/45)

Kendal 3^{d} March 1830

Sir,
I return you thanks for the 4 shillings you last sent me, I am now Obliged on Account of the distress of the times to apply to you for further relief and hopes you will send us a trifle as soon as possible as we are in real need. I am your Humble

& Obed^{t}. Servant
W^{m}. Winder

Circumtext: *In different hand [SG]:* Granted 5s/

585 W[illia]m Winder in Kendal to the Parish of Kirkby Lonsdale, 19 May 1830 (WPR/19/7/6/23/8)

Kendal 19th May 1830

Sir/

This is to inform you that I am very ill not able to work, the Doctor says it is the plurisey fever, he has bled me twice you will be so Kind as send me some relief by saturday or I shall be Obliged to apply to Kendal

I am Your Humbl & Obedt.
Wm Winder

586 W[illia]m Winder in Kendal to the Parish of Kirkby Lonsdale, 19 January 1831 (WPR/19/7/6/24/62)

Kendal Jan. 19. 1831

Sir)

I am under the necssety of informing *[you]* that We have been Short of work for a long time; Which has reduced us in our Circumstances and we cannot do any longer without relief.

I hope you ^will^ attend to my case without delay.

I am Sir your's &c.
Wm. Winder

587 Tho[ma]s Line in Kendal to Stephen Garnett in Kirkby Lonsdale, 8 February 1831 (WPR/19/7/6/24/58)

Kendal Febry. 8th 1831

Mr Stephen Garnett
Sir/

I am requested by Wm Winder (who belongs to your Township) to request you will be kind enough to send some relief as he has been out of health for some time, and has had but very little Work your immediate attention will greatly Oblige them with what relief you Can possibly Send, or they will be under the necessity of being removed

I am Your Obt. Servt.
Thos. Line

Circumtext*: Different hand [SG]:* Feby. 11th sent 6s/

588 Tho[ma]s Line in Kendal to the Parish of Kirkby Lonsdale, 2 July 1831 (WPR/19/7/6/24/15)

Kendal July 2nd. 1831

Sir/

I beg leave to write to say that ½ a years rent is now due from W^{m}. Winder say £2. & as he is unable to pay I hope you will be Kind enough to do it for him

Your answer will
Oblige your Ob^{t}. S^{t}.
Thos. Line

Circumtext: *Different hand [SG]:* To apply personaly

589 Thomas Line in Kendal to the Parish of Kirkby Lonsdale, 2 December 1831 (WPR/19/7/6/24/45)

Kendal Decr. 2<nd> [*smudged*] 1831

Sir/

I beg leave to state that I want a year's Rent of W^{m}. Winder & as he is unable to pay any Rent I shall be under the disagreeable necessity of making distress upon the Goods unless you consider to pay the amount of – your answer in course of next week will Oblige

Your Obd^{t}. Servt.
Thomas Line

1 Year's Rent due at Martinmas £4.0.0

Circumtext: *Different hand [SG]:* Granted Rent

590 William Winder in Kendal to [Stephen] Garnet[t] in Kirkby Lonsdale, 2 November [1831] (WPR/19/7/6/24/52)

Kendal Novth 2

Mr Garnet

I have sent you these few lines to let you know that my Wife was brought to Bed yesterday morning & is in a very weak state & you must be so kind as send us som[***] [*page torn*] with the Carrier on Saturday as it is <not> [*page torn*] possible I can do without your assistance being eight a Family & I am very short of work

Yours
William Winder

Notes: *Although no year is given in this letter, its place in the sequence strongly suggests that it was sent in 1831.*

591 W[illiam] Winder in Kendal to [Stephen] Garnet[t] in Kirkby Lonsdale, 3 October [1832] (WPR/19/7/6/25/51)

Mr Garnet Kendal Octob. 3
I Return you many thanks for your Kindness and am Sorey to Say I was takin very poorley the thusday after you was at hour hous if you will be Kind as send me a smal trifle to asist my smal famley I will be much abliged to you
your humbl Servent
W. Winder

Notes: *Although no year is given in this letter, its place in the sequence strongly suggests that it was sent in 1832.*

592 Thomas Line in Kendal to the Parish of Kirkby Lonsdale, 1 December 1832 (WPR/19/7/6/25/68)

Kendal Decr. 1st 1832

Sir,

I beg to inform you that a Year's Rent is due from W^{m}. Winder say £4. which I find he is quite unable to pay – he desires me to write to beg you will be kind enough to pay the amount for him & oblige
I am your Obt. Servt.
Thomas Line

Circumtext: *Different hand [SG]:* Granted £3.0.0

593 Tho[ma]s Line in Kendal to the Parish of Kirkby Lonsdale, 1 June 1833 (WPR/19/7/6/26/30)

Kendal June 1st 1833

Sir)

I beg leave to inform you that the Whitsuntide Rent is due for a Cottage Occupied by Wm Winder & also £1 which was short last remittance together £3 – I shall be Obliged by your sending the above
& am Your Obt Servt.
Thos. Line

594 Thomas Line in Kendal to the Parish of Kirkby Lonsdale, 2 November 1833 (WPR/19/7/6/26/22)

Kendal Novr. 2nd 1833

Sir/

I beg to Know whether the Parish of Ky. Lonsdale intends Paying Wm. Winder's Rent which will amount at Martinmas to £5.0.0 His wife is very ill & they are quite unable to pay any Rent. Your immediate answer will Oblige

Your Obt. Servt.

Thomas Line

Balance of Rent	1.0.0
1 Years Rent due at Martinmans	4.0.0
	£5.0.0

595 H Kay in Kendal to the Parish of Kirkby Lonsdale, 7 December 1833 (WPR/19/7/6/26/70)

William Winder has been a patient of the Dispensary for the last month for a severe attack of Rhumatism and is still not in a fit state to follow any employment

Kendal H Kay

Decr. 7 Surgeon

1833

Circumtext: *Different hand:* John Hudson Vicar

596 R Hawley to the Parish of Kirkby Lonsdale, 1 November 1834 (WPR/19/7/6/27/20)

I certify that Wm. Winder is ill, requiring your relief

R Hawley

1st Novr. Surgeon

1834

597 W[illia]m and Eliz[abeth] Winder in Kendal to the Parish of Kirkby Lonsdale, 2 November 1834 (WPR/19/7/6/27/21)

Kendal Novr 2nd 1834

Gentlemen

I now address you under ~~If~~ circumstances of a very hard Kind I myself am confined to my bed in sickness and my Wife likewise on a bed of sickness & child-bed of which you will see by the inclosed note from the Doctor Gentlemen if you have any compassion shew it for it is now a house of distress and poverty. it is now two months since the Doctor told me I was unable to work and I cant offer to rise out of bed without the assistance of two men We are now nine a family and I will leave it for you to judge the state we are in and hopes you will shew your compassion and relief at this critical moment and so I remain your ~~affection~~ Obedient

Servant
Wm. & Eliz. Winder

598 Sarah Winder in Kendal to the Overseer of Kirkby Lonsdale, October [1835] (WPR/19/7/6/28/23)

Kendal October

Sir,

I humbly beg leave to inform you that my Husband ^Wm. Winder^ is Labouring under a severe illness and has ^been^ for some time unable to follow his Employment which renders me under the necessity of asking for some assistance towards the support of our family as it is impossible for us under present circumstances to put on without assistance in some manner therefore I do most humbly beg you will have the goodness to favour us with your ansr. as soon as you can make it convenient to write as we have no desire to make application to Kendal which certainly must at this time be the case if we don't here from you soon our family consists of my self & Husband & 7 Children, which now implores assistance at your hands therefore I beg you will not fail to ansr. this as soon as convenient

To the Overseer
of the Poor
of Kirkby Lonsdale

and you will
truly oblige
Sir, your Humble Sert.
Sarah Winder
Capt French Lane

P.S. 5 out of the 7 children
is unable to earn anything
towards thier maintainance

Notes: *Although no year is given for this letter, its place in the sequence strongly suggests it was sent in 1835.*

599 Sarah Winder in Kendal to [Stephen] Garnet[t] in Kirkby Lonsdale, 28 October 1835 (WPR/19/7/6/28/21)

Kendal Octr 28 1835

Mr Garnet
)Sir

I am sorry to Informe you my husband William Winder still Continues verry ill and is quite Confined to his bed I will be verry much Oblidged to you to send us some Relief by return of Carrier as it is not possible for Can do any longer I remain your humble Servt

Sarah Winder

Bibliography

Manuscript sources

East Sussex Record Office
PAR 496/37/3, Mary Harte of Alresford, Hampshire, to Mr. Eagle of Uckfield, West Sussex, 1 February 1728.

Kendal Archive Centre
Because we have used only around half of the extant Kirkby Lonsdale letter collection and organised 'our' half by surname group, there is no single intuitively obvious way to present the manuscript source references for a bibliography. Here we retain the primary organisational category for the book – name – but group the individual letter references by year. For clarity, the Kirkby Lonsdale Township Letter collection is ordered chronologically and the cataloguing number for the letters can be broken down as follows:

WPR/19	– Kirkby Lonsdale, St. Mary's Parish
/7	– Overseers of the Poor
/6	– Township letters
/1–29	– Year of letter (/1 = 1801–6; /2 = 1809, /3 = 1810; /4 = 1811 et. seq., to; /29 = 1836)
/1-XXX	– Individual item number (ordered chronologically, with a few anomalies)

Bainbridge

WPR/19/7/6/4/20, 23
WPR/19/7/6/7/2
WPR/19/7/6/9/3, 8
WPR/19/7/6/15/44
WPR/19/7/6/16/36
WPR/19/7/6/17/22
WPR/19/7/6/18/2, 16, 23, 31
WPR/19/7/6/19/1, 13
WPR/19/7/6/20/29, 37

Beck

WPR/19/7/6/2/22, 28
WPR/19/7/6/5/24, 36
WPR/19/7/6/15/23
WPR/19/7/6/20/46, 48
WPR/19/7/6/24/41

WPR/19/7/6/25/2, 7, 15, 19, 23, 25, 32, 41, 46, 57, 62, 72
WPR/19/7/6/26/8–9, 12–13, 26, 44, 58
WPR/19/7/6/27/3, 10, 23, 43, 53
WPR/19/7/6/28/2, 18, 34
WPR/19/7/6/29/1, 4, 12, 21, 31

Boothman

WPR/19/7/6/2/36
WPR/19/7/6/3/16, 24
WPR/19/7/6/4/6, 17, 28
WPR/19/7/6/5/15–16, 18, 25, 27, 32
WPR/19/7/6/10/39
WPR/19/7/6/12/13, 19
WPR/19/7/6/15/14
WPR/19/7/6/16/32
WPR/19/7/6/17/8
WPR/19/7/6/18/6, 15
WPR/19/7/6/19/12
WPR/19/7/6/20/1, 17–19, 22, 42, 45
WPR/19/7/6/21/7
WPR/19/7/6/22/3, 13–14, 21, 30, 37, 44, 50, 56
WPR/19/7/6/23/55
WPR/19/7/6/24/31
WPR/19/7/6/25/14
WPR/19/7/6/26/29
WPR/19/7/6/28/35, 46–47
WPR/19/7/6/29/10, 19

Garlick

WPR/19/7/6/9/22
WPR/19/7/6/12/5, 27
WPR/19/7/6/13/1, 9, 22, 35, 37
WPR/19/7/6/14/19–20, 42
WPR/19/7/6/15/10, 20
WPR/19/7/6/16/17, 56
WPR/19/7/6/20/39
WPR/19/7/6/21/16
WPR/19/7/6/23/27, 51
WPR/19/7/6/24/44
WPR/19/7/6/25/6, 21, 35, 60
WPR/19/7/6/26/36, 38, 41, 46, 72
WPR/19/7/6/27/27, 30, 36, 45, 50

Garnett

WPR/19/7/6/9/21
WPR/19/7/6/10/27, 37, 43

WPR/19/7/6/13/15, 28, 44
WPR/19/7/6/14/28
WPR/19/7/6/15/4, 37, 46
WPR/19/7/6/16/39, 53
WPR/19/7/6/20/23
WPR/19/7/6/21/36–37
WPR/19/7/6/23/1, 12, 35
WPR/19/7/6/24/1, 24, 27–28
WPR/19/7/6/26/39, 42, 49, 54
WPR/19/7/6/29/18

Gill

WPR/19/7/6/20/9, 47, 49
WPR/19/7/6/21/15, 29
WPR/19/7/6/22/23, 49
WPR/19/7/6/24/42
WPR/19/7/6/25/56
WPR/19/7/6/26/11, 19
WPR/19/7/6/28/1, 39
WPR/19/7/6/29/32

Grime

WPR/19/7/6/10/21, 45
WPR/19/7/6/11/11, 23–24, 31
WPR/19/7/6/12/9, 18, 29, 34
WPR/19/7/6/13/23, 43
WPR/19/7/6/14/4, 16, 21, 31, 37, 45
WPR/19/7/6/15/3, 8, 35
WPR/19/7/6/16/16, 28–29, 35, 38, 40, 54, 66
WPR/19/7/6/17/24
WPR/19/7/6/18/1, 34–35
WPR/19/7/6/20/16, 36, 43, 52
WPR/19/7/6/21/4, 10–12, 18, 31
WPR/19/7/6/22/18, 40, 51
WPR/19/7/6/23/9, 11, 52, 54
WPR/19/7/6/25/55
WPR/19/7/6/27/56
WPR/19/7/6/28/11

Hall

WPR/19/7/6/2/29
WPR/19/7/6/3/2
WPR/19/7/6/5/3–4
WPR/19/7/6/6/5, 16
WPR/19/7/6/9/14, 21
WPR/19/7/6/10/22

WPR/19/7/6/15/46
WPR/19/7/6/16/22, 24–25
WPR/19/7/6/17/39, 48

Hodgson

WPR/19/7/6/1/2
WPR/19/7/6/5/11, 37
WPR/19/7/6/8/3
WPR/19/7/6/9/7
WPR/19/7/6/10/35, 38
WPR/19/7/6/11/32
WPR/19/7/6/14/11, 40, 46
WPR/19/7/6/15/31, 40
WPR/19/7/6/18/17, 21
WPR/19/7/6/19/10
WPR/19/7/6/20/30
WPR/19/7/6/23/25
WPR/19/7/6/24/14, 39, 47, 55
WPR/19/7/6/25/1, 3, 11, 16, 32, 61
WPR/19/7/6/26/32
WPR/19/7/6/27/11, 49

Kitchen

WPR/19/7/6/13/4, 8
WPR/19/7/6/14/35
WPR/19/7/6/15/27, 36
WPR/19/7/6/16/57
WPR/19/7/6/19/11
WPR/19/7/6/23/30–31, 57
WPR/19/7/6/26/28
WPR/19/7/6/27/22

Langhorn

WPR/19/7/6/5/17
WPR/19/7/6/8/12
WPR/19/7/6/9/23
WPR/19/7/6/9/10
WPR/19/7/6/10/4, 51
WPR/19/7/6/11/1–2, 8, 20, 36
WPR/19/7/6/12/4, 7, 15, 17, 32
WPR/19/7/6/13/3, 10, 18, 20, 29
WPR/19/7/6/14/9, 22, 26, 33, 44
WPR/19/7/6/16/12, 43, 61
WPR/19/7/6/17/3, 33

Lowry

WPR/19/7/6/15/5, 43
WPR/19/7/6/16/20, 55
WPR/19/7/6/17/23, 41
WPR/19/7/6/19/8
WPR/19/7/6/20/6, 14, 32, 40
WPR/19/7/6/21/5
WPR/19/7/6/22/1
WPR/19/7/6/24/40, 48
WPR/19/7/6/25/34

Moore

WPR/19/7/6/9/11, 17
WPR/19/7/6/10/9, 33
WPR/19/7/6/11/19, 39
WPR/19/7/6/12/23
WPR/19/7/6/13/31, 34, 39
WPR/19/7/6/14/48
WPR/19/7/6/15/2, 6, 9, 33
WPR/19/7/6/16/30, 52
WPR/19/7/6/17/20, 30
WPR/19/7/6/18/36
WPR/19/7/6/19/2, 3

Nelson

WPR/19/7/6/2/20, 24, 51
WPR/19/7/6/3/10, 30
WPR/19/7/6/4/4, 10, 18, 21, 25
WPR/19/7/6/5/7, 9, 14, 29, 33, 35
WPR/19/7/6/6/1–2, 4, 11
WPR/19/7/6/7/5, 9, 11, 14–15
WPR/19/7/6/8/2, 4, 6–7, 10–11, 15–16
WPR/19/7/6/9/2
WPR/19/7/6/10/8, 10, 12, 41
WPR/19/7/6/11/21
WPR/19/7/6/12/3, 22, 24, 28, 33
WPR/19/7/6/13/16, 38, 45
WPR/19/7/6/14/14, 27, 29–30, 34
WPR/19/7/6/15/1, 11, 30, 42
WPR/19/7/6/16/10, 34, 47, 60
WPR/19/7/6/17/7, 11, 13, 29, 34, 36, 45
WPR/19/7/6/20/21
WPR/19/7/6/21/22, 39
WPR/19/7/6/22/5, 22, 27, 29, 48
WPR/19/7/6/23/36, 40
WPR/19/7/6/24/2, 12, 25, 34, 57

WPR/19/7/6/25/9, 18, 27, 37, 73
WPR/19/7/6/26/50
WPR/19/7/6/27/4
WPR/19/7/6/28/31

Pearson

WPR/19/7/6/2/8, 25, 30
WPR/19/7/6/4/29
WPR/19/7/6/5/1–2
WPR/19/7/6/6/3, 10, 17
WPR/19/7/6/7/3
WPR/19/7/6/9/12
WPR/19/7/6/11/29, 33, 38
WPR/19/7/6/12/31
WPR/19/7/6/13/19
WPR/19/7/6/14/1, 39
WPR/19/7/6/15/7, 34
WPR/19/7/6/16/3, 7, 14–15, 21, 58–59
WPR/19/7/6/17/9, 17, 21
WPR/19/7/6/26/45, 52
WPR/19/7/6/28/41

Robinson

WPR/19/7/6/17/6, 12, 31, 35
WPR/19/7/6/21/1, 23–25, 28, 32
WPR/19/7/6/22/32–33
WPR/19/7/6/23/7, 10, 41
WPR/19/7/6/24/29, 33
WPR/19/7/6/27/7, 14, 16, 31–32
WPR/19/7/6/28/9, 15, 32, 50
WPR/19/7/6/29/9, 28

Sill

WPR/19/7/6/10/2
WPR/19/7/6/11/18
WPR/19/7/6/12/20, 25–26
WPR/19/7/6/21/33
WPR/19/7/6/26/4, 55, 56, 59, 73
WPR/19/7/6/27/33
WPR/19/7/6/28/4, 29
WPR/19/7/6/29/3, 6

Thistlethwaite

WPR/19/7/6/2/17, 37
WPR/19/7/6/3/13

WPR/19/7/6/15/19
WPR/19/7/6/17/14–15, 19, 28
WPR/19/7/6/18/5, 7, 38–39
WPR/19/7/6/19/4
WPR/19/7/6/21/14
WPR/19/7/6/22/34
WPR/19/7/6/23/44, 49
WPR/19/7/6/24/16
WPR/19/7/6/29/7, 22

Wilson

WPR/19/7/6/15/12–13, 16, 21–22, 29, 39, 41, 45
WPR/19/7/6/16/4, 23, 26, 33
WPR/19/7/6/17/16
WPR/19/7/6/20/15, 26
WPR/19/7/6/26/2, 27, 31
WPR/19/7/6/29/15

Winder

WPR/19/7/6/3/15
WPR/19/7/6/10/26, 32, 43
WPR/19/7/6/19/5
WPR/19/7/6/20/4, 34–35, 51
WPR/19/7/6/21/26, 19
WPR/19/7/6/22/11, 35, 39, 53
WPR/19/7/6/23/8, 24, 38, 45, 53
WPR/19/7/6/24/15, 45, 52, 58, 62
WPR/19/7/6/25/51, 68
WPR/19/7/6/26/22, 30, 70
WPR/19/7/6/27/20–21
WPR/19/7/6/28/21, 23

Other Kendal Archive Centre

WPR/19/7/18/29, Stephen Garnett to John Scorah, 1 November 1825.

Lancashire Record Office
PR 866 and 867, Lancaster Overseers' Letter Books, 1809–1840.

Printed sources
An Act for the Relief of the Poor (43. Eliz. Cap. 2), 1601.
An Act for the Better Relief of the Poor of this Kingdom, better known as the Settlement and Removal Act (14. Carl. 2. Cap. 12).
Mannex, P. J., *History, Topography, and Directory, of Westmorland; and the Hundreds of Lonsdale and Amounderness in Lancashire* (London, 1849)

Report from His Majesty's Commissioners for Inquiring into the Administration and Practical Operation of the Poor Laws: Appendix (B.2.). Answers to Town Queries, in Two Volumes, Vol.1.

Secondary sources

Bailey, J., '"Think Wot a Mother Must Feel": Parenting in English Pauper Letters, c.1760–1834', *Family and Community History* 13 (2010) pp. 5–19.

Earner-Byrne, L., *Letters of the Catholic Poor: Poverty in Independent Ireland, 1920–1940* (Cambridge, 2017).

Charlesworth, L., *Welfare's Forgotten Past: A Socio-Legal History of the Poor Law* (Abingdon, 2010).

Green, D., *Pauper Capital: London and the Poor law, 1790–1870* (Aldershot, 2010).

Healey, J., *The First Century of Welfare: Poverty and Poor Relief in Lancashire, 1620–1730* (Woodbridge, 2014).

Hindle, S., *On the Parish? The Micro-Politics of Poor Relief in Rural England, c.1550–1750* (Oxford, 2004).

Hitchcock, T., 'A New History from Below', *History Workshop Journal* 57 (2004) pp. 294–98.

Hollen Lees, L., *The Solidarities of Strangers: The English Poor Laws and the People, 1700–1948* (Cambridge, 1998).

Houston, R., *Peasant Petitions: Social Relations and Economic Life on Landed Estates 1600–1850* (Basingstoke, 2014).

Hurren, E., and King, S., 'Begging for a burial: Death and the poor law in eighteenth and nineteenth century England', *Social History* 30 (2005) pp. 321–41.

Innes, J., King, S., and Winter, A., 'Settlement and Belonging in Europe, 1500–1930s: Structures, Negotiations and Experiences', in *Migration, Settlement and Belonging in Europe, 1500s–1930s* ed. S. King and A. Winter (Oxford, 2013) pp. 1–28.

Jones, P., and King, S., 'Voices from the Far North: Pauper Letters and the Provision of Welfare in Sutherland, 1845–1900', *Journal of British Studies* 55 (2016) pp. 76–98.

Jones, P., and King, S., 'Introduction: Obligation, Entitlement and Dispute: Navigating the English Poor Laws, 1600–1900', in *Obligation, Entitlement and Dispute under the English Poor Laws* ed. P. Jones and S. King (Newcastle, 2015) pp. 1–19.

Jones, P., and King, S., 'From Petition to Pauper Letter: The Development of an Epistolary Form', in *Obligation, Entitlement and Dispute under the English Poor Laws* ed. P. Jones and S. King (Newcastle, 2015) pp. 53–77.

Jones, P., 'Widows, Work and Wantonness: Pauper letters and the Boundaries of Entitlement under the Old Poor Law', in *Obligation, Entitlement and Dispute under the English Poor Laws* ed. P. Jones and S. King (Newcastle, 2015) pp. 139–67.

Jones, P., '"I Cannot keep my place without being deascent": Pauper Letters, Parish Clothing and Pragmatism in the South of England, 1750–1830', *Rural History* 20 (2009) pp. 31–49.

Jones, P., 'Finding Captain Swing: Protest, Parish Relations, and the State of the Public Mind in 1830', *International Review of Social History* 54 (2009) pp. 449–53.

King, P., 'The rights of the poor and the role of the law: The impact of pauper appeals to the summary courts 1750–1834,' in *Obligation, Entitlement and Dispute under the English Poor Laws* ed. P. Jones and S. King (Newcastle, 2015) pp. 235–62.

King, P., 'Social inequality, identity and the labouring poor in eighteenth century England', in *Identity and Agency in England, 1500–1800* ed. H. French and J. Barry (Basingstoke, 2004) pp. 60–87.

King, S., and Jones, P., 'Testifying for the Poor: Epistolary Advocates and the Negotiation of Parochial Relief in England, 1800–1834', *Journal of Social History* 49 (2016) pp. 784–807.

King, S., *Writing the Lives of the English Poor 1750s–1830s* (Montreal, 2019).

King, S., *Sickness, Medical Welfare and the English Poor 1750–1834* (Manchester, 2018).

King, S., 'Poor Relief, Settlement and Belonging in England, 1780s to 1840s', in *Migration, Settlement and Belonging in Europe, 1500–1930s: Comparative Perspectives* ed. S. King and A. Winter (Oxford, 2013) pp. 83–93.

King, S., '"In these you may trust". Numerical information, accounting practices and the poor law, c.1790 to 1840', in *Statistics and the Public Sphere: Numbers and the People in Modern Britain, c.1750–2000* ed. T. Crook and G. O'Hara (London, 2011) pp. 51–66.

King, S., 'Negotiating the Law of Poor Relief in England, 1800–1840', *History* 96 (2011) pp. 410–35.

King, S., 'The residential and familial arrangements of English pauper letter writers, 1800–1840s', in *Accommodating Poverty: The Housing and Living Arrangements of the English Poor, c.1600–1850* ed. J. McEwan and P. Sharpe (Basingstoke, 2011) pp. 145–68.

King, S., '"I Fear You Will Think Me Too Presumptuous in My Demands but Necessity Has No Law": Clothing in English Pauper Letters, 1800–1834', *International Review of Social History* 54 (2009) pp. 207–36.

King, S., 'Friendship, Kinship and Belonging in the Letters of Urban Paupers, 1800–1840', *Historical Social Research* 33 (2008) pp. 249–77.

King, S., 'Pauper Letters as a Source', *Family and Community History* 10 (2007) pp. 167–70.

King, S., '"Stop This Overwhelming Torment of Destiny": Negotiating Financial Aid at Times of Sickness under the English Old Poor Law, 1800–1840', *Bulletin of the History of Medicine* 79 (2005) pp. 228–60.

King, S., '"It is impossible for our Vestry to judge his case into perfection from here": Managing the Distance Dimensions of Poor Relief, 1800–40', *Rural History* 16 (2005) pp. 161–89.

King, S., and Tomkins, A., 'Introduction', in *The Poor in England, 1700–1850: An Economy of Makeshifts* ed. S. King and A. Tomkins (Manchester, 2003) pp. 1–38.

King, S., *Poverty and Welfare in England, 1700–1850: A Regional Perspective* (Manchester, 2000).

King, S., 'Reconstructing lives: The poor, the poor law and welfare in rural industrial communities', *Social History* 22 (1997) pp. 318–38.

Levene, A., *The Childhood of the Poor: Welfare in Eighteenth-Century London* (Basingstoke, 2012).

Lyons, M. (ed.), *Ordinary Writings, Personal Narratives: Writing Practices in 19th and Early 20th Century Europe* (Bern, 2007).

Macfarlane, A., *The Origins of English Individualism* (Oxford, 1978).

Marshall, D., *The English Poor in the Eighteenth Century* (New York, 1969).

Moring, B. and Wall, R., *Widows in European Economy and Society, 1600–1920* (Woodbridge, 2017).

Muldrew, C., and King, S., 'Cash, wages and the economy of makeshifts in England 1650–1800', in *Experiencing Wages: Social and Cultural Aspects of Wage Forms in Europe since 1500* ed. P. Scholliers and L. Schwarz (Oxford, 2003) pp. 32–56.

Murdoch, L., *Imagined Orphans: Poor Families, Child Welfare, and Contested Citizenship in London* (New Brunswick, 2006).

Pooley, C., and Turnbull, J., *Migration and Mobility in Britain since the Eighteenth Century* (London, 1998).

Sharpe, P., 'Parish women: Maternity and the limitations of maiden settlement in England, 1662–1834', in *Obligation, Entitlement and Dispute under the English Poor Laws* ed. P. Jones and S. King (Newcastle, 2015) pp. 168–92.

Sharpe, P., 'Survival Strategies and stories: Poor widows and widowers in early industrial England', in *Widowhood in Medieval and Early Modern Europe* ed. S. Cavallo and L. Warner (London, 1999) pp. 220–39.

Shave, S., 'The impact of Sturges Bourne's poor law reforms in rural England', *Historical Journal* 56 (2013) pp. 399–429.

Snell, K. D. M., 'Belonging and Community: Understandings of "Home" and "Friends" among the English Poor, 1750–1850', *Economic History Review* 65 (2012) pp. 1–25.

Snell, K. D. M., *Parish and Belonging: Community, Identity and Welfare in England and Wales, 1700–1950* (Cambridge, 2006).

Sokoll, T., 'Writing for relief: Rhetoric in English pauper letters 1800–1834', in *Being Poor in Modern Europe: Historical Perspectives 1800–1940* ed. A. Gestrich, S. King and L. Raphael (Bern, 2006) pp. 91–112.

Sokoll, T., *Essex Pauper Letters 1731–1837* (Oxford, 2001).

Sokoll, T., 'Negotiating a living: Essex pauper letters from London, 1800–1834', *International Review of Social History* 45 (2000) pp. 19–46.

Sokoll, T., 'Old age in poverty: The record of Essex pauper letters, 1780–1834', in *Chronicling Poverty: The Voices and Strategies of the English Poor, 1640–1840* ed. T. Hitchcock, P. King and P. Sharpe (Basingstoke, 1997) pp. 127–54.

Solar, P., 'Poor relief and English economic development before the industrial revolution', *Economic History Review* 48 (1995) pp. 1–22.

Taylor, J. S., 'Voices in the crowd: The Kirkby Lonsdale township letters 1809–36', in *Chronicling Poverty: The Voices and Strategies of the English Poor, 1640–1840* ed. T. Hitchcock, P. King and P. Sharpe (Basingstoke, 1997) pp. 109–26.

Taylor, J. S., 'A different kind of Speenhamland: Non-resident relief in the Industrial Revolution', *Journal of British Studies* 30 (1991) pp. 183–208.

Taylor, J. S., *Poverty, Migration and Settlement in the Industrial Revolution: Sojourners' Narratives* (Palo Alto, 1989).

Taylor, J. S., 'The Impact of Pauper Settlement, 1691–1834', *Past and Present* 73 (1976) pp. 42–74.

Thompson, E. P., 'The Moral Economy of the English Crowd in the Eighteenth Century', *Past and Present* 50 (1971) pp. 76–136.

Tomkins, A., '"I mak Bould to Wrigt": First-Person Narratives in the History of Poverty in England, c.1750–1900', *History Compass* 9 (2011) pp. 365–73.

Turner, D. M., *Disability in Eighteenth-Century England: Imagining Physical Impairment* (London, 2012).

Webb, S., and Webb, B., *English Poor Law History Part I: The Old Poor Law* (London, 1963 reprint).
Webber, M. C., 'Troubling Agency: Agency and Charity in Early Nineteenth-Century London', *Historical Research* 91 (2018) pp. 116–36.
Wells, R., 'Migration, the law and parochial policy in eighteenth and nineteenth-century southern England', *Southern History* 15 (1993) pp. 86–139.
Whyman, S., *The Pen and the People: English Letter Writers 1660–1800* (Oxford, 2009).
Whyte, I. D., *Migration and Society in Britain, 1550–1830* (Basingstoke, 2000).
Williams, S., *Poverty, Gender and Life-Cycle under the English Poor law, 1760–1834* (Woodbridge, 2011).

Index